To My Son,

As you embark on this road of coaching which is filled with bumps, disappointments, joy, fun, challenges, victories and defeats remember that above all be a man of integrity. Be honest and truthful always.

Stay grounded, never too high and never too low as you go through winning and losing.

Never lose sight of the most important things in your life — your wife and your family. As my brother Stephen said, "Be moral and ethical and don't kiss anyone's ass"! You are, and will continue to be a very talented coach.

With love,
Mom

The Sports Leadership Playbook

Principles and Techniques for Coaches and Captains

MIKE VOIGHT

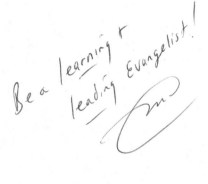

McFarland & Company, Inc., Publishers

Jefferson, North Carolina

ISBN 978-0-7864-9411-8 (softcover : acid free paper) ∞
ISBN 978-1-4766-1544-8 (ebook)

LIBRARY OF CONGRESS CATALOGUING DATA ARE AVAILABLE

BRITISH LIBRARY CATALOGUING DATA ARE AVAILABLE

Cover image © 2014 Fuse/Thinkstock

Printed in the United States of America

*McFarland & Company, Inc., Publishers
Box 611, Jefferson, North Carolina 28640
www.mcfarlandpub.com*

To my H & S, Jenny, Bradley, Ally, and Julieann for your love and support, and for taking me away from my books, laptop, and blue chair to enjoy life, one game at a time. I dedicate this also to the best family and friends a guy can have. My family continues to be there for me and my kids, which I never take for granted. Lastly, I dedicate this work to one of my beloved mentors, Dennis Viollet, who took a chance on a young coach so many years ago. His lessons on life and leadership continue to guide me.

Table of Contents

Part IV. Building Teams Who Lead and Follow

Acknowledgments

I would first like to thank those leaders, leaders-in-training and their followers who continue to allow me access to their lives and experiences. I so appreciate your confidence and willingness to be open-minded, to listen, respond, question, learn and practice to become more effective leaders for yourselves, your team members and your communities. Thanks for having me as a performance team member, but more importantly, as a friend. Thanks also for my current clients who continue to believe in the work we do together and for putting up with my constant questioning and desire for more feedback/feed-forward information! Thanks for spoiling me on my visits as well!

This project would not have made it anywhere close to the publishing stage without astute editing from my friend Megan Donovan. I drove her crazy with my creative use of the language and assiduous grammatical issues. I am indebted to her for the time and care she took with it, which I know took her away from her wonderful family.

Lastly, I also need to thank my colleagues and friends at Central Connecticut State University in the Physical Education and Human Performance and Athletic Departments for their patience and for covering for me when I was away or at home working. Go Blue Devils!

Preface

Poor examples of sport leadership are ever present in today's sports-crazed society, such as professional coaches who organize a "pay for injury" bounty program on the opponents, athletes who take performance-enhancing drugs and get arrested for all sorts of malfeasance, coaches and players from the youth, high-level amateur and professional ranks "bending" rules and cutting ethical corners to gain a competitive edge, parents on the sidelines going on shocking tirades across all competitive levels, and the lack of high moral standards that lead to the scandal that rocked Penn State University. Too many examples exist of poor, ineffective, and negative leaders in the sports arena. Not valuing leadership for its own sake, nor taking advantage of opportunities to assist today's students and athletes to improve upon their leadership skills, is a loss for the players, coaches, teams, schools, communities, and society as a whole.

Today's newest generation of students and athletes need coaching on how to become productive leaders, yet those who should be empowering them to do so—coaches, administrators, and parents—have limited resources for this much-needed information. This is the imperative I have attempted to launch in this thought-provoking, empirically-driven book for sport participants and professionals. This first-of-its-kind book reveals what the most referenced scholars and icons from the leadership and business fields know about leadership theory, research, and practice, which I have tried to deftly apply to the world of sport in a methodical, easy-to-follow manner.

Scholars and icons representing the best minds in leadership and business have been cited throughout the book: Warren Bennis, Jack Welsh, Peter Drucker, Daniel Goleman, Alan Murray, Joan Goldsmith, John C. Maxwell, James Kouzes, Barry Posner, Marshall Goldsmith, Rayona Sharpnack, John Kotter, Bernard Bass, Noel Tichy, Jim Collins and Jay Conger, to name a few. Also integrated are the leadership philosophies and practices from some of the most

1

effective and successful leaders in sport, including John Wooden, Vince Lombardi, Bill Walsh, Phil Jackson, Dean Smith, Anson Dorrance, Lou Holtz, Pete Carroll, Pat Williams, Sue Enquist, Mike Krzyzewski, Tony DiCicco, Colleen Hacker, Pat Summitt, and many others. Integrated throughout the book also are readily usable principles and applications from my own research and leadership consulting work with professional athletes, coaches, Olympians, and top collegiate coaches, athletes and teams. Features of this work include a practical leadership model for sport leadership effectiveness, educational assessment tools, and advice on implementing formal leadership development programs to sport organizations.

This is a book coaches, administrators, sport professionals and consultants can use to maximize their personal leadership potential, as well as a reference guide on how best to create, use, and teach leadership for those under their charge. Sport participants can use this book as a resource about the leadership "A-B-C's," namely, what leadership is, how it relates to individual and team performance, how to gain awareness of strengths and weaknesses, and how to improve and apply leadership skills, techniques, and tactics to their sport and life. Valuing leadership in this fashion will optimize the collaborative efforts of coaches, players, and administrators, which can help to maximize performance and the sporting experience, while empowering today's generation with much-needed leadership skills.

Introduction

Today's millennial students and athletes are simply unprepared with critical life skills for the pressure, stress, and heightened expectations that are all a part of the fabric of modern society, technology, education, employment, and even athletics. The president of Student Life University, Jay Strack, believes this to be so, and he is far from the only professional who feels this way: "Our universities and the military are realizing that the young people who stream into their halls and barracks are not well prepared to lead. We have produced a generation that is neither deep nor wide in leadership ability."[1] Being "on the same page" with today's young people is one thing, but empowering them with critical life skills, especially leadership skills, takes a more proactive approach and process.

This approach and process begins with the value placed on leadership, followership, and the importance given to teaching leadership skills by those in positions to do so. In the world of sport, one of the most successful women coaches ever, Pat Summitt, who led her Tennessee basketball team to six national championships, believed her job as coach was to help develop leaders: "More than winning, I believe our job as coaches is to develop our players into responsible leaders. Sure we teach them how to be better athletes. But that's not all I want to be known for. I want the young women who come into our program to be better people and better leaders by the time they leave."[2] Coach Summitt goes even further and believes teams cannot win consistently without good team leadership: "You won't win consistently without good team leadership. It's just that plain and simple. You've got to have players who are willing to buy into your system, demand the best from themselves and their teammates, and hold their teammates accountable."[3] A perennial contender in NCAA men's basketball year in and year out has been Duke University. Their leader, Mike Krzyzewski, believes the "single most important ingredient after you get

3

the talent is internal leadership."[4] Jerry Yeagley, a six-time national champion soccer coach at Indiana University, had this to say about the value of leadership training: "Because I understand how important leaders are to the success of the team, I've worked hard at selecting the captains and helping them develop the leadership qualities that I feel are important."[5]

Although the aforementioned quotes from some of the most effective and successful coaches speak to the value of leadership and the importance of training effective team leaders, a dearth of resources exists in the sport arena for sport coaches, administrators, professionals and participants to study and apply to their respective organizations and teams. Due to this, most of the leadership training coaches and team captains receive consists of either a recommended reading list of books or articles about leadership or a list of responsibilities accompanied with little or no guidance or instruction. Others may focus on both these items with active discussion in the off-season, yet when it matters the most, during the competitive season, time spent on leadership instruction and follow-ups becomes an afterthought at best. Still others will subscribe to a commercial program that represents a "one-size-fits-all" approach to teach predetermined leadership behaviors via experiential activities in short workshops with brief practice opportunities, doing little to truly empower leaders with realistic, real-world problem solving and authentic leadership techniques and tactics.

Fortunately, the topic of leadership and development has been given massive amounts of attention in the areas of business, management, and organizational psychology for many years now. Relying on the written works of some of the best minds from these fields, in this book I present the most recent and cutting-edge research and applied content on leadership and its development. To aid in its readability and application, the rich content is organized into a contextual model, the Leadership IQ Model (Chapter 4, Figure 3). In formulating this model, I acknowledge the important work on sport leadership conducted by Rainer Martens (creator of the sport publishing giant Human Kinetics) by including three important factors from his early model, including the *qualities* of leader and follower, *leadership styles* and *situational factors*.

In order to integrate the valuable work from business, management and organizational psychology, I wanted to also highlight the importance of knowing more about leadership theory and other key contributors to effective leadership as indicated by this vast literature. To capitalize on the notion of improving one's knowledge and intelligence of these critical leadership variables, these variables are labeled using a similar moniker used to identify general intelligence, IQ or intelligence quotient. For example, the focus of Chapter 4 is on becoming more knowledgeable on leadership theory, practice and application, thus this variable was labeled "Leadership LQ," or Leadership Intelligence Quotient. In similar fashion, Chapter 5 was given the label "Leadership ERQ," to signify acquiring knowledge about emotional and relational intelligence. Other model components include delving deeper into the recent literature on leadership styles (leadership quotient) (Leadership LSQ—Chapter 6), the significance of leadership talents, techniques, and tactics (Leadership TQ³—Chapters 7–9), the declarative and procedural knowledge of organizational dynamics, and the subtleties of managing and leading teams and organizations (organizational quotient) (Organizational OQ—Chapter 10), as well as the substantive task of developing leadership strengths through a formalized process rather than through commercial programming (Leader Development Program-LDP—Chapter 12). Many of the applicable situational factors were addressed in the first three chapters, while effective followership (Followership FQ) is addressed in Chapter 11.

This heuristic model integrates the science-theoretical (Leadership LQ) and the art of leadership (Leadership ERQ, LSQ, OQ, FQ), along with the careful execution of the most effective leadership strategy for the particular situation, while considering the impact of these decisions on the followership. The primary goals of the leadership development process (LDP- 6 T's) are to mobilize these processes to assist the team in accomplishing their ultimate goals (e.g., winning conference and national championships), while improving team functioning and effectiveness via fostering a culture of leadership, collaborative connections and sustained relationships, effective followership, and empowered individual leaders. Subsequent goals include improving upon individual leadership skills of team members and orienting the up-and-coming team leaders to the process and programming for the future. This model has been employed with numerous high-level teams at the top collegiate level, but applications can be made to higher and lower competitive levels, as shared in the appendices, and to be further addressed in future books and resources.

Using this model as a framework for the organization of this book, there are four definitive sections. Part I, entitled "Situational Leadership (SLQ): These Kids Today" goes into great detail about describing who today's generation is and what shaped their generational personality. In Chapter 1, the particular agents of socialization are addressed, which include historical perspectives and world events, but also the impact of technology, media, diversity, pop culture, shifts in education, and the fallout of invasive parenting. Also included are the ten common generational traits of the Millennials according to the published research on the topic, which include: feeling special, sheltered, confident, motivated, pressured, competitive, team-oriented, conventional, technologically savvy, and needy. When generational preferences are not met, incompatibility can result in many consequences, including emotional responses such as dissatisfaction, contempt, and frustration, which can lead to actions such as transferring from school, team mutinies and insubordination (Chapter 2). The last chapter in this section (Chapter 3) outlines the "top 10" techniques derived from the research, qualitative work, case studies, and consulting work from business professionals, those on the sidelines (coaches), and those playing, the millennials themselves.

Part II, "The Artful Science of Leadership: Theory, Research and Application," contains chapters that orient the reader to the art and science of leadership, namely the theories and practical models used to define, explain, interpret and apply the behavioral, technical, tactical, emotional, and even the spiritual sides of leading others to collective productivity and potential greatness. Chapter 4 sets out to define leadership and outlines the most cited theories of leadership, in the process posing several reflective, philosophical questions. A leadership model is reintroduced, with each of the model's eight components being detailed throughout this book.

Focusing on the emotional and relational sides of leadership is the objective of Chapter 5. Daniel Goleman's work on Emotional and Relational Intelligence, aptly termed ERQ, differentiates between personal competence and social competence. Personal competence helps determine how people manage themselves, whereas social competence determines how relationships are managed. Personal competence improves when individuals or teams have heightened levels of emotional self-awareness, which include the ability to control emotions, displaying honesty and optimism, and being flexible and adaptable. Social competence is displayed when people are able to sense others' emotional states while understanding their perspectives (empathy) as well as the perspective of the organization or team, while serving the needs of everyone involved.[6] The last chapter in this section, Chapter 6, delves into what is called "leadership LSQ," because it goes deeper than the definitions and theories addressed in Chapter 4, and covers the *substance* (applied leadership strategies) and *styles* (different leadership styles) of leadership that are important for present and future leaders to discern and integrate into their arsenal as this information can be quite useful in improving how one handles the myriad of situations in which leaders find themselves.

Part III, "Tools of the Trade: Talents, Techniques and Tactics (TQ³)," contains three chapters that represent key components to the sport leadership training process. This section summarizes what the good and effective leaders *have* (talents), as well as what they *do* (techniques) and *how* they get it accomplished (tactics). Chapter 7 summarizes the qualities, or *talents* of good and effective leaders and the survey that is used to discern the six components, which include humility, toughness, character-in-action, competence, communicative abilities, and being passionate-inspired. The next two chapters represent a compilation of the techniques and tactics used by effective leaders from the research and applied trade literature. The six techniques detailed in Chapter 8, interestingly enough, all begin with the letter "C": collaboration, connections, confidence enhancement, communication, competitive climate, and conflict-change management. Chapter 9 includes six of the more cited tactics used by effective leaders, which include the use of debriefs, facilitating effective meetings, gaining perspective, being a change agent and a go-to leader, and making the most of leadership moments.

Part IV, "Building Teams Who Lead and Follow," contains the final three chapters. Chapter 10 details one of the more important responsibilities for sport team leaders—building the team into a cohesive, compatible, and fully functioning unit. In order for lasting team building to occur, every single teammate must be "on board" and "bought in" to the standards and work to meet these expectations consistently. For this to occur, all members of the team, including the leaders, must be better informed on the importance of followership, a most neglected aspect of the vast leadership literature. This is the primary focus of Chapter 11, where five topics are covered: defining followership, examining current followership theories cited in the literature, the reasons people follow leaders, detailing followership styles and the tools and teaching of followership skills. The last chapter, Chapter 12, specifically focuses on the process of developing a culture of leadership on teams, to include the six T's to Leadership Development: test, teach, train, transfer, transform and tradition. The Appendices include surveys and sample leadership process plans used by me in high-level sport so followers and leaders alike can maximize their influence and impact on others via formalized process plans applied to sport from the vast literature on leadership.

> *"One of the most important things you can do*
> *as a leader is to develop other leaders.*
> *Those leaders will affect hundreds, if*
> *not thousands, of other people."[7]*
> —Lieutenant Colonel Kail,
> *Leadership Lessons from West Point*

Part I

Situational Leadership (SLQ):
These Kids Today

– 1 –

Today's Millennial Athletes

"I think the athlete of today is much more savvy. They want to know
why they are doing what they are doing and I think that is good."[1]
—Jerry Yeagley, former champion soccer
coach at Indiana University

Open up any newspaper, website or magazine and it will be clear as day. Or tune into the nightly news, especially the sports segment, and it almost jumps off the screen. The "it" refers to the ever-changing landscape that is our society, its members, and our societal playground, the world of sports. Through the ages society has continued to evolve with the only constant being that change will continue to occur at blazing speeds. Societal change has led to a generation of children, adolescents, and young adults who are asked to navigate a society so technologically advanced that staying current with it all is almost an impossibility, with new devices leapfrogging the "old" technology at record pace. This generation lives in a post–9/11 society at war with terrorism, which has led to a new level of security and national apprehension. The U.S. public school system is characterized by students who are less literate and less mathematically competent than a generation ago, with an annual high school dropout rate of approximately 1.3 million students, with more than half of these being students of color.[2] According to the College Board, 857 students drop out of high school every hour each school day. About 1 in 4 high school students do not graduate from high school with their class, and nearly 4 in 10 minority students do not graduate with their class.[3] Recent statistics do show a slightly higher graduation rate overall (75.5 percent, up from 72 percent in 2001).[4]

Violence among this population continues to escalate, with homicide rates among teenagers doubling every decade since 1970 (although rates have decreased since the late 1990s). In 2010, the homicide rate was 8.3 deaths per 100,000, the lowest it has been since before 1980.[5] Teen suicide rates have also climbed in the past few years, from 6.3 percent in 2009 to 7.8 percent in 2011. According to a semi-annual survey conducted by the Centers for Disease Control and Prevention (CDC), nearly 1 in 6 high school students has seriously considered suicide, and 1 in 12 has attempted it.[6] These numbers also reveal the trend that more teen suicides are reported as a result of bullying. Moreover, according to the CDC survey, about 20 percent of high schoolers said they had been bullied while at school, while 16 percent said they had been "cyberbullied" through email, chat, instant messaging, social media or texting. According to the National Education Association, it is estimated that 160,000 children miss school every day due to fear of attack or intimidation by other students, and that 15 percent of all school absenteeism is directly related to fears of being bullied at school, and 1 in 7 students in Grades K-12 is either a bully or a victim of bullying.[7]

Incidents like the tragedy at Columbine High School (1999), Virginia Tech (2007), and Sandy Hook Elementary (2012) are becoming more frequent, from big cities to small towns in Anytown, USA. Youth gang membership is burgeoning, as is the number of new gangs in all the major U.S. cities. Based on law enforcement reports published in 2010 by the National Criminal Justice Reference Service, there were an estimated 29,400 gangs and 756,000 gang members throughout 3,500 jurisdictions across the United States, and gang-related homicides increased more than 10 percent from 2009 in cities with populations of more than 100,000.[8]

Drug use also is steadily rising. The drug of choice for today's youth appears to be prescription drugs. The recent numbers reveal that among teens and young adults aged 12 to 25, one-third of those who use illicit drugs say they recently have abused prescription drugs. Among kids 12 to 17, 3.3 percent had abused psychotherapeutic drugs in the last month. Among 17- to 25-year-olds, 6 percent had abused prescription drugs in the last month.[9]

Some encouraging statistics from the Centers for Disease Control's National Center for Health Statistics show the U.S. teen pregnancy rate has declined 40 percent from its peak in 1990 and is now at a nearly 40-year low. In addition to the overall national declines, teen pregnancy has also decreased dramatically among all racial and ethnic groups, despite the reality that nearly 3 in 10 girls get pregnant by age 20.[10]

Less severe indicators of societal challenges reveal disappointing facts and figures, namely, the fitness levels of today's youth and their use of free time. First, teenage obesity levels are rising steadily, with obesity rates tripling since 1980 linked to a rise in late-onset diabetes. Young people do not have the best models in regards to eating and exercise behaviors, since all U.S. states except one (Colorado, 19.8 percent) have adult obesity rates above 20 percent, with two Southern states at a whopping 34 percent and 32 percent (Mississippi and Alabama, respectively).[11] When not in school, today's young people watch four to five hours of television on weekdays, and eight to nine hours of television on the weekend.[12] One recent study published in the *International Journal of Behavioral Nutrition and Physical Activity* tracked the habits of 1,314 children at 2.5 years of age and 4.5 years of age, revealing that every extra hour of TV watched per week translated to an added half a millimeter to children's waistlines.[13] The amount of time searching the internet, instant messaging, texting, on social networking sites, blogging and playing video games is more time away from school work, time with family, free play with friends, and physical fitness activities.

Who is to blame for the current state of affairs facing today's youth? The sources of social strife are as varied as its effects on the youth of today. Sociologists and generational researchers have posited that societal decline is due to factors such as the economy, demographic shifts, population changes, and changes in family living.[14] One of the more salient sources of present-day youth problems is the manner in which our young are raised. It brings to question what parents and schools are doing to help socialize children into today's world, especially a world full of fear, violence, racial tension, destructive peer influence, economic woes, and continual change. Defining factors include instruction and learning, relationship development, help-seeking behaviors, challenging expectations, self-esteem messaging, discipline and reward, and moral atmosphere. According to these same sociologists, social agents such as the family, schools, community organizations, even youth sports, are failing to adequately socialize today's youth. Like anything else connected to modern society, drastic changes are commonplace, and the same goes for the sporting culture in the United States. Today's sport culture, although well intentioned by most, embodies the principles of egocentrism, elitism, privatization, specialization, win-orientation, over-involvement, and the mirroring of the professional sports model.[15] Yet before looking at the sport culture, it is important to first look at its participants.

These Kids Today

> "A lot of kids we get nowadays have grown up macho."[16]
> —NFL coach Bill Parcells

> "Players demand greater ownership of their careers, and coaches must respond to a multifaceted agenda."[17]
> —NFL coach Bill Walsh

"You tell a guy you want him to improve his free-throw shooting and he takes it that you don't like him. You know, 'You're dissing me!'"[18]
—Boston University's Dennis Wolff

"You must understand the uniqueness of each individual. There are different push-buttons with each individual player."[19]
—University of Florida's Mary Wise

As indicated by these quotes, there are coaches out there who perceive today's athletes are different, especially when compared with athletes from the past. It does seem like a right of generational passage to complain about the current generation ("these kids today") while reflecting upon personal history ("when I was your age"). Coaches are not the only professionals who share this perception. The primary focus of this first chapter is to detail the work conducted by sociologists and generational researchers and practitioners on the current generation and insight into their perceptions, preferences, and how best to communicate, relate, motivate and teach them.

Two noted generational researchers-consultants, Lynne Lancaster and David Stillman, embrace the idea of generational comparisons as an example of yet another diversity movement and value it as a new way to help people get along as well as be more productive in the process. They believe gaining a more astute understanding of the generations can be a "strategic tool" in "reaping bottom-line rewards" such as increased success and higher satisfaction.[20] According to Jean Twenge, author of *Generation Me* and co-author of *The Narcissism Epidemic,* many of the studies she and colleagues used and cited in their books have indicated *when* you were born influences personality more than how you were raised. She even quotes an Arab proverb that fits the topic nicely: "Men resemble the times more than they resemble their fathers."[21] As Lancaster and Stillman state in their book, *When Generations Collide,* "The generations can't help but be influenced by the events and conditions that have shaped who they are and how they see the world."[22] These authors, and many like them, are at the forefront of this generational diversity movement, and according to an article in *The Chronicle of Higher Education,* colleges and corporations pay experts such as these "big bucks to help them understand the fresh-faced hordes that pack the nation's dorms and office buildings."[23]

With more and more attention given to generational analysis and discourse, some critics believe this generational analysis is a form of "generationally stereotyping" which puts some professionals on the defensive. On this particular point, Twenge noted: "Everyone belongs to a generation. Some people embrace it—while others prefer not be lumped in with their age mates.

Yet like it or not, when you were born dictates the culture you will experience. The society that molds you when you are young stays with you the rest of your life."[24] Since we are dealing with humankind, there are certainly no clear cut answers, and the inquiry into this topic assimilates many fields, including sociology, psychology, cultural studies, anthropology, and philosophy/morality, which represent a knowledge-base as complex and varied as the subjects (e.g., millennials) being surveyed, interviewed, polled, marketed, and behaviorally analyzed. Moreover, as a disclaimer, whenever an attempt is made to characterize a group of people (players, coaches, and students), some will fit this description, while others will not. In *Generation Me,* Twenge addresses this point: "I'm not trying to stereotype the generations. The studies I discuss here show what people from certain generations are like on average. Many of these studies show very strong, consistent change, but of course there will always be exceptions to the rule."[25]

In a similar vein, the important work that applied generational consultants provide to educational and business institutions is cited here to show that the overwhelming majority of the generational generalizations fit this newest generation, which only helps to offer this readership greater understanding of today's youth from a different perspective. One of these experts, Diana Oblinger, echoes this sentiment: "There is no single formula, particularly since students often span broad ranges of ages, learning styles, and communication preferences. Though each institution will find its own answers, a common set of principles may emerge that will help guide decisions and directions. The first step will almost undoubtedly be to better understand the 'new' learners."[26] Lancaster and Stillman believe people can make generalizations about others across generational lines, such as comparing those who grew up in the Great Depression to those of the Dot Com boom, and thus, "we can make some assumptions about how they are likely to believe and behave in the marketplace."[27] These authors assume their readers "have the moral sense to try earnestly not to use this information to stereotype people, but rather to become better listeners, better observers of the human condition, better bosses, and better friends. Our goal is not to put people in a box, but to open up the box so that we can all get a better glimpse of who and what is inside."[28]

Historical and Societal Influences

The majority of the literature on today's generation of young people looks at the generations born between 1980 and 2002, with current statistics having them at 76 million strong. This is almost three times the size of the previous generation, referred to as "Gen Xers," who arrived throughout the 1960s and 1970s.[29] These statistics have some believing the new generation could be the first 100 million-person generation.[30] Though the term "Millennial" is common, other words have been coined to name this new generation, from Generation Y, the I Generation, Generation Next, Generation Tech, Echo Boomers, to Generation ME. The generational experts most referenced throughout current scholarship are Neil Howe and William Strauss, authors of *Millennials Rising* and *Millennials Go to College*. Howe and Strauss wrote that the millennials are "the babies on board of the early Reagan years, the 'Have You Hugged Your Child Today?' sixth graders of the early Clinton years, the teens of Columbine, and the high schoolers/new college students of 9/11."[31]

Howe and Strauss, along with others, have reported all generations are shaped and influenced by the world events that happen during their lifetimes. These experts believe that life experiences assist in molding our attitudes, beliefs, and sensitivities. For example, the Boomer Generation, 72 million strong and born between 1945 and 1965, had Truman and Kennedy as presidents, world affairs including the space race, the civil rights movement, Korea, and Cuba, and included the television set, 8mm film, and mainframe computers as the premier technology of the day. The Gen X generation, referenced earlier, born between 1965 and 1985, had Johnson and Carter as presidents, with world events such as Vietnam, the fall of the Berlin Wall, AIDS, the Chernobyl nuclear accident, the Exxon Valdez oil spill, the Challenger explosion, the killings at Tiananmen Square, and the Iran conflicts all at center stage, and the technology of the day including cable television, videocassette recorders, cassettes, compact disc players, and the world wide web.[32]

Now enter the Millennials, over 76 million strong, who have had Reagan and the two Bushes as presidents, with President Obama currently in office, with world affairs ranging from Iraq to Kosovo to the War on Terrorism, with the technological advances of the day ranging from MP3s, DVDs, personal computers, audio-video streaming, instant messaging, blue-ray disc players, HD and now 3-D television sets, to phones that do so much more than make phone calls, to social networking websites (Facebook, Twitter), and beyond. What will the next 10 years bring to your local RadioShack, Best Buy, or Apple stores?

Technological Natives

Technology appears to be one of the first influences brought up in casual conversations about today's young people. "They have so much today that we didn't have" is a common phrase shared among people today. The majority of them are so tech savvy, having always had computers, 100 cable channels, and cell phones, that they proudly refer to themselves as "tech or digital natives," while using the moniker "tech or digital immigrants" for the older generations.[33] It is the cell phone that continues to transform and define this generation. In 2000, 38 percent of college students were cell phone users, yet by 2004, 90 percent of college students had them.[34]

In *Nation of Wimps,* Hara Marano notes that the cell phone is one way overprotective parents keep track of their kids despite the studies being done on how it may have negative neurodevelopmental effects on adolescents via "interfering with the maturation of brain circuitry underlying mood and decision making."[35] She refers to the cell phone as the "eternal umbilicus—the new and pervasive instrument of overprotection" used by parents, which is a cheaper method than subscribing to a computer program service called Zangle, used by many affluent school districts in Michigan to track students' homework due dates, grades, tests, behavior issues.[36] Marano quoted a sociologist who avows that parents buy their children cell phones (most beginning cell phone usage at the age of 12) because "they hope to keep a certain control on the whereabouts of their offspring. Second, they use them for conditional purposes, helpful for arranging pickups on the fly and accommodating schedule changes. Third, they use them for security—for assuring themselves that the kids are safe and well."[37] Marano insists the children are the ones "paying the bill for parental security" with the cost being their autonomy and self-regulation abilities, and how this type of dependency actually "infantilizes" young adults, causing them to take longer to actually grow up.[38] Another sociologist quoted by Marano affirms that only 31 percent of males in 2000 had reached adulthood by the age of 30, compared to 65 percent in 1960. Among women, in 2000, 46 percent had met the adulthood benchmarks (e.g., leaving home, finishing school, getting married, having children) compared to 77 percent in 1960.[39] This is apparent in the number of times students call home, especially to talk with Mom, which for some can be upwards of five times a day![40]

Technology provides its users with so much, from information to entertainment, but also convenience. The recent numbers reveal the time today's children spend on multimedia electronic devices as simply astonishing. Two Kaiser Family Foundation studies revealed in a recent *USA Today* article that Asian American, African American, and Hispanic children spend an average of 13 hours *a day* using mobile devices, computers, TVs, and other media. White children in the United States spend the least, with an average of 8 hours a day. A clinical psychologist with Children's National Medical Center in Washington, D.C., was quoted as saying: "Everyone is using too much media across the board. There are only so many hours in the day. They're going to miss out on a lot of important things, especially face-to-face contact."[41]

Youngsters are not the only ones getting carried away with the use of media. According to a recent article, college athletes and teams are getting themselves in a heap of trouble by posting pictures of team hazing practices on social networking sites, providing evidence of violation of their university anti-hazing policies and/or codes of conduct.[42] University teams mentioned include Northwestern University, Catholic University, Loyola Marymount, UC Santa Barbara, and Claremont-Mudd-Scripps, which does not include the dozen more teams identified by Bad Jocks (*www.badjocks.com*) for hazing incidents. Then there is the criminal and civil litigation of the 12 former members of the famed Florida A & M marching band who are facing manslaughter charges for fatally beating one of their own, Robert Champion, on the band's bus after a football game in 2011.[43]

According to a study conducted on college sport team hazing by a University of New Mexico professor, Colleen McGlone, more than 48 percent of Division I women athletes surveyed said they had been hazed. Her research reveals 31 percent said they witnessed hazing while more than 33 percent said they took part in hazing activities. It is important that coaches and athletic administrators take notice of research results like these and do all they can t o oversee these networking sites on a consistent base. One college coach found an interesting way to police the (social networking) posting practices of his athletes. Former Colorado football coach Dan Hawkins would do the following: "Usually during the year, I'll pull up a few guys' names, and if there is anything derogatory on there, I'll just make a copy of it and send it to their mom."[44]

Another technological/networking medium giving coaches and administrations headaches is tweeting (via personal Twitter accounts). Some consider the inability to control one's impulses to type out their immediate reactions as a social media disorder. As early as 2008, pro and college players were being fined or suspended for their 140-character missives.[45] One college football coach believes Twitter impacts his program directly: "Twitter has allowed the outside world to come into your locker room—I think that's affected coaches' ability to keep things in-house and to build team unity and togetherness. Many other coaches, at college and professional levels agree." According to *USA Today* study results, more than half of the NBA players and more than 1,000 players in the NFL from all 32 teams, along with an undetermined number of NCAA athletes, primarily from basketball and football, have active Twitter accounts. In the professional leagues rookies are even lectured about the dangers of social media in educational classroom sessions.

At the college level more universities are either banning athletes from social media or have staff members monitor the sites and alert coaches of any questionable tweets. In a recent *USA Today* article, four college football coaches removed Twitter from their players' playbooks: Bobby Hauck (University of Nevada Las Vegas), Steve Spurrier (South Carolina), Turner Gill (Kansas), and Chris Petersen (Boise State).[46] Despite some coaches taking a firm stance, Twitter is not going anywhere anytime soon, so this issue will continue to escalate. Another social media issue that until recently has been under the radar is "catfishing." Former Notre Dame linebacker Manti Te'o's experience with "catfishing" put it on the national scene. Catfishing occurs when individuals engage in an online relationship with a person who is not who he or she says he or she is. In Te'o's experience, he believed his online relationship was with a woman named Lennay Kekua, who supposedly died, until it was discovered that she was very much alive (and turned out to be a man). Don Yeager, a former *Sports Illustrated* writer who runs a consulting firm that conducts social media training for schools and athletes, uses Te'o's experience as a valuable learning tool. "If there's anything good that can come out of Te'o's situation, weird as it was, it's a heightened awareness of the damage it could cause, not just to the athlete but to the institution. Anybody that thinks Notre Dame didn't suffer because of the Te'o hoax is just wrong."[47]

Lastly, another technological issue coaches, strength coaches, and athletic trainers are showing frustration over is websites that athletes seek out to obtain a "second opinion," or as one college athletic trainer calls it, "website trolling." These second opinions are sought to either confirm, deny, or obtain additional options of different types of sport training and practice drills on the court or field, or conditioning or training exercises for the weight room, or even other ways of rehabbing injury or more information on injury protocol. The frustration comes when athletes are presenting these second opinions to their coaches to challenge original assumptions and decisions. At issue is not only coaches and trainers having their expertise challenged, but internet websites and blogs, which may or may not be valid and based on science and research, being used as the source of the information.

Convenience is not limited to technology, however. Today's society is predicated on making things close, easy, and fast. Instant gratification is at a premium amongst a generation who has always had multimedia experiences at their fingertips, from the internet, to innumerable television channels, streaming movies, YouTube videos, texting (and its sinister counterpart, "sexting") to picture-video cell phones, and social networking sites of all shapes and sizes. One guidance counselor believes all this instant technology leaves little time for kids to reflect and use their imaginations, and it all demands even more instant gratification. This counselor also posed an important question: "I don't know if they know how to be patient anymore, or how to be alone."[48] These influences can easily be seen in our classrooms when students demand to know their grades right away, or on the sport fields/courts in how much playing time they get and how they crave immediate feedback.

The Spotlight on Specialness, Cheating and Debt

Something else today's generation has over those in the past is the proverbial "spotlight." Not only are they the most researched generation, especially from big business, marketing firms, and Madison Avenue who know, according to one expert, that "generational styles influence consumer buying power as much or more than sex, income, and education."[49] This generation is also held in such high esteem not only by their parents, but by government ("No Child Left Behind" legislation, for example), movie and television studios (e.g., more child-themed feature films and television channels just for them, 24 hours a day), even adult playgrounds like Las Vegas, which went "family" in the '90s (with family-themed vacations and attractions) before returning to their old standby, "What happens in Vegas stays in Vegas." In a CBS News special on today's generation entitled *Echo Boomers,* Neil Howe was quoted saying, "They came along at a time when we started to re-value kids. During the '60s and '70s, the frontier of reproductive medicine was contraception. During the 80s and beyond, it's been fertility and scouring the world to find orphan kids that we can adopt. The culture looked down on kids. Now it wants kids; it celebrates them."[50] This is evident in the amount of popular press singer-entertainer Madonna and actress Angelina Jolie received in their celebrated adoptions of children from third-world countries. The millennial generation has also been given the label "ME Generation," for how special they are viewed as well as how special they view themselves. Some have coined this generation the "Entitlement Generation" because they have had it all. A vice president for human resources had this to say about this generation: "They all had their own cell phones, their own cars, everything they wanted. But we are also beginning to see more clearly the advantages they bring to the workplace. They bring a whole lot of skills that previous generations didn't have."[51]

This sense of "specialness," mixed with a greater perception of pressure, has resulted in some unethical decisions made in the classroom by today's generation. A child psychologist at Tufts University believes the dramatic increase in cheating and plagiarism is a result of the pressure to get good grades, leading students to break the rules in order to gain an advantage.[52] An educator was quoted as saying that "too many of my students are too interested in the grade and not at all interested in what they are learning."[53] According to the American Association of Higher Education Bulletin, more A's are being given in high school, from 12.5 percent in 1969 to 31.6 percent in 1997.[54] According to the Josephson Institute of Ethics (a nonprofit organization that conducts research and training in ethics), a survey of 36,122 high school students revealed interesting results about the ethics adopted by these millennials: 61 percent had cheated on an exam in the past year; 28 percent had stolen from a store; 23 percent had stolen from a parent or relative; and 39 percent had lied to save money.

The president of the Josephson Institute of Ethics, Michael Josephson, asks, "What makes us think these kids won't cheat or steal at work? It puts huge pressure on the workplace to retrain these kids."[55] Keep in mind that fewer than 2 percent of cheaters are ever caught and of those who do cheat, only half get punished. A recent study of high school student-athletes, also conducted by Josephson, signifies a higher rate of cheating in school by student-athletes when compared to their non-athlete classmates. Results also reveal a greater acceptance of cheating on the sports fields, with 65 percent of athletes surveyed admitting to cheating on an exam at least once this year (2012), compared with 60 percent of non-athlete students. Other notable figures include: 72 percent of football players and 70 percent of hockey players admitting to cheating, whereas 72 percent of softball players, 71 percent of cheerleaders and female basketball players acknowledged cheating.[56]

Due to these results, Josephson believes, "the fact remains that for most kids, sports promotes rather than discourages cheating," and "there is reason to worry that the sports fields of America are becoming the training grounds for the next generation of corporate and political villains and thieves."[57] Many reasons have been proffered for these results, including a dearth of experienced coaches, coaches who do not teach at the high school level, too many inexperienced, young coaches, poor role models in professional sports, prevalence of amateur teams who do not follow set ethical boundaries and rules, and over-involved parents, or as one coach calls them, "illogical" parents.

The millennials will also be known as being the most indebted generation in modern history, especially for the oldest of the millennials (late 20s), which only adds more pressure for them to go to the best schools and get the best jobs. With the cost of higher education up by 63 percent (public) and 47 percent (private), more students have to borrow tens of thousands of dollars to attend, so they will be paying off their student loans well into their 40s. It has also been reported that one-quarter of graduates will be paying more than 12 percent of their income. The median debt for college grads in 2004 was 15K, an increase of 66 percent since 1993. According to *Business Week*, "This is a generation with an unusual sense of entitlement. They were brought up as consumers, comfortable, with prosperity, certain of their eventual success. For those who graduated when they were in their early 20s, America was at its most exuberant. Then came the recession, Sept 11, a slow economic recovery, growing job insecurity, and pressure all around."[58] Moreover, real earnings for full-time workers between the ages of 25 and 34 have dropped by 10 percent since 2000, by 5 percent in 2004 alone. This will only exaggerate the burden of their debt.

Millennial General Characteristics

Since today's generation of young people are believed to be influenced, positively and/or negatively, by its history, people, places, technology, and world events, the pundits have generated a listing of general characteristics shaped by these influences: protected, confident, realistic, multi-taskers, stimulation junkies, team-oriented, always "connected" to either each other or to a technological device, or both. This generation identifies with their parents' values and schedules, are fascinated by new technology, seek leadership from those who can help them accomplish their lofty goals, favor frequent feedback from those in authority, and appreciate diversity of people and philosophies. They also learn best by working in groups and doing experiential activities. In the book *Millennial Leaders* by Bea Field, Scott Wilder, Jim Bunch, and Rob Newbold, many examples of successful millennial leaders are shared, highlighting the positive skill sets today's generation bring to the world, including being tech savvy, having a high tolerance of others, a blasé attitude about race and gender issues, entrepreneurial prowess, a status as information gatherers, having a legitimate thirst for knowledge, and an adventurous spirit.[59]

This book also showcases some up-and-coming millennial leaders who hold leadership positions at their colleges and churches, those who started their own businesses (ranging from software companies, to moving/storage companies for colleges, to one company assisting in disaster relief efforts) while still in school. A *USA Today* article extolled the entrepreneurial spirit of today's generation. Examples include a college sophomore whose company imports iPod accessories from China, a couple who revolutionized the tattoo industry by redesigning the standard instrument, a relocating firm, a company that makes ultra light backpacking gear, and a couple who do entrepreneurship consulting for college students.[60] Moreover, a recent Bureau of Labor Statistics study showed some 370,000 young people between the ages of 16 and 24 were self employed.[61] There are now even college programs designed for these entrepreneurs. A professor at Michigan State University believes today's generation "view work as part of life, but they don't live to work the way we were socialized as boomers."[62]

The millennial generation even got some notice at the 2004 Athens Olympic Games. On the NBC telecast, Jimmy Roberts wrapped up his segment by stating that Michael Phelps (who won eight medals that Olympics) and the other American medalists were "Athens class replacing Sydney crass." Mike Webster wrote in the *Daily Lobo,* "Roberts might as well have said we saw Millennial class replacing Gen X crass."[63] According to Webster, Gen X celebrities are known for being "super cocky, eccentric, or both, embodied in Charles Barkley's public proclamation, 'I am not a role model,' and that the Xer sport culture, like most Xer culture, has been a mess." It is quite telling that in future Olympics, and in all other sport contests, these Millennials will be the athletes we are rooting for and will surely be put to the test of meeting sky-high expectations. One can only imagine what was said of Phelps when he won more gold (eight) in the 2008 Beijing Olympics and six more medals, five of them gold, in the 2012 London Games.

Similar to the *Millennial Leaders* book, the books Howe and Strauss have published (see *Millennials Rising* and *Millennials Go to College*) paint a very uplifting viewpoint of today's generation. One of Howe and Strauss's ardent critics, Jean Twenge, based her bestselling book, *Generation ME,* on a collection of 12 generational research studies centered on survey responses from 1.3 million young people to provide a more valid look at generational differences.[64] Despite these experts agreeing on the importance given to the influence of a given generation, they differ significantly on how to view the millennial's generational personality traits, including level of optimism and self-esteem, attachment to duty, attractiveness to group cohesion, motivational drive, perceptions of one's own importance, and quality of mental health.

In another bestseller, *A Nation of Wimps,* Hara Estroff Marano paints a picture similar to the one postulated by Jean Twenge. Today's generation is not as "confident and optimistic, team and rule oriented, and hard workers" as Howe and Strauss would lead us to believe.[65] According to Marano, overbearing parents are front and center to the mental health crisis she believes exists in our colleges and high schools due to what she calls "hothouse" child rearing practices. Marano details statistics showing a rise in anxiety disorders, depression, sexual assaults, and self-destructive behaviors including binge drinking, cutting, suicide, and eating disorders, which she links to the fallout of invasive parenting practices. Other negative consequences of this type of invasive parenting include a 400 percent increase in attention stimulant drug prescriptions for kids 6–14, antidepressant use up 333 percent, little to no free play (which "deprives kids of opportunities to discover themselves"), and fewer young people meeting the classic benchmarks of adulthood (e.g., leaving home, finishing school, getting a job, getting married with children).[66]

Specific Generational Traits

The ten common traits of millennials, along with the implications for parents, teachers, coaches, and mentors, are listed in Table 1. These characteristics and implications for sport are taken from numerous sources, and again, these are traits believed to be representative of today's generation.

Table 1: Ten Common Traits of Millennials and Their Implications for Sport

Trait	Descriptive	Sport Application
Special	Most endeared generation	Entitled attitude due to being pampered by parents and sport coaches/teammates/fans
Sheltered	Have been protected by others	Lacking coping skills critical to handle pressure and adversity of competition
Confident	High achievers with false pride	Used to receiving praise on a regular basis
Motivated	Motivated for success with little patience for paying one's dues	Lose motivation in repetitive drills
Pressured	Pressure and guilt from internal and external sources	Over-scheduled due to pressure to achieve in all areas, not simply sport
Competitive	Set high goals	Will pursue high goals yet when the going gets tough will seek the help from significant others
Team-Oriented	Prefer group-think	Prefer to be involved in decision making and problem solving and will grumble if not included
Conventional	Identify with parents' values and schedule	Parents are involved, sometimes over-involved, with child's many activities, potentially distracting, interfering, and meddling

| *Technological* | Digital natives | Can be useful digital mentors to improve coaches' uses of technology |
| *Needy* | Prefer frequent feedback | Coaches should prepare to be asked "why" certain drills and strategy are being taught as well as to provide frequent feedback |

Today's generation is considered *special,* and due to this pervasive attitude, many believe they are oftentimes "pampered, coddled, favored, given extra benefits, undue attention, and have unrealistic expectations."[67] With all of the attention they have been given by their parents, school, even society, it is no wonder they feel entitled to be the best and have the best. Also, those who feel entitled will be less than enthusiastic to "pay their dues" and "start from the ground floor" on their teams. Some even perceive themselves as "gamers," who feel they can save their maximal efforts for big games and cruise through the "insignificant" practices and games against weaker opponents.

From their earlier days, today's youth are believed to have been *sheltered* by having their physical selves protected ("baby on board signs," special laws protecting them, special cribs, strollers, car seats, food, clothing, etc.) and their egos protected by not being allowed to fix their own mistakes or handle adversity themselves (hovering parents do that for them). Thus, they have not developed time-tested coping and problem-solving skills, and when faced with adverse conditions (like a bad game or not making the team) some just crumble, which leads some experts to believe they lack critical leadership skills as a result.

Millennials are *confident,* are known for having a high need for achievement, and have a "false pride" after being told how great they are and that they can accomplish anything. They have received praise for less than praiseworthy standards and accomplishments, primarily from their over-involved parents. True confidence comes from being able to optimally prepare, remain tough in adverse situations, learn from mistakes, and take responsibility for one's actions and life. Some millennials are not given this freedom or responsibility, so they lose out on a prime opportunity for self-discovery and true self-confidence. A study by Ypulse, surveying over a thousand millennial college students, revealed that college students themselves believe they are more self-promoting, narcissistic, over-confident and attention-seeking than previous generations, with 20.4 percent strongly agreeing to this statement, 45 percent agreeing somewhat, and 19.7 percent taking a neutral position. Interestingly, the students blamed social networking sites as a partial contributing factor to these narcissistic traits.[68] A similar survey study conducted with 16,000 college students revealed almost two-thirds had narcissism scores above the average 1982 score, and 30 percent more students showed elevated narcissism from then to now.[69] Although these studies are not stating that more students today have the narcissistic personality disorder (meaning excessive self-love) needing formal treatment, they reveal that some narcissistic traits are much more evident than in the past.

According to Howe and Strauss, the millennials have a limitless supply of *motivation* to take on the world and make something of themselves. Others report that some of these millennials have overinflated views of what they can accomplish, so once adversity hits they are unable to cope effectively, thus lowering confidence levels and motivation to continue. They want the "corner office" right away without working their way to the top via paying their dues. Some coaches believe some of their players are motivated in practice when they are doing "fun" drills, but lose their motivation when doing skill repetitions or a drill bringing them discomfort and stress. One coach, who had the privilege of playing for John Wooden at UCLA, had this to say about today's athletes' level of motivation: "Maybe they're not hungry enough. I wanted to be the best basketball player I could be. I don't know if the kids this day in time are really concerned about that. They have cars. They have jewelry. They have video games. Their parents are supporting them still. What else are you hungry for? You have everything you want to have in life, that's what an 18-year-old is thinking."[70]

Millennials look through what has been referred to as a "distorted mirror." To get ahead they need to be the best, to be involved with many different activities to improve their chances of getting to the prestigious schools, clubs, and so on. This *pressure* comes from their over-involved parents, as well as the internal motivation to accomplish their high goals. They also feel the pressure and stress covertly from all of the private coaching, tutoring, expense of travel and equipment, and how the family sacrifices holidays and weekends to watch their millennials compete. Today's students and athletes do not want to let anyone down, especially those who are making the financial and emotional investment for their futures. Due to pressure put on them by their parents, and pressure that is self-imposed, millennials' pre-set goals are very high and difficult to reach. Due to a high motive to succeed and insufficient coping and leadership skills, they will work the system to ease the perceived adversity they are experiencing, or ask a parent to work the system on their behalf.

The parents of today's generation asked them from a very early age for input regarding what they would like to eat and do on a daily basis, basing the family meal menu and schedule on this input. Thus the generation grew up to be very *team-oriented,* preferring to work within a team, or "group-think." They enjoy working and collaborating in groups, whether at school, in sports, and when they are older, on the job. Some of the generational experts, and some coaches too, believe this is so they can share the responsibilities with others rather than taking on a task (and the risk from going it alone) for themselves. Being as tech savvy as they are, staying connected with their peers is a strength via cell phone, texting, email, IMing, Tweeting, and of course, social networking sites. An important member of the student-athlete's "team" is his or her parents. Millennials tend to identify with their parent's *conventional* values and schedules, making them multi-tasking specialists who are spread very thin. They also have a different relationship with one or both of their parents, much closer to being "friends" than in the past, and parents and their millennials tend to keep in continual contact throughout the day. Moreover, usually one or both parents are called to solve issues and make problems go away.

It goes without saying that millennials are fascinated by new *technology* and some expect everyone (parents, teachers and coaches) to know it and use it as much as they do. A big asset is this generation can reverse mentor their boomer or Gen X coaches in the finer points of anything technological! Teachers and coaches should take advantage of this skill set to maximize their use of today's technology, such as incorporating *Ti Vo* with fundamental repetition drills, breaking down video to specific plays and opponent tendencies, or using sophisticated stat programs to improve upon game preparation. Millennials also require frequent feedback, helping feed their sense of competence and motivation to excel, without necessarily paying their dues. This contributes to the perception of being *needy*.

Despite the proposition that an individual's attitudes, preferences, and values are shaped by their generational ethos, including the history, people, places, technology, and events, even the present economy, this should not limit the impact and importance of how today's youth are raised. The generational experts exhibit a mixture of enthusiasm for how special today's generation is treated with a sharp cynicism, depending on which you choose to read, again referring to the contradictions among the experts and the complex study of human nature. Despite this discourse, both sides agree there is an increased level of involvement that parents, and others, have in their children's lives compared with the past.

From Helicopter Parents to Jet-Powered Turbo Attack Model: No Parent Left Behind

Overprotective parents are generating fallout from the doting pervading our neighborhoods, schools, and athletic fields. Despite their best intentions, their child-rearing practices are contributing to the ME generation. This type of parenting has been given many names in the past few years, including invasive parenting, hothouse parenting, professional parents, helicopter parents, intrusive parenting, among others. In *A Nation of Wimps,* Hara Marano quotes a school principal from Colorado who began referring to helicopter parents back in the '70s, and is astonished at how they have evolved since: "They want discipline in schools, but they don't want their kids to be held accountable for anything. These parents are constantly running interference and intimidating teachers to give kids better than they deserve. They're doing the homework for the kids, even lying for them. Today they are a jet-powered turbo attack model."[71] After surveying 1,700 teachers across the United States about what they believed to be the most difficult aspect of teaching today, the answer with the highest frequency was dealing with today's generation of parents. Others have used the term "snowplow parents," who work hard to clear the path for little Jimmy and Susie, pushing obstacles out of their way for smooth traveling.

As a parody to the "helicopter parenting" syndrome, the writers of the popular sport-themed comic strip *Tank McNamara* in 2007 had a series of comic strips dedicated to the "helicopter parent bowl" football game. Commentary and pictures showed bowl participants talking with their parents from their helmet phones, parents staging protests arriving at the NCAA headquarters via their chopper hats, and parents text messaging the field officials about their calls. "It seems we're too inflexible, oh, and insensitive to the players' specialness as individuals," was one text, to which the other official responds, "Shoulda quit when we saw the helicopter parents duct-taping nanny cams to the goalposts." One comic ends with the helicopter parent credo, "No parent left behind!"[72]

There are many documented consequences to this type of invasive parenting. One of these is how today's generation are over-everything: over-scheduled, over-protected, over-pressured, and over-achieved. The over-scheduling and over-monitoring of kids does little to empower them with opportunities to discover themselves, but instead deprives them of the valuable assets that come from free play, mostly human development. Morano has argued this point: "Play is actually critical to healthy development, a biological imperative for higher animals. It sharpens and limbers intelligence. It is the only activity that directly prepares people for dealing with life's unpredictability. Delay play and you delay adulthood."[73] A child psychologist from Tufts University, David Elkind, said, "Society has changed so rapidly parents can't look to their own childhood for guidance, or their own parents. They look to experts, but they often disagree with one another. So they look to other parents, and that creates a great deal of parent peer pressure."[74]

Dr. James Dobson, a minister, in his *Focus on the Family Bulletin,* spoke of the curious value system young people have and why they test their parents' disciplinary boundaries so much. "When parents refuse to respond to their child's defiant challenge, something changes in the relationship. The youngster begins to look at his parents with disrespect. More important, he wonders why they would let him do such harmful things if they really loved him. The ultimate paradox of childhood is that boys and girls want to be led by their parents but insist that their mothers and fathers earn the right to lead them."[75] How about sport players? How far do they go to push disciplinary lines? What reaction is appropriate?

Becoming cognizant of these generational traits and characteristics has hopefully provided a different perspective of the millennial generation. The next chapter will detail some of the negative consequences of misunderstandings between the generations in the classroom, at home, and on the athletic field.

> *"Do these revolutionary times suggest anarchy in the gym?"*[76]
> —*ESPN the Magazine* article title

– 2 –

The Ills of Incompatibility: General to Generational Misunderstandings

*"Talking 'bout a revolution: Is player power
out of control? Depends who you ask"*[1]
—*ESPN the Magazine* headline

In his book *The Last Season: A Team in Search of Its Soul,* longtime NBA coach Phil Jackson wrote about the 2003–2004 Los Angeles Lakers season, and in it, he states how difficult it was to get teams to play his system, the triangle offense, with today's players.

> In the 1960s and '70s, players asked: How do I fit in? How can I help this team win? Now they ask: How do I get what I want? Given this selfish mind-set, it is remarkable, actually, that teams play with any cohesiveness. I can't help but believe that for both the players and the fans, the purity of this wonderful game has been compromised in the process, perhaps for good.[2]

Despite these generational attributes and frustrations, Coach Jackson, staff, and team found a way to coexist just fine as evidenced by their five national championship rings preceding his retirement in 2011.

Generational Clash Points

In *When Generations Collide,* Lancaster and Stillman refer to the generational misunderstandings in the workplace as "generational collisions," referring to the source of these conflicts as "clash points." These authors listed some of the potential consequences of these generational collisions in the workplace, including "everything from reduced profitability to the loss of valuable employees, higher payroll costs, poor customer service, derailed careers, wasted human potential, and even potentially serious health problems caused by stress."[3] Examples of clash points provided by the authors include how millennial employees would rather build parallel careers (some predict millennials will have anywhere from 3 to 10 career changes in their lifetime[4]) rather than just one career, and how when it comes to rewards, millennials desire work that is meaningful rather than work that provides satisfaction (traditionalists), money (Baby Boomers), or freedom (Generation Xers). Other clash points involve how the generations view having a work-life balance (a true balance) and retirement.

In the sport world, "collisions" or "clashes" can take numerous forms. For example, I have had coaches and clients share some of these generational disconnections between coach and player, which can be seen in Table 1.

Table 1: Coaches and Athletes Clash Points

CLASH POINTS	COACH QUOTE
Athletes do not take their sport as seriously as they should	"They have too many other things going on"
Athletes are not punctual	"They show up when it works for them"
Do not dress professionally (piercings, self and tattoos, etc.)	"Do not have the same respect for others like we did"
Work rate lower and less consistent	"I need to do more motivating than I ever have"
Not students of the game	"Most don't watch the game like I used to"
Fail to communicate face-to-face	"Most would rather leave an email or text than come by the office to talk with me, especially about an issue"

Sport psychology consultant Harvey Dorfman, who has worked for years with many teams in professional baseball, cautions coaches about putting too much emphasis on today's players' stylings: "You do have to coach and teach a pitcher with a nipple ring and a 'dude' mentality. That's a contractual obligation. The player's styling is not his substance. You've got to know more about him than how he looks and speaks."[5]

Clashes or collisions between people can obviously take on many forms, from personality differences, conflicting styles of problem solving, or generational misunderstandings. In sport, besides those presented in Table 1, additional sources of conflict relate to the player's perceived roles on the team (role ambiguity), which includes playing time/starting status, leadership style of the coach, communication style used by the coach, and the ability of the coach to establish real relationships with players.[6] It can be difficult to pinpoint the exact "clash point" or source of the disagreement, but keep in mind the primary goal of this chapter is to improve understanding of today's generation through a greater comprehension of why they do, say and think what they do. The secondary goal is to share strategic generational "tools" from the generational experts to improve generational relations and the amount of productive collaboration and cooperation among teams and their leaders.

Twenge, in *Generation Me*, views today's young people as products of their culture, and specifically, "a culture that teaches them the primacy of the individual at virtually every step, and a culture that was firmly in place before they were born."[7] She goes further by stating, "Asking young people today to adopt the personality and attitudes of a previous time is like asking an adult American to instantly become Chinese."[8] The more salient generational misunderstandings are that today's generational traits and trends are this generation's fault and our charge is to change them, even in our own likeness of attitudes and beliefs. Thus, the ideal is to use the knowledge of today's generational traits and trends to your advantage. The old adage "Knowledge is power" is indeed apropos and underscores the importance of applying appropriate strategies to improve connectedness, collaboration, and productivity. Not simply using the strategies contained herein to "change" today's players, but to use their skill sets on and off the field more wisely. Ways of doing so will be discussed in detail in Chapter 3.

Sport Team Cohesion, Compatibility and Clash Points

In the world of sport, the term used to describe the relationship between player and coach is compatibility. How well a group of people work together (task) and enjoy being together (social) is referred to as cohesion. Research in sport psychology shows player-coach compatibility is known to be an important determinant of team success and personal and team satisfaction. Interventions designed to "bridge the gap" between coach and athletes include improved communication and interacting skills, role clarification, improved conflict resolution skills, goal setting, reinforcement modification (productive feedback), coping skills, and finally, an acceptance of responsibility to improve from both parties.[9] Similarly, studies in sport consistently show the higher the level of team cohesion the greater the team success. This also applies in the other direction as well. A more successful team breeds greater perceptions of conformity and cohesion. In their text, *Foundations of Sport and Exercise Psychology*, Robert Weinberg and Dan Gould described numerous studies showing a positive relationship between cohesion and performance. One such analysis reviewed over 30 studies on cohesion and found 83 percent of the studies showed positive relations while another review used 66 studies and found a positive effect in 92 percent of these studies. A more recent review of sport teams used 46 studies (including almost 10,000 athletes and 1,000 teams) and found moderate to large cohesion-performance effects.[10] Besides improved performance, other factors are related to high levels of compatibility and cohesion, such as improved effort, collective efficacy (confidence), stability (lower turnover), social support, group goals and norms, and team satisfaction.[11]

A quote from NBA coaching great Phil Jackson opened up this chapter, stating how remarkable it is that teams can play with any sort of cohesiveness nowadays due to the generational attributes he referred to as a "selfish mindset." He is not the only sport personality who has chimed in on the challenges of coaching today's athletes. These quotes are a continuation of those mentioned in the previous chapter.

> *"If you can't relate to today's player, you're through as a coach.*
> *I think you can be a gentlemen and succeed and treat players*
> *fairly and like men; this is not old Rome with the gladiators."*[12]
> —Former college and NFL coach
> Steve Mariucci

> *I've realized in the last 5 years that kids*
> *come in here less confident and more fragile."*[13]
> —University of Tennessee women's basketball coach
> Pat Summitt

> *"Young people today, not only with the referees but with each other,*
> *give me an Excedrin headache ... all they do is talk, talk, talk.*
> *They don't play anymore. They'd rather talk."*[14]
> —University of Louisville men's basketball coach
> Rick Pitino

> *"I could probably quit somewhere this season. There are too*
> *many changes that have taken place in young people that I*
> *just don't like. There's no sense of urgency, no sense of awareness."*[15]
> —Former Temple University basketball coach
> Don Cheney

In addition to the *ESPN the Magazine* headline beginning this chapter, a voluminous amount of headlines underscore the consequences of clashes between coach and team, including this sampling:

"Athletes' voices heard"[16]

*"Dissatisfaction: Player displeasure and
fan frustration played a part in coach firing"*[17]

"Gauchos mutiny against Pimm"[18]

"A wildcat strike may take flight"[19]

"How tough is too tough"[20]

"Generational issue cited for brawl"[21]

"A new way for athletes to bargain: Sabotage"[22]

"Coaches too tough: Lines hard to find"[23]

"Coaches rough behavior in spotlight"[24]

Behind each of these headlines are a surfeit of additional articles, blogs, and reports across all levels and types of sports about a coach and team in turmoil due to conflicts and clashes, incompatibility, poor team cohesion and poor results. From these articles are stories of high-profile, collegiate coaches getting fired due to claims of player abuse, as was the case with former Texas Tech basketball coach Billy Gillispie,[25] Kansas football coach Mark Mangino,[26] former South Florida football coach Jim Leavitt,[27] former Texas Tech football coach Mike Leach,[28] and of course the well-publicized oust of Bob Knight at Indiana and the alleged verbal abuse of Jason Collier and the physical altercation with Neil Reed and the IU student eventually leading to his firing.[29] There have been recent incidents of abuse accusations against several coaches: Stanford University men's basketball coach Mike Montgomery admitted he made a mistake for shoving his star player, Allen Crabbe, during a game[30]; Texas Tech men's basketball coach Billy Gillispie was fired due to mistreatment including practicing more than 4 hours a day (one accusation stated they practiced all day into the night)[31]; Idaho football coach Mike Kramer was investigated for shoving a player to the ground during a practice session, injuring the player's neck[32]; Tommy Tuberville, football coach at Texas Tech, was publicly reprimanded for an altercation with a graduate assistant football coach during a game.[33]

Still other coaches were targets of alleged team revolts, including Tom Penders at Texas,[34] Matt Kilcullen at Western Kentucky,[35] Matt Doherty at North Carolina,[36] Bobby Williams at Michigan State,[37] and John Mackovic at Arizona.[38] Regarding Mackovic, it was reported at his school, the University of Arizona, that 55 players marched into the school president's office to complain about his coaching style, and shortly after many of these same players almost refused to board a plane for a game in California. A women's basketball coach was fired by a PAC 10 school after several losing seasons, and four players and an assistant coach left the program in the span of a week.[39] Other reports detailed the firings of two more women's basketball coaches (2005 and 2003, respectively), one accused of being abusive in her treatment of students and staff,[40] the other for "pulling a player's hair and making a sick player run until she collapsed and was hospitalized."[41]

Many other coaches, though not as high profile as those listed previously, have been fired due to alleged abuse, team conflict, or player revolts that made headlines in recent years, including coaches from all kinds of sports, but especially basketball, football, baseball, hockey, wrestling, track and field, soccer, even Olympic speed skating. In this rare case of athlete revolt on this stage, the United States short-track speed skaters accused their coaches of abuse and stated they would not compete in the coming World Cup season if the head coach, Jae Su Chun, and his assistant coaches were not replaced. Examples of the accused abuse include slamming an athlete into a wall, calling a female athlete a "fat cow" and other instances of "unchecked abuse."[42] The head coach and staff did resign shortly after the accusations became public.[43]

Player revolts are nothing new, especially at the professional level. An internet search reveals many in the last two years alone, most notably from the NBA's Detroit Pistons. According to Stephen A. Smith of ESPN, players Tracy McGrady, Tayshaun Prince, Richard Hamilton, and Chris Wilcox failed to show up for a pre-game shoot-around in February 2011, as a formal protest against coach John Kuester. "As the reports of player mutiny in Detroit began circulating throughout the NBA community on Friday, detailing disdain, disrespect and total disregard for a head coach—and ultimately for a Pistons organization once considered the gold standard—a palpable level of disappointment should have permeated throughout professional sports."[44] In the sport of hockey, Peter Laviolette was fired after two seasons coaching the New York Islanders due to a player revolt, and for what the general manager termed "losing the team." This firing occurred despite consecutive playoff appearances.[45] There was a player revolt of players versus commissioner. The commissioner is Carolyn Bivens of the LPGA, who the players believed did not do enough to keep the tournaments they have, losing seven tournament sponsors in two years. According to *USA Today's* Christine Brennan, "that's why top players including Lorena Ochoa, Paula Creamer, Morgan Pressel and Cristie Kerr are leading the palace coup."[46]

These revolts are not simply an American issue. Outside of our borders, there have been many such occurrences in international football (or soccer) especially, on such famous clubs or teams (with the date of its occurrence in parentheses) as Aston Villa (2011), the French national team (2010), the English national team (2004 and 2010), Manchester City (2009), Newcastle (2009),[47] Wolfsburg (2005), River Plate (2006), Manchester United (2004), and Borussia Monchengladbach (2003).[48]

Other articles contain stories of players quitting or transferring due to conflicts with coaches over playing time, treatment, and unfairness accusations. In other stories players refuse to take up a new position due to injuries. One such story appeared in the *Los Angeles Times* detailing USC football player Allen Bradford refusing to move to the position of fullback due to injury.[49] One example of mistrust between coach and athlete happened to a college coach who was having his usual end of the season debrief with one of his soccer players, but unbeknownst to him, she had her father, an attorney, on the other end of her cell phone hidden in her handbag so the father could hear all that was being said.[50] Another story involved a coach whose basketball players were dissatisfied with the treatment they were getting from him. Instead of going to the coach to talk about it, they locked themselves in the locker room prior to a game and would only go out onto the floor for the game if the athletic director was summoned to the locker room. As the story goes, the athletic director came, listened, then the players took to the court for the game, but the coach was fired prior to the next scheduled game.[51]

Legal System as Clash Point Coping Alternative

The use of the legal system is fast becoming another method millennials use for handling dissatisfaction. There are several reports of players who sued their respective universities for not having their scholarships renewed (University of Central Michigan[52] and the University of Rhode Island[53]) for alleged discrimination practices. In a discrimination lawsuit, a former Penn State basketball player states the coach discriminated against her by claiming she was a lesbian (she asserted she was not) and because of that tried to force her off of the team. The player then transferred to attend and play at James Madison University. The coach was fined $10,000 for violating the university's nondiscrimination policy and resigned a year later.[54] Another report details an athlete who decided not to sue his university but instead went after the "big fish," the NCAA. The *New York Times* chronicled the case of Joseph Agnew, a former football player at Rice University, who lost his scholarship for his senior year, then filed a class-action lawsuit in U.S. District Court in San Francisco against the NCAA, "arguing the one-year limit on athletic scholarships amounts to a price-fixing scheme between the association and member universities."

According to the article, this came five months after the NCAA "acknowledged that the antitrust division of the Justice Department was looking into the one-year scholarship rule."[55]

Another lawsuit was filed in the spring of 2011 against the NCAA, this time by a group of junior college football players, headed by Reginald Davis, a student-athlete from City College of San Francisco. According to the article, "In the suit filed in San Francisco this week, Davis and six other players from across California are challenging a rule that forces them to achieve higher academic standards before they can transfer to a four-year university, get financial aid, and play Division I sports."[56] These "higher academic standards" refer to non-qualifier students who are required to attend junior college and achieve a 2.0 GPA while completing 48 semester hours. Yet one particular conference, the SEC, added even more academic requirements in 2009, which players believe hurt, not help, student-athletes who are ready to transfer and play at more competitive levels. In the wake of the North Carolina football scandal, where seven players were forced to sit out the 2010 season due to alleged acceptance of improper benefits and academic misconduct, one player, James Michael McAdoo, filed a lawsuit in July 2011 against the school and the NCAA.[57] McAdoo was signed by the Baltimore Ravens in 2011. His case against UNC and the NCAA was dismissed by the North Carolina Court of Appeals in early 2013.

In a bizarre lawsuit filed in 2010, three former football players at Feather River College in California allege "discrimination, disparate treatment and violations of civil rights and federal statues" charges against the defendants, which include the college, football coaches, and athletic director. According to the plaintiffs' attorneys, "The new lawsuit alleges that once Small (assistant head football coach) was no longer in the college's employ, Trueblood (athletic director), Johnson (football coach) and Josh White, another member of the coaching staff, insulted, unfairly criticized, abused and taunted the team's African American players, including the plaintiffs, while Caucasian players were not treated in such a manner." It is also alleged the "coaching staff decided to change the 'face' of the team from 80 percent African American to 80 percent Caucasian under the guise of the 85-player cap the college instituted for the 2010 season."[58] Additionally, the three plaintiffs were not told they would not play until it was too late to transfer to other schools. In another football-related legal case, a former college football player hurt lifting in the football weight room sued the university and ex-assistant conditioning coach alleging negligence in the accident that crushed the player's throat.[59] The player, Stafon Johnson, recovered and was drafted by the Washington Redskins. Johnson settled out of court for unspecified damages in early 2012.[60] Another instance of legal litigation involves a high school football player who sued the University of Hawaii for allegedly revoking his scholarship offer after his coach, June Jones, resigned to take another position elsewhere.[61]

Another occurrence that generated a lot of publicity and airtime was the case of a women's basketball player at Rutgers University who sued the notorious radio host Don Imus for slander, libel, and defamation. This occurred during a live broadcast in April 2007, when the shock jock referred to members of the highly ranked team as "nappy headed hos," causing a firestorm of attention ultimately leading to his firing by CBS Radio and MSNBC.[62] In another case featuring a very public individual, one of the lacrosse players from Duke University, who was not indicted in the 2006 wrongfully accused rape case, sued Duke University and a professor for failing him in a course he was passing, as a form of retaliation after the Duke lacrosse sex scandal hit. Interestingly, this professor was one of the "Group of 88" professors who published an advertisement in the Duke *Chronicle* calling the rape scandal a "social disaster." The Group of 88, perceived by critics as attacking the lacrosse team, at one point thanked protesters who posted "wanted" fliers containing photos of all or nearly all of the lacrosse players.[63]

In another case against Duke University, the son of former New York City mayor Rudy Guliani sued the school in 2008 over being cut from the golf team because the coach wanted to cut the size of the team from 13 to half that.[64] There was even a report of a civil rights lawsuit filed by two former players and a manager from Rutgers University seeking unspecified damages accusing the basketball coach, Kevin Bannon, of making them run wind sprints naked during a practice as a punishment. This case was dismissed in 2000 and the coach was fired in 2001.[65]

This next case can be filed as "A win for the little guy!" In a rare loss for the NCAA in court, an Oklahoma State University pitcher won his court case and was reinstated to the team, when, according to the article, "an Ohio judge threw out an NCAA rule that prevents college baseball players from hiring advisers who are in direct contact with big league clubs. Oliver filed a lawsuit after he was ruled ineligible. The NCAA suspended him last spring because it said advisers he had hired listened in on contract negotiations after he was drafted by the Minnesota Twins in June 2006."[66] In doing so, the judge ruled the NCAA cannot restrict a student-athlete's right for legal representation when negotiating a professional contract, especially since baseball players are the only athletes allowed to be drafted before they enter college and usually retain advisers to help with the draft process. Another pitcher, this one from Mississippi State University, filed a lawsuit against his coach, John Cohen, accusing him of intentionally breaking NCAA rules while "conspiring to force the player to quit the team." The rules mentioned include practicing for more than the allowable 20 hours per week and taking away his scholarship without due process. The player also asserts he was forced to pitch while injured, causing further injury which required surgery.[67]

The previous example is reminiscent of another controversial player versus coach fray, although no lawsuit came of it. In this particular instance, accusations were lobbied at former Michigan football coach Rich Rodriguez in 2009 by current and former players that he willfully broke NCAA rules regarding practice time. As one article goes, "Numerous players on the 2008 and 2009 teams said the program far exceeded limits intended to protect athletes from coaching excesses and to ensure fair competition." Two players called Michigan's off-season requirements "ridiculous." The players described the coaches' expectations as an ongoing concern among many teammates. Parents of several players agreed. As the report indicated, "The players and parents agreed to talk only if they were not identified because they said they feared repercussions from the coaching staff."[68] Rodriguez was fired one season later.

Whether it is in the court of law or the court of public opinion, today's athletes are not passive, submissive bystanders who follow their leaders blindly. Due to their generational make-up, including their transitory ways, high level of motivation, and how interconnected they are with players from other schools, if they are not getting what they were told they would get, or getting the most out of the present experience, or they do not see the current path they are on as the right path to get them where they want to go, they will not only confront the issue but they will use anything at their disposal to alter the situation in their favor. This could entail calling on their parents, their lawyers, or the media to assist. Players today are not fearful of coaches or of confronting them or their bosses.

A special report written for the *Los Angeles Times* states that "today's athletes have been shaped, for better or worse, by two unavoidable influences that have mushroomed like an atomic cloud in the last 10 years: money and media."[69] The writer of this exposé, Mike Penner, believes professional sport stars may not be so different today from what they used to be, they are just paid a lot more and are in the spotlight much more. Both present and past players had their share of clashes with the other generation, such as physical abuse of coaches (Latrell Sprewell in 1997 choking his coach, PJ Carlisimo, and Lenny Randle punching his manager in 1977), getting coaches fired (Los Angeles Laker Magic Johnson got his coach fired in 1981), and contract holdouts (commonplace today, but also staged by Joe Di Maggio back in 1938). It was not long ago that Gary Sheffield demanded a trade from the Los Angeles Dodgers, saying he would honor his contract if he had to, but then stating, "I'm not 100 percent mentally here and I've never played baseball like that before. You never know what you're going to get out of that. I'm going to do my best, but I can't stitch it in stone how I'm going to do every day."[70] He also stated he might not hit as many home runs if he were forced to stay. Shortly thereafter he was traded. A veteran NBA coach, Chuck Daly, also believed that athletes have not changed much in their behaviors over the years: "Every player wants 48 minutes, wants to shoot the ball 48 times and make 48 million. The only thing that's changed is the money."[71] Even legendary coach John Wooden said, "Your players change, but you don't," when asked how much one should change from year to year by former USC football coach Pete Carroll at a fundraiser in 2005.[72]

Despite some detractors, the majority of those in athletics do believe in singer/songwriter Bob Dylan's classic lyric, "the times they are a-changin'." For example, George Raveling, a veteran college coach, analyst, and supporter of grassroots basketball development, states, "We're going through a lot of societal changes in our country—kids are different, values are different, parents are different. All of our norms and standards are being questioned today and we have a spillover of societal problems into intercollegiate athletics. And we're not used to it."[73] Another veteran, former Arizona Wildcat coach Lute Olsen, stated it is so important today's athletes take responsibility for their actions: "Kids have to understand they are responsible for what they do. It can't always be somebody else's responsibility or somebody else's fault. You're 18 years old, you know what's right and what's wrong. When do you start taking responsibility for your own actions? If that's how it is now, it makes me wonder how its' going to be in another 10 years."[74] That was stated over 14 years ago. Times continue to change and Coach Olson's question remains: what will things be like in another 10 years?

Player Dissatisfaction and Consequences

Quotes and incidences of player dissatisfaction were shared in an earlier section of this chapter. One particular case led me to choose this topic of athlete dissatisfaction for my doctoral dissertation. The men's soccer coach at the University of Wisconsin, Jim Lauder, led his team to a national title, and a year later was fired. The associate athletic director cited poor player evaluations, yet from the fired coach himself, "the official reason was I did not run organized practices or motivate players. I don't discuss it because I don't understand it."[75]

The results of my doctoral dissertation reveal the primary cause of dissatisfaction among a sample of collegiate athletes was the coach, and specifically, the following behaviors and actions: unequal player treatment, questionable leader strategy and ethics, poor training and instruction, burnout experiences, negative team climate, and poor communication skills.[76] How these dissatisfied athletes reacted and attempted to cope with their perceptions of dissatisfaction ranged from decrements in their practice and game performance, to seeking other options, such as transferring to another school, to seeking council from athletic directors, deans of students, even lawyers, to insubordination, rebellion and revolts, and finally, simply tolerating the perceptions of dissatisfaction.[77] It is worth noting that having players transfer out of a program carries consequences in light of NCAA academic reform policies set in motion by former NCAA president Myles Brand. Athletes who do not stay at a university or do not graduate can hurt a program's APR (Academic Progress Report) index, a statistic each team gets for keeping athletes eligible and for graduating them in a timely fashion. A poor APR index could result in loss of postseason play, practice time, scholarships, or more severe punishments for a consistently poor APR score. It is usually the actions of insubordination, rebellion or revolt that make the national headlines, and in most cases, cost the head coach, and sometimes the athletic directors, their jobs.

Traditional Versus Modern Coaches: Exchanging the Old Model

Mentioned by many of the athletes surveyed in my dissertation, and quoted in several national articles and blog postings since, is how negatively perceived "old school" or "traditional" coaches are by today's athletes, and how this could be a potential clash point. Coaches often use the prefix "In my day" to kick start a motivational speech (or a tongue lashing). A more modern version is continual reference to a team in the past who did all the right things, that quintessential team. For example, "That 2000 team did this so well, and did that so well," usually does not have the desired motivational effect, and often, the opposite tends to occur. Statements such as these do little to bridge the generation gap and usually demotivate and lead to resentment of this past, great team. Coaches who utilize such language may be referred to as "old school" coaches by today's generation. Sport psychology consultant Bill Beswick charted his comparisons between the traditional, "old school" coach and the more modern coach. In dichotomous categories, traditional coaches are characterized as being too task-centered, results-dominated, instinctive, player-dependent, isolated, authoritarian, with yelling and training and hard work. Conversely, modern coaches are player-centered, excellence-dominated, careful planners, coach-influenced, mentors, democratic in decision making, sales-like, teachers, and smart workers.[78] It is an important exercise for coaches to become more aware of what their behaviors say about whether they are "old school" or "new school" in their behaviors and styles.

An article appearing in the *Chronicle of Higher Education* entitled "Coaching the Coaches" highlights the need for athletic program directors to develop educational programs to help coaches relate and communicate better with their athletes. An academic counselor quoted in the article stated that "some of the old coaching methods won't work with them," referring to today's athletes.[79] Jim Haney of the National Basketball Coaches Association agrees: "Communication is a key element in one's ability to be successful as a coach. Discipline is still very important, but coaches can no longer get away with the old 'it's my way or the highway' kind of approach."[80] A coach for more than 26 years at the high school level, Liz Miller echoes the importance of communication when coaching today's athletes: "Communication is the key, you have to be able to work with the athletes. I think of all the changes that have occurred over that span. Staying in coaching is about changing your approach with regard to athletes."[81] For coaches today, there is no better time than the present to bring about change if in fact change is needed. For one coach, this realization came a little too late. Under siege of his players and administrators, Arizona football coach John Mackovic vowed to change his approach after reportedly 40–50 of his players met with the school president to voice their displeasure about him and his coaching. Despite getting a stay for the remainder of the 2002 season, his style must not have changed much, as he was fired five games into the following season.[82]

In an *ESPN the Magazine* article written by John Hunter, many college football players were interviewed regarding what it takes to coach their generation.[83] The questions asked included: What does it take to relate to young college athletes? How old is too old to coach? What makes an effective football coach? Is it harder for coaches from different eras to relate to today's student athletes? The answers were quite intriguing. The majority agreed age does not matter, but there were some who offered conflicting opinions. For example, a punter from Purdue states, "It is hard to define what is meant by an 'older' coach. Is Bobby Bowden [former Florida State University coach] old and therefore ineffective? Well, he has a multitude of rings that would suggest otherwise." A running back from West Virginia had this to say: "I think a good coach has a way to motivate and encourage his players, and that really doesn't have much to do with his age." A quarterback from Kansas says, "I see a lot of old coaches who work well with the players just fine." A free safety from Navy had a different spin on older coaches: "Older coaches may have a hard time relating to today's players off the field, but this should not hurt the effectiveness of older coaches. When a coach and player are on the football field, they share a common bond, football." A quarterback from Ole Miss mentioned what a challenge it is coaching today's player: "It definitely takes a special person to take on the challenge of coaching today's athletes. Athletes today are much different than they were ten years ago, and the coaches of today have to be extremely patient." A center from Baylor said, "I think it takes a different type of coach to coach in today's game. You need a coach that you can relate to and that you can feel comfortable with." A wide receiver from Colorado agrees it is a challenge and coaches must adapt to the changing of the times, saying, "Yes it is hard for coaches to relate. Times change and you have to change with the times." A player from Baylor agreed: "But today's coaches still have to modernize and stay with the times in order to relate well with their players."

World Cup–winning coach and sport psychology consultant Tony Dicicco and Colleen Hacker, respectively, detail in their book, *Catch Them Being Good,* that the old model of coaching champions got results, albeit in the short run.[84] Those coaches who typified this old model included the likes of Woody Hayes (Ohio State) and Bobby Knight (Indiana, Texas Tech). According to the authors, this old model did not distinguish one player from another and treated them all in similar fashion, which was "relentlessly driving them to perfection." The authors believe the new model of the champion must change with the times because athletes do not practice blind obedience, they often ask the question, "why" (are we doing this, doing that), and each player needs to be motivated differently. An "old school" coach would not allow players to ask the "why" question but the modern coach must let the players have a say and ask questions and make decisions. Dicicco calls this "inspiring my players with my humanity" and not simply "leading with my intensity" which was characteristic of the old model of champions. The authors outline important steps coaches can take to "exchange their old model for a new one." These are: teach your players how to compete, ask advice of your captains and other leaders, learn to listen to your players, be flexible, allow for individuality, create community, teach tolerance of others' mistakes (and your own), and my favorite, foster leadership![85]

Another term used often to characterize a certain type of coach is "player's coach." Some equate this term to mean a modern coach, while others believe a player's coach is a "powderpuff" whom teams take advantage of. Before the classic matchup that was the 2006 Rose Bowl between USC and Texas, a *Los Angeles Times* writer wrote both of the coaches are far cries from the archetypal football coach of yesteryear, but instead, are player's coaches who "prove that nice guys don't finish last." Despite both coaches (Pete Carroll and Mack Brown) having been characterized as too soft early in their careers, both of them are now "sitting atop college football and observers of the game wonder whether their 'humanistic' style will gain respect." A coach known for his authoritarian ways at Arizona State University in the 70s, Frank Kush, was quoted in the article: "I would call them soft in comparison to me, but I don't think either one of them is truly soft. It comes down to teaching. The way to evaluate a coach is, are the players improving?"[86]

Jackie Sherrill, former head football coach at Arkansas, Pitt, Texas A&M, and Mississippi State, who retired in 2003, was asked if he thought his former head coach, Bear Bryant (University of Alabama great), could still be successful coaching today's athletes. Sherrill was certain of it. "A player's coach is not somebody that's going to hug and kiss you and do all those things. A player's coach is a person that you know will be there when you need him."[87] Rick Carlisle, coach of the NBA's Dallas Mavericks who led his team to the 2011 NBA title, and who played for the Boston Celtics' legendary coach Red Auerbach, had this to say about his former mentor: "A lot of people think that Red Auerbach could be a menacing guy to be around. I found that he had a great feel for getting his point across and also softening it up and encouraging you."[88]

Coaching Today's Athletes—Lessons Learned

Based upon numerous years consulting in sport and the research conducted by generational experts, Table 2 is a compilation of "lessons learned" regarding generational collisions between coach and athlete, coach and team, and the importance of modernizing coaching approaches to help players become their best. These "lessons learned" act as a springboard for Chapter 3, which goes into greater detail about ten specific methods modern coaches can utilize to get the most from their millennial athletes while maximizing their potential by how they reach, teach, relate, motivate, and lead these athletes.

Table 2: Lessons Learned About Generational and Team Collisions

NUMBER	TITLE	LESSON LEARNED—TECHNIQUE
1	Awareness of generational misunderstandings	Realize these misunderstandings could be factors in how coach, player and team attempt to cope and problem solve con-

		flicts, whether they be issues with role identification, clarification, acceptance, playing time, or communication issues.
2	Awareness of generational personalities	Improve your understanding and connection with players through considering their generational personalities and current skill set (accentuate their strengths). It will be time well spent and will have the desired impact.
3	Awareness of own behaviors	Improve awareness of the effect personal behaviors and decisions have on players and how behaviors and decisions relate and differ from those of athletes (compatibility).
4	Establish standards and roles	Spend time establishing expectations, standards, and roles for each player and team while considering player preferences and allowing them to collaborate in this process.
5	Enhance training	Organize challenging, upbeat, varied, and updated training sessions. Doing the same drills over and over will do little to improve today's teams. Ensure players see how what they are doing transfers onto the game court or field.
6	Importance of meetings	Holding informal and frequent meetings, especially individual meetings, even if they are text or emails to offer a kind word or to check in on them after a hard session.
7	Balanced approach	Establish a balanced approach to sport, classes, and social commitments for players. Have a weekly or monthly schedule detailing all of their responsibilities and try to stick to it. Today's athletes are a busy group and will need to pack a lot into the available "free time." Continually changing the schedule will frustrate them beyond belief.
8	Personal expectations/goals	Help individual players establish personal expectations and goals, and ensure these

Number	Title	Lesson Learned—Technique
		are referred to often and updated if needed. This will show true concern for their personal pursuits and goals.
9	Enhance the experience	Be accountable for enhancing the student-athlete experience. The following questions can help leaders achieve this goal: What makes the relationship with players special? What do they learn in addition to their sport in this program? What life skills are being taught and reinforced? Are players active in the campus community?
10	Keep communication open	Players will network and fight for what they believe in, and administrators are listening to them more and more. Consider the articles shared throughout this chapter. Today's athletes have a voice and will not hesitate to use that voice, to the media, to the top administrator, or to a lawyer. Keep the lines of communication open and treat athletes with respect.
11	Cope with adversity adaptively	Assist dissatisfied athletes in coping with adversity in an adaptive fashion by being aware of athletes' common behaviors and emotional reactions to challenging times. When they deviate from these normal responses will be the cue to intervene.
12	Players are people first	Coaches must appreciate their players as people first, athletes second. The active sharing of respect and trust is a collaborative exercise, which in most cases begins with the coach. They will follow the leader's lead. The old adage applies: "They don't care how much you know until they know how much you care."

"In these days of two-career couples and the failure of the traditional family, we as coaches have the responsibility to educate our players on what it takes to become successful leaders and adults."[89]

—Roby Stahl, former professional
soccer player and coach

– 3 –

Techniques for Reaching, Teaching, Relating, Motivating and Leading the Millennials

*"Adjustments are not frivolous abandonments of philosophy.
If the philosophy is based on application, rather than just theory,
then the coach will consistently be observing how his players respond
to him and to his techniques. The ability and willingness to make
adjustments are signs of a number of positive attitudes."*[1]
—Harvey Dorfman,
author/sport psychology consultant

Helping students and players become not only leaders, but good and effective leaders, begins with parents, coaches, teachers, and mentors. Even with the knowledge of who today's young people are and how they got to where/who they are, along with realizing the importance of generational and team clash points, while applying the "lessons learned," there is still much to learn. Generational researcher and consultant Claire Raines offers additional strategies to inform and educate present and future leaders. She warns those in authority to be prepared for high expectations from these young people and moderate to high parental involvement, while not expecting players to pay their dues, nor dousing their enthusiasm or discounting their ideas for lack of experience. Raines encourages leaders to encourage, mentor, respect, and learn from today's young people while working hard to meet their high expectations.[2] This chapter includes ten additional strategies that complement Raines' list of "readiness strategies," based on my leadership consulting, and the work of generational consultants and coaches who have modernized and continue to empower young athletes.

A story about crossing the generational divide occurred with a professional team from Major League Baseball, pointing to the importance of being prepared for coaching today's generation. Harvey Dorfman, sport psychology consultant, shares in his book, *Coaching the Mental Game,* what he told members of the St. Louis Cardinals organization during a meeting when a question was raised about "today's kids." In his words, "I reminded them (coaches) of the date on the contract they signed. That date indicates that you're all leaders in the new millennium. You're not being hired to coach kids of the '60s or '70s or '80s. The effective leader addresses the credo of the organization and the need of each player. No compromise of principle and standard; no intolerance for the individual. Whatever his age or yours."[3]

The ten strategies that can help leaders bridge the generational gap include: Relating (previously mentioned in Chapter 2), Connecting, Respecting, Trusting, Envisioning, Empowering, Enabling, Collaborating, Competing, and Adjusting. Prior to detailing the strategies, a quick review of the applicable, specific characteristics is presented, termed the "*Scouting Report*," which rationalizes the use and application of a particular strategy, titled the "*Game Plan.*"

Connecting to the Millennial

The *Scouting Report* recognizes this generation as a very social group, preferring and craving social stimulation because they have always had it at their fingertips via cell phone, computers, email, instant messaging, websites, and social networking. With these tendencies, there is a strong desire to be part of what is going on while seeking opportunities for greater involvement. As mentioned previously, technology is second nature to millennials. They truly are "digital natives," leaving Boomer or Generation X coaches, teachers, and parents playing "technological catch-up" since we are "digital immigrants." Connecting to today's athlete must include a *game plan,* detailed below, to also connect with their parents since they are so active in their kids' lives.

(1) Ask about and refer to student-athletes' goals and their plans for the future.
(2) Open-door policy is expected, and so is being available after-hours for texting and emailing. They need to know there is availability for them, outside of "banker's hours."
(3) Continually reinforce the idea of keeping team issues "in house." With how connected these athletes are, team "dirty laundry" could be in cyberspace in seconds, and fodder for opponents' bulletin boards.
(4) Be very clear about expectations as a coach and respond consistently across situations and challenges because today's athletes are always watching, comparing,

and sharing their situations with their parents, friends, and even friends on opposing teams.

(5) Build in time for the team to be able to have "team" time, even during practice, such as a fun activity to start and conclude practice, or allowing catch-up time before stretching, or the use of team outings, even team fundraisers.

(6) Ask each player often about how they are doing and continually work to build a relationship with each player that is not only based upon the sport. Moreover, connect to their parents as a continual practice. Having success teaching today's student-athletes entails forging a relationship, not only with the student-athlete, but his/her parent(s) as well since parents are the role models (conventional characteristic). "You recruited me when you recruited him" is a common quote from recruit's parents as told to college coaches.

(7) I have included ten points to a millennial parent connection plan in Table 1.

Table 1: Millennial Parent Connection Plan

NUMBER	TITLE	LESSON LEARNED—TECHNIQUE
1	Parent meetings	Conduct several parent meetings prior to the start of the season for youth, club, and high school programs. For college programs, ensure this information is shared on recruiting visits. Use this time to discuss philosophy, playing time rules, the role of parents in practices and games, and the communication process (how to engage the coach about issues).
2	Moderately involved	Stress the importance of being a moderately involved parent. This includes parents showing interest in their child's sporting endeavors but at a moderate level. Attending all practices is not a moderate level, nor is critiquing play and trying to coach from the sideline. Include these "moderate level" practices on a handout for them.
3	Over-involved	Describe the effects of over-involved parents. Similar to the above list, detail these on a handout for them. The take-home message is parents are not helping their athlete by behaving this way and are taking away from the full experience for their child. Parental behavior that is considered over-involved includes embarrassing

NUMBER	TITLE	LESSON LEARNED—TECHNIQUE
		the player, adding pressure to play well and making play less fun by making it about them and not the child.
4	Embarrassments	Ask parents if they are partaking in behaviors that embarrass their player. Again, outline what these behaviors are in verbal and written terms. For example, are they too intrusive, too loud, criticizing everyone and everything? Do they give unsolicited advice to coaches and do they get angry when things are not going well on the field or court?
5	Mistakes teach	In these meetings also discuss how making mistakes on the court or field, along with losing, teaches valuable lessons and is important to the learning process. For example, some lessons learned in losses include learning to analyze and make adjustments, the development of mental toughness as well as a greater appreciation of success, and how it usually helps to improve motivation to work harder.
6	Be a model	Also explain how parents reinforce and model good sportsmanship (or sportspersonship) behaviors, rather than gamesmanship (gamespersonship) behaviors. Gamesmanship refers to behaviors used to gain a winning or advantageous edge over opponents, such as bending the rules (holding the jersey) or trying to get into an opponent's head by distracting him/her. Parents can send a strong message to their player if they punish their child's unsportsmanlike or gamesmanship behaviors.
7	Model values	Parents must be models of important values, such as showing self-control (handling their emotions), self-reliance (allowing players to handle their own adversity), responsibility (leaving it up to

		the athlete to ready themselves for practice or game), perseverance (helping the player to keep working hard despite adversity, like lack of playing time, losing, etc.), and perspective (winning is not the sole objective to playing sport).
8	Parental feedback	Ask for parental feedback and for their assistance in menial (getting water, pumping up soccer balls, providing snacks) to important (travel plans, parental committees, etc.) tasks. The parents want to be part of it and will force themselves in if needed, so they might as well be given the opportunity to help.
9	Debriefings	Address how to best offer practice and game debriefings to these parents. With patience and the right values and practices, sport parents can be a great source of support, motivation and inspiration. Some of the correct practices to offer feedback post-practice or post-game include parents speaking when spoken to (let the player ask you what you thought of the game and their play), ask questions such as, "Did you have fun? What did you work on today? What did you improve upon? What did your team do well today?"
10	Share the joy	Parents should be encouraged to share the enjoyable sport experience with their athlete, win or lose, and with other players and their parents. Make it a fun, family social activity.

Respecting the Millennial

To begin this *Scouting Report,* it is important to review the important characteristics applicable to these particular strategies. First, an article written in the *National Federation of High Schools Coaches Quarterly Magazine* stresses the importance of changing one's approach when coaching today's athlete.

The author, William Berard III, believes students today view authority differently than in the past due to what they watch on television and view on the internet and social networking sites, and notes these sources present mixed messages about how to respect those in authority. He continues: "Although it is imperative that a coach demand and receive respect from their players, that respect must be more of a mutual one today than in years past. It is much more of a two way street and give and take relationship in how a coach deals with their athletes."[4]

In their book, *The Seven Secrets of Successful Coaches*, Jeff Janssen and Greg Dale highlight five ways coaches earn the respect of their athletes: treating athletes with respect by abiding by the golden rule (treat people the way they would like to be treated), being honest and trustworthy, not being afraid to show how much you care about your athletes, creating an environment where athletes feel valued, appreciated, and challenged, and building your athletes' confidence while guiding them toward their goals.[5] Athletes today want their coaches to invest in them as people and as performers, so coaches must plan on spending a lot of time teaching, coaching, mentoring, and conversing with athletes. Today's younger coaches must be made aware of this level of commitment. Anson Dorrance, the highly successful women's soccer coach from the University of North Carolina, wrote in his book, *Training Soccer Champions,* "Some coaches no longer make the emotional commitment needed to motivate players to attain the standard required of them to compete successfully at the highest level. Coaches sometimes are not willing to make that commitment because it's so exhausting."[6] Although he used this to detail the commitment it takes to lead players on the soccer field, it can be applied to the plight of the modern coach taking on the challenge of coaching today's players and teams. Moreover, the story used to kick-start this chapter from Harvey Dorfman was a strong endorsement for respecting each player and the standards put in place to assist individual and team. The following quotes offer additional support for the importance of respect:

> *"If your players respect you, you can have a very good working environment. If they respect you and like you, you can have a very harmonious working environment. If they dislike you and don't respect you, then it's just poison— it's your death. So if you can only pick one, you choose respect."*[7]
>
> —Rhonda Revelle,
> University of Nebraska softball coach

"It's interesting to me because you hear coaches say all the time,
I don't want to be liked, I just want to be respected. Believe me, if
players like you and respect you, they'll do just about anything for you."[8]
—Marcus Allen,
former NFL Kansas City Chiefs player

The *Game Plan* consists of:

(1) Understanding the generational differences and how misunderstandings and clash points can occur.
(2) Effectively establishing a balanced approach to your coaching by respecting your athletes' free time when scheduling the days, weeks, and months. They are a very busy generation and time must be given for other interests.
(3) Coaches being accountable to enhancing student-athlete "experience" by doing more than simply coaching the sport, such as embracing the value and opportunity for community service, fundraisers, or scholastic or university events.
(4) Coaches/teachers appreciating their student-athletes as people first, student-athletes second. Their experience on the field and court must mean more than simply training and playing their sport. What life lessons and skills are being experienced, taught, and learned?
(5) Continually having informal/formal reviews of progress and areas to work on. This is a must with this generation of players.
(6) Asking for and respecting opinions and feedback on a regular basis. They have been asked for their feedback from their parents since before they could speak, literally! It is what they are used to. Athletes want a voice and want to be listened to. They expect it.

Trusting the Millennial

Today's athletes have very high expectations of themselves and of their mentors as well. They are open to being led by those with the right skills, ethics, and by those who can help them accomplish their goals. Keep in mind this generation is multi-media driven and in turn can be skeptical since they are so used to being bombarded with so much information, 24–7. The majority of this information can be conflicting about the world and its rulers, and they are thus untrusting from the onset. Their conventional beliefs cause them to question almost everything, yet at the same time this conventional thinking also places a great importance on the ethics and values of their mentors. Speaking of trust, it has been found to be an important determinant in establishing close relationships, and even in winning basketball games. In a 2000 study published in the *Journal of Applied Psychology,* researcher Kurt Dirks found only two factors had a significant effect on conference record. The first was talent, followed closely by trust in the coach. How this works, said Dirks, is "trust in leadership allows the team members to suspend their questions, doubts, and personal motives and instead throw themselves into working toward team goals."[9] Also, trust in coaches' leadership is both a product and a determinant of team performance. Given trust is so important, leaders should use trust-building strategies such as role modeling, being fair in the treatment of players, and asking players to collaborate with decision making. Other points to add to the *Game Plan* include:

(1) "Do as I do and as I say." This is a zero tolerance generation and will thus lose respect and trust quickly.
(2) This is a generation who is willing to be led if their motives are met, so leaders must take the time and effort to get to know what these motives are. All coaches have to do to gain access to this important information is ask.
(3) Today's athletes are a loyal bunch, albeit a bit skeptical in the beginning, but they will also keep their options open. Some coaches refer to athletes today as "free agents," as they are open to new opportunities if they perceive their current place and people are not helping them to accomplish their goals.
(4) Studies have shown the following coach behaviors hurt athletes' performances: too uptight in competition, not enough feedback asked for, overtraining, and poor organization.
(5) These same studies cite the coach behaviors that help athletes' performances, which include: not overly instructive, good communicator, works to build chemistry, well-organized, provides good training and conditioning, and is calm and relaxed in stressful times.
(6) Treat athletes as people first, thus establishing real relationships.
(7) It is very important players know their coach will be there when things get tough.

Coach Roy Williams from the University of North Carolina shares his thoughts on the importance placed on trust in his program: "They know that I'll never put my personal goals or wishes in front of what's best for the program. I think that trust is something that really is important."[10] "Trust, that loyalty, that feeling that we're in this together is the most important thing with our team."[11]

The importance of being a good model, and practicing what one preaches, is never as apparent as in this story. In New Jersey, a father wanted to teach his 16-year-old daughter a lesson about drinking when she came home drunk one night, so he proceeded to call the police. Upon their arrival, the daughter told them her father had weapons and illegal drugs in the house. She then led them to a crawl space where they found four semiautomatic guns and more than 600 vials of cocaine.[12]

Envisioning the Process for the Millennial

Since this generation is so goal driven, athletes want to consistently feel they are achieving and working toward something while continually developing and improving. They do expect success due to their overinflated confidence from over-parenting and mature relationships with parents and from them living in "mini-adulthood" for much of their lives. Combined with their affinity for group interaction, these athletes are ripe for team bonding and team building activities. Today's most successful coaches have known for several years the importance of including their teams in the envisioning process and having them assist in developing the team standards and team identity points, namely, what they want their team to look like, sound like, and play like. Considering these characteristics, the *Game Plan* should include:

(1) Players are driven by a strong team ethic and an unquenchable thirst for achievement. Coaches and players can be on the same page while designing the road map for the season. Ask for feedback on all sorts of different matters.
(2) Despite being strong team players, they also need to receive personal attention often. For these athletes, being underutilized and overlooked is a huge source of anxiety and frustration.
(3) Seasonal and personal goals must be continually evaluated and adjusted. It is time well spent because of how this process motivates.
(4) Helping athletes focus more on the process of getting better than simply on the outcome of winning is an important practice for modern coaches. Since these athletes are so goal driven toward achievement (which is a downside to their drive), watch how much emphasis is placed on rankings, "must wins," and remain composed and consistent regardless of outcome.
(5) Setting team/individually accepted vision and standards is a fun, motivating and empowering activity for teams. By doing this collectively, it will increase affiliation motivation while clarifying team standards and norms and helping the athletes commit to something beyond themselves.
(6) More information on helping players and teams with this process can be found in Chapter 10.

Empowering the Millennial

A consistent theme throughout the first three chapters of this book has been the importance of modern coaches allowing their athletes and teams to assist in the process of building the vision and standards of the program. If these things are already established, then it is important to allow the team to add their own signature to these goals and traditions. With the athletic programs I work with, especially those consults lasting many years, each new team's challenge is to add to the list of team traditions from past teams, leaving their own legacy on the fabric of their championship program. Today's generation loves challenges almost as much as they love collaborating in groups and having the opportunity to be heard. Since they have always been asked by their parents for their opinions and preferences ("What do you want to eat for dinner? What will you wear to school today? What do you want to do this weekend?"), they have come to expect it in the majority of situations they find themselves in, classroom, ball field, or when older, board room. Coaches should use this attitude to their advantage by giving players more of a say and more responsibility, even the responsibility of helping coaches lead the team. This way, some of the day-to-day tasks, such as keeping the team updated on schedule, assisting in recruiting, upkeep of locker room and practice facilities, can be put on the shoulders of these captains, giving them a bigger stake in the program, thus entrenching them into the workings of the program. This helps in increasing their commitment to the program's goals, which hopefully becomes contagious throughout the team. With how mobile these athletes are, with the increasing number of them transferring from club to club, or university to university (some call this trend "surfing"), the deeper the commitment and sense of contribution, the more buy-in there will be and thus, the lower the chances of seceding. Dr. Lapchick's quote emphasizes the importance of leadership for today's young people.

> *"I would advise any adult who has a responsibility for young people—*
> *whether that adult is a parent, coach, counselor, or teacher—*
> *to treat every single young person as a potential leader."*[13]
> —Dr. Richard Lapchick,
> director of DeVos Sport Business Management Program
> and co-director of TIDES, University of Central Florida

The *Game Plan* to empower athletes and teams should include the following:

(1) Replace the "me" with the "we" in planning and promoting the program, including assisting in establishing team goals, standards, and program's traditions. Many of the collegiate programs I have consulted embrace the concept of a "player centered/player driven" program, characterized by players earning leadership responsibility when expectations are met, with the appropriate support and guidance (see the next strategy, Enabling, for more details). Giving players more control over decision making and the vision and direction of the program can truly empower them to commit and contribute more toward the collective effort on the field or court.

(2) Emphasize the importance of "peer-team" pressure and influence, which the sport psychology literature terms "team norming." Acclaimed University of North Carolina basketball coach Dean Smith had this to say of the importance of peer pressure: "We were fortunate at North Carolina to have many great junior and senior leaders. Peer pressure is often a wonderful thing."[14] Coaches should ask themselves about their use of productive peer pressure on their teams.

(3) Be open to all sorts of challenges due to today's young person's multitasking ways and how their attentional capabilities work. They are used to continual stimulation from their technological devices and media since whatever they want or need is at their fingertips, so boredom sets in quickly, especially in repetitive drilling if they do not see how this work fits into the bigger picture. According to J. Bradley Garner, author of *A Brief Guide for Teaching Millennial Learners*, it is important to "intentionally connect content with practice. Always ask yourself the 'so what?' and 'now what?' questions. These questions help us evaluate the content of what we are teaching and how we are connecting the content to real world scenarios."[15] This is the desired "big picture" viewpoint referred to earlier.

(4) Establish a leadership council of captains, along with a formal leadership development program so captains and other senior level players can offer insights to the coach and staff.

(5) Always be on the look-out for young players who may be showing leadership potential. Buck O'Neil, who broke the color barrier for coaches when he was hired to coach the MLB Chicago Cubs, believes anyone can be a leader, they just need to be recognized and given the chance. In his words, "Young people can be leaders, so pay attention to them. Give them a chance. They have wonderful ideas—ideas that we grown-ups would never think of. The more chances they have to lead, the more their abilities and confidence will develop and grow."[16]

Enabling the Millennial (Mentor)

Enabling is a term usually denoting a negative, whereby we enable or help someone to continue their bad habits, whether those be overeating, behaving childishly, using the English language poorly, or even more serious issues, such as eating disorders, drug use, overexercising, and so many other maladaptive coping behaviors. Dean Smith states in his book, *The Carolina Way,* most of the basketball players he ran across on the recruiting trail, and even those who decided to come to play for him, were enabled by coaches, parents, and teachers because of their athletic skill. "Many of the most highly recruited high school players had been pampered and spoiled. They had been told for as long as they could remember how special they were, how great they were going to be. Adults waited on them hand and foot."[17] Regardless of the sport coached, many coaches and teachers have come across some of today's athletes who have been enabled in this fashion, leaving them, staff, and teammates to work hard at breaking some selfish, narcissistic habits.

The word "enable" means "to make able, give power, means, and competence."[18] Leaders of leaders must be able to *enable*, to give power, competence, and the ability to lead others through self-responsibility, self-awareness, and the maximal use of personal leadership strengths. As Coach Dean Smith wrote, despite getting some prima-donnas into his program, he and his staff began the minute they walked on campus to help acclimate them to a different culture: "We worked to break them of habits and characteristics that we thought would be detrimental to our team's success as well as to theirs. We wanted the 'Harry High School' mentality checked at the door."[19] Confronting the impact of negative enabling practices, replacing them with productive peer pressure and positive enabling take conscious work and effort from all parties. This is where the *Game Plan* begins, focusing on addressing these issues in as productive and collaborative an effort as possible, especially if one has leaders already established, who can be of great assistance in acclimating the "negative enabled ones" into a different culture. More will be discussed about developing team culture in Chapter 12.

(1) Use team leaders to help the prima-donnas learn the culture of the team their first day on campus.

(2) Conduct informal and frequent meetings especially with individual athletes.

(3) Help individual players establish personal expectations and goals regarding other aspects than just their game, and ask them important follow-up questions, such as these: Do they want to be in a leadership role? Do they believe they can contribute more? If so, in what specific areas? What is holding them back from doing those things already?

(4) Mentor athletes to improve not only their play but needed life skills, such as leadership, risk taking, and problem solving. Talking about it and doing it are obviously two different things. True mentoring takes time with consistent meetings spent on teaching, practicing, and following-up.

(5) Reverse mentoring works well with today's athletes. Leaders can learn from the athletes not only about technology but about ways they can help with team bonding, leadership initiatives, dealing with prima-donna teammates, favorite drills, game preparation procedures, etc. They will welcome the effort and actually learn different ways of doing things (see Buck O'Neil's quote in the previous strategy write-up).

Collaborating with the Millennial

As has been stated many times already, today's athletes prefer and thrive while working in groups, and they want to include their mentors, teachers, and/or coaches in this process and their group, and to make the team agenda their agenda, team goals for the program their goals for the program. Marketers state that younger people today want to be different, just like everybody else, in that they express their individuality yet seek to fit into a group, regardless of the environment (school, sport, work). If they are a welcome part of the process, these goal-directed players will work hard and smart for the team. Yet, if they begin to think that what they are doing is counter to their goals, they will be quite negative and will question authority, or even rebel if pushed, evidenced by the team revolt article cited in Chapter 2. That is why keeping in contact and offering continual feedback, even if it is critical feedback, is so important to gauge their motivations and attitudes. Another positive is they welcome structure, because they have always had it in school and in sports, and will "buy in" if they see what they are doing will contribute to achievement/success. Keep in mind also they have always been immersed in "organized" sport, with adult coaches, referees, uniforms, schedules, and the like. It was the Gen Xer generation who would partake in "free play," who not only played the game but were also the coaches and referees who made all decisions and solved all problems that arose. Today's athletes are not privy to this wonderful learning lab, but on the flipside, they do know structure, prefer it, and operate well within its guidelines. Leaders today should take advantage of their preferences for structure, for greater contribution to a collaborative team effort, and their goal-driven tendencies. The *Game Plan* to enhance collaborating with the millennial includes:

(1) Establish individual and team expectations, standards, and roles with their assistance. Following up and evaluating progress made on these expectations, standards, role clarity and acceptance will be both educational and motivational.

(2) Celebrate their team spirit and establish team traditions. Have them brainstorm vision posters, team quotes, design T shirts, and continually add to their list of team traditions and practices.

(3) Welcome assistance in marketing their program via car washes, fundraising, community service, and representing the program around town or around campus.

(4) Capitalize on players' desire for a "player-driven" climate and desire to work, play, and chill with their teammates while embracing the fun aspect of working together and accomplishing their goals together.

(5) Give feedback as to how they contribute to the group's effort and execution, which in most cases is as empowering, if not more so, as telling them how they are playing individually.

(6) Help them to take pride in their positional units or special teams. Defensive players have a team identity as a "steel curtain," or the power play unit will always produce shots, or the defensive power play unit is always ready and working to score short-handed goals. Today's athletes believe they work with coaches, not for coaches, so their sense of affiliation motivation can be used to the team's advantage.

(7) Open up the communication process and allow players the opportunity to voice their opinions to improve the collaborative process, and improve trust between coach, players, and team. One of the big generational clash points reported by millennials is their ideas are discounted due to their lack of experience. Although realistically this may be the case, the upside of allowing for open feedback is huge, even if it is not based upon time-tested experience.

Competing and the Millennial

"I think the athlete of today is much more savvy. They want to know why they are doing what they are doing and I think that is good."[20]

—Jerry Yeagley,
former men's soccer coach, Indiana University

The *Scouting Report* for this particular characteristic includes the fact millennials are "stimulation junkies" and love to be challenged. They are savvy to how competitive life is out there, from how they place on their standardized exams throughout their school years, to how competitive their sport is, to how competitive the job market is. They are achievement-driven and want to be the best, now, therefore they are not the most patient bunch. Millennials are not used to being told "no" since the majority of the parents out there fail to do so. The resulting effect of this is players today will work the system if a rationale is not provided to them, which could mean the player and/or parent or both go above the coach's head to the athletic director or even further up the chain. College professors and university administrators have commented on the increasing number of parent complaints about grades and advising issues.[21] Students and athletes are used to having things done for them, so when they hit a rough patch the problem is escalated and there is usually someone else to blame for it.

It becomes essential for millennials to be taught by their mentors that they will not always get their way, while also learning that this is the time to handle things on their own instead of deferring to parents or other adults. The same could be said about sport-related adversity that may strike any time, and usually will, such as not getting the starting position or playing as long as one wishes. Players need to realize that getting better takes time and adverse situations are a part of the learning process. Each adverse situation presents them with the opportunity to improve their ability to handle difficulties as they arise. Moreover, the more teachers, coaches, and mentors and those who support their efforts (parents) allow them to fend for themselves in these times of adversity, the more they strengthen their conflict management and coping strategies by trying them, testing them, and finally adding them to their arsenal. The *Game Plan* should include:

(1) Enhancing training, which includes a deliberate setup and organization that includes challenging, upbeat, and updated sessions.
(2) Offering lots of feedback while letting them know *what/why/how* they are doing.
(3) Stressing the importance of tempering their cathartic release of competitive tendencies in a fun and collaborative way. The term "productive rivalry" should be used because it is important their competitive focus be in the direction of improving the team process and collaborative system, whether it be the offensive, defensive, special team plays, positional responsibilities, and so on. Teams need to allow themselves to compete so at the end of the day, teammates are still teammates and not enemies, and know that each player is still working toward the same goals.
(4) Initiating structure and consequences for rule breakers since today's athletes will lose trust and respect for the leadership of the program if this is not done. Players will network and collaborate to fight for what they believe in, which is part of their competitive nature. They want to be treated fairly and consistently.
(5) Continue establishing real communication and relationships with players. This mantra is very real with today's athletes: "Rules without relationships leads to rebellion." They do prefer structure and rules but without the prerequisite relationship between them and the coach, there will be a disconnect. Players will work hard and smart if they are lead by a mentor and allowed to have fun in the process.

Adjusting with the Millennial

> *"I think some coaches will not adapt or adjust.*
> *They think this is the way we've been doing things*
> *for 15 years and this is what I am comfortable with."*[22]
> —Gail Goestenkors,
> former Duke and University of Texas
> women's basketball coach

The take-home point from this strategy is for leaders of today's young people to be aware of personal biases, attitudes, and behaviors as they apply to teaching and mentoring today's student-athletes. Taking time to be reflective by asking questions such as those asked thus far in the book, and actively reflecting on the responses will be a valuable process. Some educators and coaches may not believe today's athletes are different, some may, and others may believe there is nothing we can do to change them, and still others may believe we should not try to change them but change ourselves. Others may have already started to change their own approach, to adjust, to the changing of the times and personnel. Some additional adjustment strategies to reflect upon include:

(1) When addressing teams, try to stay in the *present* and limit talk about *past* teams and players.

(2) Appreciate players' affinity for technology and use it in your coaching and staying in touch and communicating with your team (videotaping, texting, emailing, Tweeting, Skyping).

(3) "Modernize"—know some of what your players are into, including their interests, hobbies, etc.

(4) Be real! Realize not every player wants what the coach wants. As mentioned previously, it is so important to get to know players and their primary motives for playing. As the very successful volleyball coach from the University of Florida, Mary Wise, has stated, "You must understand the uniqueness of each individual. There are different push-buttons with each individual player."[23]

(5) Chapter 5, Emotional and Relational Intelligence, delves into the emotional side of coaching, an often ignored area for coaching education and workshops, yet a very important one with the challenges faced in coaching today's athletes.

(6) Embrace the opportunity of working with tomorrow's leaders who have valuable skills and a desire and attitude unlike any who has come before. Maintaining a balance of working hard, working smart, and enjoying the process are elements coaches like to teach their teams, but how many coaches practice what they preach? Highly successful football coach, Mack Brown, was noted in one article because he "became a better coach when he realized there was more to life than winning a football game." In this same *Sports Illustrated* article, Coach Brown made a conscious decision to "start having fun or quit coaching." His quarterback, Vince Young, who won him a national title in January 2006, noticed his coach's transformation: "He's relaxed, not uptight. He'll get on you if you drop a ball or make a mistake, but he jokes around, asks about your family or your girlfriend."[24] Another tough, "old school" type of coach has admittedly changed his ways— New York Giants coach Tom Coughlin. As the story goes, "After the Giants fell apart in 2006, and a lot of fans thought Coughlin had contributed to the slide, this proud coach listened to his children and his wife, Judy. Good grief, he even sought input from reporters who covered the team." He chronicled these changes in his book, *A Team to Believe In: Our Journey to the Super Bowl Championship.* One such change specific to the main topic of this current book is he formed a leadership council made up of key players for regular meetings.[25]

No one is saying this is an easy process, nor is it a one-time thing. Adjusting to changing landscapes is a continual process, and according to one very successful coach, it can be a very taxing process as well. Anson Dorrance, the 21-time national champion with the University of North Carolina women's soccer team, states, "From an individual perspective, the fight against mediocrity is taxing. It is even more taxing from a leadership perspective, where you can't just take care of yourself; you have to inspire the ones around you to follow your example."[26] As Coach Dorrance has shown, he continues to win national championships, from the '80s, '90s, and now in the '00s. He has obviously made the necessary adjustments despite how taxing it can be.

Thomas Houser, a youth volleyball coach, offered tips for "coaching survival" which help coaches avoid making some very common coaching mistakes while coaching today's athletes. These tips include:

(1) Criticize your players in private yet praise them in public (yet some would prefer to be praised in private).
(2) Support your players year round and not just during the season.
(3) Only implement change (techniques, tactics, systems, rules) if you truly understand it.
(4) Your team rules must be pro-player (rules are to teach and provide structure, not to bust them).
(5) Communicate with parents.
(6) You will never plan enough (double and triple check all arrangements).
(7) Plan special events during the season to spice things up.
(8) Stay in touch with players during the off-season.
(9) Help your players play in the off-season by finding camps or run your own.
(10) Find ways to improve yourself via coaching workshops, webinars, or leadership books.[27] What a novel idea!

"Our communities need young leaders.
The future of our nation and our world depends
on whether we can raise a new generation of leaders to tackle
the increasingly complex problems we face. This is not an option.
This is an absolute necessity."[28]

—Pat Williams,
Coaching Your Kids to Be Leaders

Part II

The Artful Science of Leadership:
Theory, Research and Application

– 4 –

Leadership Intelligence (LQ)

"Leadership can be learned by any of us, no matter our
age, circumstances or challenges we face."[1]
—Warren Bennis and Joan Goldsmith,
Learning to Lead

As was discussed in the first three chapters of this book, today's millennial students and athletes have valuable skills in some areas (e.g., they're technology savvy, goal directed, conventional, accepting of diversity, socially connected), while in others, such as leadership skills, are in need of attention and improvement. The president of Student Life University, Jay Strack, states, "Our universities and the military are realizing that the young people who stream into their halls and barracks are not well prepared to lead. We have produced a generation that is neither deep nor wide in leadership ability."[2] Although Chapter 3 addresses specific strategies parents, teachers, and coaches can use to "build bridges" and work more collaboratively with today's generation, these steps represent only a starting point. Being "on the same page" with players and students is one thing, but empowering them with critical life skills, especially leadership skills, takes a more proactive approach and process. The stance I take is to use sport as the vehicle for such a proactive process for improved leadership for today's generation.

Sport as a Vehicle for Leadership Development

Jay Coakley, a well-known and respected sport sociologist, believes sport provides athletes with opportunities to explore and develop their identities and relationships, while providing insight into their competence knowledge and assisting in providing life learning experiences.[3] Jim Loehr, a respected sport psychology consultant who operates the Human Performance Institute in Orlando, Florida, a facility that helps professionals from all sorts of fields improve their human potential and leadership abilities, also believes sport is an ideal place for leadership initiatives: "The personal and interpersonal dynamics of competitive sport provide rich opportunities to develop leadership skills that are, in many ways, prerequisites for success in life. Competitive sport can be a powerful laboratory for teaching discipline, social skills, conflict resolution, responsibility, attention skills, adversity management, goal setting and leadership."[4]

Research reveals sports can be a valuable medium to develop both social character and moral character, two important components of leadership. This work defines social character as the values of teamwork, friendship, loyalty, self-sacrifice, work ethic, and mental toughness. Moral character on the other hand is defined as the values of honesty, fairness, sportspersonship and integrity.[5] Additional research has shown sport participation in the right setting, namely the deemphasizing of winning as sole outcome of sport participation, can improve important life skills such as goal setting, positive thinking, problem solving, performing under pressure, meeting challenges, handling success and failure, and working within a team. The results of such skills include improved intrinsic motivation, self-esteem, competence, personal control, confidence.[6] It has been noted that sports can also enhance team building, communication skills, civic responsibility, and leadership. The incomparable John Wooden reinforces the value of sport in this quote: "I have always believed and taught that the game of basketball is of small importance compared with the totality of the life we live. The true importance of basketball is this: Every great virtue and principle that applies on the basketball court is completely transferable to everyday life."[7]

Considered by many to be one of the greatest coaches ever to grace a sideline with his ten national championships (at UCLA) and his "pyramid of success" as proof, the words and wisdom of Coach Wooden will continue to teach generations to come. NBC's Bob Costas says, "The America that produced John Wooden is gone. The principles which guided his life and career endure."[8] I certainly hope so.

Another pair of sport researchers, David Shields and Brenda Bredemeier, well-known for their work with sport and character development, stress the importance of coaches prioritizing time in their team meetings to discuss moral and character issues relevant to sport and life in general, with student-athletes benefitting tremendously from these discussions.[9] Not only can and should this be done at the early levels of competitive sport, but as one NBA coach exemplifies, it can be done at the upper echelon of sport as well. It has been reported that now-retired Los Angeles Lakers coach, Phil Jackson, took time in meetings to discuss moral issues, such as gun control and ethics, and even distributed books for the players to read on topics such as character and morality, sociology, history, Zen Buddhism, mindfulness, and even spirituality.[10]

One of the moral issues to address in team meetings with players of all ages is leadership. In one of his many wonderful books, Pat Williams, executive with the NBA's Orlando Magic and father of 19 children, states the number one desire of every parent, teacher, coach, pastor and youth worker is to help the youth of today become leaders. A professor of management was quoted in this book as saying, "If today's kids do not become leaders, where does society go?"[11]

> *"I think a lot of players burn out, and subsequently quit because they*
> *are missing consistently positive, productive leadership."*[12]
>
> —Anson Dorrance,
> *The Vision of a Champion*

Valuing Leadership in Sport

John Maxwell, an expert in leadership development and training, and author of more than 20 books on the subject, learned about leadership in the home. His parents valued leadership so much they were always reading books about leadership growing up. Maxwell states, "I read every weekday until I graduated from high school."[13] Another leadership guru, former chairman and chief executive officer of General Electric, Jack Welch, credits his mother as one of his most important influences on leadership, with the other influence being team sports.[14] Pat Williams simply states: "If you want to raise young people to be leaders, you must begin teaching and modeling leadership from the very earliest years of their lives."[15] One of the most successful women coaches, Pat Summitt, who led her Tennessee basketball team to six national championships, believed her job as coach was to help develop leaders. She states, "More than winning, I believe our job as coaches is to develop our players into responsible leaders. Sure we teach them how to be better athletes. But that's not all I want to be known for. I want the young women who come into our program to be better people and better leaders by the time they leave."[16]

In their book, *The Seven Secrets of Successful Coaches,* Jeff Janssen and Greg Dale interviewed coaches from the top collegiate to the professional ranks. A common theme throughout the many interviews, which covered the respective games' greats, was the value given to leadership development and training.[17] Coach Summitt believes teams cannot win consistently without good team leadership: "You won't win consistently without good team leadership. It's just that plain and simple. You've got to have players who are willing to buy into your system, demand the best from themselves and their teammates, and hold their teammates accountable."[18] Gary Barnett, former football coach at several top universities, echoes this sentiment: "Because team leaders are often the difference between successful and unsuccessful seasons, we as coaches must invest the time to develop them."[19] A perennial contender in NCAA men's basketball year in and year out has been Duke University. Their leader, Mike Krzyzewski, believes the "single most important ingredient after you get the talent is internal leadership."[20] A Naismith Basketball Hall of Famer, Kay Yow, also believes this to be true: "The quality of your team leaders can make or break your season."[21] In my younger days as an aspiring collegiate soccer coach, I was most impressed and star-struck with Jerry Yeagley, six-time national champion coach, who was known for winning the right way and was a true gentleman. Coach Yeagley had this to say about the value of leadership training: "Because I understand how important leaders are to the success of the team, I've worked hard at selecting the captains and helping them develop the leadership qualities that I feel are important."[22]

The aforementioned quotes highlight the importance and value given to leadership skills and leadership development at the highest levels of sport. Janssen lists seven benefits effective leaders provide their teams in another book on leadership: Good captains ensure high standards and a strong work ethic, help the team handle adversity, build better team chemistry, help the coach obtain the pulse of the team, minimize and manage conflict, help in recruiting, and are the best insurance against stupid acts committed by teammates.[23]

Other benefits I have seen in my leadership consultations over the past ten years can be seen in Table 1, which include labeling specific contexts and leadership responsibilities.

Table 1: Benefits of Sport Team Leadership

CONTEXT	RESPONSIBILITIES
Team organization	With how busy teams are these days, captains keep the team alerted of these schedule commitments and changes to it.
Team connections	Captains are responsible for connecting with their teammates on a daily basis to ensure each teammate feels a part of the program.
Locker room climate	Captains try to keep the locker room talk and banter productive and motivating, win or lose.

Practice leader	Captains keep the practice climate productive, energetic, and efficient.
Go-To's	Captains always want the ball with the game on the line and will make the plays that need to be made.
Lead by example	Captains are first to speak in team meetings, first to go in a drill, and know the system and plays.
Competitive	Captains are responsible for setting the competitive tone by getting the most out of every rep, drill, practice, and game opportunity.
Challenge teammates	Captains ensure their teammates follow the competitive tone set.
Improved teammate play	Captains help reinforce coach teachings and strategy instruction while helping their teammates make adjustments during game play.
Improved team play	In most sports, play on the field is dictated more by the players (adjusting and decision making) than by the coaches, and the captains are the "coaches" on the field or court of play.

This leadership business is hard work and it is much easier to simply be a follower, yet even being a follower has its own unique challenges, especially if players want to be effective followers. Much more on effective followership will be detailed in Chapter 11. So why then would someone want to take this on? Steve Gilbert, former football coach at Jacksonville University, told his players, "It feels good to be a leader and there are great rewards for being a good leader. Those rewards include a sense of satisfaction and a feeling that what you are doing is meaningful and significant."[24] Athletic director Stan Morrison, at the University of California Riverside, states, "Young people need to understand that the rewards of leadership far outweigh the rewards of following," and those who mentor young people "need to help them see that there are few things in life more exciting and uplifting than leadership—the challenge of determining their own destiny and even the destiny of their entire team or organization."[25] Donna Lopiano, a former athletic director at the University of Texas and Executive Director of the Women's Sports Foundation, believes everyone should be given the chance to captain because they are rewarded with increased self-esteem and confidence, along with improved "basic people skills, organizational skills, and communication skills."[26]

Lieutenant Colonel Eric Kail, leadership instructor at the U.S. Military Academy, includes in his chapter for the edited text *Leadership Lessons from West Point* three reasons why leader development must not only be included in an organization's mission but should also be a deliberate process:

(1) If leaders do not get personally involved in leader development they will be missing out on a rewarding experience of watching leaders learn and grow.

(2) Good leaders take advantage of factors that could directly affect personal and organizational effectiveness.

(3) Since leaders very seldom develop themselves into effective leaders without any assistance from others, why then would they decide to let their subordinates develop themselves as leaders. This is considered bad reasoning.[27]

An additional reason includes the notion that good leaders look to maximize all factors that could influence productivity, thus, having improving individual and team leadership can greatly improve a team's chances of succeeding. Another is knowing more about the newest of generations, the millennials, who are in need of improved leadership and followership skills to overcome their alleged shortcomings as a generation. Colonel Kail also states, "Every organization should be arguing that you cannot afford not to do any leader training."[28] Appreciating leadership for its own sake is a very important first step for coaches, players, and teams to make, followed by knowing and defining what leadership is and how best to perform effective leadership skills and strategies.

Defining Leadership

What is leadership? How administrators, coaches, captains, players, and teams define it sets the tone for leadership development. The task of defining such a grandiose concept is no easy feat, as much discourse revolves around this very task. The following quotes from legendary leaders will depict the esoteric nature of defining such a concept.

> *"There are no hereditary strata in leading.*
> *They're not born; they're made. There has to be an*
> *inclination, a commitment, a willingness to command."*[29]
> —Vince Lombardi,
> NFL Green Bay Packers

> *"Leadership is the ability to achieve goals through people.*
> *Leaders get things done—not through their own effort,*
> *but through the combined efforts of people."*[30]
> —Pat Williams,
> NBA Orlando Magic

*"Leadership is getting people to do what they don't want
to do, to achieve what they want to achieve."*[31]
—Tom Landry,
NFL Dallas Cowboys

*"The position of authority identifies the leadership role. The degree to
which one appropriately influences others identifies the leader."*[32]
—Harvey Dorfman,
MLB sport psychology consultant

*"Many of the world's greatest leaders demonstrated relatively little
aptitude for leadership in their youth, but instead learned this
esoteric art through study, apprenticeship and practice."*[33]
—Steven B. Sample,
former president of the
University of Southern California

*"Leadership involves getting others to willingly move in a new direction
in which they're not naturally inclined to move on their own."*[34]
—U.S. president Harry Truman

One can ascertain from the above quotes the notion that leaders are not born, but made, and leadership is about doing and working in collaboration with others (followers), while sometimes influencing and "moving" them in new directions. In a recent lecture, former New York City mayor Rudy Giuliani told the audience all leaders are born, literally, but after that, they are "made" into leaders by what they read, what they learn, who they work with and lessons learned from them, and other important life experiences.[35] In an attempt to prove the "leaders are made" axiom, one particular study conducted by business giant Johnson and Johnson reveals top performing leaders' first awareness of leadership competence began to show in late childhood or adolescence. Moreover, leadership excellence develops throughout the lifespan, and according to one of the researchers, "great leaders are made as they gradually acquire the competencies that make them so effective."[36] The textbook definition of leadership varies, but the definitive sport psychology textbook for university sport psychology programs, *Foundations of Sport and Exercise Psychology*, written by Dan Gould and Robert Weinberg, defines leadership as "the behavioral process of influencing individuals and groups toward set goals."[37] Another textbook on coaching theory written by former coach and current sport psychology researcher/practitioner Robin Vealey defines leadership in a similar way: "The behavioral, psychological, and social process of influencing individuals to move toward the achievement of specific objectives."[38] Dr. Steven Sample, former president of USC, put a different spin on this discussion, emphasizing instead *who* the leader is leading: "My definition of a leader is someone who has identifiable followers over whom he exercises power and authority through his actions and decisions."[39]

Leadership vs. Management

To add another layer to the definitional discourse, the organizational literature details a clear distinction between *leadership* and *management*. As an aside, in Chapter 11, a third concept not given its due attention in the literature is detailed regarding *followership*. Without followership there can be no leadership or management. Dr. John Kotter, professor of leadership at the Harvard Business School, extols those organizations who value both kinds of people: those who are strong managers (but not strong leaders), and those who are strong leaders (but not strong managers). The difference between the two, according to Dr. Kotter, is management is more about coping with complexity and leadership is about coping with change. He also asserts, "Good management brings a degree of order and consistency to key dimensions like the quality and profitability of products, and major changes are more and more necessary to survive and compete effectively in this new environment. More change always demands more leadership."[40] Dr. Abraham Zaleznik, professor emeritus of leadership at the Harvard Business School, agrees that managers and leaders are two very different types of people: "Managers' goals arise out of necessities rather than desires; they excel at diffusing conflicts between individuals or departments. Leaders, on the other hand, adopt personal, active attitudes towards goals. They look for the potential opportunities and rewards that lie around the corner, inspiring subordinates and firing up the creative process with their own energy."[41]

Leadership guru Warren Bennis writes that over the years several themes have become apparent through his interactions and interviews with leaders of all kinds, with one of them being the importance placed on knowing the key difference between management and leadership, which he reveals is: "Each of these individuals understands that management is getting people to do what needs to be done. Leadership is getting people to want to do what needs to be done. Managers push. Leaders pull. Managers command. Leaders communicate."[42] Similarly, Joe Batten in *Tough-Minded Leadership* states, "Managers push and direct. Leaders pull and expect."[43]

An article by Kotter published in the *Harvard Business Review's 10 Must*

Reads on Leadership includes his thoughts on manager versus leader: "Most U.S. corporations today are over-managed and under-led," pointing to the importance of these organizations to develop their capacity to exercise leadership. He also states, "Successful corporations don't wait for leaders to come along. They actively seek out people with leadership potential and expose them to career experiences designed to develop that potential."[44] It is important for leaders to be aware of their use of managerial and leadership behaviors by asking themselves the following questions: Do you over-manage (push and command) and under-lead (not pull or not communicate) like most corporations cited by Drs. Bennis and Kotter? Do you develop a culture of leadership where you recognize, expose and teach leadership to your players or team? What would your players perceive is the culture of your organization? Would your players view your behaviors as primarily managerial or leader?

To give some additional clarity, Kotter offers an example on how managers and leaders operate in different ways. For organizations that need to manage complexity, managers will plan and budget, whereby the leaders will begin the change process by setting a direction or vision for the future. Managers then work to achieve their plan by organizing and staffing, yet the leaders align people to commit to the vision. The next step is for managers to control and problem solve to ensure the plan is enacted, while the leaders motivate and inspire staffs to keep moving in the right direction despite the obstacles change presents.[45]

Applying these differences to sport, some additional questions should be answered: Where do you see your primary role—as a coach or captain, as a manager or as a leader, or both? Going further, what is the priority based on your particular situation? Head coaches at the national team or Olympic levels seem to hold managerial positions, while at the same time being critical agents in the setting of the direction and vision of their programs, especially at the start of a quadrennial. This may also point to the importance of this manager/head coach helping to create a leadership culture within the team to share the leadership load, especially with the use of experienced veterans who know what it takes to be successful on the international stage. Similarly, coaching at the collegiate level brings with it so many organizational tasks, the enormity of time it takes to recruit, and then the development of players on the practice field/court. How much time can be left to consistently push the right leadership buttons of individual players and the whole team through the season? Chapter 10 details a team building program, part of my leadership development program, which actively involves team captains, experienced players and the followers in the process of daily leading themselves toward their team goals.

In his book, *The Contrarian's Guide to Leadership,* Dr. Sample posits most people confuse good leadership with effective leadership. His example is Adolf Hitler, who was an extraordinarily effective leader due to his rise in power from very humble beginnings. Few would classify him as a good leader, rather an evil one, since one's moral values are put into play when evaluating a leader's goodness.[46] Peter Drucker, renowned scholar of management, had this to say of great leaders: "The three greatest leaders of the 20th century were Hitler, Stalin, and Mao. If that's leadership, I want no part of it."[47] I tend to agree with Michael Useem, director of the Wharton School's Center for Leadership and Change (University of Pennsylvania) and author of *The Leadership Moment,* as he writes, "A precise definition is not essential here; indeed, it may be impossible to arrive at one. But I take leadership to signify the act of making a difference."[48]

Making a Difference: Theories of Leadership

Despite Steven Sample's supposition, "Leadership is an art, not a science," many theories have been posited to explain the mechanisms of leadership. The early theories, *Trait* and *Behavioral,* focused on consistent personality traits for leadership effectiveness (trait theory) or the consistent behaviors of effective leaders (behavioral theory), which proved to have limited predictability and little support for their validity and applicability. Although this was the thinking of the day in the 1920s, and an attractive approach at the time, the research has shown leaders are not born (trait theory), and though interesting to determine the traits of the most successful leaders, its applicability to many situations (does a leader on the basketball court lead to a leader in the community) has not been shown. Likewise, studying the behaviors of successful coaches adds credibility to the argument that leaders are made, as generalizing these behaviors to the myriad of situations we find ourselves in, whether it be as a coach, teacher, businessperson, military leader, politician, clergy, and so on, is very limited and does not consider the interaction between people (coach-player, teammate to teammate) and the particular situation.

To combat these shortcomings, researchers and practitioners in organizational psychology, business and sport posited the interactional approach, whereby the effectiveness of leaders is the interaction between some common personality traits and leadership styles that best fit the particular situation. For example, many types of leadership styles exist, and the most referenced will be covered in Chapter 6, yet in the sport literature the more common coaching styles include authoritarian, cooperative, relationship-oriented, or task-oriented. Those coaches who are believed to be authoritarian are win-centered and make all of the decisions, while cooperative coaches are more process-centered and ask for feedback from their players. The relationship-oriented coaches develop interpersonal relationships as part of their coaching, whereas the task-oriented coaches work to develop players to accomplish the task, which is winning ballgames. More attention now is being given to two additional coaching styles, transactional and transformational leadership.

Transactional leadership is similar to the authoritarian style mentioned earlier by the way the leaders manage others and how much control is taken away from the followers. Vealey defines this type of leader as those who "influence followers via behavioral transactions such as providing resources or doling out rewards and punishments."[49] Transactional leaders are characterized as those who exact their authority on their followers through rewards and punishments, manage the operational side of their jobs well, and hold true to the pre-set standards and traditions. The rewards and punishments involved in the transactional approach are driven by contingent rewards (CR) based on high levels of development and performance, and management-by-exception (MBE). According to Bernard Bass, director of the Center for Leadership Studies at the State University of New York at Binghamton, the transactional style represents a "corrective transaction," a more ineffective method when compared to the use of CR, since in MBE, the "leader arranges to actively monitor deviances from standards, mistakes, and errors in the follower's assignments and to take corrective action as necessary."[50] The final component of transactional leadership is actually an absence of leadership, or an inactive or non-transaction leadership, referred to by Bass as laissez-faire leadership (LF).

Contrary to the transactional approach is the transformational style of leadership which, according to Hargrove, has been conceptualized as a process of "altering people's frames of reference or ways of thinking so as to produce profound shifts in their perceptions and ways of being, living, and responding."[51] Leaders who lead primarily with this style are able to attract followers while influencing team members through their collaborative methods and shared governance. They take risks to achieve greatness and rely on a shared vision. In *Transformational Leadership: Industry, Military, and Educational Impact,* Bernard Bass writes that civilian studies based on business and government, along with research conducted by the military, "have supported the greater effectiveness of transformational leadership in contrast to transactional leadership in generating subordinate extra effort, commitment, satisfaction, and contribution to military readiness."[52] According to Bass, there are four components to transformational leadership: *charismatic leadership* (leaders are admired for their leadership skills by followers), *inspirational motivation* (leaders motivate and inspire followers through setting goals and a vision and by communicating expectations), *intellectual stimulation* (leaders stimulate followers' efforts to be creative and innovative), and *individualized consideration* (leaders pay special attention to individual follower's needs and growth).[53]

Transformational leadership has also been shown to have a positive impact on performance and members' satisfaction across a wide range of organizations and contexts, including business organizations, educational institutions, church congregations, the military, and sports management. Although there is no right way to manage and coach across all situations, good and effective leaders are able to switch instinctively from one style to the next depending on the needs of the given personnel and situation. Much more will be discussed on this very important skill-set in both Chapter 5 (emotional-relational intelligence) and Chapter 6 (leadership styles).

Sport Models of Leadership

Multidimensional Model of Leadership

To best address the needs of leaders in sport, two theories have been developed specifically for this setting. The first is the multidimensional model of sport leadership, developed by Packianathan Chelladurai from The Ohio State University. This model posits leadership effectiveness in sport varies depending on the characteristics of the athletes and situation. Specifically, the degree of congruence among the three states of leader behavior (required, actual, and preferred behavior of the leader) determines the effect on group performance and member satisfaction. The predicted antecedent influences on the three types of leader behavior include the characteristics of the situation, the leader's own characteristics, and those of the team members.[54]

The required behavior indicates the standards of behavior dictated by the organization, its environment, and its members. Athlete characteristics, which include age, gender, ability, or personality traits such as need for achievement or affiliation and competence in the task, can all influence the athletes' preferences for particular coaching behaviors. The actual behavior of the coach is not only a function of his/her personality, ability, and experience, but also the situational requirements and the preferences of the athletes. Examples of situational characteristics include the competitive level, types of task (individual or team), social norms, and organizational climate (process or win oriented). All of these factors combine to influence the actual behavior of the coach. As can be seen in Figure 1, a positive outcome (satisfaction and optimal performance) is predicted to occur if the three aspects of leader behavior agree,

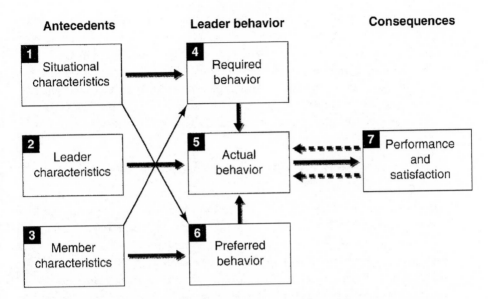

Figure 1: **Multidimensional Model of Sport Leadership. Reprinted, with permission, from R.S. Weinberg and D. Gould, *Foundations of Sport and Exercise Psychology,* 4th ed. (Champaign, IL: Human Kinetics, 2007), 216.**

namely, if the leader behaves appropriately to the situation and these behaviors match members' preferences.[55]

If the prescribed and actual behaviors are different from the behaviors preferred, optimal performance may still result, albeit with a corresponding lowering of satisfaction. Alternately, if the actual and preferred behaviors are different from the required behavior, then satisfaction will result, yet with a lowered performance level as predicted. If this pattern exists long enough, one can also predict the leader (coach) will not have the job any longer.[56]

Research on this model reveals interesting results for coaches and teams. Weinberg and Gould summarize the study results as they pertain to antecedent influences, which includes the finding that as athletes get older they prefer an autocratic coach (similar to a transactional coach) who is also supportive (similar to a transformational coach).[57] Moreover, younger players prefer coaches who allow athletes to participate in decision making and give lots of instruction. Males prefer more autocratic coaching and strict training and instruction, whereas females prefer a democratic coaching style that allows for collaborative decision making. Athletes who play team sports (basketball, soccer, football) prefer autocratic coaching more than individual sport athletes (tennis, track, golf). Research results pertaining to the consequences of leader behaviors have also been summarized by Weinberg and Gould. The greater the discrepancy between actual and preferred leader behaviors, especially with training, feedback, and support, the lower the satisfaction, leading back to study results about the consequential actions of dissatisfied athletes presented in Chapter 2. Also, many studies have found the relationship between optimal performance and satisfaction when the actual and preferred coaching behaviors match. Lastly, results found a relationship between coaches who are perceived as good trainers who provide positive feedback while allowing for feedback from team members.

Loehr's Energy-Management Model of Leadership

The second leadership model was developed by renowned sport psychology consultant Jim Loehr, who first used this model in his consulting work with top amateurs and professional athletes, but now applies his rich experience to industry, business, law enforcement, medical, and military fields. His energy-management model of leadership continues to be an important aspect of the work he does at his Human Performance Institute in Orlando, Florida. This model of peak performance for leaders is predicated on the importance placed on the management of energy, in the forms of physical, emotional, mental, and spiritual energy. According to Loehr and a colleague, Tony Schwartz, effective energy management has two key components. The first is knowing the difference between energy expenditure (stress) and energy renewal (recovery), with the realization that stress is not the real enemy of high performance, but actually a stimulus for growth. Instead the problem lies in the absence of recovery. The second component of high performance for leaders is the practice of rituals promoting the "oscillation" between what the authors call "rhythmic stress and recovery."[58] These authors also state that "sustained high achievement demands physical and emotional strength as well as a sharp intellect. To bring mind, body, and spirit to peak condition, executives need to learn what world-class athletes already know; recovering energy is as important as expending it."[59]

Loehr's four energy sources are represented by a pyramid shape, with the *physical capacity* forming the foundation since the body is the fundamental source of energy.[60] With an optimal physical capacity, the leader builds endurance, which aids in promoting mental and emotional recovery by oscillating between energy expenditure and energy recovery via rituals. Some have reported (to the authors) that with improved physical capacity in this fashion they can work fewer hours and get more done. The next step up the pyramid is the emotional capacity. This stage is highlighted by the importance placed on positive emotions. They are said to ignite the energy that drives high performance, while on the other side, negative emotions drain this energy. Rituals believed to help with the production or maintenance of positive emotions include the use of music, productive body language, reframing experiences, acting differently, and taking advantage of social support and close relationships.

The second-to-the-last step up the pyramid is the *mental capacity.* Here the majority of the performance-enhancement, mental training strategies come into play. This type of mental or cognitive training seeks to improve one's focus, time, and energy management, belief of self, and positive and critical-thinking skills. Reframing one's own verbalizations, from negative to more positive statements, can have profound consequences on mental state and subsequent actions.

Also practicing meditation and relaxation techniques can assist in slowing brain activity and minimizing the clutter and static experienced during stressful times. Moreover, shifting the mental activity from the left hemisphere to the right by doing something to "get our minds off of something" can aid in problem solving via this mental oscillation. The authors pose the question, "Have you ever suddenly found the solution to a vexing problem while doing something 'mindless' such as jogging, working in the garden, or singing in the shower?"[61] This is what occurs in this simple process of mental oscillation, an important cognitive technique, along with the power of mental imagery, or visualization. Being able to visualize success not only produces more energy and assists in building what the authors call "mental muscles," but it also increases strength, endurance, and flexibility due to foreseeing one's achievement.

Spiritual capacity, the fourth and final step to the pyramid model, has been defined by the authors to mean "the energy that is unleashed by tapping into one's deepest values and defining a strong sense of purpose. This capacity, we have found, serves as sustenance in the face of adversity and as a powerful source of motivation, focus, determination, and resilience."[62] It is this capacity coaches should strive to reach when they want to get to know their players as people, not just as competitors. Do we get to know what our players dream of doing in their sport, or how they plan on using this sport experience to propel them to their life's ambition? What are their goals for the short term, like this season, conference play, even the upcoming contest? As was addressed in the first three chapters, today's athletes are very goal driven, ambitious, competitive, and are generally people-pleasers, so those leaders/coaches who are able to identify with these ambitions and are able to be enablers of the personal visions of their athletes will have athletes who will be very committed and loyal to the cause and trust the process undertaken. A critical ritual the authors believe should be practiced to add more spiritual energy to the system is personal reflection, which could take many forms, including journaling, meditation, prayer, and service to others. Another important reflective ritual is to achieve a proper balance of recovery-renewal and expenditure while connecting to the deeper source of purpose and priorities, such as one's family, friends, and hobbies. The importance of achieving this balance will be repeated often through the remainder of this book because of the saliency to continued high performance across the four energy systems: physical, emotional, mental and spiritual capacities.

Loehr believes leadership through his model is about managing energy. The 12 principles of energy management can be of great assistance in helping you achieve sustained high achievement in any leadership endeavor (see Table 2).[63]

Table 2: Loehr's 12 Principles of Energy Management

Number	Principle	Defined Applied
1	Growth follows energy investment	Effective leaders help team members to make the right investments at the right time.
2	Growth ceases when energy investment supply ceases	Leaders must ensure an adequate energy across the four capacities including physical, emotional, mental and spiritual.
3	The best energy produces the most growth	Leaders help team members fully engage when it is significant to the team.
4	Whatever receives energy gains strength	Investing in positive emotions stimulates positive growth, while negative or toxic emotions stimulate defensive growth.
5	There are four energy sources (physical, emotional, mental, and spiritual)	The power of full engagement is the skillful management of these human energy forces.
6	Energy investments must be balanced	Both overtraining (too much energy expenditure with energy deposits relative to recovery) and under-training (too much recovery relative to energy expenditure) threaten the success of a mission. Using recovery techniques like taking advantage of renewing energy opportunities between points, or deep breathing, muscle relaxation, positive

		self-talk, mental routines, and imagery can help renew energy and prepare for the next challenge.
7	Players must push beyond their comfort	Any form of energy expenditure prompting zone discomfort has the potential to expand capacity. Effective leaders know this discomfort is important for growth.
8	Positive rituals and routines	Achieving energy management takes habits used to manage energy such as pre-competition, pre-performance, sleep, and hydration rituals-routines.
9	Energy is highly contagious	Great leaders are quick to recognize individuals who have the potential to carry and transmit positive or negative energy to the team and encourage or discourage this type of behavior.
10	Negative energy should be kept outside of the comfort zone	Effective leaders help team members to create boundaries to contain their negative energy so it does not contaminate the team.
11	Self-esteem deficiencies require energy	Great leaders recognize that those with low self-esteem can create a powerful drain on the team. They work to ensure that energy investments in these individuals do not compromise the team's mission.
12.	Repeated energy investment makes a difference	Great leaders understand that a positive individual can be contaminated by too much negative energy, so this negative energy must be contained.

Reprinted, with permission, from R.S. Weinberg and D. Gould, *Foundations of Sport and Exercise Psychology,* 4th ed. (Champaign, IL: Human Kinetics, 2007), 223.

Leadership IQ Model

A recent contribution I have made to the sport leadership literature is a modified version of Rainer Martens' leadership model, first published in his classic coaching book, *Coaches Guide to Sport Psychology*. As Figure 2 indicates, in Marten's model there are four distinct components of effective leadership, which show leadership behavior comes from an interaction between the personal qualities of leader and follower, and the situational factors inherent with the team. These four components consist of the *leader's qualities* believed to be consistent across successful leaders, the particular *follower's qualities* and how

Figure 2: The Four Components of Effective Leadership. Reprinted, with permission, from R. Martens, *Coaches Guide to Sport Psychology* (Champaign, IL: Human Kinetics, 1987), 35.

coherent and *compatible* the leader's actions are compared with the preferences and perceptions of the followers, the *leadership styles* used by the coaches (discussed in detail in Chapter 6), and the *situational factors,* such as type of sport, competitive level, team dynamics, and the impact these have on the coaches' decisions, and vice versa.[64]

In my model of effective sport leadership (see Figure 3, the *Leadership IQ Model*), the importance Martens placed on the qualities of leader and follower, leadership styles and situational factors remain key aspects, yet there needed to be greater importance placed on knowing more about leadership theory. This is referred to as the leadership intelligence quotient, similar to IQ (intelligence quotient), but applied to knowing more about leadership theory, practice, and application (Leadership IQ). Other model components include emotional intelligence (EG) to leadership to include relational intelligence (Leadership ERQ, Chapter 5, delving deeper into the recent literature on leadership styles (Leadership LSQ, Chapter 6), the significance of leadership talents, techniques, and tactics (Leadership TQ, Chapters 7–9), the declarative and procedural knowledge of organizational dynamics, and the subtleties of managing and leading organizations (organizational quotient, Chapters 10–12), as well as the substantive task of developing leadership strengths through a formalized process (Leader Development Process, Chapters 10–12).

Many of the applicable situational factors are addressed in the first three chapters, while effective followership (Followership FQ) is addressed in Chapter 11. This heuristic model of effective sport leadership (*Leadership IQ Model*) integrates both the science (Leadership IQ) and the art of leadership (Leadership EQ, LQ, OQ, FQ), along with the careful execution of the most effective leadership strategy to the particular situation, while considering the impact of these decisions on the followership (Situational Leadership). The primary goals of the leadership development process (LDP- 6 T's) are to mobilize these processes to assist the team in accomplishing their ultimate goals (e.g., winning conference and national championships), while improving team functioning, communication, and overall effectiveness. Subsequent goals include improving on individual leadership skills of its members and orienting the up-and-coming team leaders to the process and programming for the future. This model has been employed with numerous high-level teams at the top collegiate and international levels, but applications can be made to all competitive levels, which I will share in subsequent books and resources.

Science of Sport Leadership

Empirical studies reveal how and why sport can be a fertile learning lab for leadership development. For example, in 1963, a researcher named Oscar

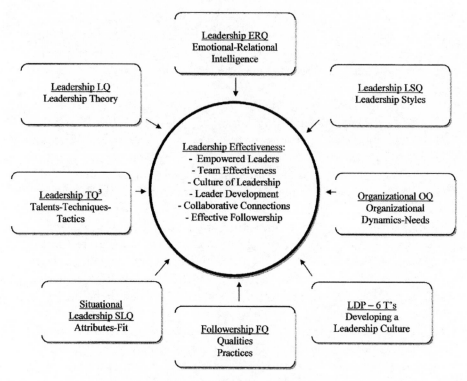

Figure 3: Leadership IQ Model

Grusky published a study based on a random sample of baseball players from the *Official Encyclopedia of Baseball* and found the catcher and infielder positions produced the greatest percentage of managers. He theorized that "central positioning was pivotal to leadership development, as individuals in central locations interact with others more frequently than peripherally positioned players."[65] Other studies, most specifically a study on rugby players in New Zealand[66] and a sample of major league baseball players from the States,[67] have found similar conclusions. Another study had conflicting results when compared to these studies, suggesting that positions of low interaction rated higher in leadership than the higher interaction positions, and perhaps the nature of the position is of greater importance and more salient in developing leadership. For example, in this study on a women's varsity field hockey team, the goalies were rated highest in leadership and attraction to follow despite their low level of interacting with teammates on the field.[68]

Besides the spatial location, nature of task, and frequency of interaction, another variable found to influence leadership in sport is the types of social and verbal interactions. This variable was explored in two studies that found the number of years of experience and players' popularity were significant in perceived leadership, as well as the ability of the player-leader to influence both task (practice energy, game execution)[69] and social interactions of team-mates.[70] A qualitative, interview-based study with high school soccer players and their coaches reveals the coaches' ratings of their players' leadership tendencies were most strongly associated with skill level, yet the peer evaluations reveal "athletes who were perceived to have high self-esteem, soccer competence, psychological androgyny[71] and lower competitive trait anxiety" were rated highest for leadership. This research finding highlights additional variables believed to influence leadership in sport, namely, personal and psychological characteristics of player-leaders.[72]

Another interview study with Canadian sport participants discloses that peers valued four central characteristics in their peer leaders, including high levels of skill, strong work ethic, advanced tactical sport knowledge, and good rapport with teammates. What makes this study even more interesting is it is the only published work exploring how these leadership tenets were developed through their sport experience. The authors, Wright and Cote, shared the commonalities between the patterns of development in "being exposed to a lot of fun, nonthreatening sport environments, having parents who provide various forms of support and act as play partners, as well as early participation with older peers may result in early skill development. Furthermore, early recognition and encouragement provide the motivation to develop further skills."[73] Some of the additional influences summarized by Weinberg and Gould include parents who mentor players on complex cognitive sport issues and decision making, coaches who appoint athletes to leadership positions, players who maintain good relationships with peers and gain trust, and coaches who provide an excellent training environment to help develop skills.[74]

The later chapters in this book look to expand player-leaders' skill-sets beyond these four central tenets (high skill, strong work ethic, enriched cognitive sport knowledge, good rapport with people), although these represent an excellent start. In a recent case study, Voight reveals that collegiate athletes who are named captains value the experience of not only being a leader, but also in learning how to become a better leader via a formalized leadership development process.[75] In their words, "it forced us to do some of the things we talked about in meetings," and "I felt that it was extremely valuable learning all of the essentials of what it takes to be a leader and how to lead a team. Also, the program helped me to connect with my teammates on an individual level," as well as "the leadership program helped everyone on the team feel involved and that they had a voice." Lastly, "being able to talk with each other throughout the season worked out great because of how much we learned from this but also how much I felt part of the interworking of this team." These same captains helped lead their teams to the NCAA Final 4 in their sport, and as an ancillary, the leadership development process these captains trained under is the same process detailed within these pages. More about this case study and the specific leadership development process, which includes the 6 T's (Testing, Teaching, Training, Transferring, Transforming, and Tradition), will be detailed in the final chapter.

"An army of deer led by a lion is more to be feared
than an army of lions led by a deer."[76]

—Philip II of Macedon
quoted in Anson Dorrance and
Gloria Averbuch's *The Vision of a Champion*

– 5 –

Emotional and Relational Intelligence (LERQ)

"Effective leaders are alike in one crucial way:
They all have a high degree of emotional intelligence."[1]
"Gifted leadership occurs where heart and head—
feeling and thought—meet."[2]

—Daniel Goleman

The term "Leadership ERQ" refers to Leadership Emotional-Relational Quotient, used here in similar fashion to an individual's IQ, or Intellectual Quotient, the measure of one's intelligence. Emotional quotient, or the more commonly and referenced term, Emotional Intelligence, was originally coined by Peter Salovey and John Mayer, and is defined as "the ability to monitor one's own and others' feelings and emotions, to discriminate among them and to use this information to guide one's thinking and actions."[3] In his book *Emotional Intelligence,* Daniel Goleman conveys "a person's emotional quotient (EQ) is a more reliable predictor of success than a person's intelligence quotient. People with a high EQ are better equipped to empathize with, understand, relate to, and connect with other people."[4] Harvard Business School Professor Joseph Badaracco, Jr., cites ancient philosopher Aristotle, from his classic work, *Ethics,* in that people's feelings can be used to help them make sense of an issue. Badaracco, Jr. summarizes Aristotle's statement: "In other words, our feelings and intuitions are both a form of intelligence and a source of insight."[5]

One of the more important responsibilities of leaders is to motivate and inspire their followers, and according to John Kotter, professor of leadership at the Harvard Business School, this is best done by "satisfying basic human needs for achievement, a sense of belonging, recognition, self-esteem, a feeling of control over one's life, and the ability to live up to one's ideals."[6] He continues by stressing the importance of these emotional states: "Such feelings touch us deeply and elicit a powerful response."[7] In Pat Williams' book, *Coaching Your Kids to Be Leaders,* a former state representative and founder of a management company speaks about the importance of emotional and relational intelligent traits: "There are children who demonstrate an ability to communicate with their peers, connect with them and organize them for almost any activity, and then coach them to the fruition of the project. These children have excellent people skills, excellent leadership skills, though in some cases they may not test out as geniuses on an IQ test."[8]

Beyond Simply "Service with a Smile"

Reflection is such an important leadership technique, it will be mentioned many times throughout this book. On the topic of emotional and relational intelligence, reflection should be employed by leaders to self-evaluate their awareness of not only their emotional and relational behaviors but the impact they have on others. This reflective process begins by asking the following questions: Would you play for a coach like you? Would you want your son or daughter to play for a coach like you? Have you worked for a boss you did not like? What was the experience like? How productive were you in that class you had with that teacher you did not respect? How motivated or inspired were you by that coach you did not respect? How did you feel when the salesperson in that store was unprofessional and rude in his dealing with you? What impact do negative emotions and moods have on your decisions, emotional state, and performance? As these reflective questions and responses probably confirm, whether it is sport, education, business, or retail, emotions and moods are not trivial matters. Emotions and moods do impact the bottom line, whether it be a win, a passing grade, a profitable quarter, or a sale.

A voluminous amount of research supports the consequences of negative moods and emotions on the process, practice, and work being accomplished in the business setting especially, but more attention must be given to this topic in sport. Chapter 2 detailed the myriad of consequences of dissatisfied athletes and those who were hit by "clash points" in sport. Negative emotional states such as anxiety, worry, frustration, anger, sadness, and dissatisfaction can all contribute to a decrement in mental abilities, attention, and production. This also entails influencing a person's emotional intelligence through his or her inability to effectively use his or her personal coping skills and maintain his or her relationships in times of stress and distress.[9] Goleman and colleagues noted the importance of feelings while working, saying, "The percentage of time people feel positive emotions at work turns out to be one of the strongest predictors of satisfaction, and therefore, for instance, of how likely employees are to quit."[10] The authors conclude, "Leaders who spread bad moods are simply bad for business and those who pass along good moods help drive a business's success."[11] Some additional reflective questions to aid in improving personal awareness of emotional and relational intelligence include: What types of moods do you consistently spread? How much value is placed on the moods and emotions spread with your team, and what impact do these have on team climate and performance?

A commonly accepted logarithm is used in business to accentuate the "Service with a smile" mantra (about improved emotional intelligence and service to others), which has shown that for every 1 percent improvement in the organization's climate, there's a 2 percent increase in revenue. This improvement is attributed to climate, which is driven by customer satisfaction, which is predicted by how employees perceive the emotional climate of the job.[12] The term "climate" refers to the individual or collective emotional perception of the situation-specific environment, like the workplace, sport team, classroom, or household. For example, a negative team climate can be characterized by an old school coach who motivates through fear and punishment, while rewards are only attached to the outcome of winning, not on progress and improvement. Goleman and colleagues cite a study of 19 insurance companies that highlights the importance of the climate created by the leader: "In 75 percent of cases, climate alone accurately sorted companies into high versus low profits and growth."[13]

A similar term is used in sport research to describe the group or team environment and its influence on leaders and team members—motivational climate. As the research tells it, the majority of social climates in sport take the form of either a strong task-oriented climate (focused on improvement and progress) or a strong outcome-oriented climate (focused on winning and being the best when compared to others), with others having a combination of both.[14] Task-oriented climates are linked to more adaptive motivational patterns such as positive attitudes, higher levels of confidence and motivation to improve and strive for challenging situations, strong work rates and persistence, and effective use of learning strategies.[15] Conversely, outcome-oriented climates are characterized by less adaptive motivational patterns, including low effort and persistence in adverse situations, lower perceptions of ability and competence, and negative self-talk and thoughts about progress and play.[16] Team members can take on the goal orientations of the motivational climate of the team, so those players who play in a task-oriented climate take on these personal orientations, where their focus is on adaptive motivational strategies.[17] However, those who operate in an outcome-oriented climate can take on the maladaptive motivational strategies previously mentioned. Coaches play very important roles in the creation of these motivational climates and should be aware of the positives and drawbacks of their particular climates and their impact on team members. Coaches should "check themselves" for the particular type of motivational climate they are endorsing on a regular basis. Much more will be discussed in Chapters 10 and 12 on climate and culture.

Personal and Social (Relational) Competencies

Goleman writes that emotional intelligence (EI) is a "powerful combination of self-management skills and the ability to work with others."[18] In the book *Primal Leadership,* he and colleagues detail the EI leadership competencies, beginning with the two most salient EI competencies—personal and social competence.[19] *Personal competence* helps us to determine how we manage ourselves, whereas social competence determines how we manage our relationships. According to these authors, personal management begins with a heightened awareness of self through reading emotions, an accurate evaluation of self, and a realistic sense of level of self-confidence. This process continues with maximizing self-management skills, which includes the ability to control emotions, display honesty, be flexible and adaptable, and strive for achievement with optimism. Leaders who have high self-awareness and self- management (high personal competence) are those who are attuned to their strengths/weaknesses, are authentic in their caring of their own and others' emotional states, stay clear-headed and optimistic in crisis, are adept at changing environments, and are willing to take the initiative to problem solve and create change.

In describing the important competencies to improving how one manages relationships, the authors depict how valuable it is to be socially aware, as well as the use relationship management strategies. Regarding *social competence,* effective leaders are able to sense others' emotional states while understanding their perspectives (empathy), as well as the perspective of the organization or team, while serving the needs of everyone involved. As is commonly known, the relationships in our lives do require attention, time, and work to keep them current in the hope of continuing a flourishing connection with those we love, like, respect, or need. To best manage these relationships, managing conflict, change, and our collaborative efforts become important skills, as does inspiring and developing others through our example and influence. An important reflective question for leaders is to ascertain how one consistently manages relationships on the team and in other social spheres (work, school, home). Leaders who have high social competence are able to get along with others, especially those from diverse backgrounds, are politically and organizationally astute, concern themselves with the emotional climate of the program and its members, and are active in developing future leaders in their program through their strong vision, influence, problem solving, collaborative and team building abilities.

Another reflective exercise to improve awareness of emotional and relational intelligence is for leaders and those who aspire to be better leaders and followers to reflect on the leaders they have in their lives who they just naturally gravitate toward. As part of my leadership consulting practice, I facilitate this exercise with teams to help them identify with their leadership experiences from their past and present to learn what they can about the qualities and competencies from their favorite and least favorite leaders. The exercise is most meaningful when athletes learn from their own experiences and apply these lessons to their present mindset and knowledge base. An important step to this process is to determine which attributes are behavioral in nature, and how many are linked to emotional competencies.

Emotional magnets are those leaders who people gravitate toward because they have the following emotional traits and competencies, which make them an emotionally resonant leader: enthusiastic, optimistic, humorous, compassionate, ethical, upbeat, energized, passionate, approachable, inspired, confident, creative, genuinely happy, and visionary. Opposite of these magnets are those who repel would-be followers, referred to as dissonant leaders, due to the following negative descriptors: irritable, moody, touchy, domineering, autocratic, aloof, unapproachable, anxious, easily frustrated, sarcastic, caustic, rude, apathetic, selfish, depressed, angry, dissatisfied, and out of touch with their constituents.[20] Another reflective question for leaders to ask themselves is how many of their players (for coaches) or teammates (for captains) would rate them as an emotional magnet (a resonant leader), or instead as an emotionally dissonant leader and one who repels?

Chapters 7–9 cite additional emotional and relational intelligence competencies highlighting the talents, techniques, and tactics of effective leaders based on the voluminous research and literature on the topic, and the consulting experiences of expert leader consultants, as well as the opinions of good and effective sport leaders.

> *"One of the key duties of leaders is to manage*
> *the emotions of group members."*[21]
>
> —Ronald Humphrey,
> professor of management at Virginia Commonwealth University

Team Emotional Intelligence (TEI)

Emotional intelligence competencies relate to both the individual and the group or team. Work teams and athletic teams are similar in that they both have specific needs, standards, shared moods and emotional states, and an appreciation for similar goals and the vision of what is needed to achieve these goals. As was referenced earlier, a team's motivational climate can impact shared moods, emotions, and could impact attitudes, progress, productivity, and performance. Teams from all settings (sport, education, business) could learn a lot about themselves by improving their EI competencies, such as self and social (team) awareness, self and team management, and relationship management. Similar to what occurs on a work team in the business setting, or a sports team, the leaders, whether they be the captains or coaches, set the tone and help create "the group's emotional reality—how it feels to be part of the team," according to Goleman and colleagues.[22]

A leader who is in touch with his or her EI competencies and feels the pulse of the team is able to balance what needs to be done to achieve team goals with ensuring that each team member feels valued and that their contributions are required. The examples shared in Chapter 2 about the consequences of incompatibility are rife with emotional intelligence overtones, especially in those cases where the coach's style of leadership was not accepted by the athletes. In some of those cases the players believed they were not having their emotional needs met or they were having to play in a culture of emotional abuse. Although there is always blame to be assigned, this is the reality of coaching in the new era. Today's athletes know what they want and need, and if the present staff is not getting it done, either the player will leave (which in some cases is an adaptive coping method for all involved) or work the system to displace the staff.

Goleman and colleagues link the EI of teams with the creation of team norms, which represent those tacit rules team members learn as they go, by their day-to-day interactions adopted for the betterment of the team. These norms help to determine the course the team will take in pursuit of their goals, whether it is the high performing or low performing path.[23] It is indeed a pleasure when teammates enjoy each other's company, are respectful in their expectations and questioning, support each other, and if needed, motivate each other (high performing). Then there are those teammates who operate from many individual agendas and resemble a collection of individual talents who do their own thing (low performing). According to Goleman, the leaders need to be effective managers of "the silent language of both emotion and norms."[24]

Coaches who casually pit one teammate against the other to motivate both players competing for the same position can be counterproductive on a team where the team norm is a collective spirit, all working as one. Another incongruent setting is a team captain who puts herself in the front of the line for meals or airline tickets. Despite this being a somewhat innocent decision, especially if this person is a senior believing she has paid her dues and deserves this little perk, it does not reinforce the team norm of "putting your team first in all you do."

One of the bigger mistakes leaders can make, according to Goleman, is, "ignoring the realities of team ground rules and the collective emotions in the tribe and assuming that the force of their leadership alone is enough to drive people's behavior."[25] Another reflective question for coaches and captain to ask themselves is: How effective are you, and your captains, at assessing the team norms and the emotional needs (emotional reality) of the team? The answer to that question could equate with the number of "clash points" leaders have experienced with their teams. In my own particular example of team dissatisfaction (collegiate team organizing themselves to successfully get the head coach fired for not providing a substantial student-athlete experience), I was totally unaware of the emotional reality of that team and thus was blind to the fact they were working the system in their successful attempt for a new coach. Could I have done something to save the head coach's job if I had known? This question continues to haunt.

Once an accurate assessment is ascertained, what next? Maximizing the powerful influence of team norms and the team's emotional intelligence competencies encompasses improving on their *self-awareness* (being mindful of shared moods and emotions), *self-management* (team members take care of their responsibilities and put to action the standards/norms), and practicing *empathy* (triggering sense of team pride). Especially in the case of underling leaders (team captains), how receptive are they to the verbal and nonverbal cues the rest of the team is signaling? One of my collegiate teams had a captain who was totally unaware of the impact her strong judgments and aggressive manner during halftimes and especially after losses was having on the team. As a result, the team disconnected from her, thus leaving the team one leader down, with an awful lot of resentment in its wake. It was only through reflective exercises, carefully facilitated team meetings, a patient head coach, and some wins that this particular team issue was resolved.

Assisting teams with being better self-managers can be boiled down to two words: responsibility and accountability. To be a high functioning team, every player must know his or her role, accept this role, no matter how distasteful it might be (reserve role), and fulfill this role to the best of his or her ability. Easier said than done with today's athletes because of how confident, goal driven, and competitive they are. Chapter 10 shares a team building process in which team leaders, members, and coaches are all a part of, and thus, can be used to assist in not only letting the players be active agents in the creation of team standards and norms, but also ensuring everyone is on the same page regarding the "silent language" of team norms and emotional reality. Maximizing the role process, as well as having all team members create the team standards, and then police themselves and others in the adherence to these norms and standards, is at the core of effective team management. The final EI team competency, being an empathetic team, is predicated on every member and each positional unit feeling and believing their contributions are integral for this team to function at a high level.[26] Chapter 11 addresses this particular competency, and in it are many ways to improve the followership on teams via promoting team pride through traditions, improved listening, communication practices and problem solving, embracing diversity of people and ideas, appreciating the roles and contributions of others, and confidence building techniques.

Emotional Intelligence Studies in Sport

Applying the emotional intelligence content from the organizational and business settings to sport is a relatively new proposition, yet some studies do exist. Sam Zizzi and colleagues sampled collegiate baseball players with an emotional intelligence survey, comparing their feedback with their performance statistics, studying the link between emotional skills and athletic performance.[27] Significant results were found for the pitchers. Those who had better stats (strikeouts and earned runs) maintained better emotional recognition, monitoring, and control of emotional states. However, no conclusive results occurred for the hitters in the sample, possibly due to the reactionary demand of the skill, thus not allowing much time to regulate one's emotional states. Zizzi and colleagues posit the research conducted in sport psychology on negative emotions (anxiety, anger, depression) and the many techniques to gain control over these performance decrement variables (self-talk, productive thinking, visualization, and relaxation training) can overlap with the construct of emotional intelligence, despite the paucity of studies focused specifically on emotional intelligence.

Some in sport believe emotions are the ultimate determinants of athletic performance success. It is a costly mistake for coaches and leaders to not know more about emotions, and also their influence on play and how to maximize their use. In *Applying Sport Psychology: Four Perspectives,* edited by Jim Taylor and Gregory Wilson, the topic of emotions in sport takes center stage due to its impact on every aspect of an athlete's performance, including the physical, psychological, technical, tactical influence on team norms, team functioning, and leadership.[28] The influence of emotions on the physical game is evident whenever an athlete gets amped up, motivated, and excited. There are obvious physiological reactions, such as an increased heart rate, blood pressure, and muscle tension due to the "flight or fight" psychophysiological reaction, whereby the body readies itself for the impending challenge. When athletes are technically sharp they are usually operating from a state of euphoria or in a "zone" or "flow" state, where they are automatically reacting to their environment and allowing their bodies to play the way they have trained, relinquishing conscious control and letting play happen. Athletes equate this automaticity with a sense of calm, happiness, high confidence, and a deep reserve of energy. When an athlete is technically playing automatically, he is also strategically making decisions and problem solving "on the run" as he helps his team win the ball back, or possess the ball, restart the ball, or put it in the back (or bottom) of the net, using invasion sports such as basketball, soccer, lacrosse, or field hockey as examples.

In the mental game, emotions play an even bigger role as they are believed to impact motivation, confidence, focus, and coping with adversity. Yuri Hanin, a professor and researcher at the Research Institute for Olympic Sports in Finland, postulates that optimal emotions (e.g., excitement, satisfaction) motivate athletes to continue to give the required effort to successfully accomplish the task, whereas dysfunctional emotions (e.g., fear, disappointment, embarrassment, guilt) decrease this motivation, thus impacting the requisite effort. This same relationship can be applied to confidence, whereby pleasant emotions help bolster confidence, which in turn improves motivation and work rate.[29] Unpleasant emotions, on the other hand, are believed to be counterproductive to performance, resulting in lowered levels of confidence and disbelief in task completion.[30] With the lowering of confidence, and the subsequent rise in anxiety and other dysfunctional emotions, a person's field of focus begins to narrow, causing the performer to miss potentially important environmental cues (e.g., football quarterback who does not see the inside linebacker has positioned himself for the blitz). Performers are believed to focus more on the important performance-related cues, while attending to fewer distractions or adversity, such as the last failed play, mistake, or missed open goal, when they are experiencing positive emotions during competition.

Getting back to the research, a more recent sport-specific study went beyond linking emotional intelligence (EI) and playing ability, instead focusing on the relationship between emotional intelligence and leadership effectiveness in sport, as well as comparing the results from sport coaches with those of leaders from business. This makes conceptual sense since the worlds of sport and business have been forever linked, with each setting using research, theories, strategies, and personalities from the other to educate, inspire, and entertain. Study results show the sample of elite coaches and business leaders all scored higher than the population norms on emotional intelligence, consisting of 15 subscales of EI, such as emotional regulation/management, empathy, social awareness, optimism, relationships, and self-control. Interestingly, there were no differences between the EI scores of the elite coaches and business leaders, supporting the time-honored tradition of the applicability and transferability of sport to business, and vice versa.[31] There is more work to be done by sport researchers on linking the efficacy of emotional intelligence on athletic performance and leadership effectiveness.

Training Emotional Intelligence

What researchers have found is that emotional intelligence training programs can have either no impact or even be a negative influence on one's performance (and one's bank account) primarily because these programs focus on the wrong part of the brain. According to the work of Dan Goleman and the Consortium for Research on Emotional Intelligence in Organizations, training in emotional intelligence must focus on the limbic brain rather than the neocortex part of the brain, responsible for higher-order concepts and logic. This particular part of the brain can be useful to a point, in regard to learning the content associated with emotional intelligent definitions and the memorization of the EI competencies, as well as being able to critically analyze the actions, words, and nonverbal expressions of those around us. But the real learning and application of EI training entails the breaking and changing of old behavioral habits, which can only be achieved through the limbic system.[32] Thus, the science of emotional intelligence can be taught via these neocortical approaches, but the art of emotional intelligence has to be tapped via a limbic approach. The science and art of leadership effectiveness as prescribed by the Leadership IQ Model (see Chapter 4) and subsequent intervention programs (see Chapters 10–12) follow this same logic.

In his article re-published in the *Harvard Business Review's 10 Must Reads on Leadership*, Goleman details this limbic system approach: "emotional intelligence is born largely in the neurotransmitters of the brain's limbic system which governs feelings, impulses, and drives."[33] According to Dr. C. George

Boeree, "The limbic system is a complex set of structures that lies on both sides of the thalamus, just under the cerebrum. It includes the hypothalamus, the hippocampus, the amygdala, and several other nearby areas. It appears to be primarily responsible for our emotional life."[34] According to Joseph LeDoux, the limbic brain is our emotional center, transmitting signals to other parts of the brain that lead to actions related to emotions and survival, like how we react to stressful events.[35] According to Goleman in his book *Emotional Intelligence*, the limbic brain is the "honest brain" since many of our reactions occurring through the limbic system are without thought, and thus, genuine, which can be observed through our limbs and face.[36]

A former FBI counterintelligence agent and expert on nonverbal behavior, Joe Navarro, in his book, *What Everybody Is Saying,* refers to the neocortex as the "lying brain," "because it is capable of complex thought. This brain, unlike its limbic counterpart, is the least reliable of the three major brain components. This is the brain that can deceive. The neocortex can easily permit us to tell a friend that we like her new haircut when we, in fact, do not."[37] Navarro continues by stating our limbic survival responses are hardwired into our nervous system, making them difficult to disguise, and thus honest and reliable. So coaches or captains who are deficient in particular emotional intelligence capacities really have to work hard to change old habits into new ones that are positive and productive. As Goleman recommends, this process takes much more than a workshop due to the time it takes, as well as how individualized the approach must be. He also states, "It's important to emphasize that building one's emotional intelligence cannot—will not—happen without sincere desire and concerted effort."[38] Additional points of emphasis include obtaining feedback from colleagues and subordinates (when observed doing things better or worse), observing others who model the most appropriate behaviors, and placing importance on the persistence and practice of these new habits.

How Is Coach EQ or Captain EQ Evaluated?

In Chapter 9 (and Appendices 1 and 2) readers get an opportunity to evaluate EI competencies, as well as additional leadership qualities and practices believed to lead to good and effective leadership via an individual leadership assessment, *Leadership Skill-Set Assessment.* Some sample items are below in Table 1, with the EI competency preceding it, using Goleman, Boyatzis and McKee's model cited in their text, *Primal Leadership: Realizing the Power of Emotional Intelligence.*

Table 1: Emotional-Relational Intelligence in Sport

SUBSCALE	DEFINITION	ITEM
Personal Competence:		
Self-Awareness	Thinks before acting; Realistic in his ability and handles criticism well	Displays a confident image regardless of play
Self-Management	Stays optimistic even in the face of personal or team adversity; Looks for different ways to drive one's performance	Continues to captain and help the team despite their play
Social Competence:		
Social Awareness	Sensitive to teammates' or coaches' emotional reactions to an event; Listens to the viewpoints of teammates and fellow captains	Approachable to coaches and teammates via a genuine willingness to openly discuss on-court/ off-court issues.
Relationship Management	Builds rapport easily with teammates and staff; Knows how to support teammates and be there for them	Has a relationship with each player on the team and connects with them regularly

Emotional intelligence-related questions have been included on the team leader feedback form completed by team members to identify those who have leadership traits and perform leadership practices, entitled the *Team Leader Survey,* also cited in Chapter 9, and Appendix 1.

> *"Just like positive emotions ignite the energy that drives high performance, negative emotions—frustration, impatience, anger, fear, resentment, and sadness—drain energy."*[39]
>
> —Jim Loehr,
> Human Performance Institute

– 6 –

Substance and Styles (LSQ)

"If you want to succeed, you need to learn as much as you can about leadership before you have a leadership position." [1]
—John C. Maxwell,
The 360-Degree Leader

"Style and substance are not mutually exclusive. Leadership style in action is substance!" [2]
—Joe Batten,
Tough Minded Leadership

Leadership *substance* is the knowledge and know-how of leadership, which includes the material previously covered in Chapters 4 and 5, along with the character, ethics, and values one brings into the leadership role. As Batten's quote indicates above, style and substance do go hand-in-hand, and in this chapter greater detail is provided about leadership *styles* and how to use these leadership styles for optimal benefit, as well as helping team leaders identify and lead from the needed and desired style. As the former president of USC, Steven Sample, states in his book, *The Contrarian's Guide to Leadership,* "There is no infallible step-by-step formula for becoming an effective leader. But leadership can be taught and learned. More explicitly, a person can develop her own potential for leadership by reading about what's worked for others and then selectively applying those lessons to her own situation." [3]

Taking this quote to heart and mind, what an individual must do is immerse himself in the leadership literature to improve upon Leadership IQ (Chapter 4), LERQ (Chapter 5), and LSQ (this chapter), to best prepare for the present or future leadership opportunity. For those team captains who have been given a leadership role before they have worked on improving their Leadership IQ, LERQ, and LSQ, which probably includes the majority of leaders, this book and those cited from business, leadership, and organizational psychology become valuable resources. For sport leaders, it is important to reflect on what methods are used to personally evaluate prospective team leaders. Is it the most senior player on the team, the best player in a centralized position (e.g., quarterback in football, setter in volleyball, midfielder in soccer), the player who works the hardest, the best practice player, the most consistent player in big games, the play maker, those who lead by example on/off the field, the most talkative and motivating in huddles/locker room, the true team player who is all about the team and who is a friend to every teammate, the most popular player, or a combination of some of these or something else not mentioned here? Some of these behavioral traits and talents of potential leaders may serve the team well, but will they be enough to handle the myriad of situations teams find themselves in? Will this particular strength best fit the more global needs of the team? Can more be asked of team leaders/captains than simply doing what they already do in the locker room and on the court or field? Given what is known about today's athletes and their preferences, they want more of a say and more of the responsibility. Why not provide them with these opportunities to lead along with the commensurate teaching of leadership substance and style necessary to not just be the captain by position, but to actually practice leadership in their team setting.

As will be discussed later, the leadership development process should begin as soon as possible, ideally, for example, the first day of off-season practice for collegiate athletes. This way, it gives all involved as much time as possible to learn what needs to be learned about leadership, and their particular leadership strengths and weaknesses, and what the primary needs of the team and its followers are. J.C. Maxwell best sums up how leadership is usually learned: "Good leadership is learned in the trenches. Leading as well as they can wherever they are is what prepares leaders for more and greater responsibility. Becoming a good leader is a lifelong process."[4] This insight emphasizes the importance of not only learning about leadership and how to become a better leader, but also how to practice leadership and the continual process that being a good and effective leader entails. An important step in this process is to determine one's particular leadership style.

Leadership Styles

Leadership style is defined as "the manner in which a leader presents himself and his point of view."[5] Harvey Dorfman, a long-time sport psychology consultant to Major League Baseball teams, notes each leader has a predisposition for a particular style, which is influenced by their personalities. Yet despite this natural inclination, the adoption of different styles can be changed to best reflect the circumstances or needs of the personnel and team. For example, a person's natural style may be to lead by action instead of by voice, but if the team is in need of a more vocal leader, this leader should make the necessary adjustments in style to lead by example and by voice. The trick, Dorfman says, "is to keep the naturally instinctive behaviors that help us and change the ones that hurt us."[6] Dorfman also believes that "great leaders are great actors. They play to the needs of their audience. Circumstance will allow you that naturalness, or beg for a different style, a different approach."[7] Moreover, "your style is the way you act out your role—the substance is the script."[8] Being able to identify the particular circumstance in which one is involved and the appropriate style is difficult, which is why a systematic needs assessment at the start of the season and continual evaluation checks throughout the season become a critical process. More on this process will be discussed in Chapters 9 and 10.

When it comes to leadership styles, the most apt analogy to describe the concept is offered by Daniel Goleman in a *Harvard Business Review* article: "Imagine the styles then as the array of clubs in a golf pro's bag. Over the course of a game, the pro picks and chooses clubs based on the demands of the shot. Sometimes he has to ponder his selection, but usually it is automatic. The pro senses the challenge ahead, swiftly pulls out the right tool, and elegantly puts it to work. That's how high-impact leaders operate, too."[9] To take this analogy further, the "golfer" or "leader" would have six clubs in the bag, one for each of the more common and preferred leadership styles, including visionary, coaching, affiliative, democratic, pacesetting, and commanding. The first four styles have been found by the research to have a positive impact on climate, productivity, and personal outcomes such as satisfaction, initiative, and competence. The last two styles, however—pacesetting and commanding—have been found to "poison the climate" and are ineffective in the long run.[10] The six styles are summarized here from Daniel Goleman's book *Primal Leadership*.[11]

The Visionary Style

Visionary leaders embrace the practice of helping others move toward a set of shared goals, thus creating a collective purpose among the team while defining a standard of performance that revolves around this vision in the process. The "visionary golf club" should be chosen when a new direction is required. According to Tom Rath and Barry Conchie, authors of *Strength Based Leadership,* "Visionary leaders articulate where a group is going, but not how it will get there—setting people free to innovate, experiment, and take calculated risks."[12] With this style, leaders ask their team members not only for their feedback on issues such as what they believe could be accomplished, the process of getting there, and how they, as a leader, can help get them there, but they follow through on this feedback and integrate it into a collective, unifying vision for all. According to Goleman's research, this approach has been found to be the most effective since it is empowering for the individual while galvanizing for the whole team, with each person's goals tied into the ultimate vision of the organization or team. This style, although highly recommended, should not be the primary style used with teams who have more experience than the leader. The leader's vision for the team could be viewed as pompous or not truly applicable, and according to Rath and Conchie, could lead to cynicism toward the leader, which they believe would lead to "a breeding ground for poor performance."[13]

The Coaching Style

Leaders who coach their teammates are those who focus on helping individuals develop their games and even leadership skills, all designed to help them connect better with the team vision and desired process. This is a "one-on-one style" in which the leader has impactful conversations that delve into a player's personal goals and ambitions. The leader has continued dialogue with teammates, especially newer teammates, helping to build rapport and trust— two very important ingredients of emotionally and relationally intelligent leadership. Bill Parcells, former NFL head coach for three teams, shares his insight with the *Harvard Business Review* on the difficulty of turning around teams. An essential tool he cites in bringing about change is the one-on-one conversation. "With the Giants, and with the other teams I've coached, I've found that holding frank, one-on-one conversations with every member of the organization is essential to success. It allows me to ask each player for his support in helping the team achieve its goals, and it allows me to explain exactly what I expect from him."[14]

Using this leadership style has a strong impact on individual and team emotionality, a sentiment echoed by Goleman: "Even though coaching focuses on personal development rather than on accomplishing tasks, the style generally predicts an outstandingly positive emotional response and better results."[15] This coaching or mentoring style is seen when leaders help individuals not only assess strengths and areas needing improvement, but reinforce the pursuit of individual development by capturing teammates' "coachable moments," those moments when teammates improve or succeed in a particular area. These "high five" moments help not only an individual's pursuit, but also team collaboration, while promoting greater effort and productive emotions. According to Goleman, the coaching style works best with subordinates who are motivated to improve, yet this style will hit a wall with teammates who lack this internal drive or who are "high maintenance" (those who need continual feedback and guidance), especially if the leader lacks the patience or knowhow to deal with teammates like this. Another concern is overstepping the coaching style with the pacesetting style, where despite the coach's best intention, his guidance is perceived by teammates as micromanagement, being told how to do every aspect of their role, position, or play.

The Affiliative Style

Affiliative leaders focus on the emotional needs of their team members during the short-term goals of finishing drills or beating the next opponent. Goleman asserts affiliative leaders are most concerned with "promoting harmony and fostering friendly interactions, nurturing personal relationships that expand the connective tissues with the people they lead."[16] Leaders who prioritize team needs do so by recognizing their team members as people first, making time in their busy seasons for team bonding activities, as well as being there for their teammates with an empathetic ear or simply by giving them time to discuss personal matters. When teams are in need of a morale boost and team harmony, especially in those situations where team trust is being questioned, affiliative style works best. Goleman warns against using this style on its own, however: "Despite its benefits, the affiliative style should not be used alone. The style's exclusive focus on praise can allow poor performance to go uncorrected, and employees may perceive that mediocrity is tolerated."[17] Another consequence is leaders who become too nice because of the worry of creating disharmony among the team, trying to avoid confrontation. When this occurs, they could instead steer the team toward failure or leave the followers without direction in times of crisis. According to Goleman, leaders "tend to be overly worried about getting along with people, often at the expense of the task at hand. This 'anxious' type of affiliation has been found to drive down the climate rather than raise it."[18]

In my own leadership consulting with women's collegiate sport teams, this is such a common issue it normally becomes a continual "lesson learned" case study revisited on a regular basis. An often-used mantra, "It's OK to compete," resonates often in these meetings to keep stressing the important outcomes of confrontation and pushing each other to be better. The team strives to keep their relationships intact afterward. The highly successful women's soccer coach at the University of North Carolina, Anson Dorrance, repeatedly writes that women athletes are not as innately competitive as men and they relate "through an interconnected web of personal connections as opposed to a more traditional male hierarchical style."[19] Coach Dorrance continues by stressing the importance of leading men with the force of one's personality, but the greater effectiveness of leading women with one's humanity: "Gaining their respect, being sensitive to their strengths and weaknesses, and showing that you value their contributions."[20] Mia Hamm, one of his star pupils and former Olympic, World Cup, and professional star, when asked about this topic responds, "I don't think that we, as women, can't compete at the same level of intensity as men do. And I don't think that we, as women, can't train at the highest level of fitness as men do. We can, and we want to. We don't want to be coached differently and we don't need to be coached differently. So coach us as you would coach the most elite men's team. And at the same time, treat us like women, which means don't be in our faces, don't be confrontational. Challenge us, but do it in a humanistic way."[21] Tony DiCicco, another one of Mia's coaches on the U.S. National Team, states what Mia was referring to is coaching with a more humanistic approach via the components of emotional intelligence (main topic in Chapter 5), such as coaching through compassion, empathy, the ability to listen and relate to others. This is a much different style than the "old school model" which used aggressiveness, intensity, and macho behavior.[22] Goleman recommends combining the affiliative leadership style with the visionary style for a potent combination of a shared mission and standards, with a caring, empathetic approach.

The Democratic Style

Tapping the experience and wisdom of team members is at the heart of the democratic leadership style. Collective brainstorming becomes a most valuable tool in assisting athletes in choosing a vision, the daily standards to be met to accomplish this vision, as well as coming up with an accountability plan and adding to the traditions of the team and program. Additional specifics about a similar team building intervention process are discussed in Chapter 10. The coaching staff has their own views on the vision and daily standards, but before this is integrated, the team gets their chance to be creative, to perform a needs assessment on their own terms, weighing strengths, weaknesses, and the potential contributions of new team members. After several team brainstorming sessions, the feedback is prioritized and agreed upon, at which time the coaches' ideas are presented and integrated to form a collective action plan. After further discussion and tweaking, this becomes the collaborative plan for the team. The democratic style not only offers its stakeholders the opportunity to share their viewpoints, but genuinely incorporates the most salient of these ideas into a formulated action plan. These become the guiding principles for all. A common phrase coaches use to describe the commitment of their players to the team ideal is "buy-in." There is not a better way to get "buy-in" than to incorporate players into the most important team process, which is establishing the vision and direction of the program, and working together to follow the steps needed to accomplish this plan. Being involved in the interworking of the team also promotes a climate of respect, which as was discussed in the first three chapters of this book is a critical preference for today's millennial athletes. From their earlier days their opinions have mattered greatly. Leadership expert and former CEO of General Electric Jack Welch writes in his book *Winning,* "Every person in the world wants voice and dignity, and every person deserves them." By "voice" he means people want the opportunity to be heard, and by "dignity" he means people inherently want their work and effort to be respected.[23]

According to Goleman, the democratic style works best when there is uncertainty about the direction in which a team or organization should proceed and the leadership desires ideas from its experienced and knowledgeable subordinates. With collegiate teams especially, each new season brings with it new players with different strengths and weaknesses, and thus, what worked for last year's team may not work for the new team. This is why the coaching staff, team leaders, and players must renew and refresh this process every season, so they can capitalize on these changes and obtain feedback from the new contributors. It is important for leaders to be aware that when they ask for feedback, they have an obligation to listen to all of it.

Leaders must also prepare to hear from many different perspectives, some of which may be opposite of their own. As one CEO states, "You have to listen to some pretty tough stuff, but the first time I chop someone's head off for telling me the hard truth, that's when they'll stop talking to me. I have to keep it safe for everyone to speak up. There's no problem we can't solve if we can be open about it."[24] Jack Welch chimes in on this subject: "Some people have better ideas than others, some are smarter or more experienced or more creative. But everyone should be heard and respected." What he incorporated in GE in the late 1980s was what he referred to as "Work-Out" process meetings. Held around the world, these two- to three-day events gathered employees and an outsider facilitator to discuss how to improve efficiency and productivity. As Welch tells it, each worksite boss was to be in attendance and committed to two things: "To give an on-the-spot yes or no to 75 percent of the recommendations that came out of the session, and to resolve the remaining 25 percent within thirty days." These "Work-Outs" led to an "explosion in productivity" and helped "bring every brain into the game."[25]

The main drawback of this style of leadership, according to Goleman, includes the time it takes to garner feedback and consensus with so many meetings. Also, seeking advice from an uninformed team, for example, with little experience in the sport and/or competitive level, could be counterproductive. This particular style can be impractical in times of crisis when informed decisions must be made on the spot, and time to gather consensus among the group is not possible. The first four leadership styles—visionary, coaching, affiliative, and democratic—represent the best in practical emotional and relational intelligence and can resonate through a team, producing efficient team systems and productive action plans. The final two styles, however—pacesetting and commanding—must be carefully integrated when the situation best dictates their use. Using these styles in the heat of the moment (e.g., after bad losses, frustrating practice sessions) or in other reckless ways could have permanent, negative effects. With skillful and deliberate application, these two styles could have a profound impact, again, in the right situation.

The Pacesetting Style

Goleman presents the hallmarks of the pacesetting style as admirable: "The leader holds and exemplifies high standards for performance. He is obsessive. He quickly pinpoints poor performers, demands more from them, and if they don't rise to the occasion, rescues the situation himself."[26] He then explains that the research data indicates more often than not that this style "poisons" the climate of an organization, leading to highly anxious subordinates who collectively have low morale and little trust in the leadership. The subordinates believe the leadership is too focused on their goals and not focused enough on the team members who do all of the work.

On one hand there are the ideals of a productive organization, yet on the other exists research denouncing its usage. Why this disconnect? As explained in Goleman's *Primal Leadership,* the dilemma revolves around the use of pressure: "The more pressure put on people for results, the more anxiety it provokes. Although moderate pressure can energize people, continued high pressure can be debilitating. As people shift away from pursuing an inspiring vision, pure survival issues take hold."[27] Goleman continues by postulating this continued pressure also stifles talent and creative thinking, obviously constricting innovation and sustained productivity so critical for any team or organization in the ever-changing landscape of competitive pursuits. This pressure can take the form of "micromanaging," where minute details are obsessed over and important responsibilities are not delegated. This is mostly due to a lack of trust in subordinates, including lower performing staff, and the belief the leadership can do it better. Team captains who use this pacesetting style recklessly lose respect and credibility quickly. They have an inability to use important emotional intelligence competencies, including the absence of empathy, or ineffective listening and unproductive communication, such as negative and unwelcomed performance feedback, and another gem, taking frustration about one's own play or team play out on their teammates, indicating a lack of self-awareness and emotional self-management. It is believed the pacesetting style works well in combination with the other leadership styles, especially with the guiding force of the visionary style, the team building aspect of the affiliative style, and the collaboration of the democratic style.

The Commanding Style

Of all the leadership styles, the commanding, or coercive style, is the least effective in most situations, especially with the athletes of today. The mantra of this style, according to Goleman, is, "Do it because I say so," and it is a classic model of military-style leadership. Interestingly enough, according to Alan Murray, the author of *The Wall Street Journal Guide to Management,* even the modern military has come to realize the limited effectiveness of this command and control style of leadership.[28] This coercive style of leadership can be seen when coaches and team captains demand immediate compliance with all orders, replete with threats and intimidation, which can also be applied to negative reviews of player's play where only mistakes are mentioned. Micromanaging becomes a continual practice, with little control or shared power, thus leading to a less-than-ideal motivational climate for the team.

Goleman refers to the impact of this style on the emotional climate of an organization under the grip of a coercive leader in the following manner: "Given that emotional contagion spreads most readily from the top down, an intimidating, cold leader contaminates everyone's mood, and the quality of the overall climate spirals down."[29] The impact of not receiving praise or not being recognized for one's accomplishments can be seen in an individual player's negative attitudes and high levels of dissatisfaction, leaving the player less committed, demotivated, and alienated from the higher mission of the organization. As detailed in Chapter 2, dissatisfied athletes have been reported to cope with their dissatisfaction by staging revolts against their head coach, helping to get their coach fired due to these revolts, writing petitions, or working the system (sometimes with the help of mom and dad), quitting or transferring to other programs, thus impacting the program's Academic Progress Rate (APR) regulation, or legal action.

The particular situations in which the commanding style has been found to be important are times of crisis, such as a major team rule being broken, or after many failed attempts at mentoring, advising, and teaching problem players. This coercive style may push that "magic button" and turn one of these players to commit to a more team-oriented mission, as opposed to a selfish, "me first" approach. In times of crisis, such as after a player getting arrested for breaking a law, the command-and-control style may be needed to reinforce the team rules and carry out the pre-set consequences for such indiscretions in judgment. This style can also be used effectively when an urgent turnaround is needed, especially if a coach or captain is trying to change a team culture of bad attitudes, bad habits, and sustained poor play. In his early days at General Electric, Jack Welch, known to rule with a strong fist as he began to ignite a turnaround to this company, used this style. At that time and under that situation, it turned out to be a most appropriate style. As mentioned on numerous occasions in this chapter, Welch was also known for his EI leadership styles, including the visionary, democratic, and affiliative styles. Similarly, Michael Morris, CEO of American Electric Power, learned a valuable leadership lesson from his time in ROTC: "The lesson I took from that is you can never be soft in the early stage, and then turn hard. But you can always be a high-demand leader, and then over time, soften your approach."[30]

Four emotional intelligence competencies are critical to effectively utilizing this style: emotional control, influence, achievement, and initiative.[31] Leaders must be able to keep their anger and impatience in check, realize the influence their positive and negative behaviors have on others, enact an appropriate drive to achieve (one that is not overpowering or belittling), and also have an intuitive initiative to step up right away to solve issues and not ponder any particular course of action for too long. Aristotle best captures the effective use of the commanding/coercive style: "To be angry with the right person, in the right way, at the right time, and for the right reason."[32]

> *"What works in one context at one point in time*
> *won't necessarily work in a different context at the same time,*
> *or in the same context at a different time."*[33]
>
> —Dr. Steven Sample,
> former USC president

Choosing the Right Club

What also must be considered is it is very difficult for one person to be an expert across all six leadership styles. As Alan Murray states, "Leadership styles are not something to be tried on like so many suits, to see which fits. Rather, they should be adapted to the particular demands of the situation, the particular requirements of the people involved and the particular challenges facing the organization."[34] As the following case studies reveal, leaders who have a large repertoire of strengths in emotional and relational intelligence

(LERQ), leadership know-how and styles (LQ and LSQ), will be more effective due to the flexibility they possess in handling the myriad demands and situations that arise as team leaders. The better leaders are also able to use the right style and approach in the right moment, and even go from one to the other as circumstances dictates. It has been said about having too limited a skill set in this area, "If all you have in your toolbox is a hammer, everything you see will be a nail." In my own experience in the field of sport psychology, I have seen clinical sport psychologists who have limited experience and training in the sport sciences/coaching who automatically assume the performance issue of an athlete or team is of a clinical nature. That is what they know, so that is their particular vantage point. As Goleman states, "People who lack the underlying abilities have a narrowed leadership repertoire and so are too often stuck relying on a style that's ill matched to the challenge of the moment."[35]

Another aspect of leadership style in need of attention is how decisions are made by leaders. Weinberg and Gould in their book, *Foundations of Sport and Exercise Psychology,* detail five primary decision making styles often used by sport coaches, based on the work by Packianathan Chelladurai at Ohio State University. They include autocratic style, autocratic-consultative style, consultative-individual style, consultative-group style, and group style (see Table 1).

Table 1: Decision Styles for Leaders

DECISION STYLE	DEFINED
Autocratic style	The coach solves the problem herself using the information available at the time.
Autocratic-consultative style	The coach obtains the necessary information from relevant players and then comes to a decision.
Consultative-individual style	The coach consults the players individually and then makes a decision. The decision may or may not reflect the players' input.
Consultative-group style	The coach consults the players as a group and then makes a decision. The decision may or may not reflect the players' input.
Group style	The coach shares the problem with the players; then the players jointly make the decision without any influence from the coach.

Reprinted, with permission, from R.S. Weinberg and D. Gould, *Foundations of Sport and Exercise Psychology,* 4th ed. (Champaign, IL: Human Kinetics, 2007), 222.

Similar to leadership styles, a coach or team leader can effectively use the different decision-making styles if he or she is cognizant of the needs of the particular situation and how these decisions will be accepted by the followers/athletes. Team leaders who may be limited in their leadership style repertoire may also be limited in how they make critical team decisions, and vice versa. If a high-level team is in need of a quick turnover artist, the hope is the captain will be proficient as a pacesetter using some form of an autocratic decision-making style, versus a captain who is helping teammates brainstorm a new vision for the team and thus using a consultative-group decision-making style. Although this question relies on situation-specificity, generally, it is important for leaders to ask themselves these questions: Which decision-making style is used most often? Does it always fit the situation, is it accepted by the followers, and finally, does it lead to the desired effect? This reflective question exercise could go far in helping leaders develop a more flexible repertoire of leadership and decision-making styles.

The good news is leadership and decision-making styles can be learned, practiced, and adjusted to best suit the needs of the team. This, however, takes commitment, persistence, and practice. Speaking of practice, leaders (or future captains) should challenge themselves with the following case studies to determine which leadership and decision style (or styles) should be used to have the greatest impact for the specific situation and why that method would be chosen over another.

Case Study 1. A college basketball team has failed to make the conference tournament each of the last three years, despite higher expectations via preseason rankings in the top three of the conference for each of these years. The team returns three starters, one of whom was the conference player of the year last season, and returns four who played considerable minutes coming off of the bench. The captains are both senior starters, with one being a returning captain.

Case Study 2. A high school football team returns 8 of 11 starters on offense (junior quarterback, star from last season), six starters on defense, and were one win away from the state championship last season.

Case Study 3. A college volleyball team that missed the NCAA tournament for the first time in years, and is quite disgruntled with how the team played, brings this frustration into the off-season training period. The team returns four starters and the incoming recruiting class was ranked as the top class in the nation. This team is still picked to finish in the top four of the conference, and historically, the top five teams in the conference have made the NCAA tournament.

Case Study 4. A newly formed under–16 traveling soccer club made up of the better players from three other clubs is expected to make a run at a youth regional championship, and then a run at the national club championships. The coaches include the assistant coaches from a nearby top 20 college program and the full-time coach with the club.

Case Study 5. A coach who has had coaching success at the collegiate and youth national team levels, but has limited international experience, is hired to lead a U.S. national team. This team placed 4th at the prior Olympics, with only one team member retiring from international competition, and returns four starters (and three utility players) who played in their second Olympic games, including the setter, libero, one middle and an outside.

Leadership Style Survey

In addition to the use of case study examples, an applied tool to improve awareness of the particular leadership styles can be found in the Appendices (see Appendix 1). Since this survey is a learning tool used in educating and training leadership skills, it has not been formally analyzed for reliability or validity, and thus, is not a research tool or one to be used for psychological/selection purposes. This can be used as a self-assessment survey or a survey coaches, co-captains, and teammates can complete for a 360-evaluation. When the team completes it, many patterns can develop in the responses, particularly when it is being completed as a captain identification survey. A coach can get an overall view of who the team believes leads the team and how they attempt to do it.

Other patterns include consistent "no votes" or where there are blanks, indicating this particular leadership style has not been seen, which may indicate strengths or weaknesses, depending on the team, dynamics, and situation. This same form can be used to identify and then vote for captains, as well as recommending leadership responsibilities and duties to those who were mentioned consistently throughout. Having the team complete this again during the season can provide information regarding progress or lack of progress being made on continued leadership efforts. Another version can be used (Appendix 1) for self-assessment of leadership styles.

Strength-Based Leadership Styles

Having an arsenal of leadership styles as strengths not only makes leaders good and effective, but more flexible in handling all they face while coaching or captaining the team. There is a burgeoning field of psychology called

Strengths Psychology. Its founder, Dr. Donald O. Clifton, began surveying the unique strengths of leaders back in the 1960s. Along with his colleagues from the Gallup Organization, Dr. Clifton has conducted longitudinal research studies for decades and has interviewed or surveyed more than one million work teams, leaders, and their followers on the topic of strengths and leadership. Dr. Clifton said his greatest discovery from all of his research was "a leader needs to know his strengths as a carpenter knows his tools, or as a physician knows the instruments at her disposal. What great leaders have in common is that each truly knows his or her strengths—and can call on the right strength at the right time."[36] Out of this voluminous amount of research came four distinct domains (a term synonymous with styles) of leadership strength: Executing, Influencing, Relationship Building, and Strategic Thinking.[37] As is evident, there certainly is overlap between these domains and the previously discussed leadership styles.

Similarly stated, it is very difficult for one leader to be able to do all things and be an expert at all styles. According to this work, "individuals need not be well-rounded, but teams should be!"[38] So on a team, it is most important the captains, apprentice captains, and even some experienced players, when combining their leadership strengths while tackling a particular team issue, cover the necessary strength for the circumstance.

Executing	Influencing	Relationship Building	Strategic Thinking
ACHIEVER	ACTIVATOR	ADAPTABILITY	ANALYTICAL
ARRANGER	COMMAND	DEVELOPER	CONTEXT
BELIEF	COMMUNICATION	CONNECTEDNESS	FUTURISTIC
CONSISTENCY	COMPETITION	EMPATHY	IDEATION
DELIBERATIVE	MAXIMIZER	HARMONY	INPUT
DISCIPLINE	SELF-ASSURANCE	INCLUDER	INTELLECTION
FOCUS	SIGNIFICANCE	INDIVIDUALIZATION	LEARNER
RESPONSIBILITY	WOO	POSITIVITY	STRATEGIC
RESTORATIVE		RELATOR	

Table 2: Strengths Finder Themes. © 2008 Gallup, Inc. All rights reserved. Used with permission.

In their book, *Strengths-Based Leadership,* Tom Rath and Barry Conchie define these four domains of strength and explain how teams should maximize their use of these strengths.[39] As Table 2 indicates, under each of the four strength domains are defining themes derived from a statistical factor analysis conducted by Gallup's researchers.

The first of these strengths, *Executing,* means knowing how to make things happen, usually by simply working tirelessly and consistently toward goal attainment, which also entails being disciplined, responsible, and extremely focused on the task getting done. A leader with this strength also becomes the liaison between the team, staff, and support staff in getting things done, such as standard/vision posters, getting quotes on the back of practice tees, coordinating recruiting visits, and anything else that comes his/her way. There are also leaders who may lead the team by *Influencing* teammates daily to continue to put in a consistently productive effort toward accomplishing the team goals. This leader is a self-assured, competitive teammate who projects authority through both her actions and her communications with teammates. College captains have also extended their influence on others outside of the team, such as booster groups, youth organizations, even other departments on campus (e.g., marketing, publicity, sport information), to spread the word about the program to elicit a greater fan base. A third universal strength is a leader who is a *Relationship Builder.* This leader is the "team mom" or "team builder" who is the glue that holds the team together. He or she is able to relate to all team members by keeping everyone actively engaged, even the newer team members, by mentoring them on how the program functions and their contributions to it. This leader is positive in her workings with the team and helps to bring energy and a high work ethic to practice daily, while also being able to develop and coach teammates to bring more of what is needed for the team to be successful.

The final strength, *Strategic Thinker,* belongs to the player who is consistently in the right place at the right time on the field/court of play, is a true student of the game, and helps teammates to make better decisions during play. A leader like this is an extension of the coach in how he helps teammates integrate scouting/video cues on opponents and apply them prior to and during game play. These leaders also keep the team focused on the "bigger picture," the ultimate goal set for the team. Teams can get so stuck on the little details and the stress of their schedules that being reminded about what they are working toward can strengthen their focus and efforts, while helping them get past the emotionality of tough losses or stretches of adversity.

In their studies on leadership, Rath and Conchie have yet to find two leaders who have the exact same strength sequence. They state, "While two leaders may have identical expectations, the way they reach their goals is always dependent on the unique arrangement of their strengths."[40] Another strong indicator of the importance of working within your strengths is a study conducted by the Gallup Organization of almost 200,000 employees from 36 companies, revealing that only 20 percent of the workforce is actually working in their areas of strength. As noted by J.C. Maxwell, "The number one reason people don't like their job is that they are not working in the area of their strengths."[41] Rath and Conchie also cite research findings indicating those who have lower self-confidence reported almost three times as many health issues 25 years later, when compared with those who were aware of their strengths and had higher self-confidence in these strengths earlier in their careers. Another study indicates people who had the opportunity to use their strengths early on had significantly higher levels of job satisfaction, and income, 26 years later.[42] What an endorsement for knowing current strengths and working from them as early as possible, as well as helping others to uncover their strengths.

As a coach or team leader, how often are strengths uncovered and identified, and is this process part of the recruiting protocol as much as looking for certain strengths needed by the team or to complement those of the existing team members? Recalling the four domains of leadership strengths from above, does a team need a strategic thinker to apply what is learned from the scouting reports and video, or is there a greater need for build trusting relationships, or is it instead important to find someone who helps execute the team vision and get things done, or to find someone who can motivate from within? Being able to add these questions to the team needs assessment process in the off-season, as well as including them on the recruiting "shopping list," can be valuable toward not only uncovering leadership strengths in players already involved in the team but also in improving the screening procedures of incoming players to ascertain what they can contribute to the program from a leadership perspective.

Women and the Leadership Gap

The title of this section is from a *Newsweek* article written by Leslie Bennetts on the important topic of the lack of women in positions in power and how the battle for equality is far from over. As noted in this article, Gloria Steinem reports, "Perfectly nice guys will say to me, 'You must be so happy you've won!' I say, 'But are you working for a woman?' And they look appalled."[43] It is the objective of this section to simply highlight the importance of this topic and to share noted books, resources, and institutes dedicated to women's leadership issues.

The similarities and differences of leadership styles based on gender is an important topic that has fortunately been given attention in the field of business and leadership. This research reveals small differences between leadership styles and gender, with specific results showing women tend to use more of a democratic, participative and collaborative style than do men, and are more likely to use a transformational leadership style when mentoring subordinates.[44] Virginia Schein has done considerable research on sex-role stereotypes in business, and indicates women view themselves as being equal to men in possessing leadership characteristics, yet men's views remain unchanged from her earlier work, which shows a "think manager-think male" attitude exists.[45] A meta-analysis of leadership effectiveness finds no differences among female and male leaders overall, yet in a male-dominated setting with more male subordinates, the evaluations favored men, and when the conditions were reversed, leader effectiveness favored females.[46] Alan Murray exhorts managers to avoid creating an overly "male culture," which can serve to stunt women's advancement opportunities. Murray also cites a book by Lois Frankel, *Nice Girls Don't Get the Corner Office,* whose contents include a list of 101 "unconscious mistakes" women make that stunt their careers, including not viewing the workplace as a sporting match and using minimizing words like "I just…" or "It was only …" or offering excessive apologizing.[47] Additional books that address similar women's leadership issues can be found in the bibliography section at the back of this book.[48]

One of these books has garnered recent national attention. *Lean In,* written by Sheryl Sandberg, was recently featured in a *USA TODAY* article (March 2013). As chief operating officer of *Facebook,* Sandberg, a mother of two young children, believes the talk of finding appropriate work-life balance is hurting women's careers and halting the progress of women in top industry positions.[49] For starters, men are seldom asked how they balance work and family responsibilities, as this is targeted usually to females. Second, using the dichotomous work-life balance moniker depicts work and life as weighted against each other on a scale, with accomplishing "balance" primarily meaning working less, which is what women currently do (7.8 hours vs. 8.3 hours per workday). Third, Sandberg believes in getting rid of the word "balance," and instead using the argot "work-life fit," so "you can lean in to a career and make the pieces fit however it works for you. You take control. That's what leaders do."[50]

In addition to the Sandberg book, and the Frankel text cited earlier in this chapter by Murray, there are other excellent books, journals, and leadership institutes dedicated to women's leadership issues. For example, *Warren Bennis' Leadership Excellence: The Magazine of Leadership Development, Managerial Effectiveness, and Organizational Psychology* is replete with articles specific to women's leadership issues. One such example is an article entitled, "Women's Vision: Making the Strategic Case," written by Sally Helgesen, on the cultural reasons why women still struggle to achieve top positions in business.[51] As an aside, Helgesen has written some excellent books on women's leadership issues.[52] Additionally, there is an online journal entitled *Advancing Women in Leadership Journal (AWL Journal)*, which advertises its first book, *Women's Leadership Issues: An International Perspective.*[53] *The Leadership Quarterly* is a scholarly journal published by Elsevier, in affiliation with the International Leadership Association, which includes countless articles on women's leadership, as does the journal *Leadership in Action,* published by the Center for Creative Leadership, the *Harvard Business Review, Women in Management Review* published by Emerald, and *Business Week.*[54] Moreover, the website for *Bloomberg Business Week* has dedicated links to specific writings for women leaders.[55]

To add to the many resources specific to women's leadership, there are also numerous leadership institutes, one of them being the Institute for Women's Leadership, created by the former dean of Douglass College, Mary S. Hartman, which is a "consortium of teaching, research, and public service units" operating in close association with Rutgers University, and more specifically Douglass Campus. The Institute is composed of seven consortium members: Douglass Residential College, the Department of Women's and Gender Studies, the Center for American Women and Politics, the Institute for Research on Women, the Institute for Women & Art, the Center for Women's Global Leadership, and the Center for Women and Work.[56] There is also a Women's Leadership Institute on the campus of UCLA,[57] and a national association for women's leadership, the National Association for Female Executives.[58]

In the sport area, excellent texts exist on the topic, including *She Can Coach,* edited by Cecile Reynaud, which includes tools for success from 20 top women coaches, a monthly journal, the *Canadian Journal of Women in Coaching,* and others worthy of attention.[59]

> *"Real leadership probably has more to do with recognizing your own uniqueness than it does with identifying your similarities."*[60]
> —Sydney Pollack,
> movie producer

Part III

Tools of the Trade: Talents, Techniques and Tactics (TQ3)

– 7 –

Six Top Talents

*"For people to follow someone willingly, the majority
of constituents believe the leader must be honest,
forward-looking, inspiring, and competent."*[1]
—James Kouzes and Barry Posner,
The Leadership Challenge

For the deputy managing editor of the *Wall Street Journal*, Alan Murray,
to enthusiastically recommend a book he considers "one of the most influential
business books of recent years,"[2] it has to truly be a must-read! This book is
Jim Collins' *Good to Great*, based on a voluminous research project Collins
and colleagues conducted to investigate how many of the 1,435 large companies on their survey list made the leap from good results to great results. While
using comparison grouping, the research team identified just 11 companies
who made such a leap from good to great. These companies were able to sustain
these great results for a 15-year period.[3] Jim Collins reports on the results of
this study: "We were surprised, shocked really, to discover the type of leadership required for turning a good company into a great one. Compared to high-
profile leaders with big personalities who make headlines and become celebrities, the good-to-great leaders seem to have come from Mars."[4] He continues
by stating the leaders were quiet, reserved, with a "paradoxical blend of humility and professional will."[5] This chapter details the many talents (qualities)
of effective leaders from industry, business, and sport, beginning with
Collins' most shocking result, the *humility* portrayed by these great leaders.
The remainder of the talents addressed in this chapter include *toughness, character-in-action, competence, communicative abilities,* and being *passionate-
inspired.*

"Leadership requires distinct behaviors and attitudes,
and for many people, they debut with the job."[6]
—Jack Welch, *Winning*

The Humble, Level 5 Leader

Despite the stance taken that leadership is made and not born for the most part, there is still a fascination with the traits of successful leaders. This is illustrated vividly when one visits the "Sports" section in any bookstore, and sees the collection of leadership books written by coaches, from Coach K and Phil Jackson, to Bobby Bowden and Tony Dungy, and so many more, primarily from the "Big 3" sports: football, basketball, and baseball. Alan Murray cautions against generalizing these common traits of successful leaders because of the ever-present exception to every rule. One conclusion that emerges from the best work on leadership is "Great leaders exhibit a paradoxical mix of arrogance and humility."[7] Murray explains this paradoxical mix by saying, "Leaders must be arrogant enough to believe they are worth following, but humble enough to know that others may have a better sense of the direction they should take. They must believe in themselves, but be willing to put the organization's needs above their own."[8]

It is in the humility department where modern leaders fail.[9] This same trapping is apparent in the sport world, including all levels of competitive sport. One example is of an underdog coach who was delightfully surprised to find out her opponent spent little time doing video preparation to prepare since her team was ranked and the underdog's was not. Aside from this obvious arrogance, during the match the ranked coach did not make any adjustments to the offensive or defensive schemes, or change personnel, despite being down big early. The coach believed her system would eventually kick-in and victory would be theirs. Due to this arrogance, this team was sent packing after suffering an upset loss, dropping them out of the top 25 ranking, and costing their grip on first place in the conference. An important question to ask is, how many times has arrogance impacted your decisions and team outcomes? For some, it represents a hard lesson to learn.

Jim Collins, the author of *Good to Great,* refers to those leaders who have profound humility as "Level 5" leaders. This type of leadership is further characterized as those who "channel their ego needs away from themselves and into the large goal of building a great company. It's not that Level 5 leaders have no ego or self-interest. Indeed, they are incredibly ambitious—but their ambition is first and foremost for the institution, not themselves."[10] The other levels of Collins' leadership hierarchy are: Level 1 highly capable individual, Level 2 contributing team member, Level 3 competent manager, Level 4 effective leader, and lastly, Level 5 executive. Level 5 is the highest level, exemplifying leaders who personify all five layers of the hierarchy. As Collins states, "Level 5 leaders are a study in duality—modest and willful, humble and fearless."[11] Besides humility, Jim Murray believes a ferocious resolve is of equal importance, defining it as "an almost stoic determination to do whatever needs to be done to make the organization great."[12] Murray also believes part of this resolve is the toughness needed to truly pursue the goals of the organization. When one thinks of toughness, does the name Vince Lombardi come to mind? The venerable Hall of Fame and Super Bowl winning coach of the NFL's Green Bay Packers could be one of the most cited sources of "toughness" quotes used in coaches' offices, locker rooms, and weight rooms across the United States. Who in sport coaching has not used some of these prized quotes?

"The most important element in the character make-up of a man who is successful is that of mental toughness."[13]

—Vince Lombardi

Tough Leadership

In the sport psychology field, mental toughness is defined in numerous ways. Contained herein are toughness quotes from coaches, competitors, and sport psychology consultants.

"Do what has to be done; when it has to be done; as well as it can be done; do it that way all the time."[14]

—Former Indiana University basketball coach Bob Knight

"Being comfortable while uncomfortable."[15]

—Mental skills trainer for Major League Baseball teams Ken Ravizza

"To be and/or disciplined in one's mind is to be able to keep all possible distractions at bay while consistently focusing on and executing the task of the moment."[16]

—Former coach and mental skills trainer for Scott Boras Corporation Harvey Dorfman

"Mental toughness is having the courage to make mistakes knowing the process that follows can result in greatness.

It is the ability to feel and be vulnerable, and to overcome the demons within our own head, and those that may doubt, to look adversity in the face and say, "not this time!" And to go forward and not look back or dwell. It is the ability to trust oneself to be good enough."[17]
—Two-time U.S. Volleyball Olympian Nicole Davis

"Toughness training is the art & science of increasing your ability to handle all kinds of stress: Physical, mental, & emotional so that you'll be a more effective competitor. Your mind, body, and emotions will become more flexible, responsive, resilient, and stronger—the real meaning of tough as used here, through toughness training."[18]
—Jim Loehr, author of
Toughness Training for Sports

Sport researchers have designed a model on mental toughness that comprises four constructs: control, commitment, challenge, and confidence. Control is defined as the capacity to feel and act as though one could exert influence on the situation; commitment is the tendency to take an active role; challenge is the ability to view a situation as an opportunity rather than a threat; and confidence is simply a strong sense of self-belief in one's skills. As the model purports, confident individuals who are committed to influencing positive change are considered tough-minded leaders and individuals.[19] This particular quality, toughness, has similar descriptors cited by many in the world of business and sport. Other words used to denote toughness in the literature include courage, determined, disciplined, assertive, bold, confident, poised, conviction, and competitive.

Although many of the aforementioned toughness talents are separate constructs and time could be spent defining each, when considering them together as a grouping of leadership talents, they appear to have two things in common: control and courage. Beginning with the construct of control, people have the ability to sustain greater control over circumstances and specifically, over their schedules and how they perceive what occurs around them. When they take active steps to prioritize their activities and better manage their time and schedule, they do gain a great sense of control over their lives. Another aspect of control worth mentioning is the more control people believe they have over their situation and events that surround them, the more adaptive their appraisals will be and the more productive their reactions and actions will be. For example, if a team captain views having to talk to the head coach about a sensitive team issue (e.g., a team member who got caught under-age drinking the night before) as a threat, insomuch as she thinks the coach will get angry, and maybe blame the captain for not taking a more active role to ensure this type of thing does not happen, this captain may put off talking to the coach. This may make matters worse when the coach finds out from his Athletic Director about this occurrence, which the captain knew about before the coach did but failed to bring to her attention earlier. Instead, this captain should view this scenario of having to approach the coach as her duty as a leader and as a valuable exercise in problem solving and confrontation.

To make these productive appraisals one must have the courage to make the tough decisions. Referring to the captain above, it takes courage to confront and challenge another, but to be an effective team leader one must be willing to be courageous and do what needs to be done regardless of one's comfort zone and personality style. As Harvey Dorfman states, "Courage allows the leader to express all his other qualities—the absence of courage suppresses them, stifles them. Challenging fears elevates behavior, elevates the leader, and enhances the organization one leads. All goes if courage goes."[20]

Another toughness quality is the level of competitiveness within an individual and team. The ability to weather any storm one faces in an evaluative or competitive arena is at the core of one's competitive self. It is often said great competitors like Michael Jordan, Wayne Gretsky, and Jack Nicklaus competed against their own last great performance and were driven by the competition of self. In the true competitive sense, what could have been more difficult than being a better Michael Jordan from one day to the next? This notion of competing against self is the moral of a story shared by Vince Lombardi's son, Vince Lombardi, Jr. The story is about how his father tapped the competitive toughness of one his best players, the all-pro guard Jerry Kramer, who threw the block to seal the 1967 championship game.[21] Earlier in his career, Kramer was on the verge of quitting after getting yet another earful from Coach Lombardi during a difficult practice: "Mister, the attention span for a grade school kid is 30 seconds, for a high school kid a minute, for a college kid three minutes! Mister, where does that leave you?"[22] After calling him a "fat cow" and many much harsher expletives, Coach Lombardi left him. Later in the locker room, while Kramer was seriously considering quitting right then or after the season, Coach Lombardi found the right motivational button. He walked through the locker room and took a look at Kramer, and sized up the situation. He walked over, tousled his hair, and told him, "Son, someday you are going to be one of the greatest guards in football." According to Kramer, from that day forward he never had to be pushed or motivated again. The competitive drive to be the best guard in football drove him daily. According to his son, Coach Lombardi strongly believed in the benefits of competition and thought "it was the bedrock of the American economy and culture."[23] And lastly, Pat Williams, Executive for the NBA's Orlando Magic and author of many books on leadership, summed up this particular talent quite well in this statement: "Leadership is not for wimps."[24]

> *"Its qualities are sacrifice and self-denial; It is combined with*
> *a perfectly disciplined will that refuses to give in.*
> *It's a state of mind—you could call it character-in-action."*[25]
> —Vince Lombardi

Character-in-Action

In addition to the importance placed on a leader's humility, ferocious resolve and toughness, many others from business and sport chime in on what qualities or talents help give them and their organizations a competitive edge over the competition. The qualities referenced in this literature include emotional capacity, competence, communication abilities, and passion/inspiration, yet one of the most cited qualities of successful leaders begins with character.

As the Lombardi quote indicates, character-in-action is more salient and authentic when one *practices* one's character and doesn't simply talk about it. Dorfman adds another component to character-in-action, putting special attention on who is watching: "You identify yourself by what you do when no one is watching. The supervised athlete may be the hardest worker, the most selfless and responsible competitor. But how he practices when no one sees him, how he interacts with teammates when the coach is not within listening distance—that's when he defines himself and his character."[26] Theodore Roosevelt said this about character: "I care not what others think of what I do, but I care very much about what I think of what I do. That is character!"[27]

Coaches are obviously on the front line of showing character-in-action by their own modeling, but also how they provide the setting for character and leader development. Dorfman uses the analogy of a coach/ mentor as an elevator operator who can take the athlete from the level of his current circumstance to the height needed for success. He continues by stating, "Sociologists tell us that left to their own devices, most people will rise and fall according to circumstance, rather than self-control. The coach must take that control until the athlete can assume it for himself."[28] Any conversation about character in sport usually references one of the greatest coaches to patrol a sideline, the legendary John Wooden. Most are aware of his numbers (10 national titles, 7 in a row, 4 perfect 30–0 seasons, 88-game winning streak), and those who have been fortunate enough to listen to him speak and read from his books realize the importance he placed on character development in his teaching.

Pat Williams includes in his book *Coaching Your Kids to Be Leaders* Coach Wooden's character development lessons, beginning with Wooden's two sets of threes: "Never lie, cheat, or steal" and "Don't whine, complain, or make excuses." Williams also includes Coach's 7-Point Creed for building the character qualities of a leader. It includes be true to yourself; help others; make each day your masterpiece; drink deeply from good books; make friendship a fine art; build a shelter against a rainy day; and pray for guidance and counsel, and give thanks for your blessings every day.[29] Coach Wooden was heartfelt, authentic and truly committed to teaching character, leadership, and life lessons to his teams through the years. Coach Wooden's lessons need to continue to be taught for generations to come.

> *"These five qualities make up the quality called competence: Knowledge, Experience, Confidence, Commitment to excellence, and Competitiveness. Competent leaders produce competent teams and organizations."*[30]
> —Pat Williams,
> *Coaching Your Kids to Be Leaders*

Leadership Competence

A popular myth about leadership is debunked by Robert Goffee and Gareth Jones in their article "Why Should Anyone Be Led by You?" proposing that not everyone can be a leader. "Many executives don't have the self-knowledge or the authenticity necessary for leadership. Individuals must also want to be leaders, and many talented employees are not interested in shouldering that responsibility."[31] It is for the latter reason that those being considered for the captaincy be given the right of first refusal. Just because they were either voted or selected to be captain by their teammates does not necessarily make them the right fit. Do they even want to take on the myriad leadership and managerial responsibilities that come with being a captain on these teams? Giving these players the opportunity to turn down this position, without penalty, is critical to having a captain who will be committed to learning the competencies, responsibilities, and roles of being a leader for their team.

The competencies relevant to the position of team leader include those previously addressed in earlier chapters: leadership LQ (Chapter 4), leadership ERQ (Chapter 5), leadership LSQ (Chapter 6), and those addressed in future chapters, Leadership TQ³ (Chapters 7–9) and Organizational DQ (Chapter 10). All of these components are important in enriching the knowledge base of these future leaders, on which their leadership efforts will be based. Former San Francisco 49ers coach Bill Walsh detailed in his book *The Score Takes*

Care of Itself the importance of leaders having expertise and credibility: "Leadership is expertise. People will follow a person who organizes and manages others, because he or she has credibility and expertise—a knowledge of the profession—and demonstrates an understanding of human nature."[32]

Pat Williams uses the story of Coach Ken Carter, popularized in the 2005 movie *Coach Carter,* as an illustration for the importance of competence in sport and leadership.[33] To recap, the movie is about Ken Carter, a high school basketball coach, who during the 1998–1999 season locked the team out of the practice gym, despite their 13–0 record, because the team was in violation of the 19-point academic contract they all signed at the beginning of the season. Since their academic performance was so poor, Coach Carter had the team meet in the school library to focus on their school work instead of practicing. After forfeiting two games, amidst a clamor of protests from parents, students, and administrators, Coach Carter finally allowed the team to practice and compete only because the players' academics improved. The resultant season was a 19–5 finish and an appearance in the district play-offs. More importantly, every senior player coached by Coach Carter attended either junior college or a four-year institution. Coach Carter states the objective he had in mind when he took such a courageous stand: "My goal was to get these boys into college, where they could learn to become leaders."[34] In essence, Coach Carter believed in the importance of education and how this empowered his players to become competent as leaders in their own lives and communities. Williams similarly believes competence qualifies a leader to lead, and consequently identifies five components to competence[35]:

(1) Knowledge: A competent leader (CL) is educated and committed to lifelong learning.
(2) Experience: A CL has the hands-on, know-how from practice experience.
(3) Confidence: A CL inspires confidence in his players and teammates.
(4) Commitment to excellence: A CL demonstrates the drive for being the best.
(5) Competitiveness: A CL is a fierce competitor.

Ronald Heifetz and Donald Laurie detail that one of the toughest tasks for leaders is mobilizing people to do adaptive work through the myriad of challenges facing their organizations.[36] In collegiate athletics, for example, the NCAA is pushing for stricter academic reform legislation across many areas, most specifically mandating a certain level of Academic Progress Rate (APR) before teams can complete in post-season play. For example, the 2011 national champion UCONN Huskies men's basketball team is not allowed to play in the 2013 "March Madness" NCAA Tournament because of their low APR score. This results in coaches having to be more thorough in their evaluation and recruiting of prospective student-athletes. Any border-line students who fail out or drop out of school will count against their APR. A more concerted effort needs to be in place to assist those already in the program to continually perform well in the classroom, while meeting the continuing eligibility requirements.

This is just one evolving adaptive challenge for collegiate coaches, but the ability of coaches and team captains to weather the myriad of challenges facing them day in and day out, or as Heifetz and Laurie call it, "regulating distress," becomes a leader's most difficult job. These authors continue by avowing leaders must have the emotional capacity to tolerate these challenges while also communicating confidence that they can handle the difficult tasks ahead. They also affirm an effective leader "has to be able to raise tough questions without getting too anxious himself. Employees as well as colleagues and customers will carefully observe verbal and nonverbal cues to a leader's ability to hold steady."[37] A leader's emotional capacity, or emotional intelligence, allows him to hold steady and appear ready and able to lead. Refer to Chapter 5 for a review of the most important emotional and relational capacity components.

Leadership guru Warren Bennis, in his book *An Invented Life: Reflections on Leadership and Change,* profiles four competencies for doing the right things when leading. He believes American organizations are under-led and over-managed, "not paying enough attention to doing the right thing, while paying too much attention to doing things right."[38] Bennis' first competency is the management of *attention* through a clear vision of outcome, goal or direction, followed by the management of *meaning,* which entails leaders communicating their vision through metaphors or models to help make the vision clear and meaningful to others. The third competency is the management of *trust,* which is built on reliability or constancy; people would rather follow a leader they can count on despite disagreeing with their views, rather than leaders they agree with but who shift their stance or views back and forth. This point is clearly stated in another book by Bennis, *On Becoming a Leader:* "One thing that has become clearer than ever to me is that integrity is the most important characteristic of a leader, and one that he or she must be prepared to demonstrate again and again."[39] The final competency is the management of *self,* which denotes knowing one's skills and using them effectively. In his words, "Management of self is critical; without it, leaders and managers can do more harm than good. Like incompetent doctors, incompetent managers can make life worse, make people sicker and less vital."[40] It is important for leaders to ask themselves what types of courageous steps they take in their particular leadership situations to become a more competent leader or to help others become more competent leaders.

*"Innovation requires more listening and
communication than does routine work.""*[41]
—James Kouzes and Barry Posner,
The Leadership Challenge

Effective Listener/Communicator

Revered talk show host Larry King paints a clear picture of the importance of the listening aspect of communication: "I remind myself every morning: nothing I say this day will teach me anything. So, if I'm going to learn, I
must do it by listening."[42] This from a man who has spent his career inter-
viewing and talking with the biggest names in politics, entertainment, and
sport! Steven Sample, former USC president, asserts the average person suffers
from three delusions: (1) he is a good driver; (2) he has a good sense of humor;
and (3) he is a good listener.[43] As most probably experience, many people are
poor listeners and poor drivers! Imagine how effective people would be in
their jobs and lives if they could learn to listen first and talk later. If only they
could realize, as Larry King does, listening is how we acquire new ideas. Being
an artful listener builds trust from others, and conversely, as J.C. Maxwell
avows, "a deaf ear is the first symptom of a closed mind, and having a closed
mind is a surefire way to hurt your leadership."[44] Maxwell also affirms how
much work people must put in to become artful listeners: "You spend half
your day—about four hours—in listening activities; You hear about two hours'
worth of what is said; You actually listen to an hour of it; You understand only
thirty minutes of that hour. You believe only fifteen minutes' worth. And you
remember less than eight minutes of all that is said."[45] The next chapter (Chapter 8) addresses improving on the much-needed communication practices,
especially finding a leadership voice and artful listening.

*"Passion is an incredible asset for any person,
but especially for leaders."*[46]
—John C. Maxwell, *Leadership Gold*

Passion and Inspiration

The final grouping of talents effective leaders have in common includes
their passion and inspiration for the people and the work. Similar terms used
for passion can include a leader's loyalty and commitment to the organizational
mission and its process. This talent is very important for leaders because this

is what fills the tank and energizes the leader from one challenge to another, one day to the next. J.C. Maxwell affirms when a person does not have passion, their life and their work become monotonous, and the "want to" motto is replaced with "have to."[47] Whenever people have to do something, rather than wanting to do something, attitude, effort, and motivation is much different. This represents a "red flag" whenever an athlete or a team begins to talk about their sport participation as a "job," something they have to do to keep their coach or parents happy, or simply to keep their scholarship so they can continue to stay in college. Although the majority of athletes, and their coaches, may have days they feel this way, the issue becomes a real problem in its consistency and severity.

Another red flag indicating a lowering of passion and inspiration, often referred to in sport psychology and sport as a "brown-out" or worse, an outright "black-out," is the level of commitment players consistently show in practice and competitive games. Jeff Janssen, author of *Championship Team Building,* came up with the "commitment continuum."[48] At the lower end of the continuum is the 2 R's, characterized by those players who are *resistant,* who defy the standards of the team, and those who question them, the *reluctant* players. Those players who do just enough to get by can be placed in the *existent* category. These three categories of players represent those who have low commitment to the team and to their own pursuit of excellence, and thus, can be considered to have little passion and inspiration to be their best or to help the team be its best. The next level represents those players who are *compliant,* characterized by those who do all that is asked of them, but nothing more. The next grouping includes the *committed* players, who maximize their own individual contributions and assist the team in whatever areas will lead to success. The top level consists of those players who are *compelled.* These are committed athletes who are determined to bring others with them to this top level.

Those athletes who are committed and compelled are fueled by their passion to be consistent competitors who want to do all they can to help this team. The same can be said of passionate, compelled leaders, or as James Kouzes and Barry Posner say in *The Leadership Challenge,* "There's no one more believable than a person with a deep passion for something. There's no one more fun to be around than someone who is openly excited about the magic that can happen. There's no one more determined than someone who believes fervently in an ideal."[49]

As will be discussed in Chapters 10 and 11, leaders and followers can get their passion "jump started" when they are included in the inter-workings of the team through team building and leadership development processing. Maxwell avows, "Passion is an incredible asset for any person, but especially for leaders. It keeps us going when others quit. It becomes contagious and influences others to follow us. It pushes us through the toughest of times and gives us energy we did not know we possessed. It fuels us."[50] Lastly, Jack Welch concludes this section on passion with this quote: "The world will belong to passionate, driven leaders ... people who not only have enormous amounts of energy, but who can energize those whom they lead."[51]

Talent Identifier: Leadership Skill-Set Survey

Taking all of these heavily cited talents of leaders, combined with feedback from coaching staffs and captains, I have formulated an educational assessment, including 12 talents or qualities. The survey can be seen in its entirety in Appendix 2. Coaches may value other talents and should identify and cultivate them with players and captains. The talents included in Table 1 represent those talents cited in the leadership literature and believed to be important by coaches and captains.

Table 1: The Talents of Good and Effective Sport Team Leaders

NAME	DEFINED	QUESTION
Courageous/ Toughness	Willing to take risks and put themselves in uncomfortable positions for the betterment of the team	Willing to make unpopular decisions?
Work rate	Always leading by example by doing what needs to get done	Are you the hardest working player in practice?
Competitive	Driven by wanting to be better and make the team better	Do you look for different ways to drive your performance?
Confident	Knows and trusts her talents and skills	Do you want the ball with the game on the line?
Quality trainer	Consistently has a productive attitude toward practice	Do you consistently prepare for training?
Team player	Puts the team first	Do you continue to lead despite quality of play?
Leader-by-example	Leads the team by what they say and do	Are you the first to go in drills?
Committed/ Inspired	Counted on to fulfill his/her role	Do you inspire the team to work to accomplish team standards?

Compassionate/ Humble	Easily relatable who makes connections with teammates	Do you have a relationship with every teammate?
Character Leader	Models sound character-in-action daily	Do you represent self and program in a professional manner?
Communicator	Astute in verbal and nonverbal communication	Are you a good listener?
Competent	Knowledgeable about the sport and inter-workings of the team	Do you have a pulse on this team?

"Leaders earn the right to lead. How? They manifest character and integrity. Character is not inherited, it is something that can be, and needs to be, built and disciplined."[52]

—Vince Lombardi

– 8 –

Six Top Techniques

*"In the collaborative mode that these leaders establish,
they create stimulating, synergistic connections, support honest
interactions, build trusting relationships, and encourage
self-management across organizational lines."[1]*
—Warren Bennis and Joan Goldsmith,
Learning to Lead

The voluminous amount of literature on leadership highlights what the good and effective leaders *have* (which includes their talents, the focus of Chapter 7), as well as what they *do* (techniques) and *how* they get it accomplished (tactics). This chapter details what good and effective leaders *do* in terms of techniques they use to accomplish "good to great" things for their teams and organizations. Leadership gurus Warren Bennis and Joan Goldsmith reveal key techniques of "bold, unabashed leadership," including creating a sense of collaboration between leader and followers, while creating connections, having honest interactions, building trusting relationships and encouraging self-management among all those involved in the organization.[2]

These same authors went further in their book *Learning to Lead* on this topic by sharing six behaviors, supported by the historical figures who exemplified these techniques.

(1) *Mastering the context,* as in understanding the big picture, like Winston Churchill did during both world wars;
(2) *Knowing yourself,* in terms of enhancing one's awareness through continual learning, such as Mother Theresa did with her blessed work in India;
(3) *Creating a vision* by mobilizing others to share in the journey, like John F. Kennedy's dream of putting a man on the moon;
(4) *Communicating with meaning* by reaching those who are listening on all levels, like Dr. Martin Luther King, Jr., did by moving millions of people with his speeches;

(5) *Building trust through integrity* with ethical living, working, and playing, much like Eleanor Roosevelt did through her help in creating the United Nations; and

(6) *Realizing intentions through actions*, which points to the importance of concrete results through the collaboration of others, much like the work of Nobel Laureate Archbishop Desmond Tutu healing his country of South Africa.

What a daunting task it is to live up to these model examples of sound leadership techniques, especially when one considers how very difficult it must have been for these marvels to practice these leadership techniques in their particular circumstances. For example, Mother Theresa in extreme poverty, or Dr. Martin Luther King, Jr., having his voice heard under the oppression of hate and racism. If these most revered historical leaders could practice these behaviors under the most oppressive and/or grandiose scales, then all leaders should be able to practice these leadership ethos with their sports teams while assisting their captains in doing the same with their teammates.

Considering the platform already established by the work of Warren Bennis and Joan Goldsmith, including the six valuable leadership techniques addressed above, additional leadership techniques from the voluminous leadership research from the business and organizational fields are highlighted in this section. Interestingly enough, all begin with the letter "C": *Collaboration, Connections, Confidence Enhancement, Communication, Competitive Climate,* and *Conflict-Change Management.*

> *"Being in a band is always a compromise. Provided that the balance is good, what you lose in compromise, you gain by collaboration."*[3]
> —Mike Rutherford of
> Genesis and Mike & the Mechanics

Collaboration

For leaders to have the type of team they envision, especially considering what is known about today's athletes from a generational perspective (Chapters 1–3), the leader must establish a culture of *collaboration.* Collaboration will not occur if a true *connection* is not made between the leader (coach or team captain) and team. This connection cannot happen without active listening, continual *communication,* and *confidence* within and from both parties. Collaboration is used to denote the important technique of asking for feedback from the organizational stakeholders and doing something with the obtained feedback.

Prior to beginning any leadership consultation with a new organization, it is important to clearly state to the athletic director (if needed) and to the coaching staff that this process is a collaboration between coaches, captains, and team, and feedback will be asked for and integrated, reinforced, assessed, then applied throughout the entire season. Obtaining feedback from all team members, staff, and support staff allows everyone to have a voice and to be a part of the vision and action plan. Examples of feedback areas include wanting to know others' thoughts/feelings about team vision, daily standards of action, team rules, leadership evaluation, game preparation/warm-up activities, team building, mental toughness, or anything deemed important for the betterment of the team. This feedback is then usually prioritized by the members, then defined in observable, action terms. All parties need to know that every word typed, written or spoken will be given consideration before moving forward. After obtaining consensus, the feedback is shared with all in some tangible form (poster, handout, presentation) and the standards, vision, leadership responsibilities, whatever was brainstormed and established, are then reinforced and literally put into practice by coaches and captains, preparation procedures, and game play. Throughout the season these action points will be revisited and updated if needed, following a similar team brainstorming session and process. In this way, all team members feel a part of the process of building this team and its vision and process.

> "*Positive groups help people make positive changes, particularly if the relationships are filled with candor, trust, and psychological safety.*"[4]
> —Daniel Goleman, Richard Boyatzis, and Annie McKee,
> *Primal Leadership*

Connections

For there to be open, honest exchanges of information on this level there must be a high level of confidence and trust among the team members. The process of building confidence and trust is critical for teams to successfully wield through the many dysfunctions and potential road blocks. For confidence and trust to be fostered there must be honest and genuine *connections,* not only between teammates, but between the captains and team, and coaches and team and captains. One of the early responsibilities for team captains is to make genuine connections with their teammates, especially with the newer team members. These connections simply mean engaging teammates with casual conversation about their day, classes, and family, and not as much about the sport, because at the higher levels of competition there is so much time spent talking about it already. With continued dialogue, both parties will begin to learn about each other at deeper rather than superficial levels.

From an operational standpoint, the ideal situation is to have captains named early in the off-season training period so they can begin to "practice" being captains and initiate those connections with their teammates from this different perspective. Once named captain, these individuals are no longer "one of the boys" or "one of the girls." This changes the relational dynamics with their teammates. Bonding over being silly together, playing practical jokes or chuckling at their coaches or captains for "over the top" behavior is no longer acceptable. If the peer group has not been elevated to leadership status there could be some resentment and jealousy, further changing the dynamics. This process of change takes time for all to adjust to, so why not have the team go through it in the off-season, which is usually a time dedicated to individual improvement and lowered stress and pressure as compared with the regular season? The more these captains can *connect* with their teammates from their new perspective, the greater the rapport, the stronger the relationship, and the greater level of trust and *confidence* is shared.

> *"I wanted our players to be quietly confident. A person isn't going to wake up one morning and suddenly become confident. It's not that easy. Words aren't going to do the trick. Confidence must be earned. It takes time, work, dedication—on the part of the teacher and the pupil."*[5]
> —Former coach Dean Smith,
> UNC Chapel Hill

Confidence-Enhancement

Ronald Heifetz and Donald Laurie note an important tactic for leaders is to develop collective self-confidence among team members. They quote Jan Carlzon, CEO of Scandinavian Airline Systems, who states, "People aren't born with self-confidence. Even the most self-confident people can be broken. Self-confidence comes from success, experience, and the organization's environment.[6]

The concept of confidence has been given extensive attention in the sport psychology and sport pedagogy/coaching education fields. Robin Vealey, renowned researcher/practitioner in sport confidence, believes confident athletes not only perform better than less-confident athletes, but they also set more challenging goals, work harder and persist longer in challenging situations. Additional study results indicate confident athletes think more effectively, primarily in how they are better able to remain focused while training by not attending to the myriad of potential distractions when compared to less confident players. Confident athletes have also been found to be more productive in their attributions for success and failure; use more problem-focused coping strategies to help get the task completed; use more mastery imagery in their preparation for practice and game play; and better able to manage the range of emotions associated with competing, such as anxiety, stress and satisfaction. Vealey contends athletes need to be confident in their abilities in three particular areas: physical execution of necessary skills, mental skills to help maintain focus and make effective decisions, and confidence in their ability to be resilient and refocus after errors and setbacks. All these point to the importance given to these areas by the athletes and their coaches.

Another area of importance concerning confidence is the myriad sources of confidence, beyond simply gaining confidence from previous success, which has been found by research to be the most salient source of confidence. Vealey identifies nine specific sources of confidence leaders and players alike should become more aware of in order to develop and enhance upon confidence levels (see Table 1).[7] One of the prerequisite skills for anyone wanting to build a consistent confidence level is controllability. This means taking the responsibility to become more aware of the usage of these sources of confidence and

1. Achievement	prior success; winning; demonstrating ability compared to others; mastering skills; improving skills; achieving goals
2. Preparation	physical training; developing well-practiced strategies to execute; mental preparation and training; knowing you're prepared for the situation
3. Self-Regulation	developing and using skills and strategies to maintain focus and manage emotions, thoughts, and behaviors that lead to optimal performance
4. Models	seeing others, such as teammates, friends, and other athletes, perform successfully; watching videotape of self; using imagery to view oneself performing perfectly
5. Feedback/ Encouragement	receiving useful feedback, as well as support and encouragement, from coaches and others (teammates, parents, friends)
6. Coach's Leadership	believing that your coach is skilled in decision making and leadership in terms of running the team and program
7. Environmental Comfort	feeling comfortable in a competitive environment
8. Physical Self-Presentation	feeling that you look good in terms of your physical self (e.g., body, uniform, appearance)
9. Situational Favorableness	feeling that the breaks or momentum of the situation are in your favor

Table 1: **Sources of Confidence. Reprinted with permission from R. Vealey,** *Coaching for the Inner Edge* **(Morgantown, WV: Fitness Information Technology, 2005).**

practice using them on a consistent basis. Vealey notes similarly, "All athletes should be encouraged to define success and achievement in controllable ways to help keep their confidence stable and resilient through the ups and downs of competition."[8] Leaders should ask themselves how many of these sources of confidence they use to enhance their personal level of confidence as well as the levels of those they lead.

A term synonymous with confidence is trust. James Kouzes and Barry Posner, both professors of leadership at Santa Clara University, write, "Trust is the social glue that holds individuals and groups together. And the level of trust others have in you will determine the amount of influence you have."[9] They continue by stating the important piece of the process is earning this trust: "You have to earn your constituent's trust before they'll be willing to trust you. That means you have to give trust before you can get trust."[10] So once trust is given, it can then be received. Once this occurs, the team will support the team leaders' captaincy in the hope that collaboratively, they all will help lead the program. Former NFL coaching great Bill Walsh believed that being able to instill the concept of what a team is all about is a fundamental ingredient of organizational achievement. He believed the collaborative belief, "I can't let my buddies down" is the ultimate connection. In his book *The Score Takes Care of Itself*, he compared this level of sacrifice and trust to the battlefield when he wrote, "Combat soldiers talk about whom they will die for—not the fight song, the flag, or some general back at the Pentagon, but those guys who sacrifice and bleed right next to them. That's the ultimate connection and extension."[11] The idea of not letting your teammates down is what this coach nurtured in his very successful organization, the San Francisco 49ers, which he stated begins with the leader and staff. Leaders should ask themselves if they or their captains nurture and reinforce this ideal with their team and teammates.

> *"The best communicators start with a respect for the power of language and for the communication process itself."*[12]
> —Harvey Dorfman,
> *Coaching the Mental Game*

Communication—The Leadership Voice

In Chapter 7, active listening is considered a very important leadership talent, and knowing what is known about the importance of building trust through collaboration and connection, the act of becoming a more effective *communicator* seems warranted. Stuart Levine, author of *The Six Fundamentals of Success,* extols the importance of being a more effective communicator because of its many important functions: "Communication helps to bring the best thinking into the right conversations at the right time. It reduces fear and uncertainty and breaks down barriers. It strengthens relationships, improves products, and motivates employees."[13] He continues by stating in today's world, many people mistake sending and receiving information for communication: "They use technology to replace, instead of enhance, communication. They hide behind email and voice mail to avoid difficult conversations that should take place face to face."[14] Due to this, he states organizations are at risk of experiencing a "communication breakdown." Leaders should be aware of any communication breakdowns on their team and with their personnel, and the importance of reflecting on the causes of these and the effectiveness of the resolution techniques employed. Former president Gerald Ford, reflecting on not being voted in for a full term in office, states with regret, "If I went back to college again, I'd concentrate on two areas: learning to write and learning to speak before an audience. *Nothing in life is more important than the ability to communicate effectively.*"[15] This section will highlight many strategies leaders and followers can use to steer clear of miscommunication issues, beginning with the common characteristics of effective communicators.

J.C. Maxwell, in *The 17 Essential Qualities of a Team Player,* details five characteristics of a communicative player[16]:

(1) A player who does not isolate themselves or allow others to isolate themselves
(2) A player who makes themselves approachable, sending the message to the team they are easy to talk to
(3) A player who follows the 24-hour rule, meaning if there are any conflicts between teammates it is addressed in a day's time
(4) A player who gives attention to her teammate relationships by continually connecting with as many teammates she can
(5) The final characteristic is to get important communications in writing. For example, after captain *Skype* meetings, or in-person meetings and team meetings, notes are typed up and distributed to ensure what was discussed is noted, accurate, and can be referred back to with clarity to improve team accountability.

Emulating these characteristics takes practice. One of the important tasks of leaders is the act of mentoring others to improve their communication techniques while providing them with opportunities to practice them. According to Pat Williams, young leaders especially need to be put into situations where they can become confident communicators and effective listeners. He writes, "In the process of building them up as leaders, we will also be building their confidence to tackle the many challenges that life throws at them,"[17] with one of those challenges being to find your leadership voice and be heard! Pat Williams continues, "The *confidence* to communicate becomes the confidence to lead and the confidence to face the many challenges and character tests that inevitably come their way."[18]

The legendary CEO of Scandinavian Airlines Systems, Jan Carlzon, was quoted as stating, "The leader's most important role is to instill confidence in people. They must dare to take risks and responsibility. You must back them up if they make mistakes."[19] To do so requires the young leader to use his leadership voice and to continue to practice and refine this leadership voice. To initiate this process, Pat Williams lists several questions to ask young leaders about their communication acumen, including (for the purpose of this book, feel free to change the word "child" to "player"): Does my child enjoy speaking in public? Does my child enjoy the challenge of convincing others to follow his lead? Is my child willing to go above and beyond what is expected?[20] The answers to these questions will dictate whether the young leader is showing early leadership skills (if answered "yes") or whether it is time to begin to encourage more leadership opportunities (if answered "no"). Many resources exist to help young leaders become more effective public speakers. Williams shares 12 tips on public speaking he guarantees will help build confidence and competence of young leaders: be organized and prepared; keep it simple (use three main points when possible); prepare simple notes, not a written script; relax; become a storyteller; practice your talk; avoid a monotonous tone and be aware of other nonverbals; arrive early; never apologize for being nervous; don't worry over a few mistakes; be aware of your audience's attention span; and take questions.[21] These tips are worth sharing, practicing, and reinforcing with young leaders.

Anson Dorrance, revered women's soccer coach at venerable champion UNC, asserts one of the prevalent issues in female leadership is reluctance to be vocal leaders on the field. One reason for this is they fear they and their efforts will be resented. According to Dorrance, "So they stand there and watch disaster take place, just because they are reluctant to hear their own voice because they don't want to come across as bossy."[22] This occurs at all competitive levels, and even with some of his UNC teams, where, in his words, "we have a bunch of mute zombies out here; as a result, at times we have absolutely no leadership presence. It's such a big problem that we address it in the off-season."[23] He also stresses the importance of girls and women to find this leadership voice, with the right voice being a combination of tone and the manner in which she commands the team. This is not just a female issue, however. Male teams need to invest in sharpening their leadership voice for an enhanced, consistent leadership presence on and off the court/field.

Using the most appropriate tone is important in exercising one's leadership voice, as is using the right words. Stan Morrison, director of athletics at University of California, Riverside, states, "Words have power—the wrong words can tear down and destroy; the right words can build up and heal."[24] In their text *Applied Sport Management Skills,* Robert Lussier and David Kimball describe three barriers that can block communication, with the first one being the words chosen. Two of the more formidable barriers in effectively receiving communications are semantics and jargon. According to Lussier and Kimball, "Words mean different things to different people (semantics) and jargon excludes people outside its originating groups."[25] These authors also say to ease misinterpretation problems, the person communicating must "consider what your receivers need in the way of language to understand your message, and then tailor the language you choose to fit their needs. Effective communicators don't use jargon with people who are not familiar with the terminology and especially with people from different cultures."[26] The remaining barriers for effective communication include information overload and messages that make sense (logic and order).

Part of a young leader's repertoire must be the ability to be more aware of the words used and the tone, and to be able to ascertain between these two. As Steven Sample says, "Leaders are sentenced by their sentences."[27] Anything said or written, especially tweeted or texted, could derail any vision, action plan, or momentum overnight. A recent example of this was the tweeting issues at the London Olympics, with several athletes being removed from the games because of their remarks. Sample credits finding and using the right words in his success as president of SUNY Buffalo and at USC. In his words, "Much of the success as president of SUNY Buffalo was due to my finding ways to express the deep-seated longing of my colleagues and constituents to come out from the darkness of despair into the warm sunshine of acknowledged excellence; similarly, my biggest challenge and most rewarding experience at USC has been finding the right words with which to motivate the Trojan Family to achieve higher levels of excellence than heretofore seemed possible."[28] Moreover, he affirms the important differentiation between the written and the spoken word: "Nothing comes close to offering as wide a range of opportunities for a leader to inspire his followers, or to learn what is on their minds, as does direct oral communication."[29] For those leaders who believe a memo or email is as effective as a face-to-face conversation or a phone call, Sample believes this is playing in the "minor leagues." Leaders should ask themselves what is the frequency of them being minor league communicators with their teams and organizations.

When asked how he assesses an athlete's leadership potential, University of California, Riverside, athletic director Stan Morrison looks first to the individual's listening skills, followed closely by his/her level of comprehension of what was just heard, and finally, the individual's capacity to "paint pictures with words" through the clarity of words used and the ability to clearly communicate the desired message.[30] As leaders, how much of an emphasis is placed on players' listening and communication abilities? What is used to assess leadership potential? For those coaches who emphasize not only the communication skills of their players, but their own communication, practices will give their organization the best chance of being on the same page and limiting the number of communication breakdowns that could occur.

Harvey Dorfman, long-time mental game coach to the Scott Boras Corporation (agent for many of the Major League Baseball stars), has an interesting take on communication issues. He explains how a player's or team's perspective becomes the reality. It is so important for leaders to understand what perspective exists. "Whatever style, substance, or silence a coach employs, he's always communicating something to his athletes—and he should always be aware of what that something is."[31] He insists, "Words reflect attitude, and attitude dictates behavior; misunderstanding at any level impedes an understanding of behavior; barriers that might exist can be broken down by a mutual relationship between coach and athletes, a relationship that serves the needs of each."[32] This relationship is only strengthened through continual communication, breeding a shared reality, showing a respect for the communication process and the importance placed on the building of trust. Moreover, Dorfman believes the top priority of superior leaders is to "establish a setting in which the athlete wants to do what the coach sees as necessary and essential."[33]

Lastly, Lussier and Kimball list four additional barriers to communication, all specific to how accurately a message is received. The first barrier entails whether the receiver trusts what is being said, and this trust or mistrust can be based on past experiences (a negative past experience with the sender such as betrayal) or perception about the sender's credibility, judgments, or competence. This highlights the importance of being truthful in all communications, because once lost, trust is very difficult to rebuild. When a person allows her mind to drift while someone is talking, she is guilty of the second barrier: failure to listen. Attention drifts when individuals get bored, impatient (e.g., wanting to get to the end of the story), mistrusting of the sender, or in disagreement with the sender's message. Questioning receivers about the message, even asking them to paraphrase the message back, will help receivers listen more intently. Considering the generational attributes of today's athletes mentioned in the first three chapters of this book, this should be practiced on a consistent basis.

The third barrier listed by Lussier and Kimball is "Our emotions color how we decode messages. When we are angry, sad, or irrationally attached to an idea, concept, or person, we find it difficult to be objective and to hear the real message."[34] Becoming more aware of how emotionality can impede the communication process, both how we deliver and receive messages, can be invaluable. The final barrier, distortion, occurs when the receiver alters the information received, possibly due to personal bias, mistrust in the message or in the messenger, or to bend the message to better reflect the receiver's version of the truth. As declared by the authors, "we hear what we want to hear."[35]

Repeating the message, asking questions, getting the receiver to paraphrase, or asking for feedback can assist in improved listening and more effective communication. As cited by Stuart Levine, if it's important, say it twice: "When a doctor in surgery asks a nurse for O-negative blood, the nurse replies, 'I have O-negative blood.' Not 'Okay, here it is.' She repeats the request as part of a process that eliminates errors. The stakes are too high for a miscommunication."[36] Communication is that important.

> *"Competitiveness is a natural leadership instinct."*[37]
> —J.C. Maxwell, *The 360-Degree Leader*

Competitive Climate

As Pat Williams professed, becoming a confident communicator improves one's ability to tackle the myriad challenges that will confront a leader. One such challenge is how best to balance the ability to compete within a team setting while cooperating with teammates. J.C. Maxwell believes it is more a matter of attitude and approach and knowing that to lead teammates one cannot compete against them: "It all depends on how you handle competition and how you channel it; When it comes to your teammates, you want to compete in such a way that instead of competing with them, you are completing them."[38] This represents a dyad of mindsets, one being competing against peers, characterized by a "me-first" mindset that destroys trust through the exclusion of others. The other mindset, completing teammates, entails putting the organization and teammates first, which helps to develop trust, and is inclusionary. As is evidenced, teams who can be led to adopt a completing mindset embody the most productive attitudes and resultant behaviors.[39]

One term often used with captains and teams is "productive rivalry." Having team captains and all players adopt this superlative means the team will collectively improve the more individual players compete to get better. In team sports especially, it is critical that teams scrimmage against one another in practice every day, and in most cases the starters get to play against the second team, reserve team, or the B team or B side. In my experience, teams who have progressed to the playoffs in their sport have been those who have had their B side compete at the same level as the starting side consistently. Despite the B side players not being ultra-excited about not being the starters, they know they can play themselves onto the A side with consistent effort and execution, and as a corollary, both sides get better and the starters are challenged and best prepared for the upcoming opponent. This does not just happen because the coach wants it to. This is a process that is consistently and carefully reinforced throughout the entire season. This adage of "positive rivalry" provides additional benefits, according to J.C. Maxwell. Besides bringing out the best in people, healthy competition promotes honest self-assessment to ascertain if progress is really being made when comparing one's progress with competitors.' Healthy competition also promotes camaraderie between teammates and brings more fun to the competitive arena when one is able to put his/her best against a friend's best.

> *"Disciplined attention is the currency of leadership."*[40]
> —Ronald Heifetz and Donald Laurie

Conflict-Change Management

According to Alan Murray, "The ultimate test of leadership comes in times of crisis. That's when the rules suddenly change and most people lose their bearings."[41] Conflict can take many forms. One area is how leaders deal with negative events. Warren Bennis and Robert Thomas, based on their research written in *HBR's 10 Must Reads on Leadership,* say that "one of the most reliable indicators and predictors of true leadership is an individual's ability to find meaning in negative events and to learn from even the most trying circumstances."[42] Leaders should ask themselves the following questions: What conflict has occurred recently? What types of conflicts have the captains found themselves in over the past few weeks? How effective were these methods in both the short-term and the long-term? These reflective questions are important to ask and discuss as a collective group, including staff and captains. This dialogue can provide a blueprint for future problem solving if/when problems occur.

The conflicts that arise on teams can be labeled from small to large, easy to solve to almost impossible to get on top of, and can range from roommate issues, legal matters on/off campus, team rules violations, to petty rivalries and immature reactions to everyday team matters. Embracing the opportunity to test one's leadership prowess and problem-solving acumen is an important part of this process. Fires will always need to be put out, regardless of the competitive level, with the reality that every team member is watching to see how his leaders handle the issue at hand and how they handle themselves through the process. Captains who can achieve "disciplined attention" and consistency in action in good times and in challenging ones can make the most out of these "captain moments and opportunities" and earn greater respect from their teammates.

This adversity can also be applied to the criticism leaders must endure, especially in highly competitive arenas such as top NCAA Division I athletics, international competition and professional sport. This topic is brought up very early in discussions because captains are held to a higher standard than their teammates and they will be the first one blamed when training becomes lax or the team does not start games with energy and focus. They will also be blamed if teammates drift away from accomplishing daily standards of execution or do selfish acts, even breaking curfew or other team rules. Coaches often chastise the captains with statements such as, "You should have known about this," "Why didn't you know about this—are you not checking in with them regularly?" or "You need to be a better example!" No one tells these captains it is easy being a good and effective captain, and being criticized for acts within or outside of one's control is all part of the process of learning leadership.

As Greek philosopher Aristotle acknowledged, "Criticism is something you can avoid easily; by saying nothing, doing nothing, and being nothing."[43] Since this is not a viable option, Maxwell shares his four-step process to dealing better with criticism.[44] This process begins with having a realistic view of self and realizing the criticism may be directed toward the leadership position (authority) rather than the individual leader. If it is the latter, allow this criticism to roll right off, and then the second step is to change oneself if the criticism is accurate. Maxwell says, "I have also realized that what I need to hear most is what I want to hear least."[45] Being open for improvement is an attitude and a quality of good and effective leaders, so fighting the knee-jerk reaction of defensiveness is a good place to start. The next step is to accept yourself, and "being who you really are is the first step in becoming better than you are."[46] Noted psychologist Carl Rogers added to this when he stated, "The curious paradox is that when I accept myself just as I am, then I can change."[47] The fourth step includes the ability to stop focusing so much on self and instead serve others. This can happen if leaders become self-reliant and secure in whom they are so they can now focus more of their attention and energies on the team and individual teammates.

Besides intrapersonal change, in the ever-changing landscape of competitive athletics, leaders must be able to adjust to these changes or be left behind.

This book began with a treatise on how the athlete of today has changed from previous generations of competitors, and how this presents a challenge for coaches to sidestep generational and personality clashes not only with their players but their players' parents. Besides the participants, sport continues to evolve with the enacting of revised rules, which then cause coaches to tactically adjust their systems and strategies. Other changes to sport include the different strategies that come into vogue, such as in the sport of football with offenses like the "wildcat" and the "spread offense," which forces defensive coordinators to scramble for new ways of defending these "new" schemes. It is important for coaches to reflect on the types of rule changes and strategies that alter the game, as well as the effectiveness of the necessary adjustments made to these changes.

Changes in participants, tactics, team dynamics, and coaching practices are inevitable. Leaders need to be adept at being proactive, rather than remedial, with these changes and be agents of change for their teams. A term often cited in the business literature to reflect the change process is "adaptive work." Heifetz and Laurie say it best when they write, "Getting people to do adaptive work is the mark of leadership in a competitive world."[48] According to these authors, what tends to slow or halt the change process is the ability of leaders to not only break their longstanding patterns of behavior, but also their inability to solicit the assistance of their people. Heifetz and Laurie add, "Solutions to adaptive challenges reside not in the executive suite, but in the collective intelligence of employees at all levels, who need to use one another as resources, often across boundaries, and learn their way to those solutions."[49] Applying it to coaching, it is critical for coaches to identify the adaptive work at hand and recruit the captains, who then recruit their teammates, to offer suggestions on how to counter measure and then contribute to the solution process.

An example of crisis management that occurs frequently in sport is when a key player goes down due to injury. A more immediate crisis occurs when the star player gets injured just prior to the playoffs, for example. Proactive leaders and teams have prepared for this occurrence, so despite the disappointment and reality of the situation, each team member knows what his new role is and is able to push on without much hesitation or discomfort. For example, one team lost their star player during the "Sweet 16" of the NCAA basketball tournament. This team did not prepare for this to happen, so no one really knew what to do since two-thirds of the game was still to be played. Due to the confusion and misplaced emotional displays, this team lost the game because of being out of sync. This is a valuable lesson for consultants, coaches, captains, and the team. In the off-season this issue was addressed, and with the team's assistance, a team routine was established where the injured player's needs are met (e.g., consoling, offering good wishes during a time-out) then team needs were met (e.g., refocusing on the game plan by reciting the key focal points). This ensures when the injured player returns to the bench, he cheers for the team and offers something positive to the players on the game floor. This way, the emotionality is directed in a productive manner, and the players on the court are able to express their feelings to their fallen teammate, then focus again on making sure his injury is not in vain, hopefully finding a way to win the game for him.

Other proactive, adaptive change processes used by organizations are addressed in the next chapter. For example, the U.S. Armed Forces have for years used one such tactic, referred to as AAR's, After Action Reviews. After each training exercise there is a thorough debrief about what worked, what did not, and whether the goal was achieved. Applying this tactic to sport (referred to in Chapter 9 as After Performance Reviews—APR's) can have the desired impact, especially when these debriefs are conducted throughout the season, as well as at the conclusion of the competitive season before embarking on the next phase of training or competition.

"A university that fails to prepare tomorrow's leaders and professionals is not socially responsible, no matter how many 'good works' it engages in."[50]
—Peter Drucker, father of modern management,
The Essential Drucker

– 9 –

Six Top Tactics

*"The strategies and tactics employed by a leader may
change with the situation. But the underlying leadership qualities
remain the same—that is, those qualities which bring people
around the leader to a higher level of performance."*[1]
—Vince Lombardi, Jr.,
What It Takes to Be #1

In the previous section, six highly touted leadership techniques were
highlighted and applied (Collaboration, Connections, Confidence Enhancement, Communication, Competitive Climate, and Conflict-Change Management). When combined with the six styles of leadership (Chapter 6), this
represents the more cited leadership strategies from the vast literature. The
scope of this chapter is to detail *how* leaders use these talents, techniques, and
styles for the greater good. The six tactics most cited in the leadership, business,
and organizational literature include the use of *debriefs-APR's, facilitating effective meetings, gaining perspective-awareness-balance, being a change agent, being
a go-to leader,* and *leadership crucibles—making the most of leadership moments.*

*"Reflecting on experience is a means of having a Socratic dialogue
with yourself, asking the right questions at the right time,
in order to discover the truth of yourself and your life."*[2]
—Warren Bennis,
On Becoming a Leader

Debriefs-APR's

Mentioned at the conclusion of Chapter 8, "After Action Reviews"
(AAR's), or debriefs, have been used for years by the U.S. Armed Forces. The

use of debriefs has been a valuable tactic for sport teams and coaching staffs as well. The term I have adopted for such debriefs is "After Performance Reviews" (APR's). For example, during a competitive season I lead teams through debriefs at the end of pre-season match play, and at the end of the first and second round of conference play, as well as at each stage of post-season, which entails the opening weekend (first two rounds), the second weekend (round of 32 and 16), and part of the preparations for the championships if all goes really well. The aim of these debriefs is to get collaboration from all participants about what they believe is working currently, what is not, and what lessons have been learned along the way. Lastly, plans are made to move things forward while staying focused on team standards and game plans.

Usually the feedback is typed in email responses first, and then organized so each team member can glance through all of their teammates' feedback. This can be an eye-opening experience for all involved, especially the coaches. When the team gathers for the meetings (either in-person or via videoconference), they have a master copy of all of the responses to work from. This sharing of ideas and perceptions is critical to the process. If players do not write out their thoughts prior to this meeting, then honest and genuine perceptions are not received, but rather the safe, superficial sound bites that only serve to slow and muddle the problem-solving process. Once the team sees how this process works and how the outcome of these meetings is integrated into the lexicon of the team and in the preparation process, buy-in results and each subsequent APR becomes that much more valuable.

At the end of the season, after a short break, teams can reconvene with an end-of-the-season debrief. It is important for the team to be able to get away from the emotionality of season's end for a little while, but keep things fresh for an in-depth debrief. Whether this team finishes first in the league, or bows out of the post-season tournament sooner than expected, everything about the program, its process, and the participants can be given a once over to determine what worked and what should be brought into the next season. This time also serves to determine what did not work and what aspects of the process need to be improved. This change process takes the feedback from everyone associated with the program, especially the captains and players.

Despite this process taking a few meetings, having to relive tough losses, team and individual challenges and meeting in an open forum with coaches present (for some of the meetings), what comes of it is a collaborated, adaptive work full of nuggets that can be used to form the team's revised process and action plan. During one team's debrief after a surprisingly difficult season and early departure from post-season play, every player was challenged to identify what they contributed to the inefficiency of the team as well as how each attempted to turn things around. This type of individual reflection can be distressing, but if managed productively can be fruitful. This process helped uncover such hidden variables as petty jealousies that undercut a captain's leadership. Another valuable lesson is the importance of not sweeping the "little things" under the rug, but rather confronting issues regardless of how little they are perceived to be.

Many programs will have end-of-the-season individual meetings with each player on the team to reflect on the season and perhaps what each player envisions for the upcoming off-season. Despite these meetings being good in theory, how many of them are actually productive?

Recently, I was invited to attend a "Think Tank" a major league baseball club was hosting with experts from leadership, sport psychology, coaching, and members from the U.S. Special Mission Units (SMUs) (e.g., Navy Seals, Army Rangers). The intention of this "Think Tank" was to compare philosophies, techniques and tactics around a common theme: performance enhancement. In one of the many break-out sessions, I shared the use of APR's with my collegiate teams (described previously) with the small-group members. One of the members of the small group was the general manager of the hosting ball club. He admitted to doing player meetings at the end of the season, but was not sure they led to the desired results. After hearing the process I used, he was so impressed with it that he shared the process with the entire group and vowed to implement some of the processes the upcoming season.

Based on this experience, and others, it is important these debriefs are as productive as possible, with those involved not simply telling management and coaching staff what they think they want to hear. The general manager from above stated this was standard fare with his past debrief processes. For these meetings to be highly productive, tough questions should be asked to all parties (coaching staff, support staff, players): "What did you contribute to this team's success or shortcomings?" or "What did I do well or fall short of in helping you play to your best?" (coach to player). Heifetz and Laurie reinforce the notion of asking tough questions of team members due to the ambivalence they have about their efforts and sacrifices inherently part of the competitive arena. They continue, "Leaders have to ask tough questions—rather than protecting people from outside threats, leaders should allow them to feel the pinch of reality in order to stimulate them to adapt. Instead of orienting people to their current roles, leaders must disorient them so that new relationships can develop."[3] Leaders should be cognizant of the amount of "disorientating of roles" that occurs in the debriefing they conduct. For example, coaches should alert the current team members about the quality of the incoming recruits, what the opponents are doing to improve their chances of winning, and the difficult game schedule awaiting them.

Moreover, team members must be encouraged to ask questions of their coach in return: "What can I do to earn more playing time? How close am I to earning more playing time? What have you seen in my play that you like? Who is better than I am in my position on this team and in this league and why?" In Chapter 12 the ways of developing a culture of leadership will be addressed. One of the cornerstones of this is the ability of a team to be honest with themselves and with coaches and teammates. As former General Electric CEO Jack Welch states, "Lack of candor blocks smart ideas, fast action, and good people contributing all the stuff they've got—It's a killer."[4]

> *"Most people have the wrong idea about the purpose of a meeting.*
> *I think a lot of us think of them as time savers.*
> *Meetings are for getting things done!"*[5]
> —John C. Maxwell, *Leadership Gold*

Facilitating Effective Meetings

The first coach to hire me as a team consultant, Lisa Love, former athletic director at Arizona State University and former associate athletic director and head volleyball coach at USC, paid me a compliment I still recall after a lot of years. She told me I teach teams how to have meetings. Regardless of the type of work many find themselves in, chances are, there are mandatory meetings to be attended. These meetings can be the type that have been illustrated in the *Dilbert* cartoons or parodied in episodes of *The Office*. In business, as in sport, many meetings happen for meeting's sake. Despite many meetings having the right intentions, such as getting everyone on the same page or delivering an important message, most lack clear objectives. Meetings are oftentimes allowed to take too many tangents, are too long and try to cover too many things in one sitting. Participants are often too close-minded due to their own agendas.

Meetings—Best Practices

It is vital that leaders obtain feedback regarding their use of team meetings, either from captains, players, or staff. Though players and captains may not be courageous enough to tell the coach what he needs to hear instead telling him what he wants to hear, hopefully the staff can be honest. Yet, if they are "yes coaches," maybe a friend who the coach can trust to give the "whole truth and nothing but the truth" should be invited to attend a team meeting or two. Meetings must be organized, have a clear message or messages (but not too many, which fail to hold a group's attention), and should follow a set agenda allowing some flexibility because of participant questions or feedback. Meetings need a distinct end point, either finishing up the agenda items or a time limit, whichever may come first. If there are some leftover items, these should be discussed in a future meeting, albeit an abbreviated meeting. Whoever is running the meeting, usually the head coach or a captain in a player-only meeting, should not punish the team by staying longer than expected or scheduled because he failed to keep the team focused on the agenda and limit the distractions. Meeting facilitators need to be mindful that deliberate comments derail the direction of the dialogue, often spoken by those team members who are operating from their own agendas. These violators should be noted by the meeting facilitator and a follow-up meeting with them may need to be scheduled. It is important to not water down an important meeting agenda and messages by talking too much and too long. Being organized for the meeting and sticking to the objectives and the agenda will help deliver the desired message while improving its "shelf life" as well.

With teams I consult, besides the lengthy debriefing meetings addressed in the previous section, lasting between 45 to 60 minutes each, team meetings are scheduled to last 20 or 25 minutes. I work hard to get the teams the meeting agenda prior to the scheduled time, even if the meeting is via video conference, to keep them on target and end the meeting on time. With collegiate teams, every minute of their week is scheduled, so it is imperative to have as much information prepared prior, and to keep the feedback, discussion, and action plan wrap-up contained within the designated time frame. Nothing frustrates a collegiate student-athlete more than meetings that go over time, impacting what follows, then affecting what follows that, and on and on it goes. Their schedules are packed with sport responsibilities (not just limited to practice, but video), classes, and then the other aspects of their lives, especially the training (physical conditioning, sport medicine), eating, organizational (laundry, studying) and social aspects, so impacting these schedules by going over time with a meeting sets in motion frustration and a decrease in buy-in for the next meeting. Today's athletes across most age and competitive levels share this same, action-packed schedule.

John C. Maxwell explains another best practice for effective meetings, which is to have the *meeting before the meeting*.[6] He expresses having a meeting with key people before the bigger meeting. which serves many purposes: First, "people are down on what they're not up on,"[7] so getting people in the loop can greatly improve their perception of what is being said or sold to them. It will also give them the impression their opinions are valued in addition to their influence on the rest of the group, which is a productive corollary for future influence. Second, people react negatively to information that surprises them. Having this meeting before the meeting with the most influential team members can improve buy-in from them so when the entire group hears the news the reaction can be tempered by those who have prior knowledge and are hopefully "on board." This prepped response guides the rest of the group to be more open to new ideas. Third, having this meeting before the meeting helps others gain perspective on the particular issue in a more intimate manner, helping them to see things more from the leader's (meeting facilitator's) perspective, while also helping to develop improved trust between the leader and these most influential team members.

Today's athletes prefer to be included in the inner workings of their teams. When they are allowed this type of access, it pays dividends through their buy-in and productive influence on the rest of the team. Maxwell's fourth purpose for the meeting before the meeting is to have as many of these influential players on the leader's "side" to make it easier to be a change agent due to the influence and trust that is being built. And finally, the fifth reason for having this meeting before the meeting is to ensure the leader will not be blindsided by something she is not aware of, which could derail the vision or change process underway. Showing a blindsided reaction could lead the team to perceive the leader is not as on top of things as she should be, creating doubt in the leadership. By having this prior sit-down, the leader can be privy to anything not on the radar and avert a potential leadership miscue or miscommunication. I consistently promote these meetings before the meetings to my client leaders for all of the above reasons. This ensures captains and coaches (and consultant if available) are working from the same game plan and appear as one cohesive and organized voice.

To Use or Not Use Meeting Agendas

J.C. Maxwell also offers suggestions on holding or not holding meetings. The first has to do with when not to have a meeting: "If you can't have the meeting before the meeting, don't have the meeting; if you do have the meeting before the meeting, but it doesn't go well, don't have the meeting; if you have the meeting before the meeting and it goes as well as you hoped, then have the meeting!"[8] Another piece of advice on facilitating effective meetings came from one of J.C. Maxwell's mentors, Olan Hendrix, and entails using these three categories for a meeting agenda: information items, study items, and action items.[9] The information items contain organizational or team updates since the last meeting. The study items contain issues in need of discussion and information sharing, yet with no vote or decision needing to be taken. Action items are study items that have had due process and now require decisions or votes. By following these categories, work does get done because each meeting not only follows up on the previous one, but sets up the subsequent meeting. Stuart Levine, author of *The Six Fundamentals of Success,* is amazed at the number of meetings taking place without a formal agenda: "A well thought-out agenda is an essential tool that lets participants know what's expected of them before, during, and after a meeting."[10] The meeting agenda should be distributed several days beforehand so participants have time to prepare and organize themselves. Key components of the agenda should include:

- starting and ending times
- purpose of the meeting
- involved participants
- order of items to be discussed
- decisions to be made
- expectations—who is reporting/updating?

The meeting agenda goes a long way to keeping the meeting focused. Knowing ideas will be shared that may be counter to the purpose of the meeting, it is important for meeting facilitators to accept these by writing them on a board denoted as the "idea board" or "future thinking list" so everyone will see them and realize they will see the light of day in a future meeting. Stuart Levine also suggests if a meeting is being "hijacked" by an individual or group of individuals, the meeting facilitator should simply call a break and alert them privately of their disruption and schedule a separate meeting time for them. Concluding the meeting should be a summary of any decisions that have been made, along with individual or group assignments, as well as feedback regarding what is to happen next. These assignments are then reviewed to begin the next meeting. Following these formal meeting tips will ensure a more focused use of everyone's time and energy. Yet not everyone endorses the use of meeting agendas.

The use of informal meetings has been endorsed by the landmark study and book by Jim Collins, *Good to Great.* Those companies who went from good to great had leaders who would have meetings with no formal agenda or script. As Collins states, "Instead they would start with questions like: 'So what's on your mind? Can you tell me about that? Can you help me understand? What should we be worried about?' These non-agenda meetings became a forum where current realities tended to bubble to the surface."[11] According to Collins, these leaders used pointed questions for one reason: to gain understanding, not for manipulation or blame. Collins continues by saying, "Leading from good to great does not mean coming up with the answers and then motivating everyone to follow your messianic vision. It means having the humility to grasp the fact that you do not yet understand enough to have the answers and then to ask the questions that will lead to the best possible insights."[12]

Leaders should consistently ask themselves questions to gain understanding, as well as becoming more cognizant of their use of questions used to manipulate, such as "You don't agree with me?" or put-down questions such as, "What are you thinking?" One tactic my captains use is to informally check-in with their head coach on a weekly basis. These meetings are not scripted and can be conducted on the road, while waiting for flights or waiting in line at the cafeteria or restaurant. Both parties are encouraged to ask open-ended questions like those used by Collins, as well as these two additional questions: "What do you see from us? What do you see from the team?" This open exchange of information between the captains and the coaches can bridge any gaps in understanding between the two parties, bringing to light any problems or future challenges, and even highlighting what is presently working for the team.

Using similar lines of questioning can assist in making individual meetings more productive. The meeting begins by addressing "what's new," bringing both parties up-to-date with any recent occurrences or experiences that apply to the work. This is followed by the "what's working and what's not working" question, initiating a discussion on the progress or lack of progress of the work the individual client has committed to accomplishing (being a mentally tougher performer or a more effective leader). This then leads to the decision-making part, "what's next?" At this stage, the best course of action is to improve on the desired behaviors, attitudes, cognitions, and/or process points, which are agreed upon by coach, client, and consultant (if available). Having a system in place for any meeting, whether it is a meeting before the meeting or an individual meeting, provides an organized agenda from which productivity can flourish.

Stuart Levine offered a final point on running effective meetings: be positive. Being positive helps to create energy and momentum, which assists in not only engaging the participants but in building greater commitment levels to the common vision of the team or organization. Levine's six tips on how to maximize this positivity process include:

(1) Recognize participants' achievements.
(2) Ask participants for their suggestions and listen attentively to these suggestions.
(3) Make eye contact with whoever is speaking to communicate real concern and interest.
(4) Make it clear you like someone's idea, yet if it is unrelated to the matter-at-hand, write it on another board (mentioned earlier) or during a break let that person know it will be considered in a future team or private meeting.
(5) Address concerns productively instead of destructively, as in asking for more supportive information or "help me understand this better" instead of just shooting the idea down.
(6) Search for solutions in a collaborative manner.[13]

"The dynamics of adaptive change are far too complex to keep track of, let alone influence, if leaders stay only on the field of play."[14]
—Ronald Heifetz and Donald Laurie

Gaining Perspective/Awareness/Balance

As cited by J.C. Maxwell in the previous section, one of the benefits of having a "meeting before the meeting" is helping team members see things from the leader's perspective, since people are naturally inclined to view things only from their own perspective. Steven Sample seconded this sentiment when he wrote, "No matter how hard he tries, a single human being can never give you a completely unbiased report on any event or issue; he will always give you a view that is filtered to some extent through his own prejudices."[15] The skill, or as he describes it, the "fine art" of "listening gray" is to be able to discern the truth among the bias-ridden advice, and better still, to be able to get to know the biases of colleagues so one will be able to carefully listen to all versions of discourse before offering a judgmental response.

Listening gray is an important aspect of what Dr. Sample refers to as "thinking gray," which he considers one of the most important tactics a leader can acquire. According to Sample, most people categorize what they hear as binary judgments, as good or bad, black or white, or true or false. As he states, "A truly effective leader, however, needs to be able to see the shades of gray inherent in a situation in order to make wise decisions as to how to proceed."[16] He also cites a quote from F. Scott Fitzgerald, who observed, "The test of a first-rate mind is the ability to hold two opposing thoughts at the same time while still retaining the ability to function."[17] Thinking in this fashion is not natural, yet those leaders who are not able to suspend their binary instinct when making big decisions may form opinions before it is necessary, be guilty of flip-flopping by believing in the last opinion heard, or believe what they perceive the masses believe in. Sample refers to these as the "three dangers of binary thinking."[18] This way of thinking can be improved and practiced by, "forcing ourselves to bend over backward by thinking gray with respect to a few everyday matters as an excellent way to overcome our natural inclination to think in black and white."[19]

Team members who are blind to other perspectives because of an over-reliance on their own agenda can be perceived as non-team players, unwilling to buy-in to the leader's and team's vision, leading them to become an obvious weak link when everyone's best contributions are needed to be as competitive as possible. One question begs to be asked: Why are these types of players so close-minded and such hard sells? There are some theories. One was mentioned previously about the biases people have, while another is what we have already learned about today's athletes, that they have been raised making the calls on what to do, what to eat, and where to go. They are used to operating from their own perspective and have been praised for it by their parents and their coaches, especially if they are star players on their teams.

Another generational attribute is an inflated level of confidence, stemming from the same sources previously mentioned, mixed with a lack of coping and problem-solving skills resulting from the lack of experience dealing with adverse situations (e.g., helicopter parents always circling and swooping down to save children from adversity). Many of today's athletes are not courageous enough to leave the comfort of their own perspectives to try out someone else's. On the sporting fields, many of today's athletes fight coaches (not physically, yet there are some reports of such) for trying to teach them new techniques and tactics. Trying new techniques forces the athletes to make changes to their games, which they believe are already at a high level, and usually entails making mistakes, which is unpleasant for most. Those who have tried to make even a slight change to a golf swing can appreciate how many mistakes it takes for the new swing to become an automatic process. Making mistakes, being uncomfortable, not feeling superior or performing perfectly are all transient emotional and technical perspectives. To most athletes this process seems like punishment when compared to their old ways of playing that got them to their present level. "Why do I have to change if I'm playing at a high level now?" is often heard from these disgruntled athletes. Yet I was pleasantly surprised when a team recently addressed this issue themselves by adopting a team standard of "being coachable," which they defined as "the ability to practice new techniques in competitive drills and matches," making it "ok" to make mistakes while making changes to their games.

Athletes and teams who are able to adopt a "change is good" perspective will greatly improve their game as well as improve their chances of being successful on the game field or court. This optimistic, resilient perspective used to improve performance can also be a valuable leadership tactic applied to personal and professional life. Stuart Levine believes to gain proper perspective takes deliberate work that goes beyond simply emptying the email inbox or making small changes. It takes "time to determine what really matters in life—urgency becomes mania and your productivity actually goes down. If you're stressed all the time, chances are you're not doing your job as well as you can."[20] Levine's book has a chapter entitled "Make Room for All Parts of Your Life," and in it he writes, "Three characteristics (confidence, stability, and endurance) will help put you in a place where you can take risks and do the hard work required to get the job done right. But to stay on top of your game, you must recharge your batteries during the time you spend outside of work."[21] This entails following the limitless messages about prioritizing your life and what is most important, while holding true to these important obligations. Levine concludes his chapter by stating, "Self-care is a practical investment in your success and ultimate happiness."[22] Living a balanced life is tantamount to leading a balanced professional life.

As is written by business icon Jack Welch in his book *Winning*, "Performing balancing acts every day is leadership."[23] Brian Dyson, former vice chairman of Coca-Cola, realized this very fact and shared it as part of his commencement address at Georgia Tech in 1996:

> "Imagine life as a game in which you are juggling some five balls in the air. You name them—work, family, health, friends and spirit and you're keeping all of these in the air. You will soon understand that work is a rubber ball. If you drop it, it will bounce back. But the other four balls—family, health, friends and spirit are made of glass. If you drop one of these, they will be irrevocably scuffed, marked, nicked, damaged or even shattered. They will never be the same. You must understand that and strive for balance in your life."[24]

Based on Dyson's address, leaders should ask themselves the following two questions: What are the five balls in their life? How proficient is their balancing act?

"See change for the growth opportunity it brings."[25]
—Jack Welch, *Winning*

Being a Change Agent

Being a change agent is such an important leadership tactic, especially in sport because teams change from year to year (especially scholastic and college teams) and coaches and leaders are almost always in "change mode," bringing many challenges for all involved. As the athlete is distressed while attempting to make changes to his/her game, leaders as change agents must be proficient in regulating this distress to create productive change in team culture and standards of execution. Anson Dorrance, women's soccer coach at North Carolina, is considered one of the most successful coaches in collegiate sport due to his 21 national championships and a 93.4 winning percentage in his 33 years at UNC.[26] He asserts in his book, *Training Soccer Champions,* "Some coaches are no longer willing to make the emotional commitment needed to motivate players to attain the standard required of them to compete successfully at the highest level. Coaches sometimes are not willing to make that commitment because it's so exhausting."[27] Leaders should ask themselves how committed they have been to holding the line and holding themselves, staff, captains and players to the established standard. As is often cited by coaches, the minute one allows another to shirk his/her responsibilities, even just a little, a new standard is set that is lower than it was.

For those committed to leading adaptive work, Heifetz and Laurie write, "getting on the balcony" is one principle to be utilized to help team members and the team-as-a-whole progress through the change process. It begins with the leader. Leaders must be able to see patterns emerge as if they were *seeing things from the balcony seats:* "Without the capacity to move back and forth between the field of action and the balcony, to reflect day to day, moment to moment, on the many ways in which an organization's habits can sabotage adaptive work, a leader easily and unwittingly becomes a prisoner of the system. The dynamics of adaptive change are far too complex to keep track of, let alone influence, if leaders stay only on the field of play."[28]

The tactic of "getting on the balcony" is a prerequisite for the next strategy leaders should use for adaptive change, which includes[29]:

• *Identifying the challenges* by listening to views of others and seeing conflicts as cues.
• *Regulating the distress* among team members to change. A leader must direct, protect, orientate, manage conflict and shape the norms.
• *Maintaining disciplined attention* on the tough questions since "disciplined attention is the currency of leadership."[30]
• *Giving the work back* to the team members by keeping them updated on the progress being made via the sharing of information.
• *Protecting the voices of leadership* from below by giving a voice to all those involved.

The ability of a team to have "disciplined attention" on the vision of the team and the process subscribed to at the beginning of the season is a requisite skill set for team captains. More will be said about the brainstorming, implementation, application, and adherence to team vision and standards in Chapter 10.

In a similar vein, Warren Bennis, leadership scholar and professor at USC, shares a version of seeing things from the balcony seats from Anne Bryant, executive director of the American Association of University Women: "She used something she calls the 'hot air balloon exercise' to encourage her staff to think imaginatively. Then you examine what you see, who you see, what they're doing, and what other things they might be doing."[31] Jeffrey Krames, author of *What the Best CEOs Know,* uses the term "outside-in perspective" to describe a similar process whereby leaders must start with the big picture, the overview of the market first, then work back to create the organization's vision and processes.[32] Krames describes how several prominent CEOs practiced this perspective, including Michael Dell from Dell Computer, David Glass from Wal-Mart, Lou Gerstner from IBM, and even Jack Welch from General Electric.

Through the consistent use of APR's, meeting before meetings, and continual check-ins with team leaders, coaches can take stock of their program and allow both staff and team to think imaginatively on how to improve or grow upon the product and the process. One team I work with takes great pride in the standard they have set for the other athletic programs on their respective campus. As part of the APR agenda, the team and staff obtain feedback from support staff across campus to determine if they continue to be the model program department-wide. This support staff includes professionals from sports medicine, strength and conditioning, academics, life skills, and the administration. From time to time other sport programs from the university will watch this particular team practice and play in an attempt to learn how they do what they do. Even the coaching and support staffs who works with other programs speak highly of this program's approach and progress toward excellence. This level of excellence has been attained by consistently taking a "big picture" view of the current state of the program and looking for ways to innovate, with every player and staff member involved in this process.

> *"Those team members who can make things happen are their*
> *go-to players. They demonstrate consistent competence,*
> *responsibility, and dependability."*[33]
>
> —John C. Maxwell,
> *The 360-Degree Leader*

Be the Go-To Leader

Effective leadership starts with leading by example and being the example, always. This tactic is the foundation for good and effective leadership for team captains because if this is not the everyday standard, the remainder of the team can use the excuse, "Since our captains are slacking and not doing what is being asked then why should I?" With how teams function with the ever-present temptations to "downshift" and take drill reps or plays off, especially during training, the team leaders cannot be the accelerant to this brand of social loafing. This topic will be given much greater attention in the next chapter.

In the world of competitive sport, especially at the higher levels, it truly is survival of the fittest. For players to continue to live their dreams of being an All-American, Olympian or a professional athlete, they have to brand themselves as superstars their teams cannot do without. The path to true superstardom, says Stuart Levine, is to watch true superstars play: "You see them call out to other players throughout the game. They pass off when they don't have a shot and they protect the person who does. They believe in their teammates, and their faith raises everyone's level of play. And of course, they play a great game themselves."[34] Leading by example also includes being the type of player described by Levine: a *go-to player* when one is most needed. Being a go-to leader means the leader will most lead the team on the field or court by being the go-to player, the play-maker, especially when one is needed in those critical moments in games, moreso than off the field or court. One such go-to player who exemplifies this type of on-court leader is Michael Jordan. The six-time NBA champion with the Chicago Bulls and five-time league most valuable player, is quoted as saying, "I'd rather see it done than hear it done."[35] Another quote typifying Jordan's lead-by-example style: "I've failed over and over and over again in my life and that is why I succeed. I've missed more than 9000 shots in my career. I've lost almost 300 games. 26 times, I've been trusted to take the game winning shot and missed. I've failed over and over and over again in my life. And that is why I succeed."[36]

Although off-court leadership is certainly valued for how challenging and important this work is, especially to organize, energize, motivate, educate, and support all team members at all times, what gets done on the court or field is the true mark of sport leadership. For example, when the star quarterback from USC, Matt Barkley, decided to forego the NFL draft to return for his senior season, he was lauded for his leadership in guiding the program through two years of sanctions, and for his numbers. This leadership did not necessarily occur off the field, of course, but took place on the field on Saturdays. Highlighted in an article, "Barkley developed into a *mature leader* by his sophomore season, again throwing for over 2,700 yards, with 26 TD's, a completion rate of 62 percent and 12 interceptions."[37] There is many a televised broadcast where the term "leadership" is used to describe a player's contributions on the field. As proffered by leadership guru J.C. Maxwell, "Few things elevate a person above his peers the way becoming a go-to player does. Everyone admires go-to players and looks to them when the heat is on—not only their leaders, but also their followers and peers."[38]

Maxwell, in *The 360-Degree Leader,* details these types of go-to leaders.[39] He begins by identifying four types of people working in organizations: the *detrimental* players who never deliver, the *average* player who sometimes delivers, the *valuable* player who always delivers when in their comfort zone, and the *invaluable, go-to* player, who always delivers regardless of the situation. To improve awareness of go-to leaders, coaches should ask themselves the following questions: How many of these certain types of players exist on your team? When you have had your better seasons what was the breakdown of each? How about your most challenging seasons, what was the breakdown? Is this type of leadership tactic part of your recruiting assessment/selection plan?

Also in this book, J.C. Maxwell identifies six specific areas in which go-to leaders contribute to their teams and organizations:

(1) Go-to players produce when the pressure is on—these players do not need to be in their comfort zones to contribute.
(2) When the resources are few, when faced with adversity, the job still gets done.
(3) When the momentum is low, go-to players move things along despite resistance, through energy and enthusiasm.
(4) When the load is heavy, these go-to players will do what is needed and carry even the heaviest load if that is what is needed, even if it means carrying the team on their backs through a tough stretch.
(5) When the leader is absent, go-to players step up when needed and fill the void.
(6) When the time is limited, go-to players deliver come crunch time, like wanting the ball in the closing seconds to pull out a win.[40]

More reflective questions for leaders to ask themselves include: How many go-to players are there? Are they the same players who are the go-to leaders? How do these players handle the previously stated situations: when the pressure is on, time and resources are limited, momentum is low, intensity heavy?

> *"Usually some transformative event or experience is central to finding one's voice, learning how to engage others through shared meaning, and acquiring the other skills of leadership."*[41]
> —Warren Bennis,
> *On Becoming a Leader*

Leadership Crucible—Making the Most of Leadership Moments

The transformative event or experience referred to by Bennis in the above quote is a leadership crucible. He defines a crucible as "a severe test or trial. Crucibles are intense, often traumatic, and always unplanned."[42] In interviews with 40 top business leaders, Bennis reveals every single one of them pointed to crucible-like experiences that had "transformed them and had become the sources of their distinctive leadership abilities."[43] Bennis notes historical crucibles and the leaders who rose from them, including Nelson Mandela's 27-

year imprisonment, Sidney Rittenberg's 16 years of unjust solitary confinement imprisonment in Communist China, the Great Depression and Franklin D. Roosevelt, the death of FDR and Harry Truman's promotion to the presidency, World War II and Winston Churchill, and the resistance and imprisonment Gandhi faced while employing and organizing nonviolent civil rights and freedom movements for so many across the globe.[44]

Bennis affirms magic takes place during these leadership crucibles. The magic stems from the transformative experience of the crucible, as cited by leaders interviewed by Bennis and Thomas in their book chapter "Crucibles of Leadership" in *HBR's 10 Must Reads on Leadership:* "The crucible experience was a trial and a test, a point of deep self-reflection that forced them to question who they were and what mattered to them. It required them to examine their values, question their assumptions, hone their judgment. And, invariably, they emerged from the crucible stronger and more sure of themselves and their purpose changed in some fundamental way."[45]

The transformational experiences derived from crucibles are not limited to historically significant crucibles but can arise from positive, painless experiences. Bennis and Thomas cite other less historically significant leaders' crucible experience stories, some including the arduous training one goes through as a U.S. Marine, a death of an employee, protesting for a deeply held belief, worker rebellion, a life-changing mentoring experience, coping with prejudice, and working for a demanding boss.[46] Questions leaders can ask themselves to become more aware of crucibles include: What leadership crucible story do you have to share? What experiences have your leaders had that could be a crucible?

James Kouzes and Barry Posner in *The Truth About Leadership* chose "Challenge Is the Crucible for Greatness" for the title of their seventh chapter. In it, they describe years of responses from people they have spoken with and surveyed: "The historical leaders whom people admire most always faced and led others through major challenges. Challenge was the context in which these leaders operated, and change was the theme of all their campaigns."[47] Chances are most of the leadership crucibles of staff and team leaders may be ones in which being challenged is at the core of the crucible experience. Kouzes and Posner note many of the personal best leadership cases shared with them throughout the years "are about triumphs over adversity, departures from the past, about doing things that had never been done before, about going to places not yet discovered."[48] Thus, the authors surmise a leader's mission is to guide people through times of challenge yet in times of complacency seek to shake things up in an effort to innovate and pursue new opportunities.

J.C. Maxwell has a similar take on the notion of crucibles. He calls these "defining moments." In his book *Leadership Gold,* he notes, "I also believe that the choices we make in critical moments help to form us and to inform others about who we are. They are defining moments."[49] He also believes "defining moments tell the people following them many of the things they really want to know: who their leaders are, what they stand for, and why they are leading."[50] Moreover, he postulates these defining moments do three things: they show us who we really are, especially in times of crisis; they declare to others who we are, or as he avows, "defining moments put the spotlight on us—our character isn't made during these times, it is displayed!"[51] Lastly, defining moments determine who we will become by the choices we make in these defining moments.[52] Maxwell concludes with a statement highlighting the importance of leaders making the most of these defining moments: "My point is that the defining moments of leaders can have a dramatic effect on others. When leaders respond correctly, everyone wins. When they respond incorrectly, everyone loses."[53]

Joseph Badaracco, Jr., also uses the term "defining moments" in his chapter "The Discipline of Building Character" for the book *Harvard Business Review on Leadership.* Badaracco describes it as a moment that "challenges us in a deeper way by asking us to choose between two or more ideals in which we deeply believe."[54] He believes these defining moments force a leader to better connect to his/her core values and principles to forge a renewed sense of purpose. Moreover, Badaracco describes three types of defining moments and lists reflective questions for each.[55] The first relates to one's personal identity (Who am I?). The second concerns groups and individuals (Who are we?). The third involves defining the role of the organization and how it fits in society (Who is this organization?). Examining one's values, beliefs and how actions are influenced by the former can be an important self-organizational examination exercise.

In my applied leadership consulting, I use the term "captain moments" to depict taking full advantage of opportunities to test oneself as a leader. These captain moments can take the form of leadership crucibles or defining moments, as well as on-going leadership opportunities either missed or made. As detailed in Chapter 12, the initial stages of this sport leadership development program entail self-examination about who the leader is, his/her values and beliefs, and brainstorming how he/she came to be in this leadership role (e.g., leadership mentors and experiences). As the program is implemented, these "captain moments" become more experiential, hands-on, and applied. The objective of this stage in the process is for the team leaders to practice being leaders. To best frame these practical, teachable leadership moments is to get the assistance of others, especially the head coach.

What also aids leadership development is in capturing captain moment "hits and misses." A "hit" is an example of a captain or team leader who sees an opportunity to lead and captures it. A "miss" occurs when a player misses the chance to help a teammate off the floor after a mistake or speaks when he should have been listening, or basically fails to make an impact when one needed to be made. Coaches are already looking for so many things during training and games (X's and O's), but once coaches master looking for these captain hits and misses, a valuable layer is added to the leadership process, which helps to teach the leaders how to lead while on the job. More is discussed in Chapter 12 about implementing additional "on the job" leadership techniques and tactics.

> "*As with other tactics, the goal is to deploy them strategically in order to postpone irresponsible decisions and eventually make responsible ones.*"[56]
> —Joseph Badaracco, Jr., *Leading Quietly:*
> *An Unorthodox Guide to Doing the Right Thing*

Leadership Skill Set Survey: Technique/Tactic Identifier

Taking all of these heavily cited techniques and tactics of good and effective leaders from this chapter and the prior one, combined with the feedback obtained from the coaching staffs and captains I have worked with to date, I created a survey encompassing 12 techniques and tactics used for educational purposes. This "Leadership Skill Set" survey is in the Appendices (Appendix 3). Table 1 details the subscale variables with sample questions.

Table 1: Leadership Skill Set Survey Subscales: The Techniques & Tactics of Good and Effective Sport Team Leaders

1. *Supportive:* A leader who stands behind and shows adherence to the decisions of others.

2. *Follower:* A leader who knows when and how to follow the leadership of others.

3. *Challenger:* A leader who challenges himself and teammates to achieve a higher level of performance.

4. *Team builder:* A leader who takes it upon herself to facilitate team cooperation and cohesion.

5. *Refocuser:* A leader who realizes change needs to occur and knows how to help get players or the team back to proper form.

6. *Liaison:* A leader who bridges the gap between team leader, leaders, and the team.

7. *Problem Solver:* A leader who steps up to find a solution to individual player or team issues.

8. *Organizer:* A leader who organizes team members on specific functions and responsibilities.

9. *Go-To Player:* A leader who not only leads by example, but wants the ball with the game on the line.

10. *Energizer-Motivator:* A leader who energizes and motivates individual players or team when needed.

11. *Aware/Balanced:* A leader who is ever-present and knows what is expected and what to do in all situations, while also keeping an eye on the "big picture" and the ultimate goal.

12. *Use of Meetings/Debriefs:* A leader who masterfully uses meetings before the meetings and facilitates well-organized, opinion-sharing meetings.

> *"You have to believe that your words can inspire and your actions can move others. You have to believe that what you do counts for something. If you don't, you won't even try. Leadership begins with you."*[57]
> —James Kouzes and Barry Posner

Part IV

*Building Teams Who
Lead and Follow*

– 10 –

Organizational Dynamics and Team Building in Sport (ODQ)

"Unfortunately, bringing players to this level of team awareness remains a very challenging assignment in today's me-first NBA. System basketball has been replaced by players who want to be the system."[1]
—Former NBA Los Angeles Lakers coach
Phil Jackson

Coach Phil Jackson, winner of two NBA titles as a player and 11 as a coach for the Chicago Bulls and Los Angeles Lakers, appears to be lamenting about coaching today's athletes from the quote above. In *The Last Season: A Team in Search of Its Soul,* he surmises it is remarkable that today's teams can play with any level of team cohesiveness given the selfish mind-set of today's player: "In the 1960s and '70s, players asked 'Where do I fit in? How can I help this team win?' Now they ask 'How do I get what I want?'"[2] He assured many of his players who found his style of offense (the triangle offense) "boring and a waste of their individual skills" that "championships are secured by team, not individual performances."[3] Another highly successful professional basketball coach, Pat Riley, publicly lamented in print about how his team, the 1993 New York Knicks, was plagued with an infliction he called "the disease of me."[4] He found he had too many self-centered individuals who showed little respect for anyone other than themselves. Leaders should ask themselves how much of what coaches Jackson and Riley mention have they experienced? Also, what do they do about this particular team barrier? It begins with identifying the potential team barriers standing in the way of optimal team synergy.

*"If you're not totally on board wherever you are,
then you won't stay focused, and your team will suffer."*[5]
—Jeff Cannon and Lt. Cmdr. Jon Cannon,
Leadership Lessons of the Navy Seals

Team Barriers

A selfish mind-set is one of many barriers that can hold a team back from succeeding. Additional barriers include an unwillingness to sacrifice for the team, poor communication, lack of quality practice, inability to hold teammates accountable, unwillingness to help teammates, and a lack of committed talent. Pat Lencioni added to this list of potential team barriers in his book, *The 5 Dysfunctions of a Team*. In it, he includes absence of trust, fear of conflict, lack of commitment, avoidance of accountability, and inattention to results as potential barriers.[6] According to Lencioni, an absence of trust means team members are not open with each other about their thoughts and feelings, are hesitant to step up to help or offer solutions, hold grudges, and come up with excuses to not be around each other when possible. In such a situation, team members are not honest about their feedback for fear of conflict and of having to share real ideas in an open discussion.

Lencioni asserts teams who fear conflict have boring meetings, avoid controversial topics, partake in back-stabbing and behind-the-scenes political maneuvering, and fail to utilize their own people as resources. This inability to openly share ideas leads to team members not committing to team decisions and objectives. This lack of commitment leads to a team with little direction and too much second-guessing and overanalysis, which delays decision making, and a lack of confidence and increased fear of failure. Since team members do not share common ideals, Lencioni posits an avoidance of accountability exists, which then leads to a climate of resentment, mediocrity, missed deadlines, and a heavy burden for the leadership. A team ripe with a lack of accountability breeds an overindulgence of individual agendas, rather than a collective effort toward team objectives and results. In turn, a team not focused on results is easily distracted, loses ground to competitors, and ultimately fails to grow and prosper.

Teams who function at a high level find ways to sidestep these five barriers. Lencioni believes this is best accomplished by creating and working within the following five productive climates[7]:

(1) establishing a culture of trust characterized by asking for help, admitting mistakes, appreciating fellow team members' contributions, and apologizing for transgressions;

(2) not fearing conflict, but rather working within it by considering the feedback from team members, problem solving without delay, minimizing the politics while engaging in productive meetings;

(3) reinforcing team commitment by valuing everyone's input, establishing a collaborative vision and objectives, and being innovative and creative;

(4) creating accountability that breeds improvement from all committed parties while establishing respect for others and adherence to high standards of performance;

(5) focusing on results while minimizing individual agendas and achieving high performance results due to the collective actions of the group.

As leaders reflect on the five team barriers and the five productive climates used to combat the team barriers, they should be asking, "What is the health of our team?" What is working (productive climates) and what is not working (barriers) for them presently? In addition to the implementation of Lencioni's five productive climates, leaders could explore six additional strategies and apply them to improve the building of their teams: *team selection and upgrading, a working knowledge of team dynamics, team building intervention programming, investing in relationships, formulating a vision,* and *accountability processes,* including the sociological influences of team accountability for female teams.

> *"Those who build great companies understand that the ultimate throttle on growth for any great company is not markets, or technology, or competition, or products. It is one thing above all others: The ability to get and keep enough of the right people."*[8]
>
> —Jim Collins,
> *Good to Great*

Selection/Upgrading

One of the team barriers within a leader's control is the selection of his/her team members. Jim Collins' quote frames the importance of getting the right people. This is reminiscent of the old coach's credo, "You cannot have a great team without great players." Another popular aphorism is, "You can lose with good players but you cannot win without them." In a later section of this chapter the construction of a team vision, as part of a team building program, is discussed. As a forewarning, Jim Collins states, "Great vision without great people is irrelevant." He continues by stressing the most recommended way to move from good to great in any organization is to ensure "who" questions come before "what" questions: "Before vision, before strategy, before organizational structure, before tactics—first who, then what—as a rigorous discipline, consistently applied."[9] J.C. Maxwell has a similar take on the selection process: "You really only have two choices: train them or trade for them. You grow the players you already have into champions, or you go out and recruit championship-caliber people and bring them onto the team."[10] As a former collegiate coach, I know the importance of recruiting. There is not a coach in this country who is not striving to recruit championship-caliber players, but in most cases, coaches simply have to work with who they get, championship-caliber, close to championship-caliber, or not even close.

Despite these challenges, it is obviously vital for coaches to recruit the type of person and player who can excel in their particular program. Leaders must be cognizant of what they use as primary criterion for player selection. World Cup and Olympic Gold Medal winning women's soccer coach Tony DiCicco, in his book with Colleen Hacker, *Catch Them Being Good,* reportedly uses character, and specifically the ability to be selfless, as a criterion to select players for his championship squads. He also admits to making some errors in player selection because some players were negative contributors (selfish, wanted to be the star), which negatively influenced team chemistry and team performance.[11] Recruiting and player selection is far from an exact science. Errors can be minimized by having a clear vision of the ideal person and player and the important talents, abilities, and skill-sets sought to best complement the team and program needs. It is the matching of needs and strengths that makes the player recruiting process successful. The same goes for the selection of leaders for the team.

On the topic of strengths, the people who conduct the Gallup Polls, often cited on the evening news and in newspapers, websites, and blogs, conducted a study of more than 10,000 "followers" from around the world. Those surveyed were simply asked why they follow the most influential leader in their life. Results reveal three key findings: "The most effective leaders are always investing in strengths; the most effective leaders surround themselves with the right people and then maximize their team; the most effective leaders understand their followers' needs."[12] According to Tom Rath and Barry Conchie, authors of *Strengths-Based Leadership,* effective leaders invest in their followers' strengths by giving them the opportunity "to do what they do best every day."[13] These authors believe that by putting people in roles that enable their strengths, rather than improve their weaknesses, significant gains in confidence, satisfaction, and productivity result.

Helping others uncover their strengths is another way effective leaders invest in their followers while maximizing their teams. Jack Welch, tabbed as Manager of the Century by *Fortune* magazine for the work he did at General Electric, invested the vast majority of his time and energy in three activities, which he refers to as his "rules of leadership." The first of these was upgrading the team. In his words, "Leaders relentlessly upgrade their team, using every encounter as an opportunity to evaluate, coach, and build self-confidence."[14] Some of the defining features of this first rule of leadership include making sure the right people are in the right jobs, coaching people to improve their performance in every way, and building self-confidence through recognition and caring. Welch's second leadership rule, "vision and accountability" will be addressed in a later section of this chapter.

As suggested by Rath and Conchie, another way leaders can maximize their teams is to recruit and select people for leadership positions who best complement the existing team members, rather than selecting solely for job function. For example, a coach who names a player a "captain" only because he is vocal on the field may be filling a need on the field, but if this captain gives little to enhancing team relationships or team accountability, he may not be the right fit. This is seen also when the more talented players are given leadership roles simply because they score the most points. Matching and maximizing individual strengths of leadership talents, techniques, and tactics with existing team members and the needs of the program is a recipe for improved team functioning. Chapter 12 will highlight a template for building a culture of leadership that incorporates these important concepts.

To conclude this section, the words from the venerable UCLA basketball coach, John Wooden, remind leaders of the impact talent has on the profession of coaching: "No matter how you total success in the coaching profession, it all comes down to a single factor—talent. There may be a hundred great coaches of whom you have never heard, who will never receive the acclaim they deserve simply because they have not been blessed with the talent. Although not every coach can win consistently with talent, no coach can win without it."[15]

> *"No one of us is more important than the rest of us."*[16]
> —Ray Kroc, McDonalds Corporation

Team Dynamics

Robert Lussier and David Kimball suggest much can be learned about teamwork by watching, of all things, geese flying south for the winter, specifically their use of the V formation[17] (see Table 1). The lessons derived from such a natural display of teamwork relate quite well to Lussier and Kimball's model of group processes. Figure 1 summarizes the six primary group processes consisting of *roles, norms, cohesiveness, status, decision making* and *conflict resolution.*[18]

- Each bird flapping its wings creates an uplift (thrust) for the bird following. Flying in a V adds 71% greater flying range than flying in disorganized clusters or flying alone.
  Lesson: Travel on the thrust of each other (synergy). A common direction and a sense of community can get your team to the finish line faster and easier.

- Falling out of formation causes individual birds to feel the sudden drag and the higher (and more difficult) resistance of going it alone. This helps them continually adjust their flying to keep the formation.
  Lesson: There is strength, power, and safety in members who travel in the same direction.

- When lead birds get tired, they rotate to the back of the formation and another goose flies point.
  Lesson: Take turns doing the hard jobs.

- Geese at the back of the V honk to encourage front flyers to keep speed.
  Lesson: We all need to be remembered with active support and praise.

- When a goose gets sick or is wounded and falls out of the V, two geese follow it down to help it and protect it. They stay with the downed goose until the crisis is resolved, and then they launch out on their own in a V formation to catch up with their group.
  Lesson: Stand by each other in times of need.

Table 1: Teamwork and the V Formation. Reprinted, with permission, from R.N. Lussier and D.C. Kimball, 2009, *Applied Sport Management Skills* (Champaign, IL: Human Kinetics), 263.

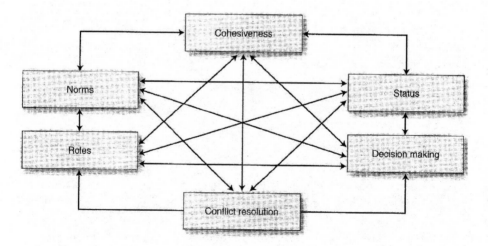

Figure 1: Group Process Model. Reprinted, with permission, from R.N. Lussier and D.C. Kimball, *Applied Sport Management Skills* (Champaign, IL: Human Kinetics, 2009), 273.

Roles

Two different sets of roles are performed on most teams. The first type of role, positional role, is specific to what each team member must do to accomplish specific tasks, which in some cases relate to the roles of their positions on the field or court. The other type of role is the team role. Lussier and Kimball report these team roles can help or hinder team functioning, and include three particular aspects: task, maintenance, and self-interest. Task roles relate to what is said and done by individuals to help the team accomplish their objectives. Maintenance roles are those that assist in developing and supporting relationships among group members. The third role, self-interest, includes those actions that help the individual at the expense of the group (e.g., individual agendas).

For teams to function at a high level, each team member must attempt to maximize her positional role, while working on her task and maintenance roles, all the while minimizing those self-interest roles. The leaders of the team are in an opportune position to ensure their teammates know what their specific roles are (positional, task, maintenance and self-interest) and accept them. Teammates who lack clarity in their roles or are not accepting of these particular roles are usually easy to spot if leaders know what to look for. For example, those who complain, are unhappy or dissatisfied, and are overt with these emotional displays, or withdraw from group activities, must be sat down and asked to explain their observable signs of role distress. In his book *Championship Team Building*, mental skills trainer Jeff Janssen uses this formula to best depict the importance of roles on success:

Role Definition + Role Appreciation + Role Acceptance = Team Success[19]

When roles and expectations are defined, and the player perceives this role will be appreciated by others, there is greater likelihood this role will be accepted by the player. When combined with the synergy from teammates' complementary roles, it is then predicted team success should result.

Norms

For roles to be accepted and adhered to at a high level, the norm of the team becomes a primary driver. Similar to the influence peer pressure has on individuals to conform, team norms represent the collective expectation of team behavior. Lussier and Kimball assert, "Norms determine what should, ought, or must be done for the group to maintain consistent and desirable behavior."[20] Highly functioning teams with productive norms usually promote them simply through the motto, "On this team, we do this," or if there is a behavior in need of correcting, the motto used to confront the guilty party (or parties) is, "We don't do that on this team—we do this instead." It is important for the leaders of a team to be aware of the team norms guiding behavior because these norms can be negative in nature, such as excessive celebrations after wins, or violent play on the field, such as the "pay for pain" allegations against the NFL's New Orleans Saints in 2012.

Cohesiveness

Team cohesiveness is a matter of how well the team members get along, referred to as social cohesion, and how well they work together to accomplish goals, called task cohesion. In the sport psychology literature many studies have been conducted on cohesion among teams, especially by Albert Carron and colleagues, who reveal a positive relationship between cohesion and performance.[21] One study reviewed over 30 cohesion studies, revealing that 83 percent of the studies reflect this positive association. In another review, 92 percent of the 66 studies assessed show this same positive relationship between cohesion and performance. In a more recent study, Carron and colleagues assessed 46 studies, which included a total of 10,000 athletes and 1,000 teams, finding a moderate to large cohesion-performance effect. These studies strongly indicate teams who have higher levels of task and social cohesion do perform better. Team leaders who work hard at including all team members in team meetings, practices, games, and other team events go a long way in improving both social and task cohesion. Additional strategies team leaders can use to enhance team cohesion are included in the next section on team building.

Status

Another important group process is the perceived status one has on the team. On sport teams, for example, the older, more experienced players tend to hold higher status levels than those who are new to the team. Additionally, those players who start the games are usually held to higher status rankings. It is the hope of the team leaders that these high-status team members play their roles well while supporting the team norms. This will lead to high cohesion and adherence to team rules, norms, and the team vision since the remaining team members will essentially follow their lead. Team leaders must be aware of what Lussier and Kimball refer to as "status incongruence," whereby conflicts arise when team members do not accept or are dissatisfied with their status and the resultant treatment.[22] Similar to role distress, team members who suffer from status incongruence may withdraw from participation, be less committed to the cause, and not invest the effort needed to perform to their best. As mentioned previously, all team members must feel their contributions to the team effort are valued, regardless of their status on the team. Players who perceive high levels of team task cohesion put less importance on achieving team status and its perceived rewards.

Decision Making and Conflict Resolution

The final two team processes include how decisions are made as well as how conflict is handled by the team. In the next section a team building intervention program will be detailed. Part of this strategy is the importance placed on collaboratively brainstorming what should be valued by this team (how decisions are made) and ways to hold team members accountable to the team objectives. It also outlines how to handle the many types of conflicts that may arise on teams, not to mention those already discussed, such as role distress and status incongruence.

> *"It's better to work on chemistry early and often*
> *in order to create and maintain a cohesive vision."*[23]
> —Tony DiCicco and Colleen Hacker,
> *Catch Them Being Good*

Stages of Team Development

As individuals begin to form into a group, and then in time into a collection of teammates, there is a documented development process originated by Bruce Tuckman, simply referred to as the stages of team development. There is no set time limit for these stages. Some teams proceed through them rapidly due to many factors. Most of these factors have been addressed previously (e.g., role clarity, acceptance, norm development and adherence, status congruence), yet others could include easy opposition, high levels of physical strengths, techniques and tactics, effective leadership, or early wins. Other teams may get stuck on a certain level for a myriad of reasons for short to long stints. Still others may never proceed to the next stage.

The four stages of Tuckman's model include the forming, storming, norming, and performing stages.[24] In the *forming* stage, individuals have not yet gelled. Everyone is busy finding his place on the team, sizing each other up, and asking himself why he is here. The *storming* stage is characterized by individuals beginning to see themselves as part of a team. However, at this stage individuals may challenge each other, and the team leader, about such things as what the team is doing and how things should be done, as well as perceived roles and status rankings. *Norming* is present when team members begin to come together socially, as well as through the sharing of ideas, establishing ground rules, clarifying who does what (roles), and determining how things will be done. The final stage, *performing,* occurs when there is an increased focus on both the task and on team relationships. When task and team come together (team synergy), the potential for team success is greatly improved.

Lussier and Kimball also include a fifth team development stage, *termination.* At this stage, the team formally closes out the season, as in a team banquet or awards night. This represents an important stage to bring closure to a hard-fought competitive season by giving credit to those who helped the team throughout the season, as well as giving the team and their significant others a final opportunity to say goodbye to friends they have made on the team and with the staff.[25] Some reflective questions leaders should ask themselves to maximize their use of these stages of team development: Have you had teams who have proceeded through these stages quickly and efficiently? What did they do, and what did you do, to assist in this happening? Have you had teams who have been stuck in the storming stage all season long? What did they do, or not do, and what did you do, and not do, to assist in this happening?

Renowned soccer sport psychology consultant Bill Beswick details strategies team leaders could use to assist their teams in proceeding through the stages previously addressed.[26] For example, to expedite the settling-in period, the forming stage, leaders can get help from the team in selecting the vision and mission of the team. This allows the team time to establish rapport and relationships with their fellow team members. Despite there being an emphasis on personal agendas, the competitive nature of the team climate (e.g., where do I rank?) at this stage gets multiplied in the storming phase where roles and status begin to take shape. Leaders at this stage must ensure every player has a role and they manage the internal competition, power struggles, and potential miscommunication in this very emotional time. If all goes as planned in the storming phase, leaders can then begin to reinforce team norms ("this is how we do it on this team"), take the time needed to manage individual role clarification and reinforcement, manage the competitive climate, and ensure individuals are balancing their individual needs with team needs. Finally, at the performing stage, the leaders remind the team of the vision and standards required to continue to work toward accomplishing the team goals. Leaders continually reinforce team norms, individual and collective roles, all while continuing to keep the lines of communication open. If issues arise the team is collectively involved in problem-solving solutions.

> *"As difficult as it is to build a cohesive team, it is*
> *not complicated. In fact, keeping it simple is critical."*[27]
>
> —Pat Lencioni,
> *5 Dysfunctions of a Team*

Team Building

Knowing the potential barriers to optimal team effectiveness and efficiency is only part of the formula to proven team chemistry. Once these barriers are identified the intervention becomes tantamount in bringing about change. In some cases there may be an immediate fix, yet others require a long-term repair. It is this intervention that needs a closer look. In my book, *Mental Toughness Training for Basketball,* I outline a team building intervention program designed to positively affect group processes and performance. The aim of these team-building strategies is to get all team members "on the same page" in terms of the team's direction and primary objectives, as well as to forge an agreement on the execution standards and everyone's particular roles and responsibilities.[28] A carefully designed team-building program is a proactive way to combat potential team barriers before they occur. Although using a program does not guarantee total team harmony, it provides coaches and players with a forum to discuss goals, team rules, and standards, and to address potential problem areas before they develop. The framework behind this sample team-building program consists of the following components:

- Team motives and preferences for team progress
- An accepted team identity—what the team will be known for
- A shared vision via setting short-term, process goals that lead to accomplishing long-term, outcome goals
- Individual and team accountability to preset standards and goals
- Collaborative communication, teamwork, and trust
- Team-bonding activities in the off-season, pre-season, and during the season

One of the primary goals for these team-bonding activities is to help teammates get to know each other and begin to form bonds, so when the pressure of the season begins, these bonds are tight enough for the team to persevere and thrive. As was addressed earlier, this process is referred to as team cohesion and consists of two interactive components: task cohesion and social cohesion. Teams who suffer from cliques, personality clashes, poor communication practices, and daily confrontations struggle with social cohesion issues. Poor social cohesion can obviously have a negative impact on how willing these players are to put in maximal, collective efforts on the field or court (task cohesion). Specifically, taking players through goal-setting, standard-setting, and other brainstorming sessions can help them get on the "same page" and improve task cohesion. Team-bonding activities have been found to be effective in improving team social cohesion as well.

A *Sports Illustrated* article details how many top collegiate football programs incorporate team-building activities into their summer "voluntary" conditioning sessions, with some even adopting the credo, "bond in the heat and we can't be beat!"[29] For example, University of Oregon players rafted down the Willamette River, while the Mississippi State Bulldogs endured Army-like basic-training exercises. Other anecdotes include players from Louisiana State University taking part in karate training, and the Fighting Illini playing in a football-player-only Wednesday night softball league. The Hokies from Virginia Tech hit several stops along the NASCAR circuit, while players from Texas Tech engaged in organized sparring sessions with local boxers. Although varied, these team-building activities were all organized to create a more closely knit team who would then (hopefully) win games in September. Some teams may go to a comedy club or have a team bowling tournament, movie night, pot-luck dinner, scavenger hunt, white-water rafting trip, outdoor adventure course, or camping trip. Coaches and captains are limited only by their imaginations.

Applying the six components of team building entails packaging them into a team-building intervention program. The following stages incorporate general implementation procedures and specific application strategies to a team-building intervention program which can be used by team leaders (see Table 2).

With the programs I consult, the team leaders, especially the captains and their support team, are integral in this process. After the first year of indoctrinating the captains and support team into the leadership roles and responsibilities, the consultant's role in this team-building process becomes that of a secondary facilitator. The lead facilitators ideally become the team captains, with guidance, support and mentorship from others including the consultant and coaches. These captains learn how to prepare the meeting agenda, what to reinforce, what not to, what to address next, and so on. Having captains so involved in this team-building process provides them with an ideal leadership opportunity, only enhancing the commitment and buy-in from the captain and the rest of the team. This process is their process, not one told to them.

The quote at the top of this section from Pat Lencioni highlights the importance of keeping this process simple. This next quote exemplifies simplicity in terms of what it takes to build and coach winning teams. Iconic football coach Paul "Bear" Bryant, who led his Alabama Crimson Tide to six national championships in 25 years, responded with the following when asked about coaching winning teams: "Winning team members need to know 5 things: tell me what you expect from me; give me an opportunity to perform; let me know how I'm getting along; give me guidance where I need it; reward me according to my contribution."[30]

Stage 1: A formal needs assessment is conducted by coaches and captains who attempt to answer the following question: What does this team need to do to be successful? Coaches and captains should think in terms of the physical, technical, strategic, team, mental, emotional, and inspirational capacities.

Stage 2: Using this information, coaches develop a specific plan that addresses how they can get the team to improve upon these needs. Decisions regarding the exact team-bonding activities and team-building meeting topics should be made at this time as well, including feedback from team captains.

Stage 3: An initial team meeting should be conducted between the team and coaches that consists of an educational orientation about what team building is and presents guidelines for optimal team communication. The coach and captains can then facilitate brainstorming sessions on what the team needs to do to be successful. Coaches can list their own comments on a blackboard, along with comments from the players. This meeting is the ideal time to have players think and record their primary motives for playing, as well as their specific preferences for coach and teammate behaviors and feedback.

Stage 4: The team prioritizes the input (i.e., the most important needs), and then additional brainstorming is conducted to define each point and how it can be assessed and accounted for in action words. This step is important because defining each strategy puts a "face on it." Another meeting point could include establishing a team identity, which defines what this team wants to be known for by people outside of the program: "What do you want opponents, fans, and followers of your sport to say about how you practice, how you play, how you conduct yourselves?

Stage 5: Follow-up meetings can be conducted to develop short- and long-range goals, action plans that detail how these goals will be achieved, team rules, and standards of execution. What will the team commit to accomplishing on a daily basis?

Stage 6: Follow-up meetings can include an evaluation of team progress on their standards and goals (via rating sheets and open discussions), and progress on team cohesion and team communication. It is absolutely critical to provide feedback and evaluation to the players for the intervention to have maximal effect. It is ideal if team captains can conduct these meetings.

Stage 7: Team meetings can then be set up to deal with conflicts that may occur during the season, as well as to incorporate some team-cohesion activities in the midst of the season, such as team meals and outings to continue to foster task and social cohesion.

Table 2: **Team Building Intervention Program. M.R. Voight & J. House,** *Mental Toughness Training for Basketball* **(Monterey, CA: Coaches Choice, 2010), pp. 99–100. Used with permission.**

"When you get along, others will go along."[31]
—J.C. Maxwell,
The 17 Essential Qualities of a Team Player

Relationships

A theme injected throughout this book is that leadership is about relationships. These relationships are built by making connections and by communicating and collaborating visions, goals, and aspirations, which then need to be continually maintained. The empowering aspect of these relationships can raise the standard of leadership across any organization into society as a whole. Don Clifton and Paula Nelson emphasize the importance of these relationships: "Relationships help us to define who we are and what we can become. Most of us can trace our successes to pivotal relationships."[32] As stated previously, teams who are more cohesive not only get along better, but work better together, and thus, have stronger relationships, which aid in improving the team's chances of succeeding. To assess the strength of the relationships on teams, J.C. Maxwell outlines five characteristics to look for on teams: (1) respecting and valuing each team member; (2) learning about your teammates through shared experiences; (3) developing trust through shared experiences; (4) relational reciprocity, in that each team member adds to the team while also gaining benefits from the team; (5) mutual enjoyment, which grows out of wanting to spend time together and not simply because one has to spend time together.

As was referred to earlier in this chapter, a team leader can improve her status within the group by establishing and maintaining good relationships with all group members, especially those team members who may be informal leaders who also have high status on the team. Moreover, according to Raymond Sparrowe, Budi Soetjipto and Maria Kraimer, the leaders also need to have good relationships with lower-status team members to assist them in feeling more comfortable with their own status levels.[33] According to Anson Dorrance, the most successful women's soccer coach in the world, the true measure of good team chemistry is "the melding of two extremes—the best and most popular player on the roster, and the worst and least popular."[34] The challenge, he says, is the ability of the leaders and/or team stars to help every player on the roster feel like an important, contributing member of the team. Noted sport psychology professors Robert Weinberg and Dan Gould believe it is the shifting of interpersonal relationships among team members that leads to the ups and downs teams may experience throughout a season. These authors also suppose leaders who have a better understanding of these dynamics are in a better position than those who do not, to structure the environment to best support individuals and the collective team as they move through each of the team developmental stages previously addressed.[35]

"Yes, Leadership is about vision."[36]

"There is nothing wrong with pursuing a vision for greatness. After all, the good-to-great companies also set out to create greatness. But, unlike the comparison companies, the good-to-great companies continually refined the path to greatness with the brutal facts of reality."[37]

—Jim Collins, *Good to Great*

Vision

A critical step in the team-building process is the construction of the vision of the team. Leadership literature is replete with references to team missions and visions and their importance. One of the better definitions of this important concept is noted by sport psychology expert and author Robin Vealey: "The power of imagination or the ability to perceive something not actually visible, which typically involved broad future aspirations or achievements that depart significantly from the status quo."[38] Peter Drucker, in *The Essential Drucker,* conveyed his belief of beginning this process of vision development with two important questions: "Common vision, common understanding, and unity of direction and effort of the entire organization require definition of what our business is and what it should be."[39] Although simple questions, how many sport organizations truly know the realities of their true purpose and mission?

Moreover, Peter Drucker explained these questions can only be answered by first taking an outside perspective, or as mentioned earlier in this book by Ronald Heifetz and Donald Laurie, "getting a view of things from the balcony." This provides the viewpoint of the primary benefactor, who in business is the customer, in sport the athlete. Drucker continued by stating: "All the customer is interested in are his or her own values, wants, and reality. For this reason alone, any serious attempt to state 'what our business is' must start with the customer's realities, his situation, his behavior, his expectations, and his values."[40] It seems apparent the importance should be placed on knowing the "customer" or benefactor in this fashion. For example, sport leaders must be aware of the values, wants, and expectations of those they lead, including the athletic directors knowing more about their head coaches, and head coaches knowing more about their captains and players. What some sport leaders assume may be the defining purposes of their program may not be compatible with that of their constituents' thoughts, drives, and motivations. At this crux there is a disconnect between the two, usually visually displayed by a reluctance or resistance to be totally "on board" and "bought in" to the philosophies and practices of the leader. Identifying this disconnect is at the core of the second question, *what should our purpose be?* If the "customer defines the business" as Drucker said, then how do the program's primary benefactors, captains and players, define the program's purpose or mission? This information can be derived by getting help from staff and players on the aforementioned questions, such as, *what is our program and what should it be and do?*

This exercise is as important to do with a team or organization that is struggling as with a team that has had success. Peter Drucker expressed an important time to ask these questions and seek answers to them is at the startup of an organization. The *most* important time to ask them however, is when the organization has been successful. In his words, "Success always makes obsolete the very behavior that achieved it."[41] In Chapter 9, the first of six leadership tactics, the use of *debriefs-after performance reviews*, was discussed. The debriefs conducted with teams during the season assist in identifying the behaviors and actions leading to the team's current strengths, in addition to areas needing further improvement. It is important to continue to remind players and teams who are having current success that "what is happening does not just happen because we want it to—it is happening because of what we are doing to make it happen." The shortened version of this reminder, "It doesn't just happen," is used more often as a reminder that the behaviors leading to success are to be performed consistently and not taken for granted or assumed they will automatically occur.

Armed with the valuable information from the question-answer exercise, the team leaders and followers can continue to collaborate on a vision for the team. Maxwell outlines seven elements to consider when crafting the vision of the team or organization from his book, *The 360-Degree Leader*[42]:

(1) *Clarity*—The vision has to be clear; one way to accomplish this is to ask these questions: "What do I want them to know?" and "What do I want them to do?"
(2) *Connection*—The vision should show how the past, present and future are connected, because Maxwell believes doing so "brings power and continuity to your vision casting."[43] A vision should include a connection to past traditions and successes, giving credit to those who have come before, while engaging the present contributors with the potential of the future and how the present work is done for a greater good, or something bigger than themselves. James Kouzes and Barry Posner also accentuated the importance of "reflecting on the past, attending to the present, and prospecting the future."[44]

(3) *Purpose*—Maxwell states, "Although vision tells people where they need to go, purpose tells them why they should go."[45] The purpose behind the vision will keep team members "on target" amidst the many distractions and challenges along the way. Similarly, Warren Bennis and Burt Nanus write, "Vision animates, inspirits, transforms purpose into action."[46]

(4) *Goals*—Goals represent the action phase to the vision process. Maxwell asserts, "When you give people a process, they realize that the vision is realistic—and that increases their confidence in you and the vision."[47] The ultimate achievement in the goal-setting process is when a team accepts the goals as their own. Author Thomas Davenport affirms as a result of his research, today's work teams "don't want to work toward a goal because someone else has set it, but rather because they believe that it's right."[48]

(5) *Challenge*—Similar to setting goals, the vision must be realistic, yet challenging, to fully engage and motivate team members. Maxwell avows, "A challenge makes good people want to spread their wings and fly; it fires up the committed people, and fries the uncommitted ones; you will actually define your people if you ask them to stretch."[49]

(6) *Stories*—Stories "put a human face" on a challenging vision, especially if these stories talk about team members from past and present. One collegiate coach tells stories to his present team of past players' sacrifices, struggles, and successes, oftentimes with tears in his eyes, personalizing these stories into more than just memories, but inspirational life lessons.

(7) *Passion*—According to Maxwell, "If there is no passion in the picture, then your vision isn't transferable; it is just a pleasant snapshot."[50] Since passion is contagious, if the leader is consistently excited and passionate about the vision, the team members will feed off of this energy, mobilizing the team's efforts. Similarly, Kouzes and Posner propose the most difficult of all of the leadership skills is expressing the vision. They continue by stating for the vision to be sustainable over time, this vision must be compelling and inspirational: "Leaders must breathe life into visions, they must animate them so that others can experience what it would be like to live and work in that ideal and unique future."[51] Moreover, Welch detailed eight rules of what good leaders do. Rule number 2 is, "Leaders make sure people not only see the vision, they live and breathe it."[52] For this to occur, team members must be passionately inspired by the vision while seeing how their role and contributions fit into this vision.

Incorporating the creation of the team vision as an aspect of the team-building process is advantageous for many reasons, most notably the inclusion of all team members in the collaboration of shared ideas. Knowing what is known about the current generation's penchant for inclusion (discussed in Chapters 1–3) it is in everyone's best interest to not only include all team members in the discussion, but to truly consider their feedback. Jim Collins also believes this to be true: "There's a huge difference between the opportunity to 'have your say' and the opportunity to be heard."[53] Moreover, organizations that do not incorporate team members in the creation of their vision are missing these ideal opportunities, especially those using what Jim Collins refers to as the "genius with a thousand helpers" model, whereby the genius leader sets the vision and the helpers ensure the vision gets carried out. This is not a model that teams and organizations who want to go from "good to great" adopt.[54]

> *"A lot of leaders have catchy slogans on their desk; many believe in them. The two-word sign on my desk genuinely summarizes my whole philosophy: 'I'm responsible.' During my time at City Hall I did my best to make those words a signature theme for every employee, starting with myself."*[55]
> —Former New York City mayor Rudolph Giuliani

Accountability

Taking the shared vision a team develops and turning it into reality demands individual members to be accountable to their specific responsibilities and roles as they apply to the action plan, including the pre-set goals and standards derived from the team-building process. Dean Smith had this to say about responsibility:

> "The willingness to delay gratification, to do the things you don't want to do, to work long hours when long hours are needed: These are the habits of mind of great leaders. These habits are formed early in life. That is why it's critical for parents not to make their children's lives too easy by solving their problems for them or letting them escape responsibility."[56]

As is stated, leaders are not doing their charges any favors by not including them in the team-building process and in not expecting all team members to be responsible for their particular roles and responsibilities. Jeff Janssen, team building specialist, avows involving players in the process of team building goes a long way to improving discipline along four distinct levels[57]:

Level One: Personal Responsibility—Players are more apt to accept responsibility for their actions while following team rules and standards because they are their rules. With that comes greater ownership. As suggested by Kouzes and Posner, "Accountability results in feelings of ownership, that you, not someone else, has the responsibility for what's going on around you."[58]

Level Two: Team Accountability—Since the standards of action and execution are from their own creation, team members realize the impact their actions have on their teammates. Since the team created the vision and rules collectively, there is some "team pressure" to abide by them. I will randomly have my teams complete "standard accountability" forms asking each teammate to anonymously record the names of teammates who have been living up to the pre-set standards and those who have not, including what they see that led them to choosing these teammates over others. This input is then organized and the captains and coaches hold a team meeting and one-on-ones regarding the input. This way, those who are hitting the standards get their proper kudos, those who are not meeting the standards get some coaching, and those in the middle who are compliant, but could be giving more, are addressed.

Level Three: Team Involvement—To ensure the team succeeds under its own pre-set rules and standards, members will police themselves to ensure compliance. Pat Summitt, the über-successful women's basketball coach while at the University of Tennessee, embraced a culture of team-involved discipline: "The entire aim of our policies at Tennessee is to get our players to discipline each other—we have evolved a system in which I don't have to do a whole lot of punishing, penalizing, or pushing them. Our upperclassmen become the disciplinarians of our team instead of me."[59] What Coach Summitt helped create for the Volunteers was a culture of "team pressure," similar to peer pressure, where team members feel compelled to conform to the high standard of execution and personal responsibility or else they are letting their teammates down or separating themselves from the team through their actions. From the business perspective, Kouzes and Posner state this form of peer pressure, whereby colleagues set high expectations on job performance is "a powerful force in motivating you to do well—the feelings of not wanting to let the rest of the group down strengthens people's resolve to do their best."[60]

Level Four: Coach Involvement—The coach, staff, and team consultant can now take the role of "team standard reminder" and at times the role of "observer" of team involvement and team accountability. From time to time it will be important to not only remind them of these responsibilities, but also to capture and compliment those times the team leaders challenge and discipline teammates in the proper manner.

Another mental skills trainer, Terry Orlick, explains in his book, *In Pursuit of Excellence,* that for teams to develop true team harmony, whereby team members help each other and rely on one another, they first must commit to the common mission or vision by putting it above everything else. As mentioned in an earlier section in this chapter, team harmony "does not just happen." It takes continual attention, maintenance, and work to continue to build and improve team harmony. There are many internal/external distractions and team barriers, such as Pat Lencioni's dysfunctions previously discussed, just around the corner waiting to dislodge a team from its harmonious state. In Orlick's words, "Harmony grows when you take the time to stop long enough to listen to others and when they listen to you; when you respect their feelings and they respect yours; when you accept their differences and they accept yours; when you choose to help them and they help you; harmony is rooted in mutual trust and respect."[61]

Sociological Influences of Team Competitiveness and Accountability for Female Teams

One of these potential barriers that could bring disharmony to teams is a teammate who gets her "feathers ruffled" by being "called out" or challenged to play better or give more effort by another teammate. This is especially true of a teammate who is perceived to be "inferior" because of age, skill level, or status on the team, or from someone who has not been pushing his own weight in recent days. This scenario is played out on most teams I have worked with at one time or another, even among teams who have a certain level of team harmony and mutual teammate respect. This event usually escalates when adversity is present, whether due to poor performance, perceptions of pressure to perform (usually by coaches), or importance of an upcoming contest. The ability to hold teammates accountable to high standards of effort and execution demands players call out or challenge each other, yet this process does present a real challenge for some teams, especially female teams (see the section entitled "Women and the Leadership Gap" in Chapter 6 for resources on the similarities and differences of leadership styles between the genders). It is my experience that most male teams are able to call teammates out for a myriad of transgressions and despite some initial backlash, their off-field relationships will be not be impacted after the training session. The ability of men's teams to integrate this into their team culture is believed to have leverage over teams who do not practice this, because of the benefits of being able to self-police in order to get the most out of everyone's contributions.

This is not the case, however, with the majority of female teams. For an in-depth examination of this occurrence, the work from one of the most-cited experts on the differences between coaching male and female athletes, Anson Dorrance, was sought. He reports, "Based on the truths in my own experience, women relate through an interconnected web of personal connections, as opposed to a more traditional male hierarchal style. To that end, what is critical in coaching women is that all players on the team have to feel like they have a personal connection with the coach, and it has to be unique."[62] Both Dorrance and his national team replacement, Tony DiCicco, speak about the importance of leading women with humanity, rather than by the force on one's personality (discussed in Chapter 7, the humble, Level 5 leader) by admitting

failures, being sensitive to individual differences among players, having tolerance of player mistakes, and valuing the contributions of all players, not simply
the star players.[63] Interestingly, one of Dorrance's most prolific former players,
Mia Hamm, considered to be one of the greatest female soccer players, when
asked how she prefers to be coached, replied, "Coach us like men, treat us like
women."[64]

In *The Vision of a Champion,* Dorrance writes about the social influences
underpinning the sociology of girls and women specifically as it applies to the
sport of soccer. This thinking, however, can be applied to all competitive sport.
He believes these social influences can interfere with their development as
competitive athletes, especially in the area of uninhibited competition, because
at a young age females prefer more cooperative play rather than competitive,
confrontational play.[65] Kathleen DeBoer, Executive Director of the American
Volleyball Coaches Association and author of *Gender and Competition: How
Men and Women Approach Work and Play Differently,* purports that many
coaches reinforce these societal influences by teaching males competitive play
through continual competitive drilling and scrimmages, while teaching females
cooperative play via technically oriented drilling with little scrimmaging.
DeBoer believes to make a female athlete and team more competitive, females
must practice competing: "We must accept that the 'me versus you' nature of
a contest can be difficult for those who choose cooperative play when left to
their own devices. For females, then, competiveness must be taught and
rehearsed."[66] The specific term DeBoer uses as a goal for female athletes and
teams to strive toward attaining is "competitive fire," while Dorrance uses the
term "competitive fury" to best depict this striving. Dorrance teaches to his
teams his "competitive cauldron," which is a competitive program based on
charting inter-team competitions ranging from one-on-one dribbling contests
to fitness training to finishing-shooting drills.[67] These charts are posted for
the team on a daily basis to see how they rank among their teammates. Dorrance believes his competitive cauldron program helps to short-circuit this
sociological predisposition, especially since females are not naturally driven
to embrace direct confrontation and competition.

Another aspect of the sociology of girls and women that can be a deter-
rent to optimal development of competitive players and team leaders is the
importance placed on their relationships with teammates and the drive to play
on a close, cohesive team. Dorrance believes this can be a double-edged sword:
"Women can be incredibly demanding; they set very high standards for each
other, and they are very sensitive, which is a difficult combination; when people
are so sensitive, any negative ripple can be picked up on and magnified."[68]
Being able to be confrontational with teammates without perceiving it will

leave a negative, permanent stain on the personal relationship is a real challenge for many female players and teams. This negative ripple can stifle a team's ability to challenge each other to be more competitive and confrontational with one other, and can also leave team chemistry in ruins if not properly managed. Adding to the challenge of achieving a competitive, close and cohesive team culture for female teams is another sociologically influenced propensity: not being vocal enough when in leadership roles. Dorrance had this to say when asked in a recent interview about ways to improve team accountability and the impact of his team leaders:

> "Well, the hardest thing to develop in terms of leadership with women's teams is what is called the verbal leader. This is a unique issue with women athletes. Men are more natural verbal leaders. Women don't like verbal leaders because they think women who are verbal leaders are bossy and they don't like bossy women. Women would rather basically agree on something through consensus and committee. And the biggest challenge in women's athletics, not just in China, but all over the world is to get the women to be verbal leaders on the field because what is interesting and different about the gender of women is they don't like verbal leadership."[69]

Despite these many sociological challenges coaches, players, and captains of female teams may face, one only has to look at those teams who have been extremely successful at the highest levels of their sport, including the U.S. women's national/Olympic soccer and basketball teams, for assurance it is attainable, especially with the right people guided by the right philosophies and processes.

> *"The best teams have not just one leader but many layers of*
> *leadership. Layers of leadership are important because when they're*
> *in place and the team is unified as to what the vision is—whether it be*
> *to win the Gold Medal, the World Championship, or even a girl's*
> *amateur tournament—there's no way you can lose your course."*[70]
> —Tony DiCicco and Colleen Hacker

– 11 –

The Art of Followership on Sport Teams (FQ)

"In many ways, great followership is harder than leadership.
But great followership has never been more important."[1]
—Warren Bennis, leadership scholar

Tom Rath and Barry Conchie disclose an often overlooked area in leadership inquiry when they ask the question, "Why do people follow?"[2] With the voluminous attention given to studying leaders in isolation via the business, leadership, and organizational psychology fields, only recently has followership been given its due. Bernard Bass refers to this one-sided view of leadership as the "great-man" theories, with the leader being the focal point of these theories. He argues, "These theories set the leader apart from followers; leaders were seen as being born with explicit traits, abilities and personalities that most common followers would not possess."[3] These earlier theories, some of which are detailed in Chapter 4, do not even consider the role of the follower in leadership. According to Lisa Burke, whose recent dissertation focuses on the topic of followership, "The follower in this approach is only a pawn waiting to be trained or influenced by the skills of the leader."[4]

One of the early leadership researchers to examine followership is Berlie Fallon, who in 1974 published an innovative article recognizing the art of the leader-follower relationship.[5] In his own words, "Additionally, the leader who survives will recognize that complete consensus is a goal but seldom a reality, and he will acknowledge that a leadership style vested in humanism will discard the illusion of the indispensable man."[6] This article represents an early prognostication about the limits of the "great man" leadership theories that dominated the leadership research in the late 1970s and 1980s. Another early pioneer in followership is David Frew, who wrote a 1977 article on followership style as it related to "the kind of leadership patterns which would be preferred by an individual in his/her boss."[7] Over a decade later, Robert Kelley's 1988 *Harvard Business Review* article, "In Praise of Followers,"[8] was published and with it came controversy due to what some considered as a "sharp rap on the knuckles of the field of leadership for neglecting followers."[9]

Lisa Burke writes, "This early view of followership resulted from observations that a manager's success was directly contingent on the acceptance of the leadership style by followers. This same perspective can be expanded to include the styles of followership although research has been slow to develop in this realm."[10] Also slow in developing is the cultural belief that followership is an important aspect of leadership and therefore, should be studied and developed in similar fashion. According to the followership literature, the current societal culture denotes followership as a negative trait and activity, especially where child-rearing practices are concerned: children are taught to lead, not follow. According to Burke, "Children are told to 'make your own decisions,' 'don't follow the crowd,' and 'be a leader not a follower.' As such, society typically does not understand and undervalues the role of the follower. Followers are as much a part of culture as leaders. Without followers, there would be no need for leaders."[11] Moreover, Patsy Blackshear in her article, "The Followership Continuum," writes, "Yet no organized effort can succeed or be sustained without followers. Just imagine the Super Bowl without a team of followers. Who would receive and carry the ball; who would block; and who would kick or punt, if everyone coached? Each of these team members provide critical, but different expertise."[12]

According to the editors of *The Art of Followership,* there is change on the horizon: "Followers, by their actions are calling attention to themselves— in massive political uprisings in diverse societies, and in incidents of individual whistle-blowing within organizations of all descriptions."[13] The "Occupy Movement" that dominated the headlines in the middle of 2012 here in the United States, the uprisings in Egypt and Libya, and even the fall of the Berlin Wall, for example, all typify the rise of the followers. Knowing what is known about the millennial, the newest generation, and the changing landscape that is interscholastic, intercollegiate and professional athletics, it is critical for today's leaders to be aware of followers' characteristics and actions. These characteristics can be both productive and counter-productive, because of the direct impact they have on leadership and the quality of play on sport teams across the levels. There are more and more examples of players and teams getting so fed up with the perceived negative treatment they receive from their coaches that they revolt. In some cases, teams lock the head coach out of the locker room, sign petitions to oust the coach, hold behind-closed-door meetings with administrators, or engage in other forms of rebellion previously discussed in Chapter 2.

The objective of this chapter is to focus on this most neglected aspect of the vast leadership literature, followership, while applying it to the world of sport. Five specific topics are covered, including: *defining followership, followership theories* cited in the literature, the *reasons people follow leaders, followership styles* and the *tools and teaching of followership skills.*

> *"Leaders may impress others when they succeed,*
> *but they impact others when their followers succeed."*[14]
> —John C. Maxwell, *Leadership Gold*

Defining Followership: The True "Team Player"

The term followership is defined as simply, "The ability or willingness to follow a leader."[15] Another definition offered by Kent Bjugstad and colleagues in their article, "A Fresh Look at Followership," is "The ability to effectively follow the directives and support the efforts of a leader to maximize a structured organization."[16] As mentioned earlier, the term "followership" is often linked to negative and demeaning words such as passive, weak, and conforming. It is no wonder this negative stereotype causes many to avoid being categorized as a follower. One research study conducted on more than 1,600 executives from all types of businesses reveals over one-third of them are followers in some capacity, yet only in rare cases did they accept they were followers, further exemplifying the stigma associated with the term follower.[17]

Bjugstad and colleagues also assert, besides the negative stigma of being labeled as a follower, there is a misconception that leadership is more important than followership:

> "The assumption that good followership is simply doing what one is told, and that effective task accomplishment is the result of good leadership, doesn't amplify the merits of the follower role."[18] Renowned followership researcher and practitioner Robert Kelley believes today's society should reconsider its outdated mindset and how this term is defined: "The words 'leader' and 'follower' bring to mind a common script in which the leader is in charge, saying 'You do this, and you do that.' Meanwhile, followers are imagined as inferior beings in need of the leader's direction, motivation, and protection."[19]

Rath and Conchie's definition of leadership underscores the important role followers play in the process of leadership when they write, "You are a leader only if others follow."[20] Joseph Rost in his book *Leadership for the Twenty-first Century* defines leadership as "an influence relationship among leaders and followers who intend real changes that reflect shared purposes."[21] Legendary investor Warren Buffett posits a similar definition: "A leader is someone who can get things done through other people."[22] In similar vein, former president of USC, Dr. Steven Sample, is quoted in his book, *The Contrarian's Guide to Leadership*, "Before one can lead, one must acquire a set of followers; followers are the *sine qua non* (translated as "without which there"[23]) of leadership."[24] Moreover, the importance placed on followers can be seen in this quote by leadership expert Max Depree: "The signs of outstanding leadership appear primarily among the followers."[25] Ira Chaleef, an executive consultant, avows, "You can't by definition have a world just of leaders; to think of leaders without followers is like thinking of teachers without students. Both are impossible."[26]

Sport Application

In the sport setting, this same logic applies: It is impossible to be a coach or a captain without players to follow. In this same setting, effective followers who portray particular "followership" behaviors are often referred to as "team players," those who put their own interests behind those of the team or leader. How coaches, captains and players define what an effective "team player" or a "good teammate" is and looks like can be a valuable springboard to active team discussion about followership. To reflect upon, then brainstorm the qualities and practices of effective teammates and team players, reveals individual perceptions, biases, and attitudes about what it takes to be an effective follower of team ideals and its leaders. The feedback may even reinforce the complexity and difficulty of being an effective follower on teams. For example, one team shares below what they believe to be an effective teammate-follower:

Being a true "Blue Devil" teammate means engaging in the following behaviors:

- Go directly to teammate to address any issues
- Have to be someone the freshmen feel they can ask questions and come to
- Consistently bring positive energy to the team
- Be the best player you can be
- Perform the best you possibly can
- Make teammates laugh, smile, and have fun together
- Help to lift teammates if they are down or lift them up when they need some inspiration
- Be a good listener—respect input
- Do not get caught up in drama, and help teammates to go to the source to solve issues
- Resolve any conflicts or issues so these issues do not get in the way of obtaining our goals

- Work at getting along with everyone
- Get everyone excited and pumped up before tournaments
- Embrace the productive rivalry that an improved "sense of team" brings
- Pack yourselves—take care of your own stuff

As this list indicates, effective team players who are good followers of their leaders and team standards and rules show their followership through these 14 actions. Although there are many more behaviors that could have been mentioned, this particular team focuses on these either because they represent current strengths or acknowledge areas that let them down in the past. Either way, this team exercise assists in defining what followership means to a group of athletes, leaving in its wake a rubric of actions that can then be used to hold each other accountable to being effective followers.

Behavioral Definition of Followership

The notion of defining followership through behavioral action receives attention in the book, *Contemporary Issues in Leadership,* by Earl Potter, William Rosenbach and Thane Pittman. In it, these authors enumerate two important forms of follower behavior sets: the amounts of *performance initiative* and *relationship initiative.*[27] Performance initiative refers to the follower who is committed to finding ways to improve his or her performance. Relationship initiative refers to the effort given by the follower to improve his or her relationship with the leader or leaders. According to these authors, "Followers differ in the extent to which they take positive initiatives in each of these domains. Effective followers are committed to high performance. At the low end of this scale one still finds satisfactory performers. At the high end one finds experts who lead in their field and whose contributions strengthen the bottom-line performance of the organization."

There are four areas mentioned by these authors that should be considered when assessing the follower's *performance initiative*[28]:

(1) What do the follower's achievement strivings look like? Does this follower go through the motions or is performing optimally important to this person? The word "pride" (in their work) comes to mind.

(2) Tied to a follower's performance is the quality of the working relationship with teammates. The term "task cohesion" is used in Chapter 10 to denote the importance placed on the shared understanding and effort needed to optimally perform. The authors describe a continuum where on one end reside those who interfere with the performance of others, or those who simply do not want to work well with others. On the upper end are followers who take advantage of the synergy of working with others, who may also take on a leader or mentor role to help accomplish the talk. To do this, the authors avow, "these followers emphasize

cooperation over competition and find their own success in the success of the whole group."[29]

(3) Effective followers see themselves as valuable resources to their organization, but also to their other social roles, including at home, in the community and among friends. For these followers to continue to be valuable contributors, they must take care of themselves physically, mentally, and emotionally by balancing their many responsibilities optimally.

(4) The final concern is how the follower views and handles change and other challenges that beset the organization. On one end of the continuum there are those who resist change and will fight the idea of changing techniques and strategies especially with the uncertainty of the results. According to the authors, the high end of this dimension includes "the followers who look for new and better ways to do things because they are committed to continuous improvement—they can be extremely effective as agents for change."[30]

Potter, Rosenbach and Pittman believe leaders can find it very difficult to lead followers with whom they have an adversarial relationship. It can be assumed the follower who perceives a similar dysfunctional relationship with the leader would make it difficult to follow orders or to offer help when and where needed. Similarly, with the performance initiative, the authors posit four evaluative criteria used to determine follower's *relational initiative.*[31]

(1) Whether a follower identifies with the leader's views and vision for the team or organization is an important differentiating variable between an antagonistic follower and an effective follower. These followers who negatively identify with their leaders could make leadership quite difficult. On the contrary, according to these authors, those followers who understand the leader will "do what they can to help the leader succeed, and take pride and satisfaction in the leader's accomplishments."[32]

(2) The efforts taken by followers to earn and build upon trust from their leaders is evident by demonstrating to the leader their loyalty and reliability. Once trust is established the leader will be more likely to be inclusive to these individuals, entrusting more responsibilities onto them. Those who dismiss these opportunities to build trust through these qualities and actions may be on the outside looking in, potentially immobilizing their position to help their careers by helping their leaders succeed.

(3) According to the authors, "A follower who exhibits courageous communication takes risks in order to be honest."[33] Some followers who are not as courageous will simply become "yes men" or "yes women," or refrain from speaking their minds when it becomes uncomfortable to be the bearer of bad news. Those followers who are able to take this initiative to speak the truth for the betterment of the organization will earn trust from the leader. The authors explain this point further: "Because leaders can suffer from being surrounded by people who are supportive

to a fault, a follower who is willing to be honest when others shy away from voicing their real opinions and evaluations can be invaluable."[34]

(4) How followers handle disagreements with their leaders can be indicative of a strong or dysfunctional relationship between follower and leader and vice versa. Those followers who have a differing of opinion with the leader, who are oriented toward improving their relationship with the leader, will put themselves in a position to mediate these differences via a real discussion with active exchange of opinions and thoughts. On the contrary, those who are not inclined to work to improve trust in the follower-leader relationship will hide their opposition, either by quickly agreeing with the leader despite true perceptions or simply keeping their opinion to themselves. The authors point out effective followers can intervene when their leader has a disagreement with other team members: "The follower can take advantage of an understanding of the points of view of both parties to try to help resolve the disagreements in a way that leads to creative solutions acceptable to the leader as well as the other followers."[35] This is a role effective team captains take on when they attempt to bridge the communication gap between the team and the coaching staff.

Referring to the list brainstormed by the "Blue Devils" sport team mentioned earlier in this section, the importance placed on those followership behaviors by the team becomes apparent. These reflect both performance and relationship initiatives among this group of athletes, with more emphasis given to the relational initiatives. For example, the performance initiatives mentioned include "be the best player you can be" and "perform the best you possibly can," "consistently bring positive energy to the team," and "pack yourselves—take care of your own stuff." The relational initiatives mentioned include "resolve any conflicts or issues," "works at getting along with everyone," and "help to lift teammates if they are down or lift them up when they need some inspiration."

Moving from sport to another dynamic organization where close coordination among team members is essential, a chamber orchestra, researchers reveal a shifting of followership and leadership roles that can be seen in the different behaviors shown by these musicians in the absence of a permanent conductor: (1) interpreting the environment to identify needed changes; (2) taking responsibility for own actions while participating in needed group decisions; (3) challenging the team members to reach desired goal; (4) adhering to the norms of the group; and (5) maintaining good relationships through effective communication practices among teammates.[36] Relating these results back to sport, in certain team sports such as soccer and hockey, most of the action is player-directed. The coaches are far removed from not only the play, but the on-the-spot decision making that must occur, thus, leaving a collaborative dynamic of leadership and followership behaviors during play up to the players. In more choreographed sports, such as football and basketball, where player movement is dictated by organized plays, called by coaches either on the sideline or in the press box, the majority of the action is followership-based. In football, the quarterback is the "field general," the leader of the team in the huddle. However, he is more of a follower since the plays (besides the audible call that changes the play call prior to the snap of the ball, which is dependent on what the quarterback sees from the opponent's defensive scheme) are primarily dictated by the coaches and communicated through the headset in the quarterback's helmet or signaled in from the sideline. This is another example of the shifting of leadership and followership roles.

Moving from sport and orchestra "teams" to the business setting, the following represent effective followership behaviors indicated by the studies: (1) demonstrating work-specific knowledge and competence; (2) building collaborative relationships with co-workers and leader; (3) supporting and defending the leader in front of others; (4) helping the leader avoid making costly mistakes through courageous influence; (5) focusing on performance while also supporting a friendly work climate; and (6) being actively involved in needed change processes.[37] Authors Jon Howell and Maria Mendez write in their chapter, "Three Perspectives on Followership," the stated behaviors above are representative of what much of the existing literature on followership studies indicates.[38] Additional forms of followership behaviors are detailed in a future section of this chapter entitled "Followership Characteristics and Styles."

To conclude, Robert Kelley states in his book, *The Power of Followership*, a leader contributes no more than 20 percent to the success of his/her organization while the followers contribute the other 80 percent. Moreover, Kelley believes 98 percent of the population is followers.[39] In his 1992 book, *Principle-Centered Leadership*, Stephen Covey suggests followers should play a larger role in the leadership discourse. He states, "A more fruitful approach is to look at followers, rather than leaders, and to assess leadership by asking why followers follow."[40] This is a question so good it is the focus of a future section. In a recent study, however, it appears there is still some room for improvement. Kent Bjugstad and colleagues posit leadership books outnumber followership books by 120 to 1.[41]

> *"A new model of followership can help us reorient ourselves*
> *and our relationships with leaders. Courageous followership*
> *is built on the platform of courageous relationship."*[42]
> —Ira Chaleff, *The Courageous Follower*

Followership Theories

Despite there being a limited number of followership resources when compared to leadership resources, what does exist is rife with theoretical and empirical information on followership. Two applicable theories and their theorists are Courageous Followership (Ira Chaleff) and Transference Theory (Michael Maccoby).

Courageous Followership

One book and subsequent theory that garners attention by the leadership community is *Courageous Follower: Standing Up to & for Our Leaders,* by Ira Chaleff, an executive consultant. In this work Chaleff posits a theory focused on the courage followers have to assume responsibility, including the courage to serve, to challenge, to participate in transformation, and to act based on morals. In his words, "I focus on the courage required to take advantage of proximity, as only with courage can we act quickly and early to ensure that the leader's power will be used well. If we practice being courageous in our mundane interactions with leaders, we will be prepared if one day we are called upon to display extraordinary courage in our relationship with a leader."[43] What the author means by proximity is the farther away followers are from a situation where power is being abused, the more difficult it is to influence it. Yet the closer followers are to this particular situation, the more they are at risk if they try to change it.[44] In sports, the assistant coaches, support staff, and team captains, are usually the closest ones to a situation such as this (abuse of power), which could take the form of the head coach playing favorites, unmerited punishment, inconsistent standards, authoritarian behaviors, and taking credit for team successes while passing blame for failures. Chaleff believes proximity and courage are tantamount in the prevention of leaders' abuses of power.

According to Chaleff, leaders and followers form an action circle around a shared purpose and vision, much like teachers and students form a "learning circle" around a particular body of knowledge/skills to be taught and learned.[45] In sports lingo, the coaches, team captains, and players will circle around the team vision and standard of play, incorporating the many aspects to optimal play, including physical, technical, tactical, team, and mental components. Mary Parker Follett, a pioneer in management (who Peter Drucker, a management icon himself, called the "prophet of management" and his "guru"), referred to the following of a common, shared purpose by leader and follower as the "invisible leader."[46] To do this entails a partnership in reciprocal following. Chaleff confirms this: "Both leaders and followers serve a common purpose, each from their own role."[47] More is shared on the reciprocal, collaborative process between follower and leader in a future section ("Tools of Effective Followership") in this chapter.

As part of this courageous follower theory, Chaleff believes in moving past the traditional definitions of a follower, including, "docility, conformity, weakness, and failure to excel" by getting comfortable with the new notion of followership, encompassing images of "powerful followers supporting powerful leaders."[48] He continues by affirming being a follower is a legitimate and necessary role and again, a person cannot have one without the other. To move beyond requires courage on the part of the follower, as noted by Chaleff's five dimensions listed next, but also from the leader. The leader needs the courage to value other's viewpoints and to include them in the discussion and implementation of planned programming to improve organizational effectiveness. The five dimensions to Chaleff's courageous followership model include the following attitudes and behaviors (Table 1)[49]:

Table 1: Courageous Follower Model Dimensions

DIMENSION	ATTITUDINAL-BEHAVIORAL DESCRIPTION
Courage to assume responsibility	Assumes responsibility not only for themselves, but for the organization; Takes advantage of opportunities to contribute to the accomplishment of the common purpose.
Courage to serve	Takes on new responsibilities to best serve the leader and organization; Is as passionate and driven as the leader in accomplishing the team vision.
Courage to challenge	Is "willing to stand up, to stand out, to risk rejection, to initiate conflict in order to examine the actions of the leader and group when appropriate."[50] Willing to confront those whose actions are deemed unethical or counter to the team's common values.
Courage to participate in transformation	Becomes active change agent when there is a need for transformation; Commits to becoming full participant in the change process.
Courage to take moral action	Takes a stand that may be counter to the leader or the group, while "answering to a higher set of values; the stand may involve refusing to obey a direct order, appealing the order to the next level of authority, or tendering one's resignation."[51] Believes service to the common purpose justifies the personal risk involved with such a decision.

Applying Chaleff's courageous follower model to sport teams, the term "team player" should now be defined to include these aspects, especially the importance placed on the interrelated workings between the leader, either a coaching staff member or team captain, and the team. Being a true team player/effective follower should include these applicable attitudes and behaviors. Special attention should be given to the ability to take responsibility for one's actions, how one attempts to maximize his or her contributions for the betterment of his/her own game and the team's game, assuming more responsibilities to better serve the team leaders and team, and the ability to challenge and confront those who are operating counter to the team vision and rules. The addition of Potter, Rosenbach and Pittman's behavioral dimensions of followership (performance and relationship initiatives), discussed earlier in this chapter, can also be included in this updated definition of a team player-effective follower.

Followership and Transference

Another theory on followership referenced in the leadership literature is the "power of transference theory" postulated by Michael Maccoby, a psychoanalyst and anthropologist, and author of *The Leaders We Need and What Makes Us Follow*. Maccoby also bemoans the lack of attention given to followership: "The problem is that followers get short shrift in the management literature, where they are described largely in terms of leaders' qualities."[52] Vince Lombardi, Jr., denotes the weighted responsibility of the follower to be accepting of guidance and direction from the all-mighty leader: "Leadership rests on followers who are ready to accept guidance. Leadership is the ability to direct people and more important, to have those people accept that direction."[53]

Although the follower's acceptance of being led by the leader is part of the leadership-followership paradigm, the objective of this chapter is to put a greater onus on the qualities, attitudes, and motives of the follower and how to maximize his/her contributions and experiences, and at the same time, improve the relationship between the follower and the leader. Maccoby appears to support this viewpoint when he writes, "What most analysis seems to ignore is that followers have their own motives and identity, and they can be as powerfully driven to follow as leaders are to lead."[54]

Maccoby notes follower motives for following leaders, or motivations, fall into two categories: the conscious and the unconscious. The *conscious* motivations consist of the desire to make money, get promoted, gain status and power, learn new skills, and be a part of the inter-workings of the organization. The *unconscious* motivations, according to Maccoby, can be even more powerful than the conscious ones, as these "are rooted in emotional attitudes in life, but in large part they also arise from the strong images s in our unconscious that we project onto our relationships with ˌ ˌ ˌ ˌ ˌ ˌ ˌ ˌ ˌave power over us."[55] The process of projecting these unconscious motives onto those who have power over us is referred to as transference. The first to uncover the follower's use of unconscious motivations was Sigmund Freud, the founder of psychoanalysis. Maccoby believes transference is the "missing link" in leadership theories and can be used to explain a great deal about the behaviors of leaders, followers, and organizations. He defines transference as "the emotional glue that binds people to a leader that makes them want to follow even when they are unclear about where the leader is taking them."[56]

This transference is based on perceived positive or negative past experiences stemming from our upbringing, including important models and mentors such as parents, siblings, extended family members, first bosses, teachers, coaches and friends. Maccoby believes in times of stress, anxiety, or fear, followers "will follow leaders who promise to protect them, transferring on to them these unconscious infantile attitudes and emotions."[57] He also infers, for today's generation especially, "growing up in families where both parents are at work and emotional support is found with peers and siblings, ties to sibling figures at work may be as strong or stronger than paternal transferences."[58] In both the workplace and the sport setting, a common transference is the "father figure," "brother or sister figure," or a "maternal figure." These represent the most common types of transferences. For example, a maternal transference could have a negative influence due to a heightened expectation of maternal qualities, such as compassion and empathy. When an employee or player is treated counter to this perception, there could be some resulting resentment. On the positive side, a maternal transference could give players an overwhelming sense of support from the coach or administrator, much like they had or have with their mother, grandmother, aunt, or female guardian.

The paternal transference works in the same fashion. Through the years company executives, CEOs, politicians, and coaches alike have promoted practices that strengthen these transferences because of the importance given to the father figure persona—the leader, protector and provider. Vince Lombardi, Tom Landry, John Wooden, and many other coaches from this same era portrayed these paternal images so well that for many aspiring coaches, even to this day, their qualities and mannerisms are emulated in an attempt to experience similar outcomes as these legends. The negative side of paternal transference is organizations and teams who uncritically worship the leader. They expect and reward what Maccoby refers to as "transferential veneration," which only acts to limit healthy debate about the vision and process standards and thus, could cause the team to become forced into doing the same thing that has been done in the past. On this point, Maccoby cautions leaders about the deleterious impact of stereotyping: "A male leader, therefore, should never assume that he is a father figure or a brother figure—nor should a female leader assume she's a mother or a sister."[59] These assumptions could have a negative impact on the transference and subsequent relationship between follower and leader. More examples of negative transference will be mentioned after the impact of positive follower transference is discussed.

Positive Transference

Followers who have a positive transference toward their leaders see them as having prerequisite skills and abilities deserving of followers' admiration. Intelligence, charisma, and compassion are some of the perceived abilities that make up the transference dynamic. Maccoby asserts followers who experience positive transference for their leader tend to give him or her the benefit of the doubt and are more open to taking on greater responsibility and risk than they would otherwise. Positive transference is also closely associated with productivity, especially when the employee or athlete views the leader in a paternal fashion for example. He or she will do all that is possible to please the leader. As long as these transferred expectations are met, the player will continue to give maximal efforts, which should improve performance for the individual and team. The term coaches use to categorize this type of player is "pleasers," those who would do anything to stay in the good graces of the coach.

A common sport analogy heard as sound bites in post-game interviews is that the team represents a "family." Here the head coach is the paternal or maternal leader of the family, and the teammates are siblings who have each other's backs in the best and worst of times. It is acceptable on the team to cajole, ridicule, or challenge each other since brothers (or sisters) do, but it is something different if someone from outside the team, or the family, attempts to do the same. Maccoby similarly asserts sibling transference can "forge bonds of affection that allow for critical ribbing as well as mutual aid."[60] Coaches and captains alike work hard to help every team member accept this transference while maximizing the benefits of the "team is family" edict, by the use of team building, team bonding, and other interactive programming plans.

Negative Transference

As mentioned previously, in times of stress and fear followers may gravitate to a negative transference toward their leader. Maccoby explains, "In such situations, followers tend to be more dominated by irrational feelings—in particular, the need for praise and protection given by all powerful parents."[61] In times of stress, the head coach may be overburdened, trying to help the organization through an adverse time, such as losing key players to injury. The coach may be spending more time developing a new game plan through video preparation and training time with the new players, while perceivably ignoring the rest of the team by not meeting their needs as much as she usually does. Today's generation of student-athletes tend to be as busy with their schedules as their parents, yet in times of stress or struggle, there is an expectation those in their support systems will be there for them at a moment's notice.

An example of negative transference shared by Maccoby was told to him by a fellow executive consultant working with a company with a very effective CEO.[62] An issue arose between the CEO and one of his chief officers. During a stressful acquisition process she perceived her boss was becoming more and more distant and did not have the same amount of time for her. This led to resentment at the unconscious level, despite her being rational at the conscious level, realizing the acquisition was taxing on everyone's time, especially the CEO's. This chief officer's resentment was concluded by the consultant to be based on the feelings of abandonment, much like she was by her distant father growing up. These unconscious feelings tapped her resentment from her past relationship with her father, which was then negatively transferred to her boss.

In the positive transference section a group of team members labeled as "pleasers" is mentioned. A downside of having pleasers on a team (especially many of them) is that to stay in their leader's good graces pleasers believe they have to continue to play well. They tend to play to their strengths rather than trying to improve on the weaker aspects of their game because this leads to making mistakes, thus putting the positive transference expectations at risk of being met. Pleasers are less likely to take risks or to try using new techniques in competitive situations. They fear making mistakes and want to avoid the predicted deleterious impact on the leader's perceptions of them as a performer and person.

Another transference concern that can have an influence on the follower-leader relationship is referred to as countertransference. Maccoby defines countertransference as a "two-way street—just as a follower projects his past experiences onto his leader, the leader responds by projecting her past experiences back onto the follower."[63] Examples mentioned include employees who get promoted over more qualified candidates because they remind superiors of a favorite friend or family member, or bosses who favor certain subordinates who show filial admiration. When coaches are recruiting new talent for their teams, or selecting starting players or captains, how much of these decisions is based on countertransference?

Managing Transference

Maccoby pronounces leaders today should understand these transference effects and work hard to help others in the organization see each other as they really are, without looking through the lens of transference. He believes there are ways of managing these transferences to not only reduce the effects of negative beliefs, but to increase the effect of positive transferences. This process begins with leaders becoming more aware of their own transferences and the use of countertransferences. Another suggestion by Maccoby includes relying on outsiders to assist the leader in making "reality checks" a part of their decision-making process. These outsiders could be wives, husbands, leadership or executive consultants, or longtime friends. Moreover, leaders who take the time to build their teams around a common purpose and vision, as well as get to know their team members on a personal level, even allowing others to get to know them as people and not simply as the head coach or the boss, will make it harder to project transferences onto others. As Maccoby affirms, "increased candor and knowledge between leaders and followers can turn a leader from being a projection of hopes and fears into a flesh-and-blood role model that collaborators can emulate."[64]

> *"If you want to lead, it is critical to know what the people around you need and expect from you."*[65]
> —Tom Rath and Barry Conchie,
> *Strengths-Based Leadership*

Why Followers Follow

Rath and Conchie ask two important questions: "If you want to know why a leader is making a difference in the lives of people, would you ask the leader for the best answer or the involved constituents?" Also, if you wanted to find out the impact the president had on the lives of Americans, "Would you look to him for the best answers—or would you ask his constituents?"[66] In a sport example, it is important to ask the head coach for feedback on the impact he is having on the team, as well as the impact his captains are having on the team. Although this is still done, greater weight is now given to how the team responds to this question. In a landmark study from 2005–2008, a team of researchers for the Gallup Poll did just this. They surveyed 10,000 followers from around the world on why they follow the most influential leader in their life. Rath and Conchie reveal three key findings: (1) the most effective leaders invest in individuals' strengths; (2) effective leaders surround themselves with the right people; and (3) *the most effective leaders understand their followers' needs.*[67] Focusing on followership, the third finding from this study will be further explored here.

As part of this study, this team of researchers studied the most commonly mentioned answers to the question, "List three words that best describe what the leader who has the most positive influence in your daily life contributes to your life." Rath and Conchie summarized the results to this question, stating, "It seems that followers have a very clear picture of what they want and need from the most influential leaders in their lives."[68] The results of the analysis of the responses from 10,000 followers reveal that the four basic needs of followers' include trust, compassion, stability, and hope.[69]

- *Trust*—Brad Anderson, CEO of electronics giant Best Buy, describes trust as "the most cherished and valuable commodity in a work environment."[70] He also explains the only way to build trust is to always be candid with people, in good times and bad. Jack Welch calls a lack of candor "the biggest dirty little secret in business," and says a "lack of candor blocks smart ideas, fast action, and good people contributing all the stuff they've got; it's a killer."[71] According to Rath and Conchie, important outcomes of strong relationships built on trust include respect, integrity, and honesty. Through their research on work teams, they also observed how little successful teams talk about trust, yet on the contrary, when involved in discussions with teams who struggle, the topic of trust was the top issue addressed.
- *Compassion*—In Gallup Polls through the years, results indicate over 10 million people who agree to the item "My supervisor seems to care about me as a person" are those employees who are more likely to stay with an organization, are more productive, more profitable, and have more engaged customers.[72] Rath and Conchie believe for people to truly love their organization it needs to have a heart.
- *Stability*—These results indicate followers desired their leaders to be there for them in good times and bad, to be consistent and lead through sound values, and to offer continual support and transparency through regular updates on goal progress.
- *Hope*—Rath and Conchie assert, "It appears that followers want stability in the moment and hope for the future. Sixty-nine percent of employees who strongly agreed to this statement (whether their company's leadership made them feel enthusiastic about the future) were engaged in their jobs, compared to a mere 1 percent of employees who disagreed or strongly disagreed."[73] These authors also differentiate between leaders who spend most of their time *reacting* to urgent matters instead of *initiating* for the future by creating hope and optimism in their followers and organizations. Leaders who are always reactionary "convey to the organization that they aren't in charge or control but are being tossed about by the demands of the day."[74] Yet those leaders who choose to initiate send the message of hope for the future, while also doing what *could* be done and not simply doing what *needs* to be done. Although being a problem solver is a critical quality and skill-set for leaders, these authors purport being more of an initiating leader is much harder work than being

in response mode day in, day out: "If as a leader, you are not creating hope and helping people see the way forward, chances are, no one else is either."[75]

Michael Maccoby writes about the hard reality of the followership-leadership dynamic in his book, *The Leaders We Need and What Makes Us Follow.* Many in the work force follow their leaders because they have to, not necessarily because they want to. Yet, these same followers may feel better about following a leader who has good character and focuses on accomplishing organizational objectives, even if they don't aspire to follow a leader. According to Maccoby and his research, one of the more salient motivations followers have is to collaborate (rather than being led) with a leader who makes their lives more meaningful. Another big reason for joining an organization and following the organization's leader is the work itself is intrinsically meaningful to them.[76]

Similarly, Kent Bjugstad and colleagues writes followers are more self-motivated by what they want out of the work experience, rather than what the leaders think they would want. It is this internal motivation that determines their level of commitment, work ethic, the type of recognition they may receive and if it will be worth it.[77] Thad Green, author of *Motivation Management,* surmises three conditions must exist for followers to be highly motivated: first, the follower must believe he/she can accomplish the expected work; second, there must be trust in the leadership that helps tie outcomes to performance, and last, the follower must be satisfied with the outcome/rewards he/she receives.[78]

Robert Kelley asserts leaders who misunderstand followers' motivations could lead to the loss of these same followers. This could impact how effective this leader will be in attracting new team members and retaining the ones he has currently. For example, too many leaders believe people follow them because of their charisma or profound vision for the organization. This could be the case for some, but as stated previously, many followers are motivated by their own vision and their own needs. According to Kelley, most people prefer "co-adventurers" who facilitate and assist in goal attainment.[79] More on the interaction between the two parties is discussed in the last section of this chapter.

Kelley's "Seven Paths to Followership" offer another view of follower motivations about why some people choose a followership role rather than a leadership one. Some of these paths serve as a vehicle for personal transformation, to improve themselves and their abilities. Those who are comfortable and satisfied with themselves (and their talents and achievements) will choose a path for self-expression purposes and to contribute to the workings of their chosen organization. These seven paths consist of the *apprentice, disciple, mentee, comrade, loyalist, dreamer,* and *lifeway* paths.[80]

- *Apprentice:* This path is chosen by those who are "aspiring" leaders because they realize they need to learn the ropes and pay their dues. This apprenticeship path is related to the coaching field in a future section in this chapter.
- *Disciple:* According to Kelley, the word "disciple" is Greek, with its origin "one who is learning from a teacher."[81] Kelley differentiates discipleship from the mentor-mentee relationship: "Unlike mentorship, which is an intensive one-on-one experience aimed at personal maturation, discipleship involves a body of knowledge being passed from a teacher to a group of students; generally, it involves intellectual not emotional development."[82]
- *Mentee:* The goal of mentoring is personal maturation. The mentoring relationship is the vehicle used for this self-improvement, yet it is not always used as a way to become a leader. These mentoring relationships also produce valuable assets to not only those involved but for the organization that supports their use as well.
- *Comrade:* In some cases people decide to follow not for the specific development of skills (apprentices) or personal maturation (mentees), but for the affiliative benefits of belonging to a group. Kelley believes some followers "follow for mutually reinforcing reasons: your feeling of goodwill toward the group and the belief that survival is more likely if you collectively share and watch out for each other."[83] Sport teams who endure demanding double or triple practice sessions in the pre-season training period may feel a tremendous closeness and mutual respect to each other as a result of these experiences. Comradeship can also be found in groups who are working together for a worthy cause, such as a political election or a fundraising campaign. On this point, Kelley affirms, "Once you feel part of something you transcend your feelings of isolation and even your feelings of self."[84] He also cautions these types of followers may become uncomfortable when asked to compete against the group or do solo work on assignments.
- *Loyalist:* As one could surmise, a loyalist follows a leader out of personal loyalty to him or her. This relationship is an emotional one, based on a commitment of trust and loyalty for the other. Leaders are fortunate to have followers like this, yet they are cautioned to not betray this trust, keeping the follower abreast of important matters and keeping them involved. In the coaching ranks it is very common to have a former player become a trusted assistant coach, one who is as loyal as the day is long and usually becomes a mainstay on the staff.
- *Dreamer:* Kelley explains followers who choose the dreamer path are people who "follow a leader not because of who the leader is, but because the leader embodies the idea or the cause."[85] Others can become so consumed by their dreams and aspirations they will follow whomever to move them closer to goal accomplishment. The author cites the term, "internalization," meaning people on this path follow because their internal goals/dreams are similar to the leaders or to the organization's purposes. The follower's dreams become the guiding force.

- *Lifeway:* The lifeway path is not simply a career choice that is made, but moreso a way of life. As Kelley states, "there is one other path of followership—it is taken by people who follow out of the conviction that no other lifeway is as rewarding; for them, following is compatible with their personality."[86] These followers actually decide following is what they want to do, and they will be happier by complementing rather than competing with the leader. Leaders are cautioned against pushing these followers into roles or positions that could be in conflict with who they are, regardless of how talented they would be in this new role.[87]

Being more aware of followers' motivations and how leaders can facilitate goal attainment can be very important information for leaders from all types of organizations, especially sport. Knowing followers' motivations are functions of both internal factors (e.g., confidence, commitment, attitude about the meaningfulness of the work, work ethic) and the climate created and influenced by the leadership (e.g., collaborative environment, trusting relationships, initiated leadership efforts, meaningful work), gives both parties an ideal opportunity to improve each others' combined efforts at becoming effective leaders and effective followers. This positively impacts the effectiveness of the organization. More is addressed on the qualities and especially the styles of effective followers in the next section.

> *"The tools of great followership are not so different from those of leadership."*[88]
>
> —Warren Bennis

Followership Qualities and Styles

A logical question at this point is to discern what distinguishes good followers from bad ones. According to Kelley, there are four essential qualities to effective followers[89]:

- Manage themselves well by determining personal goals and how to add value to organization.
- Commit to the organization's vision by word and deed.
- Build competence and focus efforts to maximize contributions to the organization.
- Are courageous, honest, and credible (what Kelley refers to as the "courageous conscience"); Warren Bennis adds the ability to always tell the truth is the single most important characteristic of an effective follower.[90]

In reviewing the seminal work conducted on the specific topic of followership qualities, Lisa Burke cites a study by Theodore Engstrom and Edward Dayton who proffer nine followership qualities, including commitment, understanding, loyalty, strong communication, competence, promise keeping, participation, getting along, and sacrifice.[91] An additional study by Robert Vecchio finds good followership relates to a sense of responsibility, maturity, commitment, openness, and loyalty, while another by Patricia Wallington presents followers as able listeners, focused, egoless, effective, and team oriented.[92] Overall, these documented qualities are remarkably similar from study to study. Moreover, according to Kelley and others, including James Kouzes, Barry Posner, Ira Chaleef, and Warren Bennis, the qualities found to produce effective followership are comparable to those qualities that yield effective leadership.

In comparison, people who are said to not have these qualities at a substantive level, or to have negative attributes and practices, are believed to be ineffective followers. Bjugstad and colleagues identify some of these negative qualities: "Ineffective followers are often critical, cynical, apathetic, and alienated; many will only do what is specifically requested of them; they tend to doubt themselves and, because they dwell on problems rather than solutions, they most often see their fears materialize."[93] Additional characteristics of poor followers include non self-starters who must be told what to do, and simply do not think autonomously.

In between the effective followers and the poor followers are the typical followers, who simply take direction and do not challenge the group or the leader. Also, negative attitudes such as these can spread not only to other team members, but to other areas of the organization, resulting in low morale, poor production, and what Stephen Lundin and Lynn Lancaster refer to as "lost human potential."[94]

With the importance placed on the followership role, the impact these roles have on organizational and leader effectiveness, and the proposed qualities it takes to become an effective follower, the followership literature goes one step further and offers distinct styles of followership. Kelley surmises, "Since most of us spend the majority of our time in the followership role, it stands to reason that how we perform as followers determines, for the most part, how satisfied we are with our day-to-day work existence."[95] To improve upon people's awareness of their followership abilities and roles, Kelley composed the five styles of followership, consisting of *Sheep, Yes-People, Alienated, Pragmatics,* and the *Star Followers.*[96]

Before detailing these five styles of followership, two underlying dimensions to these differing styles need to be addressed.[97] The first dimension is the *ability to be independent thinkers,* as opposed to looking for the leader to do the thinking. According to Kelley, the best followers think for themselves, give constructive criticism, and are innovative and creative. The worst followers must be told what to do or they do not even try to think for themselves. The typical followers simply take direction without fuss. The second dimension is the *amount of active engagement* practiced by the follower. The best followers take initiative and responsibility going above and beyond what is asked of them. The worst followers are lazy, require constant supervision and feedback, and shirk responsibility. Typical followers get the job done after being told what to do. Kelley believes the more effective followers find ways to balance these two important requirements of thinking for themselves and being willing to follow orders, while being flexible, then shifting from one to the other as the situation dictates. As the five styles are detailed below, the application of these two dimensions becomes apparent.[98]

- *The Sheep.* These are followers who are passive and let others do the thinking for them. In sport, coaches who make all the decisions and do all of the motivating are leading a team full of sheep. Red Auerbach of the Boston Celtics wrote, "In any team situation, followers will not create, they will not take the blame, and they will not experiment because of the possibility of making mistakes."[99] Kelley includes additional characteristics of the Sheep followership style: take action only when told to, rely solely on the decisions made by the leader, follow the crowd, and require a lot of supervision and feedback. These followers are usually in organizations where the leader does not properly recognize or reward efforts of their followers and in some cases, uses fear to keep people motivated and in line and micromanage all decisions that are made.

- *The Yes-People.* These self-professed "doers" or conformists are always on their leader's side being productive in following orders, but looking to the leader for these orders without questioning. They are not willing to think for themselves. These followers are believed to exemplify high amounts of active engagement, yet are low on critical thinking. In her review, Lisa Burke reports conformists do portray the image of a perfect team player, yet this may have its drawbacks: "While they are viewed as strong team players, over the long run they lose credibility because of their lack of fortitude and ability to think and stand for what they believe."[100] Kelley includes additional characteristics of the conformist followership style: team player, minimize conflict, nonthreatening to the leader, lack own ideas, unwilling to confront or attach themselves to an unpopular position and compromise own needs to please others. Kelley notes that those with this style tend to find themselves in the following organizational environment: adhering to the order of things is more important than the outcome, a domineering leader is present, and disagreeing with the leader is punished.[101]

- *The Alienated.* These followers do think for themselves, but are characterized as having negative energy because of their cynicism about the present situation or future action plans. A term used to denote these negative teammates is "energy vampires." Dr. Judith Orloff affirms the existence of energy vampires in her article for *The Magazine*: "Some people bring unexpected lightness and comfort to your life. They crackle with energy, practically electrify you with their presence. And then there are those who leave you feeling stressed out. Or guilty. Or exhausted down to your very last molecule. I call them energy vampires, and obnoxious or meek, they come in all forms."[102] A recent search on Amazon for "energy vampire" books results in over 1076 hits! Kelley also indicates these types of followers, "see themselves as the mavericks, the only people in the organization who have the guts to stand up to the boss," yet they are not moving or helping the organization move in the positive direction.[103] Moreover, Kelley adds that alienated followers believe their talents are underutilized, that the leaders have not lived up to their end of the bargain, and they question how they are treated in relation to others.

- *The Pragmatics.* Kelley believes pragmatic followers "see themselves as preservers of the status quo—leaders come and go; new visions come and go; if I just sit here and wait it out, I won't have to do all the work."[104] These followers are moderate in their level and amount of critical thinking and active engagement applied to their daily efforts. They tend to get on board with the organizational vision only when they see where things are headed, and most times, if it also is going to best serve their particular interests. Pragmatic followers know how to work the system (some would say they are too political) while maintaining the middle ground (risk averse), and have been found to be mediocre producers. These followers tend to perceive their organization as being impersonal, unstable, and having a political, transactional culture.[105]

- *The Star Followers.* These followers have been given the title of "go-to" players because they think for themselves, are positive in attitude and energy, and get on board if they agree with the leader and the organizational vision. However, if they disagree with either they will challenge it by offering alternatives. Some additional characteristics of this particular style include assume ownership, self-starters, support team and leader, are competent, and go above and beyond to add value to the organization. Kelley asserts, "The environments that bring out the best in star followers are those where the goals are shared by the followers. Companies without a clear identity, vision, or product have a harder time developing good followers."[106] More information is shared about exemplary followers and their particular skill sets in the next section.

Similar to leadership styles, followers may have a dominant followership style, yet depending on certain situations and dynamics, may move from one style to another. For example, a player may be dominant in one followership style around the head coach (sheep), yet adopt another style around the team captain (pragmatic). Moreover, each of these styles may be the most effective style depending on the situation. For example, a young team on the losing side of a game may be in need of a change in tactics or positions. During this learning process, it may be important to follow one voice in order to integrate all of the changes, thus, the most effective followership style for this team to adopt is the Yes-People style. Since the majority of the population is composed of followers, and his work indicates effective followers tend to act in similar ways, Kelley surmises the following percentages (Table 2) based on follower-ship style.[107]

Table 2: Percentage of Followers

TYPE OF FOLLOWER	PERCENT OF POPULATION
Passive followers (Sheep)	5–10 percent
Conformists (Yes-People)	20–30 percent
Alienated	15–25 percent
Pragmatist	25–35 percent
Star Followers (Exemplary)	30–40 percent

For more information on Kelley's followership research go to the Author Notes, along with a survey to be used to determine follower type based on how a person carries out the followership role and to help identify strengths and weaknesses in followership skills.[108] In the last section of this chapter, follow-ership skills are shared to assist those who are not star followers at the moment, but would like to change their perceptions, attitudes, and behavior to become one.

As with any discourse attempting to describe and predict social behavior, it is never as easy as labeling and categorizing. Case in point, referring to the player revolt issue addressed earlier, it is a matter of individual perspective, per-sonal bias, and context as to whether the team who rebelled against their coach is an example of bad followership because it dared to break the chain of com-mand or is an example of good followership because of the stand against per-ceived poor treatment against it? To muddy the water even further, does this particular scenario indicate a failure on the part of the leadership, the follow-ership, or both? Is the failure at the level of misinterpreting each party's moti-vations or is it the team environment stifling productive communication and trusting relationships. If so, who is to blame for this ineffective team climate? These particular dilemmas point to the importance of both parties, leaders and followers, being responsible agents of building and supporting a collabo-rative, sharing, and trusting organizational culture.

> *"Leaders are only as strong as the connections they make*
> *with each person in their constituency. Yet we continue to*
> *focus on leaders and all but ignore their impact on,*
> *and the opinions of, the people they lead."*[109]
> —Tom Rath and Barry Conchie,
> *Strengths-Based Leadership*

Great Leadership-Followership: A True Partnership

Earl Potter, William Rosenbach and Thane Pittman affirm the importance of modeling appropriate leadership and followership behaviors when they wrote, "The good news and the bad for every leader is that she or he is also a follower. Thus, every leader can understand what good leadership looks like to a follower. When you focus on followership, however, you gain insight into your own behavior as a follower."[110] It also helps develop strategies to support this partnership. For example, the coaching field has been following and will continue to follow an apprenticeship model of development. Here, before one becomes a head coach he/she puts in years as an assistant coach, possibly working with many head coaches before being given a shot at the top spot. Despite there being some anomalies, including Vinny Del Negro (current coach of the NBA Los Angeles Clippers) who never coached before being asked to coach the NBA Chicago Bulls after a long professional playing career, and Jay Heaps, who played professional soccer yet never coached before being given the reins to the MLS New England Revolution, the majority of head coaches at the collegiate and professional levels serve in the role of follower (head coach as boss), follower-leader (leader of players), and then leader (as own head coach). Having worked in the follower role, these head coaches can then model, instruct, and educate their followers (assistant coaches, support staff) on the most effective ways to fulfill their obligations and responsibilities. They can do this while embodying the values and contributions deemed most important to the organization as a whole, including partnership. They themselves have had to practice this on their way up the coaching ranks. For example, former head football coach at the University of Southern California, Pete Carroll (current coach of the NFL Seattle Seahawks), goes to extraordinary lengths to mentor his assistant coaches to be more effective in their current roles. He prepares them for future head coaching positions (one even replaced him at USC) by having them rehearse their meetings with their teams, even filming these rehearsals. He also grades his positional coaches on their coaching during practice with full debriefs post-practice on strengths and areas in need of improvement.[111]

Potter and colleagues posit two elements of organizational culture critical to developing partnership between leader and follower: *drive for performance* through a collective vision and a *commitment to effective relationships*. On the latter, there is an assumption that whoever has the most power (e.g., team captain, coach) is depended upon to create and foster relationships with those of lesser power (e.g., players). Yet, according to these authors, for true partnership to occur there is a shared responsibility for the quality of the relationship between boss and subordinate. According to Potter, "The greatest gains occur in those organizations where leaders take an active role in creating partnerships and build cultures that foster the independent initiative of followers who, with the same goals in mind, also work to create partnership."[112] This assumption is quite prevalent in scholastic and collegiate sport. Athletes and team captains must be encouraged to accept the responsibility of developing a relationship with their coaching staffs.

The goals of followership training, according to Kelley, are to "produce followers who can think for themselves, exercise their own independent, critical judgment, and act in the best interests of the organization or the society, even if doing so means going against the leader or the group."[113] Potter takes this even further, stating, "The leader who works in partnership with followers is one who can accept the initiative of followers and act in ways that encourage followers to continue to take initiative."[114] Again, echoing the responsibilities of both roles, followers must be courageous to take initiative and be willing to challenge authority, while the leader should not only accept the initiative of followers, but encourage more of it. What allows for this partnership is the relationship between the two, which does not just happen, but takes conscious work from all parties.

Another term used to denote this partnership is "reciprocal leadership." Joseph Raelin in *Creating Leaderful Organizations* illustrates a model he refers to as the "4 C's of leaderful practice," seen in Table 3.[115] In her review, Lisa Burke highlights the uniqueness of Raelin's model in that the emphasis is placed on the relational aspects of compassion, collaboration, and communication between the follower and leader.[116] Gene Dixon and Jerry Westbrook suggest every person in an organization who preaches and practices a partnership or reciprocal leadership culture, encourage and support "leader-followers," in that "there is leadership in the follower and followership in the leader."[117] On this point, Kouzes and Posner simply add, "The best leaders are the best followers."[118] James Georges, president and CEO of ParTraining Corporation, echoes this same sentiment when he states, "To be a leader, you'd better know what following is all about because the substance of leadership is followership. To serve is the ultimate value a human being has."[119]

Table 3: 4 C's of Leaderful Practice

TITLE	BEHAVIORAL DESCRIPTION
Concurrent leadership	Sharing of power and authority among group members.
Collective leadership	Every group member is an informal leader and mutually influential.
Collaborative relationships	Active discussions aimed at making every voice count.
Compassion	Treating others with respect.

Followership-Partnership Training

In order to maximize the partnership between followers and leaders, especially to transform it from dependency into co-dependency roles, Kelley, Chaleff, Patsy Blackshear and others believe situational changes, such as working conditions, procedures, roles and assignments, in addition to personal changes like improved attitudes, skills, supports and motivation, can all contribute to more effective followers. These changes can be and should be part of a followership development process. With any development process, it is obviously important that objectives are set for initial and summative evaluations of progress made and lessons learned. One example of a training development model is conceptualized by Patsy Blackshear with her followership continuum model, shown below in Figure 1. This model is used as a diagnostic measure and for developmental purposes. This copyrighted continuum is based on five stages of dynamic and changing followership performance (see Table 4).[120]

Figure 1: Blackshear's Followership Continuum

Employee	Committed Follower	Engaged Follower	Effective Follower	Exemplary Follower

Table 4: Blackshear's Followership Stages

STAGE	DESCRIPTION
Stage 1	Employees are hired and given payment for services rendered.
Stage 2	Committed followers are bought-into the organizational mission and his/her efforts mirror this commitment.
Stage 3	Engaged followers go above and beyond to help the organization.
Stage 4	Effective followers are always dependable and consistent with their efforts and contributions.
Stage 5	Exemplary followers lead themselves. Blackshear states these followers "could easily be the leader; instead, the exemplary follower sets ego aside and works to support the leader."[121]

A follower's stage profile does not remain static, as intrapersonal, interpersonal and situational changes can impact one's standing. It becomes imperative that consistent attention is given to the awareness of followers' stages and styles, and to the subsequent development of exemplary followers by leaders for improved personal and organizational productivity.

Besides the due diligence on the part of the leader to become more aware of the plight of the followers and in maintaining collaborative relationships with them, the followership literature provides training program strategies for both leaders and followers to assist in improving this partnership. This listing of ten strategies for both leaders and followers does not represent an exhaustive list, only a summation of the more cited works.

> *"The greatest leaders I've known are absolutely devoted to their people. There's no way to fake it. They put their people in the center of their thinking. You must be what you want your followers to become."*[122]
> —Gerald Bell, co-author of
> *The Carolina Way* with Dean Smith

Courageous Leaders

- Courageous leaders develop a culture of partnership and ownership characterized by shared responsibility. In her research, Blackshear summarizes the key elements for promoting exemplary followership, which include an organizational culture where initiative and risk taking are supported, not punished. This also involves leaders who are fair, respectful, and open, who also encourage two-way communication.[123]
- Ira Chaleff believes it takes courage for leaders to be active change agents in how the followership-leadership relationship is perceived and practiced in their organization. It also takes courage to shift to a more egalitarian culture. This begins by encouraging active exchange of ideas while actually listening, reacting to their followers.[124]
- According to John Hertig, to improve leadership-followership, a great place to start is to leverage existing strengths while improving weaknesses via continuous performance evaluation and honest feedback.[125]
- Before anyone will follow, leaders must consistently work to embody the top qualities indicated by the tens of thousands of followers surveyed by Kouzes and Posner. These qualities include always being honest, forward-looking, inspiring, and competent.[126]
- Enabling followers by allowing them to create their own goals will improve satisfaction and provide more meaning to their pursuits. This is in stark contrast to empowering followers, at least according to Kelley, who states, "Effective followership is not the same as empowerment. I prefer enabling rather than empowering. You're not giving people power. People have power—the organization simply gets in their way."[127]
- Find a mentor and be a mentor. Hertig asserts, "as a mentee you are a true follower; as a mentor, you are a leader—both roles are critical."[128]
- Make "intrepreneurs." Anthony Dadante, director of organization development at Harley Davidson, Inc., says, "We want our managers to see they can't do it all themselves. They have to give part of the business away to the people who work for them. They have to make them intrepreneurs. They have to be able to say they have the skills, knowledge and competencies to run the business as well as I can."[129]
- Kent Bjugstad suggests an integrated model of followership and leadership styles with implications for leaders specifically. This model holds that followers engage in different levels of critical thinking and these can be congruent with particular

leadership behaviors (as depicted in Hersey and Blanchard's situational leadership theory). For example, leaders who practice *participating* behaviors will include followers in the decision-making process. They will assist followers who are lacking confidence especially in becoming more involved and committed to the team vision. Leaders who use *selling* behaviors, such as clarifying expectations and explaining decisions, will engage even the most passive followers, since they will understand the rationale behind decisions being made. Leaders who use *telling* behaviors, which include providing detailed directions and thorough performance reviews, work especially well for those who are inexperienced and lack the necessary training. *Delegating* is the leader behavior most used when followers are self-directed and more than capable of handling additional responsibility.[130]

- Leaders should view their exemplary followers as "partners or co-creators." Kelley believes, "partners are viewed as equals—as equals, they decide how to work together, to share power, and to reward individual and joint contributions so that the partnership succeeds."[131] For a true partnership to occur, the following actions should occur (Kelley): (1) information must be shared; (2) evaluation should be done on both parties' performances; (3) partners co-create the vision and mission of the team; and (4) partners share the risks and rewards.[132]

- It is paramount that leaders support the conditions of courageous followership by responding productively to acts of courageous followership. They can do this by encouraging taking initiative and risk taking. They can ask for, and actually listen to, followers' opinions, supporting a culture of followership in the team or organization. Ira Chaleff includes other areas that will aid in improving the conditions for followership: "The leader's openness to diversity, empowering others, breakthrough thinking, and being challenged and learning from followers."[133]

> "If we are to attain the empowerment we crave, we must accept responsibility for both our own roles and the roles of our leaders. Only by accepting this dual responsibility do we ultimately accept responsibility for our organizations and the people they serve."[134]
> —Ira Chaleff, *The Courageous Follower*

Courageous Followers

- Chaleff asserts there are three things powerful followers must understand to fully assume the responsibility illustrated in the quote above: (1) their own power and how to use it, not succumbing to the negative stereotypes of followership; (2) value and contributions leaders provide and how to better assist them by maximizing their strengths; (3) how power corrupts and how they can help those they work with not fall prey to the "dark tendency of power."[135]

- Chaleff outlines five dimensions of courageous followership to aid in improving the leader-follower relationship for the benefit of themselves, leaders, and organization: (1) courage to assume responsibility; (2) courage to serve and work hard for the leader and team; (3) courage to challenge the leader or organization by voicing concerns that may impact personal ethics or a common purpose; (4) courage to be committed change agents for the betterment of the team or organization; (5) courage to take moral action if needed.[136]

- Learn and practice the qualities it takes to be considered an effective follower from Kelley's four essential qualities, including: being self-managers, believing in a cause greater than themselves, committing to lifelong learning, and holding themselves to the highest of professional and ethical expectations.[137]
- Seek opportunities to be one's own advocate by continual networking and seeking new opportunities for growth and advancement.
- Find a mentor and be a mentor.
- Always present solutions and alternatives to problems. Hertig believes "good followers learn not only to identify problems but also to develop and suggest solutions to the problems; you will gain more respect and develop into a successful practitioner the more you look into the solution rather than only identifying the problem."[138]
- Create one's own goals. James Georges, consulting firm CEO states, "How can anyone lead you without taking you somewhere you want to go? People with no goals of their own cannot be led because they have nowhere they want to go."[139]
- Embrace motives for becoming a more effective follower (see Kelley's seven paths to followership presented earlier).
- Ira Chaleff affirms courageous followers must be willing to be change agents for leaders who are not open to changing their philosophies and practices about followership by doing little to share their power by inviting feedback and encouraging collective participation from all parties.
- Develop the *courageous conscience*. Those courageous followers who see the need to confront leaders should follow Kelley's ten steps to courageous confrontation.[140] In Kelley's words, to do so will "substantially increase the chance that your ethical stands will carry the day and limit the fallout on your careers."[141] The 10 steps include (1) be proactive by anticipating ethical problems before they occur; (2) get agreement with the leader on the facts involved; (3) be able to bounce the facts off of a trusted, outside advisor before confronting the leader; (4) be prepared to be challenged— work on building fortitude on a daily basis; (5) work the system and show a sense of community by following the chain of command, whether that be meeting with the leader in private first or through an intermediary, whichever is the usual course of action; (6) phrase the issue or argument in terms that match the vision of the team so the leader can see the direct impact it has on team success or failure; (7) educate others as to the positive projections of the particular stand, especially as it applies to them and their needs, which follows the maxim: "you can get anything in this world if it helps people get what they want"[142]; 8) attempt to get collective support for this particular stand—there truly is strength in numbers; (9) According to Kelley, "If all your good-faith actions prove fruitless, you may have to resort to higher authorities—this is a very risky action, since many organizations have strong norms against

breaking the chain of command."[143] In collegiate athletics, it is most preferred for dissatisfied athletes to communicate with the head coach first on any issues. If that is not do-able for whatever reason, assistant coaches or support staff can be effective in airing a grievance. Finally, going to a higher authority, the particular administrator assigned to that sport, is a viable option for some. Athletic directors usually favor this procedure rather than teams or individual athletes approaching them directly. Teams should be encouraged to utilize their team leadership first (captains), then their coaching staff and head coach to communicate problem issues rather than proceeding immediately to the top administrator. This is frowned upon by most coaches and administrators; (10) Despite this not applying to collegiate athletes, Kelley's final step is to have the "financial and emotional cushions to exercise other alternatives."[144] Be prepared to have another position lined up before making a stand that could cost this courageous follower his or her job.

> *"Schools treat peer pressure as a leadership issue when
> actually it's a followership issue. They believe that if they
> teach leadership skills, they will alleviate the negative effects of
> peer pressure. A better approach may be to teach better followership
> skills. Kids need to learn how to protect themselves from leaders who
> encourage them to engage in either self-destructive or socially destructive
> behavior, as well as learn how to support positive leaders."[145]*
>
> —Robert Kelley,
> *The Power of Followership*

– 12 –

Developing a Culture of Leadership: The Six "T" Process (LDP)

"Institutionalizing a leadership-centered culture
is the ultimate act of leadership."[1]
—John P. Kotter, leadership professor,
Harvard Business School

A theme woven throughout this book is that leadership is so much more of a *process* than simply a role or a position. It can be learned and developed. It is in this *process* that young leaders can not only be identified through sound recruiting practices or discovered after their arrival (the Maryland Terrapins are addressed as an example later), but they are challenged to take on leadership opportunities. They learn best while "on the job," and with continual reinforcement, mentoring, and modeling. In time this (leadership) apprenticeship blossoms into true, empowering leadership. The *process* of identifying, recruiting, cultivating, teaching, and reinforcing leadership cannot be a one-time thing, or a once-a-month thing as part of a "leadership institute" (a concept becoming a popular methodology used by some universities and organizations). An empowering and enabling *process* must be engrained in the organization from top to bottom and referred to and reinforced on a regular basis. This entails having leadership become an integral part of the culture of the organization or team. The first step is to define what culture is and how it can be applied and its effect on corporate and sport organizations.

"I'm not saying that business is like football. I am saying that
people are people, and that the keys to motivating them and getting
them to perform to their full potential are pretty much the same whether
they're playing on a football field or working in an office."[2]
—Bill Parcells, former NFL head coach

223

Defining—Developing a Culture of Success

The word culture as it is referred to here has been defined as "the behaviors and beliefs characteristic of a particular social, ethnic, or age group."[3] Kotter in *Leading Change* defines it similarly as the "norms or behavior and shared values among a group of people" and cites its importance, "because it can powerfully influence human behavior, because it can be difficult to change, and because its near invisibility makes it hard to address directly."[4] The importance of culture is detailed as it applies to team barriers, team building, and the important work of Pat Lencioni in Chapter 10. Similar to Kotter's statement about culture's invisibility, Michael Dell, the CEO of Dell Computer, is quoted as saying. "Culture is one of those things where you know it when you see it, but it's a little bit hard to describe."[5] Despite the difficulty, he goes on to describe the culture at Dell Computer as very results-oriented, stressing the importance of setting goals, and acknowledging these goals being met as a very powerful reinforcement of this culture. Another exceptional leader, Wal-Mart's David Glass, believes most managers fail to see the importance of culture: "I think it's way underestimated how important the culture has been to the company's success."[6]

Edgar Schein in *Organizational Culture and Leadership* defines three levels of organizational culture: artifacts, values and underlying assumptions.[7] The first layer is what the public sees as representative of the culture, the *artifacts* such as company logo, slogans, branding, or vision-mission statements. The next level, *values,* can be seen by how team members interact with the leaders and each other and what beliefs the team rallies around, such as optimal play, trusting relationships, or a family atmosphere. The deepest level, *underlying beliefs,* is most emphasized and reinforced by all members of the organization. For example, according to Nick Saban and his Alabama Crimson Tide football program (repeat BCS national champions), the underlying assumption is no one can do what they do any better. This process is predicated on their "on and off–the-field performance" standard, "Be champions on and off the field." During the season there is never talk of winning a national championship, it is always about their process, and it is the collective belief in this process that will lead them to ultimate success.[8]

Complementing the three levels of team culture are the three types of culture. John Kotter and James Heskett detail these different cultures: "A *strong* culture is one in which the organization has an evident, notable style. A *strategically appropriate* culture is one that appropriately fits within its current internal and external environment. Finally, an *adaptive* culture is one that assists members to anticipate and adapt to environmental change."[9] Their research on these three types of organizational culture reveals positive correlations between strong cultures and strategically appropriate cultures with performance. However, the best performing teams were those organizations characterized as using an adaptive culture. Other results reveal that better performing organizations place greater importance on leadership and value their primary stakeholders (e.g., customers, employees) significantly more than lower performing ones.

Marshall Sashkin and Molly Sashkin, in *Leadership That Matters,* write that many leaders and consultants believe culture can be imposed on teams/organizations through the use of rituals and ceremonies, or by storytelling or rallying behind a "hero" leader. Although these activities can be useful in reinforcing an existing culture, they fall short when a change in culture is needed most. The authors suggest instead to "define values and beliefs and make them 'live' in the actions of people in an organization." This process takes the following form: (1) define the philosophy and vision of the organization; (2) work collectively to determine policies and procedures that put the philosophy into action; (3) leaders then model the values and beliefs into their daily actions.[10] A quote by Albert Schweitzer best exemplifies this last step: "Example is not the main thing in influencing others ... it is the *only* thing."[11]

There is very little empirical work on the culture of sport organizations, yet one recent study, conducted by Joe Frontiera, consists of interviews with six owners or general managers from the following professional leagues: NBA, MLB, and the NFL (including Dan Rooney from the Pittsburgh Steelers and Bill Polian from the Indianapolis Colts). These interviews inquire about the methodologies used in changing their organizations' cultures following losing seasons. Interestingly, symptoms of a dysfunctional climate vary across the three levels of climate, namely artifacts, values and underlying assumptions. For example, problematic *artifacts* include poor facilities and win-loss records, while the *values* are considered negative and not conducive to success (selfishness), and the underlying *assumptions* involve team members becoming accustomed to mediocrity, for example, "we're a mid-market club." Embedding the new culture, according to these general managers and owners, takes a consistent focus on the plan, upgrading personnel and facilities, demonstrating greater respect to players, making better decisions ("money could not be the primary driver behind decisions"), and being open to new ideas ("because you don't want to get stuck with the same ideas that were brought in 12 years ago"). Changing an organization's culture, especially in professional sport, is a risky endeavor, but one well worth the risk. Edgar Shein echoes this sentiment when he states, "the bottom line for leaders is that if they do not become conscious of the cultures in which they are embedded, those cultures will manage them."[12]

In the sport context, coaches often refer to the difficult challenge of changing a "losing culture," or a team that has been stuck in a losing spiral, into a winning culture. One former coach, NFL great Bill Parcells, who has successfully changed more than a few teams' cultures from losing to winning ones, writes about this process in an article for *Harvard Business Review*. What Coach Parcells does to build a culture of success includes: (1) establishing clear goals that are within reach (e.g., well-conditioned team, hard-playing team, prideful team); (2) accentuating the positives, especially when the team acts in a way to meet the previous goals; (3) always being honest with people, even if it leads to uncomfortable confrontations ("confrontation is healthy"); (4) applying pressure to get the most out of people ("provides an opportunity to get things straight with people"); (5) conducting one-on-one conversations with every member of the organization; (6) picking the right people. Finally, Parcells did not wait to earn his leadership, he imposed it ("to lead, you've got to be a leader").[13] Coach Parcells states that building this culture of success is not something done overnight: "You have to go one step at a time, the same way you move the ball down the field, yard by yard."[14]

What Coach Parcells did not emphasize in this article, however, was those who did not meet their performance expectations were let go. That is the harsh reality in professional football, as it is in most sports, and also in business. Alan Murray, deputy managing editor of the *Wall Street Journal,* writes getting rid of poor performers is crucial to maintaining a culture of excellence: "In the end, success at maintaining a high-performing culture requires the use of both carrots and sticks."[15] Murray includes a quote from Jack Welch, who was nicknamed "Neutron Jack" for his cutting of costs and work force in his early days at GE: "You have to go along with a can of fertilizer in one hand and water in the other and constantly throw both on the flowers. If they grow, you have a beautiful garden. If they don't, you cut them out. That's what management is all about."[16]

Bill Walsh helped turn a 2–14 San Francisco 49ers team into Super Bowl champions in 24 months. Armed with his "standards of performance," Coach Walsh set out to implement these standards to transform the entire organization. He defined his standards of performance as "a way of doing things, a leadership philosophy that has as much to do with core values, principles, and ideals as with blocking, tackling, and passing; more to do with the mental than with the physical."[17] He believed the implementation of his standards of performance would produce an organizational culture that would become the foundation for winning games. As he stated, "The culture precedes positive results. It doesn't get tacked on as an afterthought on your way to the victory stand. Champions behave like champions before they're champions; they have a winning standard of performance before they are winners."[18] Coach Walsh created a culture for the entire organization, similar to what Seth Godin writes about in his book, *Tribes*. A tribe is a "group of people connected to one another, connected to a leader, and connected to an idea."[19] Godin believes an effective leader "creates a culture around their goal and involves others in that culture."[20]

Another coach who helped turn a team's failures into success is Paul Azinger, captain of the 2008 Ryder Cup champion team. In his book, *Cracking the Code,* Azinger echoes the importance of culture: "I did whatever I could to build our culture of confidence while communicating our goal and our role in the public arena."[21] The Ryder Cup is a golf tournament played every two years, pitting the best players from Europe against their American counterparts. Prior to the 2008 Ryder Cup win for Azinger's U.S. team, the European team won three championships in a row. Azinger, with the help of team building experts, formulated his teams based on a "pod" system, linking players based on behavioral, relational and personality patterns. They even allowed these pods to choose their final roster spot, referred to as "captain's picks." By incorporating emotional and relational intelligence in the selection and building of this and embodying a culture of confidence and togetherness, captain Azinger strongly believed in the potential of this team: "I knew we were going into the matches with something America really needed: a cohesive, bonded, sell-out-for-each-other-at-every-turn team."[22]

Creating and reinforcing a particular culture for a team or organization can galvanize people collectively around the vision set forth and ultimately, a united tribe. With the university and elite teams with which I consult, the underlying mantra that defines the culture of each team is a "player-driven" team. Each team member, along with the coaching and support staff, is part of the process of establishing the vision for the team and the daily standards. Yet it is the team that drives not just the coaching staff. It is the team members who hold each other accountable to the team standards. It is the team that offers encouragement and support in tough times. It is the team members who set the tone for the practice and matches. At the center of this player-driven team culture is the work of the internal team leadership: the captains, assistant captains, the apprentice captains, and the unified voice of the followers and the collective voice of all. To enable this player-driven culture to run at peak efficiency and functionality takes much more than a leadership workshop, or monthly leadership meetings or team bonding activities. It takes a culture of leadership development and training.

"Great teams have multiple leaders, multiple voices.
A major part of building a team is discovering who those
voices will be and cultivating them, making sure their
leadership is established within your group."[23]

—Mike Krzyzewski,
Team USA/Duke University basketball coach

Defining—Developing a Culture of Leadership

In the process of creating and reinforcing a culture of success and kinship (or tribe), there are sport coaches who are subscribing to the importance of developing team leaders as an essential aspect to this global objective. The quote above by Coach Krzyzewski highlights the importance he places on establishing a culture of leadership at Duke University, where he coaches basketball, but also on the U.S. teams he has led to gold medals. More on what he does to develop a culture of leadership later.

In an issue of *Bloomberg Businessweek,* Jena McGregor shares a story about another successful college coach who stumbled upon leadership development almost by accident.[24] Mired in a disappointing 2000 season, the men's soccer coach at the University of Maryland, Sasho Cirovski, believes he did a good job recruiting talent, yet a poor job recruiting leaders. He alleges the latter was the crux of the team's problems. Frustrated by the lack of a captain who had team respect on and off the field (the two best players on the team were serving in the role of captain), Cirovski called his brother, Vancho, a human resource vice president for a health care company, for advice. Upon hearing of his brother's struggles, Vancho recommended the team complete a social network analysis survey used to identify "off-the-radar" leaders used for organizational development purposes. The results revealed one player, Scotty Buete, who was not a captain or the team's best player, as a bigger influence on the team than anyone had thought. As a result, this player was voted the third captain. Almost instantly the team rallied around him, and each other. This new captain even scored the game-winning goal in the first match since being named captain. Cirovski notes, "Scotty was the glue, and I didn't see it." Cirovski calls this change a defining moment that helped his team play in four straight college cups (soccer's version of the final four), winning the title in the fifth year. Coach Cirovski continues to use these team-leadership surveys, emphasizes recruiting leaders and not just talented players, and reinforces the culture of team leadership.

In a follow-up article about Vancho Cirovski and his team building-leadership survey method, Cirovski states there are two main components of organizational excellence: mastery (culture) and chemistry (communication, connectedness). In a sporting sense, mastery is the domain of coaches, while chemistry is the connectedness and integration of the players on and off the field. According to Cirovski, whether it's business or sport, the formula is the same. "Most organizations have some issues," Cirovski says. "It flows from trust and mutates into fear. It all hinges on leaders, their values and belief systems. The success of an organization can be found in social capital (interaction) rather than in the structure of hierarchy. It's the mesh of relationships."[25]

Although previously mentioned, Mike Krzyzewski's (Coach K) work in developing a culture of leadership is deserving of more attention, as he did not come about it accidentally. His vision of leadership comes from his experience as a cadet, then a coach at West Point. He was also mentored by some of the best coaches in the game, including Bob Knight, Henry Iba, and Pete Newell. In an interview for the *Academy of Management Learning & Education* journal, he outlines the framework for the leadership culture, not only at Duke University, but with his gold medal winning U.S. Olympic men's basketball teams. The take-away points (with quoted excerpts) from this interview are seen below as they apply to developing leaders at the highest levels of sport.[26]

(1) Coach K begins this process of recruiting leaders by watching them on their high school teams: "So I already know this kid has leadership ability, he has good communication skills, he is somebody who could lead by example or verbally."

(2) Coach K recruits leaders by looking for character: "So character is a significant part of our recruiting. I want to see that the kid is someone who will listen to his coach, that he has shown respect to his parents and other authorities he has dealt with, and that he is willing to learn."

(3) Once they join the Duke team, Coach K provides them opportunities to show their leadership: "You want to make sure that as you are developing your senior leaders, you don't stifle a freshman who has great leadership qualities."

(4) Since each season brings with it new players and a different team dynamic, Coach K has to consistently adjust systems and strategies to these changes, including adjusting to his new leaders: "I try to adjust my leadership based on who I have to help me lead the team." Yet what he does not adjust or change is the culture of success and leadership: "There are a lot of different dynamics right now in our sport. The thing that we do know is that we're going to make sure our own culture is the same."

(5) In identifying his leaders, Coach K is cognizant of not trying to change them, only to help them play to their strengths and work to improve their leadership skills: "We want to keep their strengths while working on their leadership. I have had other guys who just led the whole team, and being a leader helped them become better players. But that is not always the case."

(6) To aid in getting everybody on a team to help provide leadership, Coach K connects with many of the players on a daily basis, especially when he was coaching the Olympic team: "I made it a point to talk to four to six guys every day, and about things other than basketball. I got to know them as people, which helped me understand the dynamics that I had to work with on the team."

(7) Coach K also asks for team feedback when it comes to establishing team standards, both with the Duke team and the Olympic team: "We had a great meeting in which we came up with 15 standards. Each of those guys put their hand up; they took ownership. It was no longer just their talent, now it was also the things they said."

(8) To aid in his continual development as a leader, Coach K continues to learn about leadership by getting outside of his area: "You can learn about being a better leader from everybody. You can go and study an orchestra. You can go study a basketball team, a business, or whatever. That's why I love talking about leadership. There is so much you can do to develop it."

Coach K shares additional leadership nuggets in his book, *The Gold Standard: Building a World-Class Team,* which chronicles the gold-medal winning 2008 Olympic team he coached. In the chapter "Time to Cultivate Leadership," he mentions principles used to establish a culture of leadership on this most elite of teams. The takeaway points are below.[27]

(1) Great teams have multiple leaders, thus, multiple voices that should be cultivated, allowing the team leader to not be the only voice that is heard.

(2) Team leaders must have a solid relationship with internal leaders so they are working as one collective unit.

(3) Team leaders must realize at times the players will have a better feel or read on team situations, and those players should be trusted to guide the team: "It is their feel for the game that should guide the way you coach, as well."

(4) Team leaders also must realize that someone else may be able to express something better than they, and these additional voices should be free to step in: "A leader doesn't have an exclusive contract on getting a point across. You have to have enough confidence in your leadership to share it."

(5) Team leaders should make an assessment on how long the team's attention span is: "I am not the first to point out that attention spans seem to grow shorter and shorter with each generation." Additional leadership voices should be used to extend that if needed.

(6) With the Olympic team, the team did not name captains. "We found that the most effective way to develop leadership among this group of men and professional players was to allow it to emerge." The internal leaders Coach K relied on for leadership were LeBron James, Kobe Bryant, and Jason Kidd. "They were completely committed to the group, to me, and to our mission."

This section shared three snapshots, along with some of the methodology adopted for its consistent and effective application, from revered coaches who have firmly established leadership development programs. Based on this previously cited work, and those from experts from business and leadership, the next section delves deeper into the formulation of leadership culture through sequential stages. These stages are referred to as the 6 T's: *Testing, Teaching, Training, Transferring, Transforming,* and *Tradition.*

> *"A culture of leadership excellence and integrity is created when people at all levels genuinely expect each other to be credible, and they hold each other accountable for the actions that build and sustain credibility."*[28]
> —James Kouzes and Barry Posner,
> *The Truth About Leadership*

The 6 T's to Developing a Leadership Culture

Being an effective and credible leader and follower entails being the example by the talents one *has* (humility, toughness, character-in-action, competence, communicative abilities and inspiration), as well as what one *does* (techniques of collaboration, connection, confidence enhancement, communication, competitive climate and conflict-change management), and *how* one gets it accomplished (tactics of using debriefs, facilitating effective meetings, having perspective, awareness and balance, being a change agent and a go-to leader, and making the most of leadership moments). When one reads through the take-away messages from Coach K, the talents, techniques, and tactics he possesses and applies to create such a work of art in developing a culture of leadership become apparent. Being cognizant of seeing these qualities and practices in ourselves and in others is a valuable awareness and reflective exercise. As was pointed out by Coach K earlier, a great deal can be learned about leadership from anyone, anywhere. This process begins with each individual leader.

The 6 T process represents a compilation of techniques and tactics used by experts in organizational dynamics and leadership development programming. As stated by Albert Einstein, "The secret to creativity is knowing how to hide your sources."[29] I did not heed this advice, however. These sources are cited so if more information is desired it can be obtained through the Author Notes section. It is amazing the quality and depth of information contained in the books, newsletters, and journals from the business, organizational psychology, and leadership fields, written by the best thinkers and practitioners. Although organized for this book, the 6 T's are built and based on the work of these experts. To borrow the words of David Kord Murray, I did "borrow brilliance" in the organization of this last chapter, and for that matter, for the content throughout this book. In his book, *Borrowing Brilliance,* Murray states,

"Ideas are constructed out of other ideas, there are no truly original thoughts, you can't make something out of nothing, you have to make it out of something else. It's the law of cerebral physics. Ideas are born of other ideas, built on and out of ideas that came before. That's why I say that brilliance is borrowed."[30] I cannot agree more.

As stated earlier, this 6 T process begins with an introspection of personal leadership. Leaders who want to mentor and teach leadership to their assistants, support staff, or team captains should first go through the 6 T's themselves to learn as much as they can about their own leadership skill set. This will reveal strengths, challenges, and areas for improvement. The material will become more credible, personalized, and empowering by immersing oneself in these exercises and lessons, rather than simply deferring them to others to complete. The 6 T's include:

(1) *Testing:* Assessing the presence of leadership talents, techniques, tactics, strengths, and weaknesses, while reflecting on deeper motives and inspirations that define you and the roles you play in your social world.

(2) *Teaching:* How to analyze the material from the "testing" stage to learn more about yourself and how best to teach and mentor others about your experiences, their experiences, and about how to become more effective followers and leaders.

(3) *Training:* How to practice leadership daily while being skilled enough to use the right style for the right situation and learning from both mistakes and successes.

(4) *Transferring:* Ability to transfer leadership strengths and lessons learned from one situation to another, while looking for and learning about other potential solutions and/or methods for problem solving.

(5) *Transforming:* How to become more effective at influencing others and maximizing leadership opportunities, not only for personal growth, but for the greater good of others and the program or organization.

(6) *Traditions:* Ability to imprint leadership traditions into the fabric of the team: its standards, identity, vision, and daily pursuits, both short and long term.

> *"Leadership is first and foremost an individual capability and leadership development is first and foremost an individual experience."*[31]
> —Jay Conger and Beth Benjamin,
> *Building Leaders*

(1) Testing Leadership Talent, Techniques and Tactics

The primary aim of this first stage is to test or assess one's current leadership skill set and beliefs/knowledge about leadership and followership. This assessment step has been conducted in the business world against the backdrop of formalized assessment tools. However, another less formal method is to assess one's skill set compared with others, especially those "gold standards" such as the Coach Ks of the world, the charismatic CEOs who are in the news, or prior credible leaders in one's past, or even against what leadership experts have said "good to great" leaders do. Both methods can be quite educational in finding out more about one's predispositions, beliefs, actions, and how close or how far one is from those believed to be the models. Even though the formalized assessment tools have been found to be valid indicators of social, emotional, and psychological variables believed to be related to leadership effectiveness, no survey available can accurately predict future success as a leader since leadership is much too complex to measure.

> *"The goal of self-awareness is self-knowledge, and ultimate*
> *self-acceptance. Self-acceptance as the leader you are as*
> *well as the leader you are capable of becoming."*[32]
> —Bill George, Andrew Mclean and Nick Craig,
> *Finding Your True North: A Personal Guide*

Self-Awareness and Regulation

In this particular leadership development program, no standardized surveys are used and social comparison methods are minimized in favor of a more self-referenced method based on improving self-awareness and self-regulation. Self-awareness is defined as "the ability to recognize and understand your moods, emotions, and drives as well as your effect on others."[33] Those who are self-aware know their skill sets, are aware of any internal changes to their mental or emotional state, and the impact their behaviors may have on others. Another key process critical for improved awareness is self-regulation, defined as "the ability to control or redirect disruptive impulses and moods; the ability to think before acting and to suspend judgment."[34] According to Bill George, those who are effective self-regulators are able to gain a full understanding of matters before making decisions. They keep themselves composed in crises, and when critical feedback is delivered, they are able to receive and respond to the feedback constructively without lashing out defensively. Effective self-regulators are quite adept at employing sound emotional and relational intelligence cues and respond accordingly to maximize their effect on others.

Despite the emphasis on improving upon intrapersonal awareness at this first stage, obtaining feedback from others also stresses the importance of hearing from the prime beneficiaries and collaborators, mostly the team leaders' teammates and coaches. Becoming a more effective leader begins with being able to manage and lead oneself first. Alan Murray echoes this sentiment when he writes, "This challenge, managing yourself, is the greatest challenge you face."[35] J.C. Maxwell seconds this: "The toughest person to lead is ourselves, primarily due to the notion that we judge others by their actions yet we judge ourselves by our intentions, so despite us acting inappropriately as long as our motives were good we let ourselves off the hook."[36] He continues, "The smallest crowd you will ever lead is you, but it's the most important one. If you do that well, then you will earn the right to lead even bigger crowds."[37]

Another challenge Murray presents is the difficult task of sorting out the distinction between what feels right and what is right, then acting on it: "You must constantly ask yourself: Am I doing this because it is right for me? Or because it is right for the organization?"[38] Murray offers some advice that is revised into check points to gauge how effective one is at making this distinction daily.[39] This is a big step toward being a better manager of oneself.

- Do you resist the urge to always win?
- Do you insist on making good ideas even better?
- Do you make snap judgments about the ideas that come your way?
- Do you make sarcastic comments to others?
- Do you make comments like "I already knew that" to show how smart you are?
- Do you speak when angry?
- Do you withhold information, or dispense it sparingly?
- Do you claim undue credit or fail to give proper recognition?
- Do you make excuses?
- Are you willing to admit mistakes?
- Are you a good listener?

Testing oneself at this frequency ("constantly asking yourself ...") is why the concept of "awareness-gaining perspective" is included in the six most referred tactics of effective leaders in Chapter 9. To recall, gaining perspective and improved awareness includes rich concepts such as *thinking gray, being open-minded to other perspectives, seeing things from the balcony,* and *balancing responsibilities.* John Kotter avows that remarkably few people use simple techniques, for whatever reason, such as those previously mentioned, including listening with an open mind, trying new things, reflecting honestly on successes and failures, especially when they are doing well in their careers.[40] Being more aware, while maintaining control over oneself, will help leaders, young and old, inexperienced or experienced, continue to grow and experience new levels to their leadership.

On this point, psychologist Abraham Maslow originated the concept of "self-actualization," the top tier of his "Hierarchy of Needs," in a 1943 paper, "A Theory of Human Motivation." This model represents human potential, beginning from the most basic physical needs and progressing to higher-order needs such as esteem and actualizing one's potential and even further discovery into self-transcendence.[41] Harvey Dorfman applies this theory of human potential and self-actualization to sport coaching by challenging coaches to reflect on their personal efforts at developing these specific characteristics. Dorfman surmises the outstanding coaches, or as he names them, the self-actualized coaches, use self-examination practices for personal and professional growth. He argues this helps coaches become more aware of who they have been, who they are, and who they would like to become. The list below indicates the characteristics of self-actualized coaches.[42] To improve on awareness, read and reflect on these ten areas to identify areas of strengths, as well as those characteristics in need of more attention and improvement.

- Accepting of oneself
- Realistic in one's perceptions of oneself and others
- Independent
- Able to be a decision maker
- Spontaneous
- Willing to delegate authority to others
- Able to communicate a sense of humor
- Creative
- Concerned for the well-being of others
- Capable of having close and satisfying relationships with one's athletes

> *"Becoming a better leader requires constant reflection—*
> *making sense of your experience and then discovering ways*
> *to use your insights to increase your impact."*[43]
> —Stewart Friedman, *Total Leadership*

Self-Reflection

One of the primary tools used by self-actualized leaders to improve self-awareness and self-regulation is self-reflection. Eric Kail, leadership instructor at the U.S. Military Academy, writes, "Reflection is the ideal synthesis of what we have learned and what we have done, and there are things to be learned by reflecting on both our successes and failures as leaders. Reflection makes a leader greater than the sum of just his or her experiences and things he or she has learned."[44] In this book (evidenced by the checklists by Murray and Dorfman above, and more to come) and in the plethora of leadership books on the market, there is no limit to the number of reflective questions/exercises available to readers wanting to examine themselves in different and deeper ways. In his research, Bill George has found that authentic, self-actualized leaders use many methods of reflection for gaining deeper self-awareness, including journaling, answering self-reflective questions, meditation, prayer, speaking with close confidants about personal issues, scripting your life story and sharing with others, especially in direct reports, talking with a leadership coach, sitting quietly, obtaining direct and honest feedback from others, and physical exercise.[45] Kail recommends setting aside time each day for reflection, even if it is on the drive home from the field or on an afternoon run.

George offers two tips for making these practices effective. The first is to be honest with oneself and be able to open oneself up and bounce things off of at least one other person. Second, develop regular habits of reflection, which should be scheduled into your daily life. Although quite difficult to do since time is probably your hardest resource to reserve, it is critical that leaders take and make the time for themselves for reflection. Lieutenant Colonel Sean Hannah, director of Leadership and Management Studies at the U.S. Military Academy, also states active reflection does require a dedicated effort, especially when a leader wants to go beyond simply thinking to a deeper level. He refers to this as "thinking about thinking." Hannah describes this very important process of active reflection in the following way: "This is the difference between deciding how to best lead in a given situation (thinking) versus determining whether you are processing that decision in the best way (thinking about thinking)."[46] He mentions sample questions at this level of thinking, including, "How are my values represented in this decision?" and "How are my personality and emotions affecting the way I am leading?" Hannah believes through continual reflective practice, possibly via a leader reflective journal, leaders can focus more on where they are going (such as leading their players and team), while automating the ability to productive self-awareness habits such as thinking about thinking.

As hinted earlier, the Appendices have numerous self-reflective questions and surveys designed for improving self-awareness and self-regulation. These surveys are not psychometrically analyzed for validity or reliability, they are used as an educational and awareness exercise only. *Appendix 1* is designed to improve a leader's awareness of leadership styles across the six styles covered in Chapter 6: Visionary, Coaching, Affiliative, Democratic, Pacesetting, and Commanding styles. *Appendix 2* tests a leader's 12 leadership talents (Chapter 7) and 12 techniques/tactics (Chapters 8 and 9). *Appendix 3* is a listing of 18 reflective questions team sport leaders answer as they embark on the leadership development process facilitated here. *Appendix 4* is a form to be completed by the team leader's teammates to provide information about the leader's talents, techniques, and tactics, along with a sample summary sheet (*Appendix 5*) of the results of a team exercise utilizing this form. This form can also be used to vote for team leaders.

In their present form, these questions and surveys can be completed by the individual leader in addition to having a coach, a fellow captain, and selected teammates complete the same survey. This is an attempt to get a clearer picture of the skill sets embodied by the leader from many angles and from many positions of leadership—the leader at the top (head coach), fellow team leaders (fellow captains), supportive leaders (fellow seniors, support staff), followers (teammates), and other stakeholders (family, friends, fans, recruits). As stated by Green Bay Packers legendary coach and leader Vince Lombardi, "Leadership begins with self-knowledge."[47] The goal is for this section and the supporting Appendices to assist leaders with this important self-knowledge process.

> *"Leadership seems to be the marshalling of skills possessed by a majority but used by a minority. But it's something that can be learned by anyone, taught to everyone, denied to no one."*[48]
> —Warren Bennis and Burt Nanus,
> *Leaders: The Strategies for Taking Charge*

(2) Teaching and Learning Evangelists

Another common theme shared throughout this book is leadership can be learned by anyone. Bennis and Nanus echo this idea in the above quote. Bennis goes even further when detailing the importance of both aspects of this process, teaching and learning: "By its very nature, teaching homogenizes, both its subjects and its objects. Learning, on the other hand, liberates. The more we know about ourselves and our world, the freer we are to achieve everything we are capable of achieving."[49] He also goes so far as to say managerial skills can be taught, yet leadership cannot be taught, but rather learned through lived experience:

"Managerial skills can, of course, be taught. And they are useful skills for leaders to have. The ingredients of leadership cannot be taught, however. They must be learned."[50] Equating this to sport coaching, the managerial skills of game preparation, game planning, quality control, staff coordination of duties and player management (playing time) can indeed be taught. These skills are usually taught through an apprentice system in which an assistant coach watches and learns these skills and techniques from his head coach. Yet with leadership, the essential skills, techniques and tactics must be learned through attempted leadership, one experience at a time ("practiced" to use a sport term), and evaluated for effectiveness and appropriate fit for the specific situation. This evaluation should be done through personal reflection and feedback from others. More on the importance of intrapersonal and interpersonal feedback is found in the next section, Training. This often-cited approach to learning leadership is referred to as action learning.

> *"The more you're engaged in learning the more successful you are at leading."*[51]
> —James Kouzes and Barry Posner,
> *The Truth About Leadership*

Action Learning

Action learning describes any educational experiences using action as a primary mechanism. These primarily take the form of experiential activities since participants are active in the process of learning. Jay Conger and Beth Benjamin describe action learning for business leaders as using specific issues from their own companies, specifically: "These formats involve a continuous process of learning and reflection built around working groups of colleagues, more often with the aim of getting work-related initiatives accomplished."[52] These authors also reveal these learning experiences are not only for the individual participants, but for the organization as a whole. In the sport setting, it is important to encapsulate this view when providing leadership development training for team captains by immersing the captains in real-world, real-time team issues the coaches are presently attempting to handle. In this fashion, the coaching staff is working in collaboration with the team captains to find a solution to an issue or move the organization forward. For example, on one team the star player continued to distance herself via her hubris and entitlement attitudes. Over several meetings, the coaches and captains met, along with the captains and the team, then finally a meeting with coaches, captains and team (with the exclusion of the star player), to determine if this team was better off with or without her. All sides presented their cases and through this collaborative initiative, it was determined if the star player followed a list of team-oriented behaviors determined by the group, she would be allowed to stay. Upon hearing about the meetings and the urgency of the situation she placed herself in, this player did commit to the behavioral standards. As it turned out, she was a key contributor as this team came a few points away from winning a national championship. Throughout this process, not only did the captains learn how to problem solve in a collaborative fashion, but all involved learned valuable lessons about leadership, followership, and how much can be accomplished when people are given an opportunity to contribute to real-world, real-time organizational issues.

In *The Leadership Challenge,* Kouzes and Posner posit there are four different approaches to learning: (1) *taking action* or trial and error learning; (2) *thinking* by reading articles, books, and web references to gain knowledge; (3) *feeling* by reflecting and confronting oneself about what one is worrying over; (4) *accessing others* by using trusting relationships as a sounding board.[53] In an empirical study, these authors find that managers who are more engaged in the use of these four approaches are more effective leaders, measured by the significance of their leadership behaviors (made a big acquisition, negotiated a major contract, turned around a unit).[54] What a combination these four approaches can be for a formalized leadership development process, especially for younger leaders who have not been taught the power of reflection, the importance of developing trusting relationships, the availability of profound resources on leadership theory and strategy, and taking advantage of any and all opportunities to try new leadership behaviors.

Similar to Kouzes and Posner's first learning approach (taking action learning), Robert Fulmer, academic director of Duke's Corporate Education and prominent leadership coach, defined action learning as "learning for action as opposed to learning for knowledge alone; they (leaders being trained) are having a Just-in-Time developmental experience rather than a Just-in-Case one."[55] This process entails traditional education on leadership, but also challenges assignments, so it becomes a more interactive, real-world educational experience. In the sport arena, similar to the story above about the team who lassoed their star player back into the fold, usual challenge assignments given to new captains include ensuring they and their teammates are ready and prepared for the start of practice, organizing the team's schedule for meetings and responsibilities, and mentoring/assisting the younger players with team rules and standards of practice.

David Kolb's often-cited Experiential Learning Theory posits people learn through two processes.[56] The first is by *comprehending* aspects of an experience as it is occurring, including the feelings experienced and those of others. The second aspect is *apprehending* or better understanding the experience by formulating a model or theory. In the case of a sport team captain who has just begun to learn how to become a better leader, she will learn how to be more aware of the actions and reactions of her teammates as they respond to her statements about picking up intensity and quality of execution at practice (comprehension). After the practice, with the assistance of a fellow captain or coach, this captain will begin to "put the pieces together" and formulate a theory about what works best with this team regarding the type, tone, and frequency of the feedback needed to initiate behavior change among this group of teammates (apprehension). Both processes include intrapersonal and interpersonal reflection and activity, which Kolb refers to as active experimentation, a concept similar to action learning.[57]

> *"Promoting learning requires a spirit of inquiry*
> *and openness, patience, and building in a tolerance*
> *for error and a framework for forgiveness."*[58]
>
> —James Kouzes and
> Barry Posner

Learning Climate—Cultivating "Learning Evangelists"

Similar to action learning, Annie McKee and colleagues believe leadership competencies are learned through actual life experiences. These continue to change and evolve. However, when someone intentionally attends to these experiences as part of personal development, he/she becomes a better leader. McKee also deems personal change is possible, yet people need to want to change for these changes to be personally meaningful. Also important is the ability to try new behaviors in a safe environment: "Long-lasting behavioral change happens only when people have opportunities to try new behaviors and develop new habits in relatively safe and nonjudgmental environments."[59] Kouzes and Posner empathize with those attempting to learn new skills and strategies. It can be a risky endeavor, potentially embarrassing oneself or making mistakes: "Learning is more likely to happen in a climate in which people feel safe in making themselves vulnerable, safe in taking the risk of failure. The safer people feel the more risks they'll take and the more mistakes they'll be willing to make."[60] These authors also believe "the only way people can learn is by doing things they've never done before" and this is maximized when they can do this in a safe learning climate.[61]

One company renowned for its culture of learning is Microsoft. According to Bill Gates, his company must be a learning organization because, as he was fond of saying, "Microsoft is always two years away from failure."[62] For them to stay competitive they have to continue to pay attention to their customers and competitors, while being open to the changes in both. Jay Conger and Beth Benjamin believe the upcoming generation of leaders has to become "learning evangelists."[63] They argue, "By stressing the importance of learning and creating a context where employees want to and are able to learn, leaders can strengthen their organizations for the challenges ahead and increase their ability to compete and innovate."[64] Establishing a culture of learning evangelists obviously does not just happen. It can only occur if it is a primary objective of a formalized developmental program.

One such example is a development course offered by Federal Express. In interviews with participants of this course, Conger and Benjamin reveal that learning occurs across six categories: (1) awareness of leadership concepts; (2) awareness of skills needed to implement these concepts; (3) importance of helping relationships; (4) coaching skills; (5) feedback on leadership style; (6) awareness of the culture and values of the organization.[65] These six learning categories compare nicely with the *Leadership IQ Model* first detailed in Chapter 4. Awareness (Chapter 9), leadership styles (Chapter 6), helping relationships (Chapter 8), coaching skills (Chapters 6 and 11), and team culture

(Chapters 10 and 12) are salient constructs from which to develop effective leaders in sport organizations.

Another example shared by Conger and Benjamin of a learning organization is PepsiCo's "Building the Business" program.[66] Each of the participants chooses a significant business project. Throughout the program they are mentored and instructed on how to develop and refine a vision for this project. They create a formalized action plan, implementation schedule, as well as learn about leadership theories and feedback on their personal leadership style. Transferring this logic into the sport setting, it is recommended to challenge team captains to brainstorm a personal and collective platform for their captaincy. For example, a personal captain platform for one co-captain on an Olympic team would be to mentor the younger players who arrive to training camp as to how things are done and what the standards are. The other captain's platform may be serving as the liaison between the coaching staff and the team, having weekly meetings with each party to ensure both parties are working from the same game plan. A collective platform for both captains is to always show their professionalism in all they do, whether practicing, travelling abroad, or doing community service or appearing in public. Once these platforms are verbalized, the leadership coach or coaching staff can assist these captains in accomplishing these platforms. In this way, the more the captains' intrinsic needs and motives are met, the more they will commit to helping the coaching staff meet their own needs for the team moving forward.

To conclude, Peter Drucker, father of management theory, responded with an apt statement about the importance of *testing* oneself as a leader and learner, when asked about what makes leaders successful: "They build continuous learning into the way they live, they experiment. They are not satisfied with what they did yesterday. The very least they demand of themselves is that they do better, whatever they do, and more often, they demand of themselves that they do it differently."[67] Bill George and colleagues conducted interviews with 125 leaders, and after analyzing over 3,000 pages of transcripts were surprised that their results mirrored those of over 1,000 studies on the topic: a profile for an ideal leader does not exist.[68] George and colleagues conclude these leaders' success was not attributed to universal attributes or styles, but rather the leadership that emerged through their lived, leadership experiences: "Consciously and subconsciously, they were constantly *testing* themselves through real-world experiences and reframing their life stories to understand who they were at their core."[69]

"Leadership is a performing art."[70]
—Jim Kouzes and Barry Posner

(3) Training to Be a More Effective Leader/Follower

As with any performing artist, be it a painter, dancer, actor or sport performer, training or practice is essential to mastering one's chosen craft. Goleman and colleagues echo this sentiment when comparing business executives to athletes: "Great athletes spend a lot of time practicing and a little time performing, while executives spend no time practicing and all of their time performing. Often, a leader will try a new approach once or twice, and then apply it—without giving himself the chance to practice it."[71] These authors believe this is why leaders recycle their problems, they "short themselves" on learning to lead better due to their haste in completing tasks (performing) rather than practicing, then performing, like athletes do.

Lieutenant Colonel Eric Kail, leadership instructor at the U.S. Military Academy, believes every leader must make the most of every leadership opportunity: "There is one universal truth, though, to every leadership opportunity—it is your chance to lead and take ultimate responsibility for whatever your group or unit does or fails to do."[72] In sport, there are examples of leaders who practice their pre-game speeches over and over so they not only deliver the right message, but the most appropriate emotional state (Mike Krzyzewski, for example). There are others, like Pete Carroll, coach of the NFL's Seattle Seahawks, who had his assistant coaches at USC practice their pre-practice and pre-game meetings prior to the arrival of the players so time and the message would be maximized.

> "Give your team the information they need to determine
> how they'll continue. Then let them do it."[73]
>
> —Stuart Levine,
> The Six Fundamentals of Success

Experiential Action Learning: Leadership-in-Action

The same precept applies to becoming a more effective leader and follower. Since leadership/followership can be learned, best learned by action learning, Anne McKee and colleagues add one more layer to this line of logic: "Long lasting behavioral change happens only when people have opportunities to try new behaviors and develop new habits in relatively safe and nonjudgmental environments."[74] It is "trying new behaviors" or practicing new leadership skills, conducted in a supportive culture, which maximizes the learning and leadership potential in individuals.

Richard Boyatzis developed a model of self-directed learning that also emphasizes the important contribution training has on this important process.[75] In a sequential manner, the first step is to ascertain the answer to, "What type of leader/person do you want to be?" Next is to determine the type of leader/person you are now and the areas between the two, referred to as a gap or discrepancy. The third step is learning how to build on strengths while reducing the gaps, followed by the practice period—experimenting with the new leadership skills (behaviors, thoughts, feelings). The final step is to galvanize supporting and encouraging relationships with others. These relationships provide the context for experimentation and practice, because without involvement from others, real learning and change will not be sustained. Goleman and colleagues concur that leadership development hinges on the quality of these relationships: "Others help us see things we are missing, affirm whatever progress we have made, test our perceptions, and let us know how we are doing."[76]

As Bill George writes, "Leadership principles are values translated into action—having a solid base of values and testing them under fire enables you to develop the principles you will use in leading."[77] For example, a leadership value such as "supporting a struggling teammate" can be translated into the leadership action of taking care of a teammate like a member of the family. Consider Paul Assaiante, a highly successful squash coach at Trinity College in Hartford, Connecticut, with 13 national championship titles in a row (252 straight wins), who documents his leadership philosophies in his book *Run to the Roar*. One such leadership principle is to treat his players as family, so much so he starts his day, every morning, by calling or texting his players. He explains: "The calls showed that I cared, that from the moment I woke up and until the moment I went to bed, I was thinking about the team."[78] Coach Assaiante also has a regular routine of eating dinner with every player at least once a week.

This is one of the ways Coach Assaiante shows his love for his players. According to him, "There is no doubt that love wins."[79] As he describes, the other ways he shows his love for them is when they see him do the following: Network to help find jobs for his graduating players, go to former players' weddings and family funerals, and answer the phone on Christmas day to speak with dozens of graduates. He believes we were all born to love. "If over time my players come to believe that they are at the center of my universe, they will in return feel a commitment to me and to the program. They see that I am not coaching them for selfish reasons."[80] Another leadership principle portrayed in these actions is Coach Assaiante truly believing one cannot teach someone if he or she does not know them. He goes to the lengths he does to instill a culture of family and caring going beyond most coach-player-team relationships in collegiate sport. Considering the leadership values portrayed by Coach Assaiante above, some important reflective questions for leaders in sport to ask themselves include: What are my actions saying about my leadership values and principles? Is this the behavioral message I want to send? In the case of a gap between values and actions, what behaviors do I need to begin portraying or do I need to change my value system? Assisting sport leaders at all levels in this self-awareness process is the focus of the next section.

> *"Work on the job is essentially the best ongoing laboratory for managers to learn about leadership."*[81]
> —Jay Conger and Beth Benjamin

Feedback Practice Methods

As part of any leadership development initiative, leadership experts Conger and Benjamin believe that observing and providing for value-based, behavioral feedback in this manner should be encouraged and integrated. By taking this important step, individuals can use feedback from others to gather information about areas of deficiency and strengths. Most people tend to be inaccurate in assessing their own behavioral selves due to personal biases and psychological defense mechanisms at the ready. In response to these potential barriers to accurate self-perception, Conger and Benjamin state most people "require a mirror of some form to discern more fully our strengths and weaknesses as leaders."[82] In the business and leadership literature, this mirror usually takes the form of 360-degree assessment tools, whereby those who work with and know the leader being assessed complete lengthy survey items, which are then analyzed and shared with the leader. Other forms of feedback include simulations and role-playing activities designed to assess participants' behavioral and decision-making styles. Feedback in this form helps to clarify important behavioral skills and target developmental areas for improvement, especially as they relate to the particular situation, while also boosting self-awareness and self-confidence.

In my sport leadership consulting work, I use several forms of feedback, one of which uses the axiom "hits and misses." Appendices 1, 4 and 5 are surveys used to elicit feedback from teammates about their leader's leadership styles, talent, techniques, and tactics. If used as designed, the information derived from the prime beneficiaries (teammates) of this leadership can provide a baseline of strengths and improvements that can be referred back to throughout the season. These surveys can also be completed several times throughout a season to provide updated feedback on progress made, especially when compared to the baseline results. This information can also be used to gauge fit, whether the combined strengths of the team captains are hitting all the areas that need to be addressed for enhanced team functioning. For example, if according to the team no one is challenging them to achieve practice standards, and this is allowed to continue without intervention, a teachable moment for the leadership of this team is to step it up in this particular area. If necessary, confrontation, communication and problem-solving skills need to be learned to better assist these leaders in filling this gap, and should be facilitated by the coach and/or leadership consultant immediately.

Another form of feedback used is additional open-ended questions, usually completed during the pre-season stage. On one form, the team leaders answer these four questions: What do you need from your teammates to help you lead this team? What are the most important needs that must be met by the team leadership this season? How has your co-captain already contributed to the leadership of this team? What have you already contributed to the leadership of this team? On another form, the team (followers) answers the following questions: What does this team need the most from the team captains this season? How will you personally help these leaders lead this team? In the role of captain, how will [insert captain's name] contribute to the leadership of this team this season? Do you have any suggestions on how to maximize these contributions? This feedback is then organized and distributed to all involved parties and discussed at length. Names are only used for one of the follower questions, how will you personally help these leaders lead this team? This question is used for each follower to adopt a leadership principle/action or two and be held accountable for it throughout the season.

Since follow-up is so important, coaches and/or consultants must bring the leaders and team back to this information on a regular basis to remind and challenge them about the following: How consistently are the captains achieving their leadership goals while meeting the needs of the team? Is each of the teammates contributing to team leadership by her personal leadership actions? Is each captain consistent with his/her contributions to team leadership, while also practicing new behaviors as requested by the followers? In these follow-up, accountability meetings, teammates and captains, with the help of the coaching staff, also discuss the team's progress on improved team functioning and leadership. Examples of feedback from one of these meetings with a collegiate basketball team is below.

"Have we, as individuals and as a team, shown good leadership in December?"

- "Yes we have—in hard times we come together and AF and TF have been our guidance."
- "Yes—leadership between us could be better but people are starting to step up in positive ways."
- "Yes, I feel like everyone's leadership has risen a lot these past few months; everyone has been working super hard, not only in games but also in practice."
- "Yes, the older players have been able to set a good tempo and tone in practice, making sure everyone knows what is going on and also bringing the team together if we are struggling to stay focused."

- "Yes, one day in practice we weren't very focused and AF gathered us in and helped us refocus (a hit!)."
- "Both, at times we have shown great leadership in games. But in the State game our leadership lacked. No one person stepped up to the task [*lesson learned*]; I think we wanted to but did not know what to do."
- "Yes, I think staying focused during close games has helped us a lot. I think that an area of improvement is our energy during warm-ups. Most of the time it is down, and it seems as though everyone's waiting for one person to say something instead of taking initiative. I think it has a huge effect on the way we start games as well as the locker room environment."

Another form of feedback that helps to improve the practicing of new behaviors, while reinforcing the learning process, is the use of "hits and misses." A "hit" is an example of a captain or team leader who sees an opportunity to lead and captures it. A "miss" is when a player misses the chance to help a team-mate off the floor after a mistake or speaks when he should be listening, basically missing an opportunity at a tangible leadership moment. Coaches primarily are asked to assist in the capturing of these "hits or misses" captain moments, but in a team setting with the proper coaching and preparation, teammates can also be helpful in capitalizing on these moments. These hits and misses can then become one of the many performance points discussed at the end of a practice or game. Below are examples of hits and misses captured by a college basketball staff and team, which were discussed after a weekend game.

Hits = "In Vegas, TG told us 'this is not how we play' which helped us refocus; TA helps me calm down when I get frustrated (a button!). Yesterday we were about to run and KP volunteered to step to the line and nailed the free throw—yes!" GA celebrating 3's and we had good plays from players off the bench. AT challenging teammates to get after those rebounds."

Misses = "We missed a chance to help lead the team in Tuesday's practice with the absence of Coach. We had negative body language due to frustration with our play, and our teammates' play, which also helps fire up our opponents. Our game warm-up was not focused and could have used some energy from team leaders."

The take-away message of this section is an obvious one: action learning through practice. The next section details how learning about leadership can be transferred to other areas of an athlete's or coach's life. Approaches taken to teach, learn, and model leadership principles and values can ultimately transform individuals and organizations. In the words of contemporary inspirational author, William Arthur Ward, who synthesizes the difference between wanting to do something and actually doing it: "Do more than belong: participate. Do more than care: help. Do more than believe: *practice*. Do more than be fair: be kind. Do more than forgive: forget. Do more than dream: work."[83]

> *"Before you are a leader, success is all about growing yourself.*
> *When you become a leader, success is all about growing others."*[84]
> —Jack Welch, *Winning*

(4) Transferring Leadership/Followership Skills

In the words of SUNY-Buffalo CFO Bob Wagner, "Process is our most important product."[85] The development of leadership and followership talents, techniques, and tactics is indeed a learning process, and an important part of that learning process is to transfer what is learned to as many different life aspects as possible. Research by Jay Conger shows many executive leadership programs, especially those geared toward personal growth with an emphasis on work-life balance, improve participants' personal lives more than their work lives. Although not hitting its primary target, this research shows programs focusing on personal development and living a balanced life provide transferable life skills leading to improvements in home and family life. Goleman reveals that transferability and transformative experience can be a part of leadership development: "Very often when we work with leaders to help them cultivate a greater range or depth in emotional intelligence competencies, they tell us that the payoff for them has been not just in their work as leaders, but in their personal and family lives as well. They find themselves bringing home heightened levels of self-awareness and empathic understanding, self-mastery, and attuned relationships."[86]

As is detailed in Chapter 9, living a balanced life, which entails juggling the "five balls" (work, family, health, friends and spirit) as told by Brian Dyson, former vice chairman of Coca-Cola, is where the real challenge lies for high performers. Any assistance provided to help others accomplish this challenge through transferable skills is time and money well spent.

> *"People can't lead if they aren't psychologically hardy."*[87]
> —James Kouzes and
> Barry Posner

Psychological Hardiness

One of the transferable skills that make it possible for leaders to balance these five balls includes a class of behaviors discussed in Chapter 7, simply referred to as toughness. Other words to signify toughness in the literature include "courage," "determined," "disciplined," "assertive," "bold," "confident," "poised," "conviction," "competitive," and "hardiness." It is the last word, "hardiness," that leadership literature has determined assists people in living more balanced, stress-resistant and stress-resilient lives.

Research on stress and executives reveals that the hardy executives, those who experience high stress, but are low in stress-induced illnesses, perceive and respond to their stress in more adaptive ways than those who are high stress and high illness. The difference is primarily that the hardy executives perceive a greater sense of *control* (also addressed in Chapter 7), so they can influence the outcome due to efforts made, are stronger in their *commitment* level to find meaning and importance in their work and lives, and have a strong belief that being *challenged* will lead to personal improvement and fulfillment. Kouzes and Posner find this type of psychological hardiness in their analyses of personal best experiences among leaders they survey: "The leaders we studied experienced the change in which they were engaged, whether they initiated it or not, as a challenge out of which something extraordinary would come. They were fully engaged, curious, and committed to making something happen. They believed they had the power to influence the destiny of their own and their team's lives."[88] Moreover, these researchers also indicate leaders help the people in their lives feel the same way they do. Hardy leaders, as the research shows, can help transfer these skills to others by developing a culture of hardiness.

Kouzes and Posner believe to recruit and retain good people, leaders must create a culture fostering and promoting psychological hardiness since people will not follow leaders or a cause that distresses them. Leaders can develop this by:

(1) Fostering a greater sense of *control* among people by reinforcing the importance of taking risks and choosing challenging tasks without punishment for making mistakes.

(2) Being positive, encouraging and reinforcing innovation and creating risk taking behaviors, which will also lead to greater *commitment* to the team vision.

(3) Promoting an attitude of *challenge* by helping others view change as an opportunity for excellence.[89]

An example of a culture of hardiness is evidenced by how Google founder and CEO Larry Page responds to an employee's mistake costing the company several million dollars: "I'm so glad you made this mistake because I want to run a company where we are moving too quickly and doing too much, not being too cautious and doing too little. If we don't have any of these mistakes, we're just not taking enough risk."[90] Kouzes and Posner describe hardy leaders as those who are status-quo averse, but instead are experimenters who recognize failure is part of a learning organization: "Instead of punishing it they encourage it; instead of trying to fix blame for mistakes, they learn from them; instead of adding rules, they encourage flexibility."[91] This type of leader who reinforces a culture of hardiness helps create more innovative and creative teams. Kouzes and Posner report the hardy executives in their studies "experienced commitment rather than alienation, control rather than powerlessness, and challenge rather than threat."[92] They counter with the idea people do not produce excellence "when feeling ignored, insignificant, and threatened."[93]

Pay It Forward via Opportunities and Reminders

As the Jack Welch quote referred to earlier notes, success as a leader is not just about growing oneself but about growing others. As part of the leadership process it is imperative that followers and leaders transfer what they have learned along their personal leadership journey to others, through informal and formal methods. For example, Nick Saban, the highly successful college football coach at the University of Alabama (repeat BCS national champions), uses a peer intervention leadership program to educate players about behavior issues and how to handle stressful situations the right way.[94] In addition to a peer intervention specialist, the coaches select a small group of players in each class to serve as peer intervention leaders to oversee and teach the younger players lessons learned in their time as Crimson Tide football players. This group of peer intervention leaders also decide on rules and punishments as well.

A program like this based on transferring lessons learned from one group of players to another has reduced conduct detrimental to the team, while also heightening their awareness of the effect and influence they have on one another. The peer intervention motto, "What you do, you do to everyone in this room," is also on a sign in their team room.[95] Mike Krzyzewski at Duke University follows the old adage, "To teach is to learn twice."[96] He encourages his players to teach at the Duke basketball camp every summer because he believes, through this teaching, his players remind themselves about what they should be doing via what they say, what they show and what they do with the younger players at camp. He also believes those who teach at the camp are actually easier to teach once training camp opens up.

Programs such as Nick Saban's peer intervention program, Coach K's players teaching basketball and leadership skills in summer camp, and the leadership development processes implemented here adhere to the research findings on transfer of learning that information is learned and retained longer under distributed periods of training and feedback.[97] According to Conger and Benjamin and others, periods of extended and multiple learning opportunities are required for learning leadership. It is important to move participants beyond simply being aware of leadership skills to the actual application and ultimately, the change of targeted behaviors and perspectives.[98] Accomplishing this requires many more learning opportunities than a one-time program or once-a-month leadership academy program could ever provide. On-the-job leadership training may not even occur unless it is focused and appropriate feedback is provided on regular intervals. Spreading the learning over an extended period of time provides important opportunities for reflection and revisiting critical learning concepts and principles.

Daniel Goleman and colleagues echo the importance of making the most of these learning opportunities. They involve active reflection and revisiting key concepts through the process of formal reminders: "Because leadership skills are part of an unconscious repertoire of habits learned long ago, the old response won't magically disappear. It takes commitment and constant *reminders* to stay focused on undoing those habits. Over time, the need for reminders will diminish as the new behavior becomes a stronger pathway in the brain."[99] This active reminder process can take the form of capturing leadership moment "hits and misses" discussed earlier, or through the use of "reminder process points." Leadership gurus Marshall Goldsmith and Howard Morgan believe leadership development is enhanced when the leader-trainee can rely on those around her to achieve pre-set objectives through the use of reminders: "The trainer's role is to remind the person being trained to do what he or she knows should be done."[100] Coaches, captains, and leadership consultants can apply these reminders as part of leadership meeting agenda notes, as a summary of the progress being made across the reminder process points. A sample pre-leadership meeting agenda is below.

Captain Meeting: Update on Process Points

(1) Team issue with the new ruling about the limited number of players who can travel.
(2) Update on weekly meeting with head coach. Issues addressed and solutions.
(3) Detail the conversations you three have had with your "assigned" teammates this week.
(4) Team process on the new team standards—who meets them regularly and who does not?
(5) Have these been further defined and displayed for your teammates?
(6) What lessons were learned during the UOF match that have been applied to the team preparations for UTM?
(7) What team outings have been scheduled? Have you had a good showing of teammates?
(8) Are any teammates in need of some additional attention or feedback from you captains or coaches?

(9) In our pursuit of getting you three captains "out in front of the team more," what progress has been made? How have you done this more?

(10) M and C, as part of your captain platform, you mentioned wanting to be more vocal on the court—what progress has been made there? Have you asked for feedback from coaches on this pursuit? *THANKS for taking the time to make this team better via working through these ten process points.*

As mentioned previously, sport leaders today cannot assume on-the-job (or on the court or field) leadership will automatically occur; that simply does not happen unless there is a deliberate focus on learning, practice, and transferability. The literature on expertise, how people become experts in their respective fields, has shown it takes at least ten years of focused preparation, learning, and practice to become an expert. One of the leading researchers in this knowledge area is K. Anders Ericsson, whose research shows support for this "ten year" rule, as well as support for the importance of what he terms "deliberate practice." According to Ericsson and colleagues, with deliberate, focused and repeated practice, people begin to develop not only transferable declarative and procedural knowledge, but also tacit knowledge.[101] The latter represents knowledge of implicit information learned through innumerable opportunities for experimentation along with specific coaching or mentoring. Conger and Benjamin state their endorsement of deliberate practice in their book, *Building Leaders:* "The expertise literature would argue that leadership, like any form of expertise, requires intensive, focused learning over extended periods of time to be developed."[102]

In sport leadership consulting, it becomes paramount to maximize the number of learning opportunities for team leaders. In most cases captains (especially at the college level) and team leaders have six to eight months to learn as much as they can about leadership and followership skills and principles before their team is engaged in competitive, in-season play. In Olympic play, despite having four years between the Games, the challenges differ depending on the sport. Generally, players are in and out of training camp as schedules permit, and many have professional playing careers elsewhere, so the team is together only for short periods of time. Thus, maximizing these opportunities with focused, deliberate, and repeatable learning and mentoring is a great challenge. With the importance of the development of empowered individual and team leaders, these challenges can be overcome with adaptable and flexible leadership development programming.

> *"Empowerment means taking responsibility for getting something done, and being willing to be held accountable."*[103]
> —Bill George, Andrew McLean and Nick Craig,
> *Finding Your True North*

(5) Transforming Leadership

As is obvious by now, transforming or empowering individuals and teams into genuine, effective leaders may be one of the more difficult, yet most rewarding aspects of sport coaching. This process begins with the leader, first and foremost. A common theme found in the many writings, articles and books on leadership is to motivate and transform others to become more effective leaders who assist team members in maximizing their contributions for the common vision and enhanced productivity, all leaders need to *take responsibility* to improve their own personal leadership first, before they can begin working to mobilize the best in others. As Annie McKee and her co-authors point out, "Beginning with you is essential because professional leadership development cannot happen without personal growth."[104] Bill George refers to this specifically when he writes: "First, you must be an authentic leader yourself, and then foster a climate of mutual respect by treating others as equals, listening to them, and learning from them."[105]

You cannot create a culture of leadership without being a model leader yourself. As J.C. Maxwell states, "Improving yourself will add value to the team. But if you have a leadership role on your team, it's especially vital. Why? Because you can effectively teach only what you consistently model. It takes one to know one, show one, and grow one."[106] Linda Hill, author of *Becoming a Manager: Mastery of a New Identity,* reveals some insight into what it takes to become an effective leader, namely, a transformation. She notes, "Becoming a manager requires a profound psychological adjustment—a *transformation.* The new managers have to learn how to think, feel, and value as managers instead of as individual contributors."[107] According to Hill, to transform themselves these new leaders have to proceed through four learning processes[108]:

- Learning what it means to be a manager/leader (addressed in Chapter 4)
- Developing interpersonal judgment or perspective (Chapters 5 and 9)
- Gaining self-knowledge and awareness (Chapters 4 and 9)
- Coping with emotion and stress (Chapters 5 and 12)

This book and the conceptual model that provides the framework for the leadership development content, curricula and processes (cited in Chapter 4) encompass the most referred, topical and cutting-edge principles and practices of leadership by some of the greatest minds and practitioners in the leadership field. I hope that each leader has taken steps to *transform* his own leadership talents, techniques, tactics, and styles before applying this rich information on his own team of followers and leaders-in-training.

"Succeed with a process—not a program. No discrete program
will add up to transformation of the person or the company."[109]
—Daniel Goleman, Richard Boyatzis, and
Annie McKee, *Primal Leadership*

Process Over Programming

Successful individual and team leadership cannot be captured by a program meeting once a month (in a lecture or team bonding activity format) and is not focused on actual leadership efforts such as helping institute team standards, changing team culture, and finding real solutions to real problems. Mike Myatt, a top CEO coach, believes leaders cannot be trained, instead they must be developed: "You don't train leaders you develop them. Development is nuanced, contextual, collaborative, fluid, and above all else, actionable."[110] Cited earlier, but applicable here, is SUNY-Buffalo CFO Bob Wagner's proclamation, "Process is our most important product." Leadership gurus Goldsmith and Morgan believe leadership development involves a process approach occurring over time, which must also be action oriented. In their words, "It's like physical fitness. Imagine having out-of-shape people sit in a room and listen to a speech on exercising, or watch tapes on how to exercise. These people will still be unfit a year later. Their challenge is not in understanding the practice of leadership—it is practicing their understanding of leadership."[111]

Goleman and colleagues use the term "process" when describing the best practices of leadership development: "What many organizations need aren't just one-time programs but a process built as a holistic system that permeates every layer of the organization."[112] They continue by stating true change and transformation occurs through a multifaceted process permeating three particular levels, namely, individuals, team, and the culture of the organization.[113] These authors provide additional characteristics of the best leadership development processes, including:

- Create a safe space for learning that is challenging, yet supportive.
- Incorporate experiences relevant yet different from the usual.
- Focus on emotional and intellectual learning.
- Base experiential learning on active, participatory work (action-learning).
- Rely on team-based simulations used to examine personal behaviors and those of others.
- Incorporate a "bold mixture" of teaching techniques.
- Conduct them over a period of time, which "takes the culture head on."[114]

Sean Hannah of the U.S. Military Academy insists true leader development consists of a process that positively changes "who this person is" and is not simply a one-size-fits-all program of teaching new styles or behavioral techniques. He believes purposeful, integrated leader development takes time and must be an integral part of the organization and its daily operations: "Such development should be targeted at raising the ability and motivation for self-awareness and self-regulation ("thinking about thinking") and through moral development."[115] Former Navy Seals Jeff Cannon and Jon Cannon postulate that true leadership development not only changes who this person is, but what this leader shows through his or her actions: "You're a leader. Your people are watching you every time they see you. They're looking at every action, every moment. When they don't see you, they assume that you're working on their behalf. When they do see you, what you do confirms or destroys their assumptions."[116] For example, if players see the coach or captains blame others for mistakes or shirk responsibilities, it will leave an indelible, negative impression. If instead they see the coach or captain stand up for what is right or go down fighting, according to the authors, "they won't care whether you're dressed well or whether your grammar is correct. They'll swarm up in your defense, work overtime, and go the extra mile."[117]

> *"Empowerment is the collective effect of leadership."*[118]
> —Warren Bennis, *An Invented Life:*
> *Reflections on Leadership and Change*

Transformational Leader Effects on Teams

Warren Bennis and others have declared leadership can be felt through a team and organization by its passion, energy, and effect. Being empowered or transformed is truly the collective effect of resonant leadership and followership. In his book, *An Invented Life,* Bennis details four areas where empowerment is evident[119]:

(1) People feel significant—they feel they make a difference and what they do matters.
(2) Learning and being competent matters—there are no failures just mistakes that give feedback for improvement.
(3) People are part of a community—where there is leadership, there is a team.
(4) Work is exciting—where there are leaders present, training and getting better become a fun process.

Sport teams who function at a high level are characterized as those who play for one another, perceive their team as a family, are always trying to improve on their on-field product, and take pride and have fun in the process.

Another effect of empowerment can be seen when leaders or teams transform from an "I" to a "We" orientation. George points out the negative impact leaders with an "I" orientation have on others, mainly, followers respond with caution, a lack of commitment and unproductive output.[120] Applying George's ideas to sport, coaches who rise through the ranks have a primary focus on themselves about how they perform, what they can achieve and what rewards will come their way to improve their stock so they can have their own program one day. George believes these leaders "envision themselves in the image of an all-conquering hero who can change the world for the better."[121]

As the authors attest, this archetypal hero is a useful initial stage, especially in a program rebuild, but many get stuck in this role and have a tough time moving beyond it. Success at this initial stage tends to reinforce this approach. However, according to George and colleagues, especially in turbulent times, leaders question their philosophy and practices: "At some point, authentic leaders begin to rethink what their life and leadership are all about. They may start to ask, 'Do I have to do it all myself?' 'Why can't I get this team to achieve the goals I have set forth?'"[122] Leaders who have this change of heart and approach, a transformation from "I" to "We," can have a humbling experience. At the crux of this transformation is what George believes is a shift from a hero role into more of a servant role: "This newly found humility stems from the recognition that leadership is not just about them."[123] David Rooke and William Torbert believe leaders can create change, even transformational change like previously mentioned, in their leadership and their lives: "Those who are willing to work at developing themselves and becoming more self-aware can almost certainly evolve over time into truly transformational leaders."[124]

> *"Major internal transformation rarely happens*
> *unless many people assist."*[125]
> —John Kotter, *Leading Change*

Transformational Leadership Development Methods

For effective leadership development to occur, coaches and consultants need to engage all four of the principal learning methods identified in Jay Conger's research, namely, the four particular teaching-training approaches: Conceptual awareness, Feedback, Skill building, and Personal growth.[126] As a note of caution, it is critical these approaches do not come to represent programs with a definite beginning and an end. As stated earlier, for there to be any lasting impact, leadership development must be an integrative process continuously referred to with active reminders and follow-ups, not simply a program scheduled from time to time. These approaches and accompanying learning methods are described in greater detail below[127]:

Awareness training programs focus on improving awareness of important leadership skills through the use of lectures on theories and conceptual models, case study work, and reflective exercises. In my sport leadership developmental process, players answer detailed reflective questions in addition to learning more about the important concepts of leadership via studying key historical leaders as well as leaders from contemporary society and sport. Other content areas include learning more about emotional and relational intelligence and learning styles of leadership and followership. Conger and Benjamin cite the principal advantage of this type of approach: "The hope of such programs, of course, is that after exposure to essential ideas about leadership the learners will be motivated to seek out opportunities to develop their leadership capabilities."[128] Gaining a further understanding of leadership does represent an important first step to becoming a more informed and effective leader, despite it having little transference into actually implementing the prescribed leader behaviors.

Feedback approaches seek to acquire strengths and weaknesses by survey or personal feedback methods, in addition to obtaining feedback from others. In the business setting a popular system of feedback is the 360-degree review. Others will use formal surveys and interviews. My version of a feedback approach is to ascertain specific information from leaders via pre- and post-survey completion, as well as feedback from significant others, including coaches, support staff, and team members. Other feedback comes in the form of "hits and misses" or coaches, co-captains and support staff helping captains to capture those captain moments. The goal is to learn from what worked and what did not work, even with those missed captain moments. In this way, participants are not overloaded with information, with the continual reminders and the capturing of leader moments. Leaders will not forget the important objectives of their personal behavioral changes. Programs that focus on 360-degree feedback and other systems do not provide enough practice to create real change. According to Conger, "Because the training environment is limited in its ability to help participants make profound adjustments, participants tend instead to gravitate to changes that are more superficial in terms of dispositional traits."[129]

Skill building entails practicing behavior modification feedback from the above methods through formal exercises, simulations and modeling from trainers or mentors. Most of the programs undergoing leadership development will give team leaders the opportunity to transfer and practice their leadership skills in the off-season, while also providing teammates with the opportunity of improving their own followership and leadership skills. For example, Paul Assaiante, successful squash coach at Trinity College, allows his seniors to run the team for their nine-week pre-season training period. He refers to this as a nine-week "course in ownership development." The seniors manage off-court training runs, hold bi-weekly strength sessions, run drills and practices, arrange travel and even sort out which players are late for things and why.[130] For skill building to be most effective, however, there needs to be continual practice and training time. Integrating skill building as a process, moreso than a program, allows for more learning experiences. Conger and Benjamin believe to build expertise, skill building programs fall short of expectation because there is just not enough time to practice what is being learned. Rather, the experience must simulate actual team and sport environments: "As a result, participants often receive only a single opportunity to practice a particular skill and received feedback—with so little exposure, the experience simply builds awareness rather than true understanding and skill development."[131]

Personal growth approaches emphasize active reflective exercises to learn more about personal impact on others, as well as planning and working toward achieving personal life goals. A drawback of this type of programming is that it does not reflect realities of university or athletic life. Oftentimes a program becomes a welcomed distraction, like a team engaging in ropes-course activities. As Conger and Benjamin indicate, "A few days of training cannot substitute for the insights and opportunities that multiple work experiences can provide."[132] Working on risk taking, enhanced communication and teamwork, while team members are 200 feet above the ground zip lining and rappelling, does not directly transfer to the pressure of competing for a national championship on the football field. Although a fun distraction, the emotional high achieved while doing these activities will fade rapidly upon returning to 6:00 a.m. positional meetings and the daily grind of training and conditioning.

The final section of this chapter, *Traditions,* outlines my sample leadership development processes, which incorporates the cognitive, feedback, skill-building, and personal development approaches. Emphasized is how these processes have not only become integrated into the sport organization, but how they continue on, season after season. As pointed out by Alan Murray, "Change sticks only when it becomes the way we do things around here."[133]

> *"In our leadership meetings we try to imprint traditions."*[134]
> —Anson Dorrance and Gloria Averbuch,
> *The Vision of a Champion*

Traditions of Leadership Excellence

After a season or two of design, implementation, follow-up, reminders, hits-and-misses captain moments, evaluations, re-tooling then repeating the process, the leadership development process adopted by the coach, captains and team in most cases becomes "what this team does." Put another way, it becomes part of the *tradition* of the program. In this way, leadership development becomes just another part of the program, along with the other essentials, such as practice, match preparation, travel, strength and conditioning, academics, nutrition, team meetings, and the other usual programs and processes. Many of the coaches will even keep a detailed and organized folder of the leadership development process paperwork and bring it with them on the road to show recruits and their families.

Former Navy Seals and authors Jeff Cannon and Jon Cannon know the importance of traditions and how they can be used to strengthen the company or team by representing the culture and values of the organization. In their book, *Leadership Lessons of the Navy Seals,* they ask some pointed questions about traditions for all leaders: "What purpose does a tradition at your company serve? Morale? Teamwork? Pride? In the end, all of these have a direct influence on productivity. Likewise, what damage is your tradition causing? Lost workdays? Low productivity? Add up the pluses and minuses. Then keep the traditions or get rid of them fast."[135] Having a keen awareness of what organizational traditions best represent values and practices and which ones do quite the opposite becomes vital for leaders to ascertain.

Establishing a culture of leadership that becomes an integral part of the athletic program will be a novel tradition. What some coaches do is start something like this with all the best intentions, but *tradition*ally, the new initiative loses steam when conference play hits, for example. Players are well aware of a team tradition characterized by their coaches failing to stay with a process designed to assist player and team alike. Coaches of these teams will often wonder why there is so little "buy-in" and adherence to a start-up program or process. These players realize what is started will not be around long enough to have any lasting impact. Other examples of programs that coaches initiate but fail to follow-through on include: individual and team goal setting, team building and team bonding activities throughout the season (when they are needed the most), meeting with athletes individually, guest speakers addressing their teams, alumni networking, honoring past teams, and adding new traditions to their program to separate them from the rest. Good and effective leaders are aware of the present team traditions, especially any negative traditions. They look to change the debilitating ones that arise from their own actions or inactions.

Speaking of good and effective leaders, über-successful women's soccer coach, Anson Dorrance, shares a team tradition he has followed for all of his years winning championships at UNC Chapel Hill. During the spring season he meets with his rising seniors weekly to discuss the team's core values for that spring and the upcoming season. They discuss how they can live the core values and help their teammates live them as well. In his words, "Human nature being what it is, some leaders embrace the personal and public challenge of our discussions and some don't; just as some people within the culture live the core values and some simply don't have the strength."[136] Examples of these team values include: "We choose to be positive; we don't whine; we are noble and support the team and mission even if we don't play as much as we'd like; we are well led; the truly extraordinary do something every day; we play for each other; we want our lives to be never-ending ascensions; we want these four years of college to be rich, valuable and deep."[137] With team values and traditions like these, how can this program not be considered as one of the best in the country, regardless of the number of championships they have earned!

Mentioned earlier is the work of another very successful leader and coach, Mike Krzyzewski, Head Basketball Coach at Duke University, and what he does to reinforce the culture of leadership. In his own words, "It's tough to find a lot of leaders," so it is in Coach K's best interest to support and cultivate a tradition of leadership, for all involved.[138] He does state to do so requires hard work year in and year out, yet, as he reflects, "all the hard work is worth it because once you make it happen, confidence, excellence, unity, and pride will grow. Tradition builds pride, fosters team unity, and reinforces confidence. It lets people know they are part of something grand."[139] Helping to make all those involved in the team and organization feel a part of something grand is another ideal leadership practice for good and effective leaders.

A final endorsement for the conscious, deliberate implementation of productive team traditions again comes from Coach K: "Great tradition is like the moisture that prepares the soil. It helps the ground absorb more water, become more fertile, and it allows important things to grow to their fullest capabilities. That's what I want for all the kids who play basketball for me. I want them to grow into men of strong character, men who are leaders themselves."[140]

As can be ascertained by the volume of content contained here, becoming a good and effective leader can be learned, yet it entails an immense amount of knowledge, specifically, leadership concepts and theories (LQ), emotional and relational knowledge (ERQ), leadership styles (LSQ), situational leadership (SLQ), leadership talents, techniques, and tactics (TQ³), followership concepts and theories (FQ), organizational dynamics (OQ), and the six T's to developing a leadership culture via a leadership development process (LDP), namely testing, teaching, training, transferring, transforming, and traditions. Pursuing such a knowledge base entails adopting a "learning evangelist," lifelong learner mindset, along with much support, help, hard work and practice in maximizing those leadership opportunities that present themselves.

To conclude, there are just some final leadership lessons to share, beginning with the importance of becoming your own personal leader and not trying to become someone else. To this end, Kevin Sharer, Amgen CEO/president, points out the importance of being yourself in the leadership role: "Leadership has many voices. You need to be who you are, not try to emulate somebody else."[141] Another lesson is the importance of being a servant leader who helps build a legacy for those who are being led. As another CEO, Gary Strack, points out, "The purpose of leadership is to create a legacy and not a legend."[142] As Max Depress, author of *Leadership Is an Art,* states, in support of a legacy based on servitude, "The first responsibility of a leader is to define reality. The last is to say thank you. In between, the leader is a servant."[143] When a leader is authentic, speaks and models honesty and ethics in action, and focuses on serving others, the work and effort this will take will be seen and greatly appreciated by those on the team and in the organization. Lieutenant Colonel Eric Kail shares the content of one of his last conversations with his father, a career Army officer of 32 years, which is an important lesson for all. In it the younger Kail wanted to know how he will know if he is a successful leader. The elder Kail responded by stating: "True measure of success is found in the eyes of your direct reports, the embrace of your spouse, and the hearts of your children."[144]

Another lesson Kail passed along that must be shared: "One of the most important things you can do as a leader is to develop other leaders. Those leaders will affect hundreds, if not thousands, of other people."[145] In this way, in the words of Rath and Conchie, "The best leaders get to live on."[146] Continue to read, to learn, reflect, and practice being an authentic leader. Above all, be a leader who lives on in the lives of your family, friends, teams and players.

– Appendix 1 –

Leadership Style Survey

Team Feedback: Please write in the name of the teammate who you feel/think best typifies the particular leadership characteristic and/or practice. If no one fits then leave it blank.

Individual Feedback: If a leader would like to complete this on him/herself, insert a 0–5 where appropriate.

KEY:			
Never = 0	Very Rarely = 1	Rarely = 2	Sometimes = 3
	Often = 4	Very Often = 5	Always = 6

Visionary:

(1) _____ asks us for feedback about what we want to accomplish this season.

(2) _____ stays optimistic even in the face of personal and/or team adversity.

(3) _____ consistently has a good attitude and energy at practice sessions.

(4) _____ inspires the team to work toward collective standards and vision.

(5) _____ is optimistic about the future and shares this with teammates.

(6) _____ helps the team learn lessons from the past to help us move ahead.

(7) _____ reminds the team to keep an eye on the big picture (team goals).

(8) _____ is passionate about the possibilities for this team.

Coaching:

(9) _____ leads through encouragement and energy.

(10) _____ helps players when they are struggling during matches.

(11) _____ keeps team energized and focused when training gets difficult-repetitive.

(12) _____ is a vocal leader in practice.

(13) _____ is consistently in the right place and knows the system.

(14) _____ leads by example in practice, in weights, on the road, in classes.

(15) _____ helps pump the team up when needed during matches.

(16) _____ is good at helping us pick up our intensity at practice.

Affiliative:

(17) _____ steps up and attempts to resolve problems and "drama" right away.

(18) _____ organizes team functions to enhance teamwork and cohesion.

(19) _____ keeps the team organized about meetings, events, and schedule changes.

(20) _____ has a good rapport with each player on the team.

(21) _____ makes teammates feel comfortable going to them for questions or to talk about things.

(22) _____ connects with teammates regularly and keeps them all included and appreciated.

(23) _____ does not allow teammates to drift-get quiet-shut down when their play begins to struggle.

(24) _____ is the liaison between the team and coaching staff.

Democratic:

(25) _____ strategically calls for team meetings to discuss issues.

(26) _____ stands behind the decisions of the coaches and fellow team captains.

(27) _____ puts the team first in all decisions and actions.

(28) _____ helps keep both players and coaches "on the same page."

(29) _____ helps keep the locker room climate productive and cohesive.

(30) _____ asks for feedback from the team on important matters.

(31) _____ helps teammates feel empowered to take on more responsibility to better themselves and team.

(32) _____ is able to listen to team feedback and help the team come to a consensus on the next steps to take to improve things.

Pacesetting:

(32) _____ is one of the most competitive players on the team.

(33) _____ displays a real commitment to being the best player they can be.

(34) _____ is one of the hardest working players in practice.

(35) _____ demands the ball with the game on the line.

(36) _____ is our go-to player when the game is on the line.

(37) _____ is consistently the first to speak in a team meeting and first to start a drill.

(38) _____ is a change agent who can create change by what he/she says and does.

(39) _____ sets the tone in practice and workouts by being the example.

Commanding:

(40) _____ confronts teammates to create change if necessary.

(41) _____ challenges teammates to achieve team standards.

(42) _____ helps enforce team rules and standards.

(43) _____ is willing to challenge teammates when they know they can do better.

(44) _____ is able to notice a letdown in intensity and challenge teammates to pick it up.

(45) _____ takes the responsibility for own actions and expects team to do the same.

(46) _____ helps the team instill a sense of discipline and professionalism.

(47) _____ usually has an opinion on how best to move the team forward.

(48) _____ will say and do what is necessary to win.

– Appendix 2 –

Leadership Skill Set Assessment

Please respond to each question on a 1 to 6 scale to evaluate your leadership qualities and practices. When rating, think about the frequency of usage/application across your typical six-day training-game play week (one mandatory day off/week). For example, "*very rarely*" means you show the stated quality or leadership practice for approximately half a day (practice session/game) per six-day week; "*often*" means you show the stated quality or leadership practice approximately three to four days in a six-day week, and so on.

KEY:
Never = 0   Very Rarely (½ day/wk) = 1   Rarely (1 day/wk) = 2   Sometimes (2 days/wk) = 3
Often (3-4 days/wk) = 4   Very Often (4-5 days/wk) = 5   Always = 6

Name: _____

1. confronts teammates if needed despite how it will be
   perceived.   0 1 2 3 4 5 6
2. approaches the head coach to talk about particular team
   issues.   0 1 2 3 4 5 6
3. is willing to make and follow unpopular decisions that are
   in the team's best interest.   0 1 2 3 4 5 6
4. is the hardest worker in practice on the team.   0 1 2 3 4 5 6
5. is the hardest worker in conditioning and strength training.   0 1 2 3 4 5 6
6. helps teammates elevate their work rate by being the
   example.   0 1 2 3 4 5 6
7. is the most competitive player on the team.   0 1 2 3 4 5 6
8. is driven to succeed on the pitch and in the classroom,
   and to helping this team succeed.   0 1 2 3 4 5 6
9. looks for different ways to drive one's performance and
   others.   0 1 2 3 4 5 6
10. wants the ball with the game on the line.   0 1 2 3 4 5 6
11. displays a confidence image regardless of his play.   0 1 2 3 4 5 6

12. looks and sounds confident in a leadership role on/off the field and in the locker room. 0 1 2 3 4 5 6
13. has a good attitude at practice sessions and in the locker room. 0 1 2 3 4 5 6
14. appears ready to practice hard every session. 0 1 2 3 4 5 6
15. consistently trains well regardless of adversity or fatigue. 0 1 2 3 4 5 6
16. continues to "captain" and help the team despite how he is playing. 0 1 2 3 4 5 6
17. continues to "captain" and help the team despite dealing with off-field issues or practice fatigue. 0 1 2 3 4 5 6
18. consistently puts the needs of the team ahead of their own. 0 1 2 3 4 5 6
19. leads through example, encouragement and energy. 0 1 2 3 4 5 6
20. consistently speaks up in team meetings and is the first to go in a drill or game activity. 0 1 2 3 4 5 6
21. leads through sharing experiences, skill/tactical instructions with teammates when needed. 0 1 2 3 4 5 6
22. is willing to put in the time and energy needed to help the team accomplish its goals any way possible. 0 1 2 3 4 5 6
23. is committed enough to mentor others to help lead the team. 0 1 2 3 4 5 6
24. inspires the team to work toward team standards and vision. 0 1 2 3 4 5 6
25. is sensitive to a teammate's or coach's emotional reactions to an event or situation and is able to empathize and assist if necessary. 0 1 2 3 4 5 6
26. stays optimistic even in the face of personal or team adversity. 0 1 2 3 4 5 6
27. is tolerant of his own mistakes and those of others. 0 1 2 3 4 5 6
28. consistently represents self, teammates, and program in a professional and ethical manner. 0 1 2 3 4 5 6
29. abides by team codes of conduct and rules of our sport. 0 1 2 3 4 5 6
30. is truthful in all discussions and follows up on what is stated. 0 1 2 3 4 5 6
31. builds rapport easily with teammates and staff and effectively manages these relationships. 0 1 2 3 4 5 6
32. is a good listener and considers perspectives from others. 0 1 2 3 4 5 6
33. is able to clearly communicate (send/receive messages) with coaches and teammates. 0 1 2 3 4 5 6
34. knows the game, positional responsibilities, and team offensive-defensive systems. 0 1 2 3 4 5 6
35. is always in the right place, knows what is going on and has a pulse on the team. 0 1 2 3 4 5 6
36. knows what to say, when to say it and whom to say it to. 0 1 2 3 4 5 6
37. stands behind the decisions of the coaches. 0 1 2 3 4 5 6
38. shows positive body language and behaviors consistently. 0 1 2 3 4 5 6
39. has a united front with fellow team leaders and coaches. 0 1 2 3 4 5 6
40. follows the decisions made by fellow leaders and others. 0 1 2 3 4 5 6

41. follows the lead of others.   0 1 2 3 4 5 6
42. puts the team first in all decisions and actions.   0 1 2 3 4 5 6
43. challenges self to expand comfort zones continually.   0 1 2 3 4 5 6
44. challenges teammates to expand comfort zones continually.   0 1 2 3 4 5 6
45. challenges teammates to achieve standards of execution
    continually.   0 1 2 3 4 5 6
46. organizes team functions so the team can improve social
    cohesion.   0 1 2 3 4 5 6
47. has a relationship with each player on the team and
    connects with teammates regularly.   0 1 2 3 4 5 6
48. ensures that no player is allowed to drift away from the
    team.   0 1 2 3 4 5 6
49. helps players when they are struggling during games.   0 1 2 3 4 5 6
50. offers encouragement and energy when team is struggling.   0 1 2 3 4 5 6
51. keeps team energized and focused when training gets hard.   0 1 2 3 4 5 6
52. is very approachable to coaches and teammates via a
    genuine willingness to openly discuss game/team/off-court
    issues.   0 1 2 3 4 5 6
53. knows how to support one's teammates and be there for
    them.   0 1 2 3 4 5 6
54. helps keep teammates and coaches on the same page and
    informed.   0 1 2 3 4 5 6
55. is willing to step up and resolve team problems right away.   0 1 2 3 4 5 6
56. is willing to seek out and utilize resources to assist in
    seeking solutions to team issues (coaches, sport psych,
    support staff).   0 1 2 3 4 5 6
57. solves problems for the betterment of the team rather
    than for personal reasons.   0 1 2 3 4 5 6
58. keeps the team organized about meetings, events, and
    schedule changes.   0 1 2 3 4 5 6
59. assists in organizing recruiting visits with coaches/
    teammates.   0 1 2 3 4 5 6
60. helps organize and enforce team rules and policies.   0 1 2 3 4 5 6
61. is our go-to player when the game is on the line.   0 1 2 3 4 5 6
62. continues trying to make plays in good and bad times on
    the court.   0 1 2 3 4 5 6
63. is dependable game in, game out.   0 1 2 3 4 5 6
64. helps teammates pursue goals with energy and persistence.   0 1 2 3 4 5 6
65. continues to raise the performance bar for self and
    teammates.   0 1 2 3 4 5 6
66. is driven to achieve optimal play and team execution
    beyond expectations by being very vocal and a rallying force. 0 1 2 3 4 5 6
67. thinks before acting (reacting), even in competitive
    environments.   0 1 2 3 4 5 6

68. is realistic in his ability and handles constructive criticism well. 0 1 2 3 4 5 6
69. is able to balance the many responsibilities of an athlete, student, teammate, and team leader. 0 1 2 3 4 5 6
70. will organize team meetings at the right times. 0 1 2 3 4 5 6
71. is a good meeting facilitator, allowing for all to have a voice. 0 1 2 3 4 5 6
72. follows-up on what is discussed at meetings and reinforces main messages appropriately. 0 1 2 3 4 5 6

USE OF THIS QUESTIONNAIRE IS AUTHORIZED BY THE AUTHOR: Copyright 2011
Mike Voight, Ph.D. voightmir@ccsu.edu

Survey Subscales:

Items 1—30 = 12 TALENTS of effective leaders:

- Courageous/Toughness (items 1–3)
- Work rate (4–6)
- Competitive (7–9)
- Confident (10–12)
- Quality trainer (13–15)
- Team player (16–18)
- Leader–by-example (19–21)
- Committed/Inspired (22–24)
- Compassionate/Humble (25–27)
- Character leader (28–30)
- Communicator (31–33)
- Competent (34–36)

Items 31—60 = 12 TECHNIQUES & TACTICS of effective leaders:

- Supportive (37–39)
- Follower (40–42)
- Challenger (43–45)
- Team Builder/Connector (46–48)
- Refocuser/Change Agent (49–51)
- Liaison/Communicator (52–54)
- Problem Solver/Collaborator (55–57)
- Organizer (58–60)
- Go-To Player (61–63)
- Energizer-Motivator-Confidence Enhancer (64–66)
- Aware-Balanced (67–69)
- Use of Meetings/Debriefs (70–72)

– Appendix 3 –

Reflective Questions

If you accept this opportunity of being a team captain, please answer the following questions.

(1) What do you think it is like being a captain in this program?

(2) What did you see from your captains last season?

(3) Why do you want to be a team captain?

(4) What are the benefits of being a team captain?

(5) What are the pitfalls/negatives of being a team captain?

(6) List some examples of profound leaders you have had in your life and what they did to make your list.

(7) How many of these qualities (and practices) do you have?

(8) What is holding you back (above)?

(9) What will you do about these barriers?

(10) What leadership positions have you held? How successful was this experience?

(11) What were your strengths? Areas of challenge? What lessons did you learn from it?

(12) What is the relationship between leadership and teamwork in your particular sport?

(13) What is the relationship between leadership, teamwork, and winning in your sport?

(14) What are the strengths of your team (think *total* game)?

(15) What primary improvement areas do you have (or did you have) to address with your team this season?

(16) So far in your captainship, are there any teammates that you know you can lean on and help support your leadership efforts?

(17) How have you already contributed to the leadership of this team?

(18) How has your co-captain already contributed to the leadership of this team?

(19) What challenges do you foresee in leading this team?

(20) What areas of leadership would you like to know more about?

– Appendix 4 –

Team Leader Survey

Please write in the name of the teammate (first name & initial of last name—no nicknames please) who you feel/think best typifies the particular leadership characteristic and/or practice. Top choice then second choice (2 per line if applicable)

(1) _____ is one of the most competitive players on the team.

(2) _____ consistently represents self and program in a professional manner.

(3) _____ leads through encouragement and energy.

(4) _____ displays a real commitment to being the best player he can be.

(5) _____ stays optimistic even in the face of personal and/or team adversity.

(6) _____ stands behind the decisions of the coaches.

(7) _____ puts the team first in all decisions and actions.

(8) _____ helps keep both players and coaches "on the same page."

(9) _____ steps up and attempts to resolve problems and "drama" right away.

(10) _____ helps players when they are struggling during matches.

(11) _____ is one of the hardest working players in practice.

(12) _____ consistently has a good attitude and energy at practice sessions.

(13) _____ keeps team energized and focused when training gets difficult-repetitive.

269

(14) _____ is good at helping us pick up our intensity at practice.

(15) _____ is a vocal leader in practice.

(16) _____ wants the ball with the game on the line.

(17) _____ is consistently in the right place and knows the system.

(18) _____ is our go-to player when the game is on the line.

(19) _____ is consistently the first to speak in a team meeting and first to start a drill.

(20) _____ leads by example in practice, in weights, on the road, in the classroom.

(21) _____ confronts teammates if necessary.

(22) _____ challenges teammates to achieve team standards and goals.

(23) _____ helps enforce team rules and standards.

(24) _____ helps pump the team up when needed during matches.

(25) _____ helps keep the locker room climate productive and cohesive.

(26) _____ organizes team functions to enhance teamwork and cohesion.

(27) _____ keeps the team organized about meetings, events, and schedule changes.

(28) _____ has a good rapport with each player on the team.

(29) _____ makes teammates feel comfortable going to them for questions or to talk about things.

(30) _____ connects with teammates regularly and keeps them all included and appreciated.

– Appendix 5 –

Team Leader Survey
Summary Sheet

Only those who received two votes were included (we had many with one vote)

ITEM #	ITEM DESCRIPTION	PLAYERS NOMINATED/ # VOTED

I. LEADER QUALITIES

#1	Most competitive	Nate (9)
#2	Represents in a professional manner	Eric (4)
#3	Leads through encouragement & energy	Nate (5)
#4	Commitment to be the best	Alex (3)
#5	Stays optimistic in adversity	Nate (8)

II. SUPPORTIVE LEADER

#6	Supports decisions of coaches	Kurt (5); Eric (4)
#7	Puts team first in decisions	Eric (5); Nate (3)
#8	Liaison between team & coaches	Eric (6); Kurt (3)
#9	Steps up and solves issues	Eric (6); Nate (3)
#10	Helps teammates when struggling	Nate (5); Eric (4)

III. PRACTICE LEADER

#11	Hardest working in practice	Nate (7); Alex (3)
#12	Consistently has good attitude & energy	Nate-Kyle (3)
#13	Keeps team energized & focused	Nate-Eric (3)
#14	Helps team pick up intensity	Nate (8)
#15	A vocal leader in practice	Nate (11)

271

IV. GO-TO LEADER

#16	Wants the ball with game on the line	Kyle (5); Nate (4)
#17	Consistently in right place/knows system	Nate-Eric (3)
#18	Our go-to player	Kyle (9); Nate (2)
#19	First to speak up &start drills	Nate (8); Eric (5)
#20	Leads by example in practice, weights	Eric (6); Alex (3)

V. ACCOUNTABILITY LEADER: Willing to Challenge Teammates

#21	Willing to confront teammates	Nate (5); Kyle (3)
#22	Challenges teammates on standards	Eric (4); Kyle (3);
#23	Helps enforce team rules & standards	Eric (7); Kurt (3)
#24	Helps pump team up when needed	Nate (6); Kyle (2)
#25	Keeps locker room climate productive	Eric (8)

VI. TEAM BUILDING–ORGANIZER LEADER

#26	Gets to know teammates	Kurt(4); Hunter (2)
#27	Keeps the team organized	Nate (5); Kyle (4)
#28	Has good rapport with teammates	Eric (5); Kurt (2)
#29	Teammates feel comfortable going to him	Eric (7); Kyle (2)
#30	Connects with teammates regularly	Kyle-Eric (5); Kurt (2)

CUMULATIVE TOTALS

	TOP PICKS	2ND PLACE	TOTAL PICKS	TOP PICKS #
Eric	= 13 top picks	3	16 out of 30 items	3/5 Support L
				3/5 Challenge L
				3/5 Team Builder
Nate	= 13 top picks	4	17 out of 30 items	3/5 L Qual's
				5/5 Practice L
Kurt	= 2 top picks	6	8 out of 30 items	
Kyle	= 4 top picks	2	3 out of 30 items	
Alex	= 1 top pick	2	3 out of 30 items	
Hunter	= 0 top picks	1	1 out of 30 items	

– Appendix 6 –

Leadership Playbook Process:
15 Stages

I. *Leadership 101: Reality Check*
- Positives/negatives (risks & rewards) of being a leader
- Responsibilities of being a team leader (your perspective & coaches)
- Daily "to-do's" for captains of this program
- Have former captains speak with the group

II *Your Call*
- Take two days to decide (no consequences for saying no)
- Ask more questions of coaches, former captains, *leadership consultant* (LC)
- Once you decide to be a captain, you are "all in"

III. *Reflective Questions*
- Motives for being captain; risks/rewards; your perceived strengths; present leadership contributions; team needs/strengths; how will you impact this team?

IV. *Sharing of Reflective Responses/Discussion*
- Open exchange of responses with co-captains, assistant captains, apprentices, coaching staff and LC
- Question and answer, discussion
- Meeting notes are typed & shared post-meeting

V. *Team Needs Assessment*
- Team completed the 30-item Team Leader Survey to vote for captain, so these results are shared with coaches and captains to look for specific patterns of responses that can be used and are referred to often throughout the season with captains

VI. *Leadership Assessment*
- Each captain, and assistant captain, completes the 60-item *Leadership Skill-Set Survey* which outlines 10 leadership qualities and 10 leadership practices; results are shared with coaches and captains

VII. Captain Platform

- Captains (captains, assistant captains), along with the assistance of "senior leaders" (upperclassmen) decided on primary leadership objectives for the season (2–4 platform points)

VIII. Team Feedback for Captains: Needs from/for Captains

- Each teammate was given the opportunity, in writing, to let the captains know what they needed from them to help them improve their game and team effectiveness
- Each teammate would also commit to helping their captains lead the team in specific ways, which were also typed and given to the captains, with names attached.
- The captains also shared with the team what they need from them to help lead the program this season

IX. Leadership Roles and Responsibilities

- Based upon the needs assessment, individual assessment, captain platform points, and from the feedback from/to team and captains, formal roles and responsibilities are defined and discussed.

X. Assign "Starter" Leadership Process Points

- Primarily dependent on team needs, but usually have captains begin "captaining" by focusing on integrating the freshmen into the team standards/routines, focusing on practice preparation (starting practice with energy and focus) and providing energy throughout practice when needed, and always being the example (lead by example)

XI. Education—How to Best Accomplish Responsibilities

- Discussions with captains, coaches, and LC about the manner in which these leadership responsibilities should be carried out

XII. Practice—Aware and Capture Captain Moments

- Coaches, captains, and teammates assess how the captains are performing their leadership responsibilities
- Captains will self assess prior to captain check-in meetings (with LC and head coach), coaches recall hits (good captaining) or misses (poor or missed captain moments), and teammates offer feedback once or twice during the season via email then captain holds discussions about the feedback

XIII. Hot Spots: Actual Problem Solving as They Occur

- As part of weekly meetings with head coach, and every 2–3 week check-ins with LC, issues and potential issues are discussed
- LC is contacted if any issue arises in-between these meetings for discussion and intervention

XIV. Follow-ups and Check-ins

- Weekly captain and head coach meetings are established, usually to start a new week of training and match preparation.

XV. Evaluation and Debriefings

- Ongoing evaluation of captain responsibilities by coaches, and self assessments (see XII above) and weekly coach meetings
- End of the season debriefing of leadership experience and leadership program

– Appendix 7 –

Leadership Development Process: Winter/Spring

DATE-STAGES	OBJECTIVE	CONTENT
Off-Season:		
June email	Season debriefing questions for past season's captains	What worked; challenges; contributions; advice
July email	Compilation of feedback	Same as above to coaches & former captains
Pre-Season Training:		
October team email	Season preparation questions	Team strengths; areas needing improvement; standards; vision
November visit	Team & captain meetings; meet with captain apprentices staff meetings	Vote for captains; prioritize standards& team identity/needs; leadership contributions last season-future Stages I-VI
Pre-Season Matches:		
January visit	Team & captain meetings; Staff meetings; watch matches	Brainstorm/define/prioritize team standards; Mental preparation—individual & team routines; Stages VII-XI Weekly captains meeting with Coach
February VC	With team captains	Progress made on platform points, individual/team issues & solutions

		Weekly captains meeting with Coach

Conference Season:

March VC	With team captains	Progress made on platform points, individual/team issues & solutions Weekly captains meeting with Coach
March visit	Team & captain meetings; Staff meetings; watch matches	Progress points; lessons learned;accountability; team-mate feedback Stages XII-XV
April VC	With team captains	Progress points; lessons learned; Weekly captains meeting with Coach

Post-Season:

May VC	With team captains	Progress points; post-season prep
May visit on-site	Final four preparation meetings	Preparation

Note. **VC = video conference**

– Appendix 8 –

Leadership Development Process: Summer/Fall

DATE-STAGES	OBJECTIVE	CONTENT
Off-Season:		
December email	Season debriefing questions	What worked-challenges
January visit	Season debriefing questions for past season's captains	What worked-challenges-contributions-advice;
	Spring season vision/standards	Stage XV; Brainstorm new
	Introduce leadership program	standards; Apprenticeship period for volunteer leaders (those who want to be involved)
February VC	Progress points	Individual/team progress
		Leading by committee (apprentices)
		Weekly leadership group meeting with Coach
March visit	Captain vote; team meetings	Captain vote; progress on
	New captains meetings	standards; Stages I-VI
		Weekly captains meeting with Coach
April VC	Team and captain meetings	Accountability; progress points
		Weekly captains meeting with Coach
Summer emails	Orient the new players	Program vision, standards
	Correspondence within team	Establish relationships

Pre-Season Training:

August email	Provide schedule for meetings	Vision, standards, traditions
August visit	Team and captain meetings	Above, Stages VII-X Weekly captains meeting with Coach

Pre-Season Matches:

September VC	Captain meeting	Progress points; Stages XII-XIV Weekly captains meeting with Coach
September VC	Team and captain meeting	Progress from pre-season matches

Conference Season—1st Round:

October VC	Captain meeting	Daily to-do's; Platform points Weekly captains meeting with Coach
October VC	Team and captain meeting	Progress points; Standards
October email	Team and captains	Feedback regarding team strengths, captain progress; Stage XII-XIII

Conference Season—2nd Round:

November VC	Captain meeting	Platform points; lessons learned Rd 1 Weekly captains meeting with Coach
November VC	Team and captain meeting	Lessons learned Round 1 conference
November visit	Team and captain meetings	Platform points; lessons learned Rd 2 of conference

Post-Season:

December VC	Captain meeting	NCAA tournament preparation
December visit on-site	Team and captain meetings	Final Four preparation

Note: **VC = video conference**

Chapter Notes

Introduction

1. Pat Williams, *Coaching Your Kids to Be Leaders* (New York: Faith Words, 2005), 6.
2. Jeff Janssen, *The Team Captain's Leadership Manual* (Cary, NC: Winning the Mental Game, 2003), x.
3. Jeff Janssen, *The Team Captain's Leadership Manual* (Cary, NC: Winning the Mental Game, 2003), xi.
4. Jeff Janssen, *The Team Captain's Leadership Manual* (Cary, NC: Winning the Mental Game, 2003), xii.
5. Jeff Janssen, *The Team Captain's Leadership Manual* (Cary, NC: Winning the Mental Game, 2003), xiv.
6. Daniel Goleman, Richard Boyatzis, and Annie McKee, *Primal Leadership: Realizing the Power of Emotional Intelligence* (Boston: Harvard Business School Publishing, 2002).
7. Eric Kail, "Becoming a Leader Developer." In Major Doug Crandall (Ed.), *Leadership Lessons from West Point* (San Francisco: Jossey-Bass, 2007), 4.

Chapter 1

1. Jeff Janssen and Greg Dale, *The Seven Secrets of Successful Coaches* (Cary, NC: Winning the Mental Game, 2002), 170.
2. "High School Dropouts in America" (September 2010). Retrieved March 1, 2013, from www.all4ed.org/files/HighSchoolDropouts.pdf
3. D. Krache, "By the Numbers—High School Dropouts: College Board Says 857 Drop Out Every Hour of Every School Day" (2012, June 20). Retrieved March 2, 2013, from http://www.krcrtv.com/news/national/By-the-numbers-High-school-dropouts/-/14285942/15172398/-/rdu52lz/-/index.html

4. L. Layton, "High School Graduation Rate Rises In U.S." In *Washington Post* (2012, March 19). Retrieved March 12, 2013, from http://articles.washingtonpost.com/2012-03-19/local/35448541_1_grad-nation-graduation-rates-robert-balfanz
5. Youth Violence Stats (n.d.). Retrieved March 10, 2013, from http://www.childtrendsdatabank.org/?q=node/174
6. M. Neal, "1 in 12 Teens Have Attempted Suicide: Report CDC Finds Suicide Among High School Students on the Rise." In *New York Daily News* (2012, June 9). Retrieved March 12, 2013, from http://www.nydailynews.com/life-style/health/1-12-teens-attempted-suicide-report-article-1.1092622#ixzz2My7gPcyK
7. O.G. Hunter, National Statistics on Bullying in Schools (2012, February 14). Retrieved March 2, 2013, from http://www.alicetx.com/news/article_87be339a-5658-11e1-a087-0019bb2963f4.html
8. A. Egley and J.C. Howell, Highlights of the 2010 National Youth Gang Survey (2012, April). Retrieved March 12, 2013, from https://www.ncjrs.gov/app/QA/Detail.aspx?Id=146&context=9
9. M. Healy, Youths' Drug of Choice? Prescription. In *Los Angeles Times.com* (2008, September 15). Retrieved March 10, 2013, from http://www.latimes.com/features/health/la-he-drugs15
10. The National Campaign to Prevent Teen and Unplanned Pregnancy (n.d.). Retrieved March 2, 2013, from http://www.thenationalcampaign.org/national/default.aspx
11. M.C. Jalonick, "Obesity Rates Soaring Over 2 Decades." In *The Florida Times Union* (2011 July 8), A1, A8.
12. M. Gold, "The Latest Figures from Nielsen Have Children's TV Usage at an Eight-Year High. Children's Health Advocates Warn of Adverse Effects." In *Los Angeles Times* (2009, Octo-

ber 27), Retrieved March 2, 2013, from http://articles.latimes.com/2009/oct/27/entertainment/et-kids-tv27

13. "Amount of Hours Children Spend Watching TV Could Impact Waistlines" (2012, July 16), Retrieved March 10, 2013, from http://www.foxnews.com/health/2012/07/16/amount-hours-children-spend-watching- tv-could-impact-waistlines/#ixzz2MyU2TytJ

14. Neil Howe and William Strauss, *Millennials Rising: The Next Great Generation* (New York: Vintage, 2000); Richard T. Schaefer, *Sociology* (New York: McGraw Hill, 2011); Jean Twenge, *Generation Me: Why Today's Young Americans Are More Confident, Assertive, Entitled-and More Miserable Than Ever Before* (New York: Free Press, 2006), 150; B. Fields, B. Wilder, S. Bunch, & R. Newbold, *Millennial Leaders: Success Stories from Today's Most Brilliant Generation Y Leaders* (Buffalo Grove, IL: Writers of the Round Table, 2008); Hara Estroff Marano, *Nation of Wimps: The High Cost of Invasive Parenting* (New York: Broadway Books, 2008), 19.

15. Jay Coakley, *Sports in Society: Issues and Controversies,* 10th ed. (New York: McGraw-Hill, 2008); Stanley Eitzen, *Sport in Contemporary Society: An Anthology,* 9th ed. (Oxford University Press, 2011); Howard L. Nixon and James H. Frey, *Sociology of Sport* (New York: Wadsworth Publishing, 1996).

16. Bill Beswick, *Focused for Soccer* (Champaign, IL: Human Kinetics, 2001), 28.

17. Jeff Janssen, *The Team Captain's Leadership Manual* (Cary, NC: Winning the Mental Game, 2003), 35.

18. Andy Murray, *Los Angeles Times* (1997, December 11), 3.

19. Jeff Janssen and Greg Dale, *The Seven Secrets of Successful Coaches* (Cary, NC: Winning the Mental Game, 2002), 103.

20. Lynne Lancaster and David Stillman, *When Generations Collide: Who They Are. Why They Clash. How to Solve the Generational Puzzle at Work* (New York: Collins Business, 2002), 333.

21. Jean M. Twenge and W. Keith Campbell, *The Narcissism Epidemic: Living in the Age of Entitlement* (New York: Atria, 2010); Jean Twenge, *Generation Me: Why Today's Young Americans Are More Confident, Assertive, Entitled-and More Miserable Than Ever Before* (New York: Free Press, 2006), 150.

22. Lynne Lancaster and David Stillman, *When Generations Collide: Who They Are. Why They Clash. How to Solve the Generational Puzzle at Work* (New York: Collins Business, 2002), 42.

23. E. Hoover, "The Millennial Muddle: How Stereotyping Students Became a Thriving Industry and a Bundle of Contradictions," *The Chronicle of Higher Education.* (2009, October 16), A28–33.

24. Jean Twenge, *Generation Me: Why Today's Young Americans Are More Confident, Assertive, Entitled-and More Miserable Than Ever Before* (New York: Free Press, 2006), 24.

25. Ibid., 9.

26. Diane Oblinger, Boomers, "Gen-Xers, and Millennials: Understanding the New Students," *EDUCAUSE Review* (2003, July/August), 37–47.

27. Lynne Lancaster and David Stillman, *When Generations Collide: Who They Are. Why They Clash. How to Solve the Generational Puzzle at Work* (New York: Collins Business, 2002), 45.

28. Ibid., 46.

29. Craig Wilson, "Millennials: We Love the 90's," *USA Today.* (2011, October 25), D1.

30. Neil Howe and William Strauss, *Millennials Rising: The Next Great Generation* (New York: Vintage, 2000), 4.

31. Ibid., 5.

32. The Echo Boomers (aired 10/3/2004). Retrieved October 4, 2004, from http://www.cbsnews.com/stories/2004/10/01/60minutes/printable46890.shtml

33. Hara Estroff Marano, *Nation of Wimps: The High Cost of Invasive Parenting* (New York: Broadway Books, 2008), 39.

34. Ibid., 180.

35. Ibid., 182.

36. Ibid., 179.

37. Ibid., 181.

38. Ibid., 180.

39. Ibid., 176.

40. Ibid., 179.

41. M.B. Marcus, "Minority Kids Use Media More," *USA Today* (2011, June 8), 1A.

42. Jerry Crowe, "Internet Propels Athlete Hazing Issue to Forefront," *Los Angeles Times.* (2006, May 19), D11.

43. Melanie Eversley and John Bacon, Manslaughter Charges for 12 in Florida A & M Band Hazing, *USA Today* (2013, March 5), 1A.

44. Jerry Crowe, "Internet Propels Athlete Hazing Issue to Forefront," *Los Angeles Times.* (2006, May 19), D11.

45. Robert Klemko, "Athlete Tweets Often Create Grief," *USA Today.* (2011, June 9), 1C.

46. Bob Kimball, "Twitter Shutdown," *USA Today.* (2011, August 17), 3C.

47. George Schroeder, "Schools Try to Keep Athletes Off 'Catfish' Hook," *USA Today* (2013, March 7), 7C.

48. Meg Kissinger, "The Millennials," *Milwaukee Journal Sentinel* (2005, June 5), 3.

49. Jean Twenge, *Generation Me: Why Today's Young Americans Are More Confident, Assertive, Entitled-and More Miserable Than Ever Before* (New York: Free Press, 2006), 9.

50. "The Echo Boomers" (aired 10/3/2004). Retrieved October 4, 2004, from http://www.cbsnews.com/stories/2004/10/01/60minutes/printable46890.shtml

51. Patricia Breakey, "Entitlement Generation Expects It All," *The Daily Star* (2005, July 2),1–3.

52. Hara Estroff Marano, *Nation of Wimps: The High Cost of Invasive Parenting* (New York: Broadway Books, 2008), 59–60.

53. Ibid., 60.

54. Meg Kissinger, "The Millennials," *Milwaukee Journal Sentinel* (2005, June 5), 4.

55. Michael Josephson, "Cheating Nation," *PARADE Magazine* (2006, October 15), D9.

56. Lance Pugmire, "Sports Teaching Kids to Cheat?" *Los Angeles Times* (2007, February 18), D1, D9.

57. Michael Josephson, "Cheating Nation," *PARADE Magazine* (2006, October 15), D9.

58. "College Debts and Broken Dreams," *Business Week* (2005, December 12), 15.

59. B. Field, S. Wilder, J. Bunch, and R. Newbold, *Millennial Leaders: Success Stories from Today's Most Brilliant Generation Y Leaders* (Buffalo Grove, IL: Writers of the Round Table, 2008).

60. Sharon Jayson, "Gen Y Makes a Mark," *USA Today* (2006, December), 1A.

61. Steven Hipple, Self-Employment in the United States (2010, September). Retrieved March 11, 2013, from www.bls.gov/opub/mlr/2010/09/art2full.pdf

62. Sharon Jayson, "Gen Y Makes a Mark," *USA Today* (2006, December), 1A.

63. Mike Weber, "Millennials Reign at Olympics," *Daily Lobo* (2004, August 31), 12.

64. Jean Twenge, *Generation Me: Why Today's Young Americans Are More Confident, Assertive, Entitled-and More Miserable Than Ever Before* (New York: Free Press, 2006), 24.

65. Hara Estroff Marano, *Nation of Wimps: The High Cost of Invasive Parenting* (New York: Broadway Books, 2008).

66. Ibid., 3–6.

67. Neil Howe and William Strauss, *Millennials Go to College* (AACRAO, 2003), 6.

68. Sharon Jayson, "Are Students Today More Narcissistic? Survey Cites Social Networks," *USA Today* (2009, August 25), 6D.

69. Larry Gordon and Louis Sahagun, "Gen Y's Ego Trip Takes a Bad Turn," *Los Angeles Times* (2007, February 27), B1, B8.

70. *The Daily Trojan* (2004, February 12), 12.

71. Hara Estroff Marano, *Nation of Wimps: The High Cost of Invasive Parenting* (New York: Broadway Books, 2008), 19.

72. Jeff Hinds, *The Republican* (2007, December), 179.

73. Hara Estroff Marano, *Nation of Wimps: The High Cost of Invasive Parenting* (New York: Broadway Books, 2008), 176.

74. Ibid., 183.

75. James Dobson, *Dr. James Dobson's Focus on the Family Bulletin* (Carol Stream, IL: Tyndale House Publishers, 2005), 5.

76. Joe Drape, *ESPN the Magazine* (1998, April 20), 103.

Chapter 2

1. Joe Drape, Talking 'Bout a Revolution, *ESPN the Magazine* (1998, April 20), 103.

2. Phil Jackson, *The Last Season: A Team in Search of Its Soul* (New York: Penguin Group, 2004), 21.

3. Lynne Lancaster and David Stillman, *When Generations Collide: Who They Are. Why They Clash. How to Solve the Generational Puzzle at Work* (New York: Collins Business, 2002), 245.

4. Carl Bialek, "A Lifetime of Career Changes," in *Wall Street Journal* (2010, September 3). Retrieved March 15, 2013, from http://blogs.wsj.com/numbersguy/a-lifetime-of-career-changes-988/

5. Harvey Dorfman, *Coaching the Mental Game* (Lanham, MD: First Taylor Trade Publishing, 2003), 21.

6. Jodi Yoder, Coach-Athlete Issues, in M. Thompson, R. Vernacchia, & W. Moore (Eds.), *Case Studies in Applied Sport Psychology: An Educational Approach* (Dubuque, Iowa: Kendall/Hunt Publishing, 1998).

7. Jean Twenge, *Generation Me: Why Today's Young Americans Are More Confident, Assertive, Entitled-and More Miserable Than Ever Before* (New York: Free Press, 2006), 18.

8. Ibid., 21.

9. Richard Cox, *Sport Psychology-Concepts and Applications* (New York: McGraw-Hill, 2001), 322.

10. Robert Weinberg and Dan Gould, *Foundations of Sport and Exercise Psychology* (Champaign, IL: Human Kinetics, 2007), 189.

11. Ibid., 194.

12. Harvey Dorfman, *Coaching the Mental Game* (Lanham, MD: First Taylor Trade Publishing, 2003), 42.

13. Jeff Janssen and Greg Dale, *The Seven Secrets of Successful Coaches* (Cary, NC: Winning the Mental Game, 2002), 139.

14. *Los Angeles Times* (2002, February 8), D4.

15. *USA Today* (2002, January 13), C5.

16. *Newsobserver.com* (2003).

17. *USA Today* (1998, February 17).

18. *Los Angeles Times* (1998, February 24).

19. *Los Angeles Times* (1997, December 17).

20. *Los Angeles Times* (2002, November 15).

21. *The Wichita Eagle* (1999, January 31).

22. *USA Today* (2006, October 20).

23. *USA Today* (2012, November).

24. *ESPN.com* (2012, August).

25. Rachel George, "E-mails Illuminate Gillispie's Fall," *USA Today* (2012, October 24), C6.

26. Dugan Arnett, "Ex-Player Accuses Mangino of Mistreatment," in *KU Sports.com* (2009, December 2). Retrieved January 28, 2010, from http://www.2.kusports.com/news/2009/dec/02/ex-player-accuses-mangino-mistreatment/

27. News services, "Leavitt Fired as South Florida Coach," in *Espn.com* (2010, January 8). Retrieved January 28, 2010, from http://sports.espn.go.com/espn/print?id=4807719&type=story

28. Steve Wieberg, "End of Leach Saga, Player Ousters at Mich. State Spice Alamo Battle," *USA Today* (2009, December 31), C5.

29. Alexander Wolff, "Knight Fall," in *Sports Illustrated.com* (2000, September 18). Retrieved January 2012, from http://sportsillustrated.cnn.com/vault/article/magazine/MAG1020376/index.htm

30. Wire reports, "Montgomery: 'I Made a Mistake,'" *USA Today* (2013, February 20), C6.

31. Mike Foss, "Texas Tech Coach Billy Gillespie Faces Allegations of Mistreatment," in *USA Today.com* (2012, September 5). Retrieved February, 2013, from http://content.usatoday.com/communities/campusrivalry/post-2012/09/texas-tech-coach

32. Wire reports, "Police Investigate Idaho State Coach After Complaint," *USA Today* (2012, October 18), 2C

33. Paul Myerberg and George Schroeder, "Coaches' Rough Behavior in Spotlight," *USA Today* (2012, November 13), 5C.

34. Joe Drape, "Talking 'Bout a Revolution," *ESPN the Magazine* (1998, April 20), p. 103.

35. Wire reports, "Dissatisfaction," *USA Today* (1998, February 17), C8.

36. Chip Alexander, "Athletes' Voices Heard," in *Charlotte Observer.com* (2003, April 1). Retrieved March 29, 2003, from http://www.newsobserver.com/sports/v-print/story/2388051.html.

37. Chris Duefresne, "A Wildcat Strike May Take Flight," *Los Angeles Times* (2002, November 15), D10.

38. Associated Press, "Arizona's Mackovic Vows to Change His Approach," *Los Angeles Times* (2002, November 19), C7.

39. Associated Press, "Wagner Fired After Player Exodus," in *ESPN.com* (2010, June 1). Retrieved July 22, 2010, from http://sports.espn.go.com/espn/print?id=5240400&type=HeadlineNews&imagesPrint=off

40. Nathan Hathaway, "Embattled Coach Fired," in *The Collegian* (2005, March 4). Retrieved March 7, 2005, from http://www.csufresno.edu/Collegian/archive/2005/03/04/news/coach.shtml

41. Associated Press, "Players: Teammate Made to Run Till She Collapsed," in *ESPN.com* (2003, February 10). Retrieved February 10, 2003, from http://espn.go.com/ncw/news/2003/0210/1506777.html

42. Erik Brady, "Coaches Who Cross the Line: Push to Win Can Become 'Abusive Tactics,'" *USA Today* (2012, September 18), C7.

43. Liz Clarke, "Jae Su Chun Resigns as U.S. Short-Track Speed Skating Coach," in *Washington Post.com* (2012, October 11). Retrieved February, 2013, from http://articles.washingtonpost.com/2012-10-11/sports/35502307_1_hyung-yeo-canadian-skater-olivier-jean-simon-cho

44. Stephen Smith, "Pistons Protest Is a Problem for Players," in *ESPN.com* (2011, February 27). Retrieved June 13, 2011, from http://sports.espn.go.com/nba/news/story?id=6159298

45. Associated Press, "Laviolette: We Have Legitimate Chance at Gold," in *ESPN.com* (2005, August 16). Retrieved June 13, 2011, from http://sports.espn.go.com/oly/news/story?id=2135849

46. Christine Brennan, "Player Revolt Against Commissioner Biven Latest Danger," *USA Today* (2009, July 9). Retrieved June 13, 2011, from http://www.usatoday.com/sports/columnist/brennan/2009-07-08-lpga-bivens_N.htm

47. Internet search retrieved June 13, 2011, from https://www.google.com/#q=international+soccer+player+revolts

48. Internet search retrieved June 13, 2011, from https://www.google.com/#q=german+soccer+player+revolts

49. Wire reports, "Magic Number," *Los Angeles Times* (2004, May 21), C6.

50. Personal experience with a client.

51. Personal experience with a client.

52. Daniel Monson, "Former Player Sues Guevara," CMU (2009, February 11). Retrieved June 14, 2011, from http://www.cm-life.com/2009/02/11/formerplayersuesguevaracmu/

53. "Staff, University Sued Over Alleged Promise of Scholarship," *Sports Litigation Alert Archives* (2006, May 19). Retrieved June 14, 2011, from http://www.hackneypublications.com/sla/archive/000284.php

54. "Staff, Former Player on Women's Basketball Team Settles Bias Lawsuit Against Penn State," *Chronicle of Higher Education.com* (2007, February 5). Retrieved June 14, 2011, from http://chronicle.com/article/Former-Player-on-Womens/38174/?otd=Y2xpY2t0aHJ1Ojo6c293aWRnZXXQ6Ojpja

55. Katie Thomas, "NCAA Sued Over One-Year Scholarships," in *New York Times.com* (2010, October 25). Retrieved June 14, 2011, from http://www.nytimes.com/2010/10/26/sports/ncaafootball/26ncaa.html

56. Erin Sherbert, "NCAA, UC Sued by College Football Players," in *SFWeekly.com* (2011,

March 16). Retrieved June 14, 2011, from http://blogs.sfweekly.com/thesnitch/2011/03/ncaa_uc_cal_state.php

57. Wire Reports, "Player Files Suit," *USA Today*. (2011, July 6), 8C.

58. Mona Hill, "Feather River College Players Bring Suit of Their Own," in *Plumas County News.com* (2011, February 2). Retrieved June 14, 2011, from http://www.plumasnews.com/home/7854-feather-river-college-players-bring-suit-of-their-own.html

59. News Services, "Former Players Stafon Johnson Files Lawsuit Against USC," in *The Seattle Times.com* (2011, January 24). Retrieved June 14, 2011, from http://seattletimes.nwsource.com/html/othersports/2014028057_digs25.html-dailysentinel.com

60. Pedro Moura, "USC and Stafon Johnson Settle Lawsuit," in *ESPN.com* (2012, January 19). Retrieved February 10, 2013, from http://espn.go.com/losangeles/ncf/story/_/id/7477966/usc-trojans-settle-ex-player-stafon-johnson-negligence-lawsuit

61. Sudhin Thanawala, "Prep Football Player Suing UH, Ex-Coach," in *Honolulu Advertiser.com* (2008, February 28). Retrieved June 14, 2011, from http://the.honoluluadvertiser.com/article/2008/Feb/28/sp/hawaii802280375.html

62. Staff, "Rutgers U. Women's Basketball Player Sues Shock Jock Don Imus for Slander," in *Chronicle of Higher Education.com* (2007, August 15). Retrieved June 14, 2011. http://chronicle.com/article/Rutgers-U-Women-s-Basketball/39393

63. ABC News, "LAX Player Files Lawsuit Against Duke University," *ABC.com* (2007, January 4). Retrieved June 14, 2011, from http://abclocal.go.com/wtvd/story?section=triangle&id=4905060

64. News Services, "Giuliani's Son Sues Duke," in *ESPN.com* (2008, July 24). Retrieved June 14, 2011, from http://sports.espn.go.com/ncaa/news/story?id=3503157

65. Tom Canavan, "Rutgers Fires Hoops Coach Kevin Bannon," in *USA Today.com* (2001, March 20). Retrieved from, http://usatoday30.usatoday.com/sports/basketba/skm/2001-03-20-rutgers-bannon.htm

66. Associated Press, "Judge Rules Player to Be Reinstated," in *ESPN.com* (2009, February 12). Retrieved June 14, 2011, from http://sports.espn.go.com/ncaa/news/story?id=3903336

67. Brandon Marcello, "Former Pitcher Suing MSU," in *ClarionLedger.com* (2011, May 14). Retrieved June 14, 2011, from http://www.clarionledger.com/article/20110514/SPORTS030102/105140343/Former-pitcher-suing-MSU

68. Michael Rosenberg and Mark Snyder, "A Look Inside Rodriguez's Rigorous Program," in *Detroit Free Press.com* (2009, August 29).

Retrieved June 14, 2011, fromhttp://www.freep.com/article/20090829/SPORTS06/90829023

69. Mike Penner, "Today's Athletes," *Los Angeles Times* (2000), 8C.

70. Jason Reid, "Sheffield Hints He Might Not Play Very Well," *Los Angeles Times* (2001, March 5), D5.

71. Wire Reports, "Magic Number," *Los Angeles Times* (2004, May 21), C6.

72. Larry Stewart, "When This Bruin Talks, Trojans Listen Too," *Los Angeles Times* (2005, June 16), C1.

73. Tim Kawakami, "Still Feeling the Tremors," *Los Angeles Times* (1997, November 20), C14.

74. Ibid., C14.

75. Dan Woog, "A Season After Getting Ousted," *Soccer America* (1998, January 19), 24.

76. Mike Voight, *A Structural Model of the Determinants, Personal and Situational Influences, and the Consequences of Athlete Dissatisfaction*, University of Southern California (2000), Ann Arbor: UMI Dissertation Services.

77. Mike Voight and John Callaghan, "A Structural Model on the Determinants and Reactions to Athlete Dissatisfaction," *International Journal of Sports Science & Coaching* 1 (2006), 37–51.

78. Bill Beswick, *Focused for Soccer* (Champaign, IL: Human Kinetics, 2001), 156.

79. Katherine Mangan, *The Chronicle of Higher Education*. (1995, February 10), 15–17.

80. Times Wire Reports, *Los Angeles Times* (2004, November 11), A15.

81. Peter Frasso, "Softball: Communication Key to Coaching Philosophy," in *The Observer On-line* (2001, April 19). Retrieved June 20, 2012, from http:www.observer.com

82. Associated Press, "Arizona's Mackovic Vows to Change His Approach," *Los Angeles Times* (2002, November 19), C7.

83. John Hunter, "Ageless Leaders," *ESPN the Magazine* (2000), 22.

84. Tony Dicicco, Colleen Hacker, and Charles Salzerg, *Catch Them Being Good: Everything You Need to Know to Successfully Coach Girls* (New York: Penguin Books, 2002), 12.

85. Ibid., 14.

86. David Wharton, "Two Head Coaches Prove Nice Guys Don't Finish Last," *Los Angeles Times* (2006, January 4), A10.

87. Associated Press, "Sherrill Discusses Coaching Memories," *Dallas News* (2005, November 29), 4.

88. Dan Patrick, "Just My Type," *Sports Illustrated* (May 23, 2011), 18.

89. Roby Stahl, *Developing the Player-Leader*, in *NSCAA.com* (2010, September). Retrieved October 12, 2010, from http://www.nscaa.com/print2.php?id=136

Chapter 3

1. Harvey Dorfman, *Coaching the Mental Game* (Lanham, MD: First Taylor Trade Publishing, 2003), 7.
2. Claire Raines, "Managing Millennials," in Generationsatwork.com (2002). Retrieved September 15, 2010, from www.Generationsatwork.com
3. Harvey Dorfman, *Coaching the Mental Game* (Lanham, MD: First Taylor Trade Publishing, 2003), 21.
4. William Berard III, "Coach Perspectives in the New Millennium," *NFHS Coaches Quarterly Magazine* (2000, Winter), 20–24.
5. Jeff Janssen and Greg Dale, *The Seven Secrets of Successful Coaches* (Cary, NC: Winning the Mental Game, 2002), 18.
6. Anson Dorrance, *Training Soccer Champions* (Raleigh: JTC Sports, 1996), 20.
7. Jeff Janssen and Greg Dale, *The Seven Secrets of Successful Coaches* (Cary, NC: Winning the Mental Game, 2002), 18.
8. Ibid., 19.
9. Kurt Dirks, "Trust in Leadership and Team Performance: Evidence from NCAA Basketball." *Journal of Applied Psychology* 55:6, (2000), 1009.
10. Jeff Janssen and Greg Dale, *The Seven Secrets of Successful Coaches* (Cary, NC: Winning the Mental Game, 2002), 134.
11. Ibid., 144.
12. Dan Doyle and Deborah Burch, *Encyclopedia of Sports Parenting: Everything You Need to Guide Your Young Athlete* (New York: Hall of Fame Press, 2008).
13. Pat Williams, *Coaching Your Kids to Be Leaders* (New York: Faith Words, 2005).
14. Dean Smith, Gerald Bell, and John Kilgo, *The Carolina Way: Leadership Lessons from a Life in Coaching* (New York: Penguin Books, 2004), 107.
15. J. Bradley Garner, *A Brief Guide for Teaching Millennial Learners* (Marion, IN: Triangle Publishers, 2007), 12.
16. Pat Williams, *Coaching Your Kids to Be Leaders* (New York: Faith Words, 2005), 43.
17. Dean Smith, Gerald Bell, and John Kilgo, *The Carolina Way: Leadership Lessons from a Life in Coaching* (New York: Penguin Books, 2004), 104.
18. http://dictionary.reference.com/browse/enable?s=t
19. Dean Smith, Gerald Bell, and John Kilgo, *The Carolina Way: Leadership Lessons from a Life in Coaching* (New York: Penguin Books, 2004), 105.
20. Jeff Janssen and Greg Dale, *The Seven Secrets of Successful Coaches* (Cary, NC: Winning the Mental Game, 2002), 170.
21. Hara Estroff Marano, *Nation of Wimps:*

The High Cost of Invasive Parenting (New York: Broadway Books, 2008).
22. Jeff Janssen and Greg Dale, *The Seven Secrets of Successful Coaches* (Cary, NC: Winning the Mental Game, 2002), 97.
23. Ibid., 187.
24. Tim Layden, Mack Brown, *Sports Illustrated* (2005, December 5), 54.
25. George Vecsey, "Living and Learning, Changing and Winning," *The New York Times* (2008, July 27), 7.
26. Anson Dorrance, *Training Soccer Champions* (Raleigh: JTC Sports, Inc., 1996), 23.
27. Thomas Houser, "Ten Tips to Coaching Survival," in volleyball.about.com. Retrieved May 18, 2006, from http://volleyball.about.com/od/coachingselfhelp/a/coachingsurviva_p.htm
28. Pat Williams, *Coaching Your Kids to Be Leaders* (New York: Faith Words, 2005), 273.

Chapter 4

1. Warren Bennis and Joan Goldsmith, *Learning to Lead: A Workbook on Becoming a Leader* (New York: Basic Books, 2010), 1.
2. Pat Williams, *Coaching Your Kids to Be Leaders* (New York: Faith Words, 2005), 6.
3. Jay Coakley, *Sports in Society: Issues & Controversies*, 8th ed. (Boston: McGraw-Hill, 2004).
4. Jim Loehr, "Leadership: Full Engagement for Success," in S. Murphy (Ed.) *The Sport Psychology Handbook* (Champaign, IL: Human Kinetics, 2005), 155.
5. Andy Rudd, "Which 'Character' Should Sport Develop?," *Physical Educator* 62:4 (2005), 205–211.
6. Georgios Giannoudis and Marios Goudas, "A Team-Sports-Based Life-Skills Program in a Physical Education Context," *Learning and Instruction* 18:6 (2008), 528–536.
7. Pat Williams, *Coaching Your Kids to Be Leaders* (New York: Faith Words, 2005), ix.
8. John Wooden, *My Personal Best: Life Lessons from an All-American Journey* (New York: McGraw-Hill, 2004), 78.
9. David Shields and Brenda Bredemeier, *True Competition: A Guide to Pursuing Excellence in Sport and Society* (Champaign, IL: Human Kinetics, 2009).
10. Phil Jackson, *Sacred Hoops* (New York: Hyperion, 1995), 124–125.
11. Pat Williams, *Coaching Your Kids to Be Leaders* (New York: Faith Words, 2005), 12.
12. Anson Dorrance and Gloria Averbuch, *The Vision of a Champion: Advice and Inspiration from the World's Most Successful Women's Soccer Coach* (Ann Arbor: Huron River Press, 2002), 54.
13. Pat Williams, *Coaching Your Kids to Be Leaders* (New York: Faith Words, 2005), 14.

14. Jim Loehr, "Leadership: Full Engagement for Success," in S. Murphy (Ed.) *The Sport Psychology Handbook* (Champaign, IL: Human Kinetics, 2005), 155.

15. Pat Williams, *Coaching Your Kids to Be Leaders* (New York: Faith Words, 2005), 16.

16. Jeff Janssen, *The Team Captain's Leadership Manual* (Cary, NC: Winning the Mental Game, 2003), 18.

17. Jeff Janssen and Greg Dale, *The Seven Secrets of Successful Coaches* (Cary, NC: Winning the Mental Game, 2002), 78.

18. Ibid., ix.

19. Ibid., xi.

20. Ibid., xiii.

21. Ibid., xiv.

22. Ibid., xv.

23. Jeff Janssen, *The Team Captain's Leadership Manual* (Cary, NC: Winning the Mental Game, 2003), xvi-xviii.

24. Pat Williams, *Coaching Your Kids to Be Leaders* (New York: Faith Words, 2005), 40.

25. Ibid., 40.

26. Ibid., 41.

27. Eric Kail, "Becoming a Leader Developer," in Major Doug Crandall (Ed.) *Leadership Lessons from West Point* (San Francisco: Jossey-Bass, 2007), 5.

28. Ibid., 12.

29. Vince Lombardi, Jr., *What It Takes to Be #1: Vince Lombardi on Leadership* (New York: McGraw-Hill, 2001), 77.

30. Pat Williams, *Coaching Your Kids to Be Leaders* (New York: Faith Words, 2005), 89.

31. Ibid., 138.

32. Harvey Dorfman, *Coaching the Mental Game* (Lanham, MD: First Taylor Publishing, 2003), 23.

33. Steven B. Sample, *The Contrarian's Guide to Leadership* (San Francisco: Jossey-Bass, 2002), 2.

34. Ibid., 142.

35. Vance Distinguished Lecture guest speaker, Rudolph Giuliani, Central Connecticut State University, New Britain, CT, March 14, 2013.

36. Daniel Goleman, *Primal Leadership: Realizing the Power of Emotional Intelligence,* (Boston: Harvard Business School Publishing, 2002), 101–102.

37. Robert Weinberg and Dan Gould, *Foundations of Sport and Exercise Psychology, 4th Ed.* (Champaign, IL: Human Kinetics, 2007), 206.

38. Robin Vealey, *Coaching for the Inner Edge* (Morgantown, WV: Fitness Information Technology, 2005), 76.

39. Steven B. Sample, *The Contrarian's Guide to Leadership* (San Francisco: Jossey-Bass, 2002), 141.

40. John Kotter, "What Leaders Really Do," in *Harvard Business Review on Leadership* (Boston: Harvard Business School Publishing, 1998), 40.

41. Ibid., 61.

42. Warren Bennis, *An Invented Life: Reflections on Leadership and Change* (Reading, MA: Addison-Wesley Publishing, 1993), 104.

43. Joe Batten, *Tough-Minded Leadership* (New York: AMACOM, American Management Association, 1989), 2.

44. John Kotter, "What Leaders Do," in *HBR's 10 Must Reads on Leadership* (Boston: Harvard Business School Publishing, 2011), 37.

45. Ibid., 40.

46. Steven B. Sample, *The Contrarian's Guide to Leadership* (San Francisco: Jossey-Bass, 2002), 107.

47. Tom Rath and Barry Conchie, *Strengths-Based Leadership: Great Leaders, Teams, and Why People Follow* (New York: Gallup Press, 2008), 81.

48. Michael Useem, *The Leadership Moment: Nine True Stories of Triumph and Disaster and Their Lessons for Us All* (New York: Crown Business, 1999), 21.

49. Robin Vealey, *Coaching for the Inner Edge* (Morgantown, WV: Fitness Information Technology, 2005), 72.

50. Bernard Bass, *Transformational Leadership: Industry, Military, and Educational Impact* (Mahwah, NJ: Lawrence Erlbaum Associates, Publishers, 1998), 7.

51. Robin Vealey, *Coaching for the Inner Edge* (Morgantown, WV: Fitness Information Technology, 2005), 76.

52. Bernard Bass, *Transformational Leadership: Industry, Military, and Educational Impact* (Mahwah, NJ: Lawrence Erlbaum Associates, Publishers, 1998), 3.

53. Ibid., 5–6.

54. P. Chelladurai, "Leadership in Sport Organizations," *Canadian Journal of Applied Sport Sciences* 5 (1980), 226–231.

55. Robert Weinberg and Dan Gould, *Foundations of Sport and Exercise Psychology,* 4th ed. (Champaign, IL: Human Kinetics, 2007), 215.

56. Ibid., pp. 218–220.

57. Ibid., p. 216.

58. Jim Loehr and Tony Schwartz, "The Making of a Corporate Athlete," *Harvard Business Review* 79 (2001), 120–128.

59. Ibid., 120.

60. Ibid., 123–128.

61. Ibid., 126.

62. Ibid., 127.

63. Jim Loehr, "Leadership: Full Engagement for Success," in S. Murphy (Ed.) *The Sport Psychology Handbook* (Champaign, IL: Human Kinetics, 2005), 155–170.

64. Rainer Martens, *Coaches Guide to Sport Psychology* (Champaign, IL: Human Kinetics, 1987), 35.

65. Andy Wright and Jean Cote, "A Retrospective Analysis of Leadership Development Through Sport," *The Sport Psychologist* 17 (2003), 269.

66. M.J. Melnick and J.W. Loy, "The Effects of Formal Structure on Leadership Recruitment: An Analysis of Team Captaincy Among New Zealand Provincial Rugby Teams," *International Review of Sociology and Sport* 31 (1996), 223–240.

67. W.M. Leonard, T. Ostrosky, and S. Huchendorf, "Centrality of Position and Managerial Recruitment: The Case of Major League Baseball," *Sociology of Sport Journal* 7 (1990), 294–301.

68. K.J. Tropp and D.M. Landers, "Team Interaction and the Emergence of Leadership and Interpersonal Attraction in Field Hockey," *Journal of Sport Psychology* 1, (1979), 228–240.

69. M.S. Kim, "Types of Leadership and Performance Norms of School Athletic Teams," *Perceptual and Motor Skills* 74 (1992), 803–806.

70. S.D. Glenn and Thelma Horn, "Psychological and Personal Predictors of Leadership Behavior in Female Soccer Athletes," *Journal of Applied Sport Psychology* 5 (1993), 30.

71. *Definition of psychological androgyny:* Term is defined as "a person's ability to be at the same time aggressive and nurturant, sensitive and rigid, dominant and submissive, regardless of gender." Chris Hsuing, Psychological Androgyny (2009, February 29). Retrieved June 23, 2011, from http://uventure.net/blog/2009/02/27/psychological-androgyny/

72. J. Weese and E. Nicholls, "Team Leadership: Selection and Expectations," *Physical Educator* 44 (1996), 269–272.

73. Andy Wright and Jean Cote, "A Retrospective Analysis of Leadership Development Through Sport," *The Sport Psychologist* 17 (2003), 287.

74. Robert Weinberg and Dan Gould, *Foundations of Sport and Exercise Psychology*, 4th ed. (Champaign, IL: Human Kinetics, 2007), 210.

75. Mike Voight, (2012) "A Leadership Development Intervention Program: A Case Study with Two NCAA Final 4 Teams," *The Sport Psychologist* 26 (2012), 604–623.

76. Anson Dorrance and Gloria Averbuch, *The Vision of a Champion: Advice and Inspiration from the World's Most Successful Women's Soccer Coach* (Ann Arbor: Huron River Press, 2002), 67.

Chapter 5

1. Dan Goleman, "What Makes a Leader" in *Harvard Business Review* (1998, Nov-Dec.), 94.

2. Daniel Goleman, Richard Boyatzis, and Annie McKee, *Primal Leadership: Realizing the Power of Emotional Intelligence* (Boston: Harvard Business School Publishing, 2002), 26.

3. P. Salovey and J.D. Mayer, "Emotional Intelligence," *Imagination, Cognition, & Personality* 9, (1990), 189.

4. Daniel Goleman, *Emotional Intelligence* (New York: Bantam Books, 1995), 34.

5. Joseph Badaracco, Jr. (Ed.), "The Discipline of Building Character," *Harvard Business Review on Leadership* (Boston: Harvard Business School Press, 1998), 93.

6. John Kotter (Ed.), "What Leaders Really Do," *Harvard Business Review on Leadership* (Boston: Harvard Business School Press, 1998), 48.

7. Ibid., 48.

8. Pat Williams, *Coaching Your Kids to Be Leaders* (New York: Faith Words, 2005), 62.

9. Daniel Goleman, Richard Boyatzis, and Annie McKee, *Primal Leadership: Realizing the Power of Emotional Intelligence* (Boston: Harvard Business School Publishing, 2002), 13.

10. Ibid., 13.

11. Ibid., 14.

12. Ibid., 15.

13. Ibid., 17.

14. Robert Weinberg and Dan Gould, *Foundations of Sport and Exercise Psychology*, 4th ed. (Champaign, IL: Human Kinetics, 2007), 67.

15. Carole Ames, "Achievement Goals, Motivational Climates, and Motivational Processes," in G.C. Roberts (Ed.), *Motivation in Sport and Exercise* (Champaign, IL: Human Kinetics, 1992), 161–176.

16. Joan Duda and H. Hall, "Achievement Goal Theory in Sport: Recent Extensions and Future Directions," in R. Singer, H. Hausenblas, & C. Janelle (Eds.), *Handbook of Sport Psychology* 2nd ed. (New York: Wiley, 2001), 417–443.

17. Carol Dweck, "Motivational Processes Affecting Learning," *American Psychologist* 41, (1986), 1040–1048.

18. Daniel Goleman, Richard Boyatzis, and Annie McKee, *Primal Leadership: Realizing the Power of Emotional Intelligence* (Boston: Harvard Business School Publishing, 2002), 11.

19. Ibid., 253–256.

20. Ibid., 11, 12, 21, 174, 235, 241.

21. Ronald Humphrey, "The Many Faces of Emotional Leadership," *The Leadership Quarterly* 13 (2002), 497.

22. Ibid., 235

23. Ibid., 177

24. Ibid., 175

25. Ibid., 176.

26. Daniel Goleman, Richard Boyatzis, and Annie McKee, *Primal Leadership: Realizing the Power of Emotional Intelligence* (Boston: Harvard Business School Publishing, 2002), 39, 253–256.

27. Sam Zizzi, Heather Deanier, and Doug Hirschhorn, "The Relationship Between Emotional Intelligence and Performance Among College Baseball Players," *Journal of Applied Sport Psychology* 15 (2003), 262–269.

28. Marc Jones, Jim Taylor, Miyako Tanaka-Oulevey, and Mary Daubert, "Emotions," in J.

Taylor & G. Wilson (Eds.), *Applying Sport Psychology: Four Perspectives* (Champaign, IL: Human Kinetics, 2005), 65–82.

29 Yuri Hanin, *Emotions in Sport* (Champaign, IL: Human Kinetics, 2000), 65–90.

30. Yuri Hanin, "Successful and Poor Performance Emotions," in Y.L. Hanin (Ed.), *Emotions in Sport* (Champaign, IL: Human Kinetics, 2000), 157–158.

31. Kurt April, Darryn Lifson, and Tm Noakes, "Emotional Intelligence of Elite Sport Leaders & Elite Business Leaders," *International Journal of Sport Science and Coaching* 2 (2011), 135–155.

32. Daniel Goleman, "What Makes a Leader," *Harvard Business Review* (1998, Nov-Dec.), 92.

33. Daniel Goleman, "What Makes a Leader," *Harvard Business Review's 10 Must Reads On Leadership* (Boston: Harvard Business School Publishing, 2011), 8.

34. C. George Boeree, "Limbic System Anatomy." Retrieved October 12, 2011, from http://webspace.ship.edu/cgboer/limbicsystem.html

35. J. LeDoux (1996). *The Emotional Brain: The Mysterious Underpinnings of Emotional Life* (New York: Touchstone, 1996), 47–55.

36. Daniel Goleman, *Emotional Intelligence* (New York: Bantam Books, 1995).

37. Joe Navarro, *What Every Body Is Saying* (New York: HarperCollins, 2008), 25.

38. Daniel Goleman, "What Makes a Leader," *Harvard Business Review's 10 Must Reads On Leadership* (Boston: Harvard Business School Publishing, 2011), 9.

39. Jim Loehr and Tony Schwartz, "The Making of a Corporate Athlete," *Harvard Business Review* 79 (2001), 124.

Chapter 6

1. J.C. Maxwell, *The 360 Leader: Developing Your Influence from Anywhere in the Organization* (Nashville: Thomas Nelson, 2005), 9.

2. Joe Batten, *Tough Minded Leadership* (New York: American Management Association, 1989), 143.

3. Steven B. Sample, *The Contrarian's Guide to Leadership* (San Francisco: Jossey-Bass, 2002), 3.

4. J.C. Maxwell, *Leadership Gold* (Nashville: Thomas Nelson, 2008), 9.

5. Harvey Dorfman, *Coaching the Mental Game* (Lanham, MD: First Taylor Trade Publishing, 2003), 35.

6. Ibid., 16.

7. Ibid., 16.

8. Ibid., 20.

9. Daniel Goleman, "Leadership That Gets Results," *Harvard Business Review* 4487 (2000, March–April), 77–90.

10. Ibid., 82–85.

11. Daniel Goleman, Richard Boyatzis, and Annie McKee, *Primal Leadership: Realizing the Power of Emotional Intelligence* (Boston: Harvard Business School Publishing, 2002), 55.

12. Tom Rath and Barry Conchie, *Strength Based Leadership: Great Leaders, Teams, and Why People Follow* (New York: Gallup Press, 2008), 57.

13. Ibid., 59.

14. Bill Parcells, "The Tough Work of Turning Around a Team." *Harvard Business Review* (2000, November–December), 180.

15. Daniel Goleman, Richard Boyatzis, and Annie McKee, *Primal Leadership: Realizing the Power of Emotional Intelligence* (Boston: Harvard Business School Publishing, 2002), 60.

16. Ibid., 64.

17. Ibid., 66.

18. Ibid., 65.

19. Anson Dorrance and Gloria Averbuch, *The Vision of a Champion* (Ann Arbor: Huron River Press, 2005), 35.

20. Anson Dorrance, "Coaching Women: Going Against the Instincts of My Gender," *US Olympic Coach* (2006, Spring), 8.

21. Ibid.

22. Tony DiCicco, Colleen Hacker, and Charles Salzberg, *Catch Them Being Good: Everything You Need to Know to Successfully Coach Girls* (New York: Penguin Books, 2002), 11.

23. Jack Welch and Suzy Welch, *Winning* (New York: Collins, 2005), 53.

24. Daniel Goleman, Richard Boyatzis, and Annie McKee, *Primal Leadership: Realizing the Power of Emotional Intelligence* (Boston: Harvard Business School Publishing, 2002), 68.

25. Jack Welch and Suzy Welch, *Winning* (New York: Collins, 2005), 56.

26. Daniel Goleman, Richard Boyatzis, and Annie McKee, *Primal Leadership: Realizing the Power of Emotional Intelligence* (Boston: Harvard Business School Publishing, 2002), 72.

27. Ibid., 73.

28. Alan Murray, *The Wall Street Journal Guide to Management* (New York: Harper Business, 2010).

29. Daniel Goleman, Richard Boyatzis, and Annie McKee, *Primal Leadership: Realizing the Power of Emotional Intelligence* (Boston: Harvard Business School Publishing, 2002), 76.

30. Alan Murray, *The Wall Street Journal Guide to Management* (New York: Harper Business, 2010), 8.

31. Daniel Goleman, "Leadership That Gets Results," *Harvard Business Review* 4487 (2000, March–April), 77–90.

32. Tom Rath and Barry Conchie, *Strengths-Based Leadership: Great Leaders, Teams, and Why People Follow* (New York: Gallup Press, 2008), 80.

33. Steven B. Sample, *The Contrarian's Guide to Leadership* (San Francisco: Jossey-Bass, 2002), 190–191.

34. Alan Murray, "Leadership Styles," *The Wall Street Journal Online* (2011). Retrieved January 3, 2011, from http://guides.wsj.com/management/developing-a-leadership-style/how-to-develop-leaders

35. Daniel Goleman, Richard Boyatzis, and Annie McKee, *Primal Leadership: Realizing the Power of Emotional Intelligence* (Boston: Harvard Business School Publishing, 2002), 84.

36. Tom Rath and Barry Conchie, *Strengths-Based Leadership: Great Leaders, Teams, and Why People Follow* (New York: Gallup Press, 2008), 13.

37. Ibid., 17.

38. Ibid., 23.

39. Ibid., 24.

40. Ibid., 26.

41. J.C. Maxwell, *The 360 Leader: Developing Your Influence from Anywhere in the Organization* (Nashville: Thomas Nelson, 2005), 238.

42. Tom Rath and Barry Conchie, *Strengths-Based Leadership: Great Leaders, Teams, and Why People Follow* (New York: Gallup Press, 2008), 16.

43. Leslie Bennetts, "Women and the Leadership Gap," *Newsweek* (2012, Mar 5). Retrieved May 5, 2012, from http://www.thedailybeast.com/newsweek/2012/03/04/the-stubborn-gender-gap.html

44. A.H. Eagly and B. Johannesen-Schmidt, "Leadership-Style Matters: The Small, but Important, Style Differences Between Male and Female Leaders," in D. Bilimoria and S. Piderit (Eds.), *Handbook on Women in Business and Management* (Northampton, MA: Edwin Elgar Publishing, 2007), 279–303.

45. Virginia Schein, "Women in Management: Reflections and Projections," *Women in Management Review* 22 (2007), 6–18.

46. A.H. Eagly, S.J. Karau, and M.G. Makhijani, "Gender and the Effectiveness of Leaders: A Meta-Analysis," *Psychological Bulletin* 117 (1995), 125–145.

47. Alan Murray, *The Wall Street Journal Guide to Management* (New York: Harper Business, 2010), 179.

48. Pamela Stone, *Opting Out? Why Women Really Quit Careers and Head Home* (Berkeley, CA: University of California Press, 2005); A. Morgan and C. Lynch, *Leading from the Front: No Excuse Leadership Tactics for Women* (New York: McGraw-Hill, 2006); Elisabeth Kelan, *Rising Stars: Developing Millennial Women as Leaders* (New York: Palgrave Macmillan, 2012); M.N. Ruderman, P.J. Ohlott, K. Panzer, and S.N. King, *Standing at the Cross Roads: Next Steps for High-Achieving Women* (San Francisco: Jossey-Bass, 2002); J. Fletcher, *Disappearing Acts: Gender, Power and Relational Practice at Work* (Cambridge, MA: MIT Press, 1999); Jill Flynn, Kathryn Heath and Mary Davis Holt, *Break Your Own Rules: How to Change the Patterns of Thinking that Block Women's Paths to Power* (San Francisco: Jossey-Bass, 2011); Joanna Barsh, Susie Cranston, and Geoffrey Lewis, *How Remarkable Women Lead: The Breakthrough Model for Work and Life* (New York: Crown, 2011); Gail Evans, *Play Like a Man, Win Like a Woman: What Men Know About Success That Women Need to Learn* (New York: Crown, 2001).

49. S. Sandberg, *Lean In: Women, Work, and the Will to Lead* (New York: Knopf, 2013).

50. L. Vanderkam, "Problem With Work-Life Balance," *USA TODAY* (2013, March 19), 6A.

51. Sally Helgesen, "Women's Vision: Making the Strategic Case," *Warren Bennis' Leadership Excellence: The Magazine of Leadership Development, Managerial Effectiveness, and Organizational Psychology* (June 2010), 14.

52. Sally Helgesen, *The Female Advantage: Women's Ways of Leadership* (New York: Bantam Doubleday Dell, 1990); Sally Helgesen, *Everyday Revolutionaries: Working Women and the Transformation of American Life* (New York: Doubleday, 1998).

53. http://womenleadershipissues.com/

54. http://www.journals.elsevier.com/the-leadership-quarterly/; http://www.ccl.org/leadership/lia/index.aspx http://hbr.org/; http://www.emeraldinsight.com/journals.htm?issn=0964-9425; http://www.businessweek.com/.

55. http://www.businessweek.com/managing/special_reports/20091014women_and_leadership.htm

56. http://www.womensleadership.com/

57. http://www.anderson.ucla.edu/x27611.xml

58. http://www.nafe.com/?service=vpage/1474

59. Cecile Reynaud, *She Can Coach* (Champaign, IL: Human Kinetics, 2005); http://www.coach.ca/canadian-journal-for-women-in-coaching-s12541; Pat Head Summitt and Sally Jenkins, *Sum It Up: A Thousand and Ninety-Eight Victories, a Couple of Irrelevant Losses, and a Life in Perspective* (New York: Crown, 2013); Even Pellerud and Sam Kucey, *Coaching and Leadership in Women's Soccer* (New York: Reedswain, 2005); Jennie Finch and Ann Killion, *Throw Like a Girl: How to Dream Big and Believe in Yourself* (New York: Triumph, 2011); Karen P. O'Connor, *Gender and Women's Leadership: A Reference Handbook* (New York: Sage, 2010); Mary A. Hums, Glenna G. Bower, and Heidi Grappendorf, *Women as Leaders in Sport: Impact and Influence* (Reston, VA: AAHPERD, 2007).

60. Warren Bennis, *On Becoming a Leader* (Philadelphia: Basic Books, 2009), 103.

Chapter 7

1. James Kouzes and Barry Posner, *The Leadership Challenge* (San Francisco: John Wiley & Sons, 2007), 29.
2. Alan Murray, *The Wall Street Journal Guide to Management* (New York: Harper Business, 2010), 11.
3. Jim Collins, *Good to Great* (New York: HarperCollins, 2001), 19.
4. Alan Murray, *The Wall Street Journal Guide to Management* (New York: Harper Business, 2010), 11.
5. Jim Collins, *Good to Great* (New York: HarperCollins, 2001), 20.
6. Jack Welch and Suzy Welch, *Winning* (New York: HarperCollins, 2005), 61.
7. Alan Murray, *The Wall Street Journal Guide to Management* (New York: Harper Business, 2010), 10.
8. Ibid., 10.
9. Ibid., 11.
10. Jim Collins, *Good to Great* (New York: HarperCollins, 2001), 21.
11. Ibid., 22.
12. Alan Murray, *The Wall Street Journal Guide to Management* (New York: Harper Business, 2010), 13.
13. Vince Lombardi, Jr., *What It Takes to Be #1* (New York: McGraw-Hill, 2001), 118.
14. Jeff Janssen and Greg Dale, *The Seven Secrets of Successful Coaches* (Cary, NC: Winning the Mental Game, 2002), 27.
15. Ken Ravizza, Personal Communication, September 2009.
16. Harvey Dorfman, *Coaching the Mental Game* (Lanham, MD: First Taylor Trade Publishing, 2003), 33.
17. Quote by Nicole Davis, Personal Communication, October 2010.
18. James Loehr, *Toughness Training for Sports* (New York: Penguin Books, 1994).
19. P. Clough, K. Earle, and D Sewell, "Mental Toughness: The Concept and Its Measurement," in I. Cockerill (Ed.), *Solutions In Sport Psychology* (London: Thompson, 2002), 32–45.
20. Harvey Dorfman, *Coaching the Mental Game* (Lanham, MD: First Taylor Trade Publishing, 2003), 38.
21. Vince Lombardi, Jr., *What It Takes to Be #1* (New York: McGraw-Hill, 2001), 154.
22. Ibid., 153.
23. Ibid., 154.
24. Pat Williams, *The Magic of Team Work* (Nashville: Thomas Nelson, 1997), 56.
25. Vince Lombardi, Jr., *What It Takes to Be #1* (New York: McGraw-Hill, 2001), 175.
26. Harvey Dorfman, *Coaching the Mental Game* (Lanham, MD: First Taylor Trade Publishing, 2003), 38.
27. Ibid., 112.
28. Ibid., 114.
29. Pat Williams, *Coaching Your Kids to Be Leaders* (New York: Faith Words, 2005), 142.
30. Ibid., 169.
31. R. Goffee and G. Jones, "Why Should Anyone Be Led by You?," in *HBR's 10 Must Reads on Leadership* (Boston: Harvard Business Review Press, 2011), 89.
32. Bill Walsh, *The Score Takes Care of Itself* (New York: Penguin Group, 2009), 99.
33. Pat Williams, *Coaching Your Kids to Be Leaders* (New York: Faith Words, 2005), 169.
34. Ibid., 170.
35. Ibid., 169.
36. R. Heifetz and D. Laurie, "The Work of Leadership," in *HBR's 10 Must Reads on Leadership* (Boston: Harvard Business School Publishing Corporation, 2011), 66.
37. Ibid., 69.
38. Warren Bennis, *An Invented Life: Reflections on Leadership and Courage* (Reading, MA: Addison-Wesley, 1993), 78.
39. Warren Bennis, *On Becoming a Leader* (Philadelphia: Basic Books, 2009), xviii.
40. Warren Bennis, *An Invented Life: Reflections on Leadership and Courage* (Reading, MA: Addison-Wesley, 1993), 83.
41. James Kouzes and Barry Posner, *The Leadership Challenge* (New York: Jossey-Bass, 2007), 177.
42. J.C. Maxwell, *Leadership Gold* (Nashville: Thomas Nelson, 2008), 75.
43. Steven B. Sample, *The Contrarian's Guide to Leadership* (San Francisco: Jossey-Bass, 2002), 21.
44. J.C. Maxwell, *Leadership Gold* (Nashville: Thomas Nelson, 2008), 76.
45. Ibid., 75.
46. Ibid., 44.
47. Ibid., 85.
48. Jeff Janssen, *Championship Team Building: What Every Coach Needs to Know to Build a Motivated, Committed & Cohesive Team* (Tucson: Winning the Mental Game, 1999), 85.
49. James Kouzes and Barry Posner, *The Leadership Challenge* (New York: Jossey-Bass, 2007), 152.
50. J.C. Maxwell, *Leadership Gold* (Nashville: Thomas Nelson, 2008), 42.
51. Ibid., 56.
52. Harvey Dorfman, *Coaching the Mental Game* (Lanham, MD: First Taylor Trade Publishing, 2003), 33–34.

Chapter 8

1. Warren Bennis and Joan Goldsmith, *Learning to Lead* (Philadelphia: Basic Books, 2010), xvii.
2. Ibid., xxi-xxii.

3. Michael Rutherford. Retrieved May 21, 2012, from http://www.brainyquote.com/quotes/keywords/collaboration.html#LsA6kJUCwZ0cX31K.99

4. Daniel Goleman, Richard Boyatzis, and Annie McKee, *Primal Leadership: Realizing the Power of Emotional Intelligence* (Boston, MA: Harvard Business School Publishing, 2002), 163.

5. Dean Smith, Gerald Bell, and John Kilgo, *The Carolina Way: Leadership Lessons from a Life in Coaching* (New York: Penguin Books, 2004), 13–14.

6. Ronald Heifetz & Donald Laurie, "The Work of Leadership," in *HBR's 10 Must Reads on Leadership* (Boston: Harvard Business School Publishing Corporation, 2011), 69.

7. Robin Vealey, *Coaching for the Inner Edge* (Morgantown, WV: Fitness Information Technology, 2005), 302–307.

8. Ibid., 309.

9. James Kouzes and Barry Posner, *The Truth About Leadership* (San Francisco: Jossey-Bass, 2010), xxiii.

10. Ibid., xxiv.

11. Bill Walsh with Steve Jamison and Craig Walsh. *The Score Takes Care of Itself* (New York: Penguin Group, 2009), 23.

12. Harvey Dorfman, *Coaching the Mental Game* (Lanham, MD: First Taylor Trade Publishing, 2003), 51.

13. Stuart Levine, *The Six Fundamentals of Success: The Rules for Getting It Right for Yourself and Your Organization* (New York: Random House, 2004), 55.

14. Ibid., 56.

15. Pat Williams, *The Magic of Team Work* (Nashville: Thomas Nelson, 1997), 64.

16. J.C. Maxwell, *The 17 Essential Qualities of a Team Player: Becoming the Kind of Person Every Team Wants* (Nashville: Thomas Nelson, 2002), 32–34.

17. Pat Williams, *Coaching Your Kids to Be Leaders* (New York: Faith Words, 2005), 110.

18. Ibid., 111.

19. Ronald Heifetz and Donald Laurie, "The Work of Leadership," in *HBR's 10 Must Reads on Leadership* (Boston: Harvard Business School Publishing Corporation, 2011), 68.

20. Pat Williams, *Coaching Your Kids to Be Leaders* (New York: Faith Words, 2005), 107.

21. Ibid., 113–115.

22. Anson Dorrance and Gloria Averbuch, *The Vision of a Champion* (Ann Arbor: Huron River Press, 2005), 56.

23. Ibid., 57.

24. Pat Williams, *Coaching Your Kids to Be Leaders* (New York: Faith Words, 2005), 116.

25. Robert Lussier and David Kimball, *Applied Sport Management Skills* (Champaign, IL: Human Kinetics, 2009), 297.

26. Ibid., 298.

27. Steven B. Sample, *The Contrarian's Guide to Leadership* (San Francisco: Jossey-Bass, 2002), 150.

28. Ibid., 150.

29. Ibid., 149.

30. Pat Williams, *Coaching Your Kids to Be Leaders* (New York: Faith Words, 2005), 118.

31. Harvey Dorfman, *Coaching the Mental Game* (Lanham, MD: First Taylor Trade Publishing, 2003), 45.

32. Ibid., 46.

33. Ibid., 47.

34. Robert Lussier and David Kimball, *Applied Sport Management Skills* (Champaign, IL: Human Kinetics, 2009), 297.

35. Ibid., 299.

36. Stuart Levine, *The Six Fundamentals of Success: The Rules for Getting It Right for Yourself and Your Organization* (New York: Random House, 2004), 59.

37. J.C. Maxwell. *The 360-Degree Leader* (Nashville: Thomas Nelson, 2005), 171.

38. Ibid., 170.

39. Ibid., 171.

40. Ronald Heifetz & Donald Laurie, "The Work of Leadership," in *HBR's 10 Must Reads on Leadership* (Boston: Harvard Business School Publishing Corporation, 2011), 57.

41. Alan Murray, *The Wall Street Journal Essential Guide to Management* (New York: HarperCollins, 2010), 17.

42. Warren Bennis and Robert Thomas, "Crucibles of Leadership," in *HBR's 10 Must Reads on Leadership* (Boston: Harvard Business School Publishing, 2011), 97.

43. J.C. Maxwell, *Leadership Gold* (Nashville: Thomas Nelson, 2008), 34.

44. Ibid., 34–38.

45. Ibid., 35.

46. Ibid., 37.

47. Ibid., 38.

48. Ronald Heifetz and Donald Laurie, "The Work of Leadership," in *HBR's 10 Must Reads on Leadership* (Boston: Harvard Business School Publishing Corporation, 2011), 58.

49. Ibid., 58.

50. Peter. Drucker, *The Essential Drucker* (New York: HarperCollins, 2001), 59.

Chapter 9

1. Vince Lombardi, Jr., *What It Takes to Be #1* (New York: McGraw-Hill, 2001), 127.

2. Warren Bennis, *On Becoming a Leader* (New York: Basic Books, 2009), 56–57.

3. Ronald Heifetz and Donald Laurie, "The Work of Leadership," in *HBR's 10 Must Reads on Leadership* (Boston: Harvard Business School Publishing Corporation, 2011), 58.

4. Jack Welch and Suzy Welch, *Winning* (New York: HarperCollins, 2005), 26.

5. John C. Maxwell, *Leadership Gold* (Nashville: Thomas Nelson, 2008), 166.

6. Ibid., 166–168.

7. Ibid., 166.

8. Ibid., 170.

9. Ibid., 168.

10. Stuart Levine, *The Six Fundamentals of Success: The Rules for Getting It Right for Yourself and Your Organization* (New York: Random House, 2004), 114–118.

11. Jim Collins, *Good to Great* (New York: HarperCollins, 2001), 75.

12. Ibid., 75.

13. Stuart Levine, *The Six Fundamentals of Success: The Rules for Getting It Right for Yourself and Your Organization* (New York: Random House, Incorporated, 2004), 118–119.

14. Ronald Heifetz and Donald Laurie, "The Work of Leadership," in *HBR's 10 Must Reads on Leadership* (Boston: Harvard Business School Publishing Corporation, 2011), 61.

15. Steven B. Sample, *The Contrarian's Guide to Leadership* (San Francisco: Jossey-Bass, 2002), 28.

16. Ibid., 7.

17. Ibid., 8.

18. Ibid., 9.

19. Ibid., 12.

20. Stuart Levine, *The Six Fundamentals of Success: The Rules for Getting It Right for Yourself and Your Organization* (New York: Random House, 2004), 193.

21. Ibid., 206.

22. Ibid., 207.

23. Jack Welch and Suzy Welch, *Winning* (New York: HarperCollins, 2005), 64.

24. J.C. Maxwell, *Leadership Gold* (Nashville: Thomas Nelson, 2008), 24.

25. Jack Welch and Suzy Welch, *Winning* (New York: HarperCollins, 2005), 18.

26. Coach Dorrance stats. Retrieved March 2011, from http://www.tarheelblue.com/sports/w-soccer/mtt/dorrance_anson00.html

27. Anson Dorrance, *Training Soccer Champions* (Raleigh: JTC Sports Incorporated, 1996), 20.

28. Ronald Heifetz and Donald Laurie, "The Work of Leadership," in *HBR's 10 Must Reads on Leadership* (Boston: Harvard Business School Publishing Corporation, 2011), 61.

29. Ibid., 64–66.

30. Ibid., 67.

31. Warren Bennis, *On Becoming a Leader* (Philadelphia: Basic Books, 2009), 97.

32. Jeffrey Krames, *What the Best CEO's Know: 7 Exceptional Leaders and Their Lessons for Transforming Any Business* (New York: McGraw-Hill, 2003), 32–35.

33. John C. Maxwell, *The 360-Degree Leader* (Nashville: Thomas Nelson, Incorporated, 2005), 145.

34. Stuart Levine, *The Six Fundamentals of Success: The Rules for Getting It Right for Yourself and Your Organization* (New York: Random House, 2004), 182–183.

35. Phil Jackson, *Sacred Hoops* (New York: Hyperion, 2006), 177.

36. Michael Jordan quote. Retrieved June 1, 2012, from http://www.brainyquote.com/quotes/authors/m/michael_jordan.html

37. QB Barkley will return to USC, AP article (2011, December). Retrieved December 22, 2011, from http://msn.foxsports.com/college football/story/USC-Trojans-quarterback

38. J.C. Maxwell, *The 360-Degree Leader* (Nashville: Thomas Nelson, 2005), 146.

39. Ibid., 146.

40. Ibid., 146–149.

41. Warren Bennis, *On Becoming a Leader* (Philadelphia: Basic Books, 2009), 226.

42. Warren Bennis and Robert "Thomas, Crucibles of Leadership," in *HBR's 10 Must Reads on Leadership* (Boston: Harvard Business School Publishing, 2011), 99.

43. Ibid., 99.

44. Ibid., xxiv, 32, 226.

45. Ibid., 99.

46. Ibid., 98–111.

47. James Kouzes and Barry Posner, *The Truth About Leadership: The No-Fads, Heart-of-the-Matter Facts You Need to Know* (San Francisco: Jossey-Bass, 2010), 91.

48. Ibid., 93.

49. John C. Maxwell, *Leadership Gold* (Nashville: Thomas Nelson, 2008), 21.

50. Ibid., 22.

51. Ibid., 21–23.

52. Ibid., 22.

53. Ibid., 22.

54. Joseph Badaracco, Jr., "The Discipline of Building Character," *Harvard Business Review on Leadership* (Boston: Harvard Business School Publishing, 1998), 89.

55. Ibid., 90.

56. Joseph Badaracco, Jr., *Leading Quietly: An Unorthodox Guide to Doing the Right Thing* (Boston: Harvard Business School Publishing, 2002), 65.

57. James Kouzes and Barry Posner, *The Truth about Leadership: The No-Fads, Heart-of-the-Matter Facts You Need to Know* (San Francisco: Jossey-Bass, 2010), 1.

Chapter 10

1. Phil Jackson, *The Last Season: A Team in Search of Its Soul* (New York: Penguin Press, 2004), 24.

2. Ibid., 25.

3. Ibid., 24.

4. Pat Riley, *The Winner Within: A Life Plan for Team Players* (New York: Putnam, 1993).

5. Jeff Cannon and Lt. Cmdr. Jon Canon, *Leadership Lessons of the Navy Seals* (New York: McGraw-Hill, 2003), 152.

6. Pat Lencioni, *The 5 Dysfunctions of a Team* (San Francisco: Jossey-Bass, 2002).

7. Ibid., 45–48.

8. Jim Collins, *Good to Great* (New York: HarperCollins, 2001), 54.

9. Ibid., 42.

10. John C. Maxwell, *Team Work Makes the Dream Work* (Nashville: Thomas Nelson, 2002), xi.

11. Tony DiCicco and Colleen Hacker, *Catch Them Being Good: Everything You Need to Know to Successfully Coach Girls* (New York: Penguin Group, 2002).

12. Tom Rath and Barry Conchie, *Strengths-Based Leadership: Great Leaders, Teams, and Why People Follow* (New York: Gallup Press, 2008), 2–3.

13. Ibid., 12.

14. Jack Welch and Suzy Welch, *Winning* (New York: HarperCollins, 2005), 65.

15. M. Buckingham and C. Coffman, *First, Break All the Rules* (New York: Simon & Schuster, 1999), 105.

16. J.C. Maxwell, *Team Work Makes the Dream Work* (Nashville: Thomas Nelson, 2002), 69.

17. Robert Lussier and David Kimball, *Applied Sport Management Skills* (Champaign, IL: Human Kinetics, 2009), 263.

18. Ibid., 269–276.

19. Jeff Janssen, *Championship Team Building* (Cary, NC: Winning the Mental Game, 2002), 98.

20. Robert Lussier and David Kimball, *Applied Sport Management Skills* (Champaign, IL: Human Kinetics, 2009), 270.

21. Robert Weinberg and Dan Gould, *Foundations of Sport and Exercise Psychology* (Champaign, IL: Human Kinetics, 2006), 189.

22. Robert Lussier and David Kimball, *Applied Sport Management Skills* (Champaign, IL: Human Kinetics, 2009), 268.

23. Tony DiCicco and Colleen Hacker, *Catch Them Being Good: Everything You Need to Know to Successfully Coach Girls* (New York: Penguin Group, 2002), 64.

24. Bruce Tuckman, "Developmental Sequence in Small Groups," *Psychological Bulletin*, 63, (1965), 384–399.

25. Robert Lussier and David Kimball, *Applied Sport Management Skills* (Champaign, IL: Human Kinetics, 2009), 276.

26. Bill Beswick, *Focused for Soccer: Develop a Winning Mental Approach* (Champaign, IL: Human Kinetics, 2001), 145–148.

27. Pat Lencioni, *5 Dysfunctions of a Team* (San Francisco: Jossey-Bass, 2002), 52.

28. Mike Voight, *Mental Toughness Training for Basketball: Maximizing Technical & Mental Mechanics* (Monterey, CA: Coaches Choice Publishers, 2010), 97–100.

29. J. McCallum, "The Gang's All Here," *Sports Illustrated* (2001), 75–81.

30. J.C. Maxwell, *Team Work Makes the Dream Work* (Nashville: Thomas Nelson, 2002), 84.

31. J.C. Maxwell, *17 Essential Qualities of a Team Player* (Nashville: Thomas Nelson, 2002), viii.

32. Tom Rath and Barry Conchie, *Strengths-Based Leadership: Great Leaders, Teams, and Why People Follow* (New York: Gallup Press, 2008), 107.

33. R.T. Sparrowe, B.W. Soetjipto, and M.L. Kraimer, "Do Leaders' Influence Tactics Relate to Members' Helping Behavior?," *Academy of Management Journal* 49, (2011), 1194–1208.

34. Anson Dorrance and Gloria Averbuch, *The Vision of a Champion* (Ann Arbor: Huron River Press, 2005), 210.

35. Robert Weinberg and Dan Gould, *Foundations of Sport and Exercise Psychology* (Champaign, IL: Human Kinetics, 2006), 178.

36. Jim Collins, *Good to Great* (New York: HarperCollins, 2001), 74.

37. Ibid., 71.

38. Robin Vealey, *Coaching for the Inner Edge* (Morgantown, WV: Fitness Information Technology, 2005), 85.

39. Peter Drucker, *The Essential Drucker* (New York: Harper, 2001), 23.

40. Ibid., 24.

41. Ibid., 26.

42. J.C. Maxwell, *The 360-Degree Leader* (Nashville: Thomas Nelson, 2005), 249–252.

43. Ibid., 250.

44. James Kouzes and Barry Posner, *The Leadership Challenge* (New York: John Wiley & Sons, 2007), 150.

45. J.C. Maxwell, *The 360-Degree Leader* (Nashville: Thomas Nelson, 2005), 251.

46. Warren Bennis and Burt Nanus, *Leaders: The Strategies for Taking Charge* (New York: Harper & Row, 1985), 30.

47. J.C. Maxwell, *The 360-Degree Leader* (Nashville: Thomas Nelson, 2005), 251.

48. Thomas Davenport, *Thinking for a Living: How to Get Better Performance and Results from Knowledge Workers* (Boston: Harvard Business School Press, 2005), 21.

49. J.C. Maxwell, *The 360-Degree Leader* (Nashville: Thomas Nelson, 2005), 251.

50. Ibid., 252.

51. James Kouzes and Barry Posner, *The Leadership Challenge* (New York: John Wiley & Sons, 2007), 152.

52. Jack Welch and Suzy Welch, *Winning* (New York: HarperCollins, 2005), 63.

53. Jim Collins, *Good to Great* (New York: HarperCollins, 2001), 74.

54. Ibid., 63.

55. R. Giuliani, *Leadership* (New York: Hyperion, 2002), 69.

56. Dean Smith, Gerald Bell, and John Kilgo, *The Carolina Way: Leadership Lessons from a Life in Coaching* (New York: Penguin Books, 2004), 35.

57. Jeff Janssen, *Championship Team Building* (Cary, NC: Winning the Mental Game, 2002), 64–66.

58. James Kouzes and Barry Posner, *The Leadership Challenge* (New York: John Wiley & Sons, 2007), 259.

59. Jeff Janssen, *Championship Team Building* (Cary, NC: Winning the Mental Game, 2002), 65.

60. James Kouzes and Barry Posner, *The Leadership Challenge* (New York: John Wiley & Sons, 2007), 155.

61. Terry Orlick, *In Pursuit of Excellence: How to Win in Sport and Life Through Mental Training* (Champaign, IL: Human Kinetics, 2000), 200.

62. Anson Dorrance, "Coaching Women: Going Against the Instincts of My Gender," *US Olympic Coach* (2006, Spring), 8–12.

63. Ibid.; Tony DiCicco and Colleen Hacker, *Catch Them Being Good: Everything You Need to Know to Successfully Coach Girls* (New York: Penguin Group, 2002); Anson Dorrance and Gloria Averbuch, *The Vision of a Champion* (Ann Arbor: Huron River Press, 2005).

64. Tony DiCicco and Colleen Hacker, *Catch Them Being Good: Everything You Need to Know to Successfully Coach Girls* (New York: Penguin Group, 2002), 11.

65. Anson Dorrance and Gloria Averbuch, *The Vision of a Champion* (Ann Arbor: Huron River Press, 2005), 212.

66. Kathleen J. DeBoer, "Practice Like a Girl, Compete Like a Boy: Training the Total Athlete," *US Olympic Coach* (2006, Spring), 13–16.

67. Anson Dorrance and Tim Nash, *Training Soccer Champions* (Greensboro, NC: JTC, 1996).

68. Anson Dorrance and Gloria Averbuch, *The Vision of a Champion* (Ann Arbor: Huron River Press, 2005), 44.

69. Jin Wang and William Straub (2012), "An Investigation into the Coaching Approach of a World Class Soccer Coach: A Case Study," *International Journal of Sport Science & Coaching* (2012), 235–245.

70. Tony DiCicco and Colleen Hacker, *Catch Them Being Good: Everything You Need to Know to Successfully Coach Girls* (New York: Penguin Group, 2002), 20.

Chapter 11

1. Ronald Riggio, Ira Chaleff and Jean Lipman-Blumen (2008), "Rethinking Followership," in *The Art of Followership: How Great Followers Create Great Leaders and Organizations* (Eds.) (San Francisco: Jossey-Bass, 2008), xxvi.

2. Tom Rath and Barry Conchie, *Strengths-Based Leadership: Great Leaders, Teams, and Why People Follow* (New York: Gallup Press, 2008), 79.

3. Bernard Bass, *Bass & Stogdill's Handbook of Leadership: Theory, Research, and Managerial Applications*, 3rd ed. (New York: Free Press, 1990), 37.

4. Lisa M. Burke, Capella University, "Correlations of Followership and Leadership Styles of Medical Science Liaisons Within the Pharmaceutical and Biopharmaceutical Industry," *US Dissertation Abstracts International Section A: Humanities and Social Sciences*, 70 (4-A), 2009, 28.

5. Bernie Fallon, *The Art of Followership: What Happened to the Indians?* (Bloomington, IN: Phi Delta Kappa Educational Foundation, 1974).

6. Fallon quote. Retrieved October 1, 2012, from http://www.eric.ed.gov/ERICWebPortal/search/detailmini.jsp?_nfpb=true&_&ERICExtSearch_SearchValue_0=ED088207&ERICExtSearch_SearchType_0=no&accno=ED088207.

7. D. R. Frew, "Leadership and Followership," *Personnel Journal* 56 (1977), 90–97.

8. Ronald Riggio, Ira Chaleff and Jean Lipman-Blumen (2008), "Rethinking Followership," in *The Art of Followership: How Great Followers Create Great Leaders and Organizations* (Eds.) (San Francisco: Jossey-Bass, 2008), 2.

9. Robert E. Kelley, "In Praise of Followers," *Harvard Business Review* 66, (1988), 142–148.

10. Lisa M. Burke, Capella University, "Correlations of Followership and Leadership Styles of Medical Science Liaisons Within the Pharmaceutical and Biopharmaceutical Industry," *US Dissertation Abstracts International Section A: Humanities and Social Sciences,* 70 (4-A), 2009, 28.

11. Ibid., p. 59.

12. Patsy Blackshear, "The Followership Continuum: A Model for Increasing Organizational Productivity," *The Innovation Journal: The Public Sector Innovation Journal* 9 (1), (2004), 3.

13. Jon P. Howell and Maria J. Mendez, "Three Perspectives on Followership," in R. Riggio, I. Chaleff, and J. Lipman-Blumen (Eds.) *The Art of Followership: How Great Followers Create Great Leaders and Organizations* (San Francisco: Jossey-Bass, 2008), 28.

14. J.C. Maxwell, *Leadership Gold* (Nashville: Thomas Nelson, 2008), 80.

15. Patsy Blackshear, "The Followership

Continuum: A Model for Increasing Organizational Productivity," *The Innovation Journal: The Public Sector Innovation Journal* 9 (1), (2004), 3.

16. Kent Bjugstad, Elizabeth C. Thach, Karen J. Thompson, and Alan Morris, "A Fresh Look at Followership: A Model for Matching Followership and Leadership Styles," *Institute of Behavioral and Applied Management* (2006), 304.

17. G.A. Williams and R.B. Miller, "Change the Way You Persuade," *Harvard Business Review* 80 (2002), 65–73.

18. Kent Bjugstad, Elizabeth C. Thach, Karen J. Thompson, and Alan Morris, "A Fresh Look at Followership: A Model for Matching Followership and Leadership Styles," *Institute of Behavioral and Applied Management* (2006), 313.

19. Robert E. Kelley," In Praise of Followers," *Harvard Business Review* 66 (6), (1988), 144.

20. Tom Rath and Barry Conchie, *Strengths-Based Leadership: Great Leaders, Teams, and Why People Follow* (New York: Gallup Press, 2008), 79.

21. Joseph C. Rost, *Leadership for the Twenty-First Century* (Westport, CT: Praeger, 1993), 102.

22. Ira Chaleff, *The Courageous Follower: Standing Up To & For Our Leaders*, 2nd ed. (San Francisco: Berrett-Koehler, 2003), 25.

23. *Google Translate:* http://translate.google.com/#la/en/sine%20qua%20non

24. Steve Sample, *The Contrarian's Guide to Leadership* (San Francisco: Jossey-Bass, 2002), 142.

25. J.C. Maxwell, *Leadership Gold* (Nashville: Thomas Nelson, 2008), 75.

26. Ira Chaleff, *The Courageous Follower: Standing Up To & For Our Leaders*, 2nd ed. (San Francisco: Berrett-Koehler, 2003), 2.

27. E.H. Potter, W.E. Rosenbach, and T.S. Pittman, "Followers for the Times: Engaging Employees in a Winning Partnership," in *Contemporary Issues in Leadership* (5th Ed.) (New York: Westview Press, 2001).

28. Ibid., 4–5.

29. Ibid., 5.

30. Ibid., 5.

31. Ibid., 6–7

32. Ibid., 7

33. Ibid., 7.

34. Ibid., 8.

35. Ibid., 7.

36. Jon P. Howell and Maria J. Mendez, "Three perspectives on followership," in R. Riggio, I. Chaleff, and J. Lipman-Blumen (Eds.) *The Art of Followership: How Great Followers Create Great Leaders and Organizations* (San Francisco: Jossey-Bass, 2008), 35.

37. C.S. Burke, S.M. Fiore, and E. Salas, "The Role of Shared Cognition in Enabling Shared Leadership and Team Adaptability," in C.L. Pearce and J.A. Conger (Eds.), *Shared Leadership* (Thousand Oaks, CA: Sage, 2003a), 250–267; "Ira Chaleef," *The Courageous Follower:*

Standing Up to & for Our Leaders (2nd edition) (San Francisco: Berrett-Koehler, 2003); Jon P. Howell and Maria J. Mendez, "Three Perspectives on Followership," in R. Riggio, I. Chaleff, and J. Lipman-Blumen (Eds.) *The Art of Followership: How Great Followers Create Great Leaders and Organizations* (San Francisco: Jossey-Bass, 2008), 28; Robert E. Kelley, *The Power of Followership: How to Create Leaders People Want to Follow and Followers Who Lead Themselves* (New York: Currency Book, 1992).

38. Jon P. Howell and Maria J. Mendez, "Three Perspectives on Followership," in R. Riggio, I. Chaleff, and J. Lipman-Blumen (Eds.) *The Art of Followership: How Great Followers Create Great Leaders and Organizations* (San Francisco: Jossey-Bass, 2008), 28.

39. Robert E. Kelley, *The Power of Followership: How to Create Leaders People Want to Follow and Followers Who Lead Themselves* (New York: Currency Book, 1992), 17.

40. Stephen Covey, *Principle-Centered Leadership* (Los Angeles: Fireside Press, 1992), 79.

41. Kent Bjugstad, Elizabeth C. Thach, Karen J. Thompson, and Alan Morris, "A Fresh Look at Followership: A Model for Matching Followership and Leadership Styles," *Institute of Behavioral and Applied Management* (2006), 304–319.

42. Ira Chaleff, *The Courageous Follower: Standing Up To & For Our Leaders*, 2nd ed. (San Francisco: Berrett-Koehler, 2003). xvii-xix.

43. Ibid., xviii.

44. Ibid., xix.

45. Ibid., 3.

46. James Maroosis, "Leadership: A Partnership in Reciprocal Following, in Ronald Riggio, Ira Chaleff & Jean Lipman-Blumen," *The Art of Followership: How Great Followers Create Great Leaders and Organizations* (Eds.) (San Francisco: Jossey-Bass, 2008), 17.

47. Ira Chaleff, "Creating New Ways of Following," in Ronald Riggio, Ira Chaleff & Jean Lipman-Blumen (Eds.), *The Art of Followership: How Great Followers Create Great Leaders and Organizations* (Eds.) (San Francisco: Jossey-Bass, 2008), 71.

48. Ibid., 73.

49. Ira Chaleff, *The Courageous Follower: Standing Up to & for Our Leaders*, 2nd ed. (San Francisco: Berrett-Koehler, 2003), 6–8.

50. Ibid., 7.

51. Ibid., 8.

52. Michael Maccoby, *The Leaders We Need and What Makes Us Follow* (Boston: Harvard Business School, 2007), 42.

53. Vince Lombardi, *What It Takes to Be #1* (New York: McGraw-Hill, 2001), 89.

54. Michael Maccoby, *The Leaders We Need and What Makes Us Follow* (Boston: Harvard Business School Publishing, 2007), 42.

55. Ibid., 43.
56. Ibid., 44.
57. Ronald Riggio, Ira Chaleff and Jean Lipman-Blumen (Eds.) *The Art of Followership: How Great Followers Create Great Leaders and Organizations*, San Francisco: Jossey-Bass, 2008), 215.
58. Michael Maccoby, *The Leaders We Need and What Makes Us Follow* (Boston: Harvard Business School Publishing, 2007), 215.
59. Ibid., 45.
60. Ibid., 52.
61. Ibid., 44.
62. Ibid., 45.
63. Ibid., 54.
64. Ibid., 55.
65. Tom Rath and Barry Conchie, *Strengths-Based Leadership: Great Leaders, Teams, and Why People Follow* (New York: Gallup Press, 2008), 80.
66. Ibid., 79.
67. Ibid., 2–3.
68. Ibid., 82.
69. Ibid., 79–86.
70. Ibid., 84.
71. Jack Welch and Suzy Welch, *Winning* (New York: HarperCollins, 2005), 25–26.
72. Tom Rath and Barry Conchie, *Strengths-Based Leadership: Great Leaders, Teams, and Why People Follow* (New York: Gallup Press, 2008), 86.
73. Ibid., 89.
74. Ibid., 90.
75. Ibid., 91.
76. Michael Maccoby, *The Leaders We Need and What Makes Us Follow* (Boston: Harvard Business School, 2007), 20.
77. Kent Bjugstad, Elizabeth C. Thach, Karen J. Thompson, and Alan Morris, "A Fresh Look at Followership: A Model for Matching Followership and Leadership Styles," *Institute of Behavioral and Applied Management* (2006), 304–311.
78. Thad Green, *Motivation Management: Fueling Performance by Discovering What People Believe About Themselves and Their Organizations* (Palo Alto, CA: Davies-Black, 2000), 20–24.
79. Robert E. Kelley, *The Power of Followership: How to Create Leaders People Want to Follow and Followers Who Lead Themselves* (New York: Currency Book, 1992), 55.
80. Ibid., 50–78.
81. Ibid., 57.
82. Ibid., 57.
83. Ibid., 67.
84. Ibid., 70.
85. Ibid., 74.
86. Ibid., 78.
87. Ibid., 85.
88. Warren Bennis, "The Art of Followership," *Leadership Excellence* 25 (4), (2008), 4.
89. Robert E. Kelley, "In Praise of Followers," *Harvard Business Review* 66, (1998), 142–148.
90. Warren Bennis, *On Becoming a Leader* (New York: Basic Books, 2009), xxiv.
91. Lisa M. Burke, Capella University, "Correlations of Followership and Leadership Styles of Medical Science Liaisons Within the Pharmaceutical and Biopharmaceutical Industry," *US Dissertation Abstracts International Section A: Humanities and Social Sciences,* 70 (4-A), 2009, 28; T.B. Harbecker, *The Otherside of Leadership* (Wheaton, IL: Victor Books, 1987).
92. Ralph Vecchio, "Effective Followership and Leadership Turned Upside Down," in R. P. Vecchio (Ed.), *Leadership: Understanding the Dynamics of Power and Influence in Organizations* (Notre Dame, IN: University of Notre Dame Press, 1997), 114–123; P. Wallington, "After You: Why Leaders Should Hone Followership Skills," *CIO* 16 (15), (2003), 1–10.
93. Kent Bjugstad, Elizabeth C. Thach, Karen J. Thompson, and Alan Morris, "A Fresh Look at Followership: A Model for Matching Followership and Leadership Styles," *Institute of Behavioral and Applied Management* (2006), 304–311.
94. S. Lundin and L. Lancaster, "Beyond Leadership: The Importance of Followership," *Futurist* 24 (1990), 18–24.
95. Robert E. Kelley, *The Power of Followership: How to Create Leaders People Want to Follow and Followers Who Lead Themselves* (New York: Currency Book, 1992), 92.
96. Ibid., 88.
97. Ibid., 93, 95–97.
98. Robert Kelley, "Rethinking Followership," in Ronald Riggio, Ira Chaleff & Jean Lipman-Blumen (Eds.), in *The Art of Followership: How Great Followers Create Great Leaders and Organizations* (San Francisco: Jossey-Bass, 2008), 7.
99. Robert E. Kelley, *The Power of Followership: How to Create Leaders People Want to Follow and Followers Who Lead Themselves* (New York: Currency Book, 1992), 123.
100. Lisa M. Burke, Capella University, "Correlations of Followership and Leadership Styles of Medical Science Liaisons Within the Pharmaceutical and Biopharmaceutical Industry," *US Dissertation Abstracts International Section A: Humanities and Social Sciences,* 70 (4-A), 2009, 65.
101. Robert E. Kelley, *The Power of Followership: How to Create Leaders People Want to Follow and Followers Who Lead Themselves* (New York: Currency Book, 1992), 88.
102. Retrieved February, 2012, from http://www.oprah.com/omagazine/Protect-Yourself-from-Energy-Vampires#ixzz2B568Ju6r
103. Robert Kelley, "Rethinking Followership," in Ronald Riggio, Ira Chaleff & Jean Lipman-Blumen, (Eds.) in *The Art of Followership: How Great Followers Create Great Leaders*

and Organizations (San Francisco: Jossey-Bass, 2008), 7.

104. Robert E. Kelley, *The Power of Followership: How to Create Leaders People Want to Follow and Followers Who Lead Themselves* (New York: Currency Book, 1992), 94.

105. Robert Kelley, "Rethinking Followership," in Ronald Riggio, Ira Chaleff & Jean Lipman-Blumen, (Eds.) in *The Art of Followership: How Great Followers Create Great Leaders and Organizations* (San Francisco: Jossey-Bass, 2008), 8.

106. Robert E. Kelley, *The Power of Followership: How to Create Leaders People Want to Follow and Followers Who Lead Themselves* (New York: Currency Book, 1992), 124.

107. Kelley did not record the percentage for exemplary followers in his book, so the recorded estimates were based on the results of a follower study. Retrieved March 2013, from http://www.journal.au.edu/scholar/2009/pdf/YanYe52-59.pdf

108. Robert E. Kelley, *The Power of Followership: How to Create Leaders People Want to Follow and Followers Who Lead Themselves* (New York: Currency Book, 1992), 88–98.

109. Tom Rath and Barry Conchie, *Strengths-Based Leadership: Great Leaders, Teams, and Why People Follow* (New York: Gallup Press, 2008), 79.

110. E.H. Potter, W.E. Rosenbach, and T.S. Pittman, "Followers for the Times: Engaging Employees in a Winning Partnership," in *Contemporary Issues in Leadership*, 5th ed. (New York: Westview Press, 2001), 3.

111. Mike Voight, "Applying Sport Psychology Philosophies, Principles, and Practices Onto the Gridiron: An Interview with USC Football Coach Pete Carroll," *International Journal of Sport Science & Coaching* 1 (4), (2006), 321–331.

112. E.H. Potter, W.E. Rosenbach, and T.S. Pittman, "Followers for the Times: Engaging Employees in a Winning Partnership," *Contemporary Issues in Leadership*, 5th ed. (New York: Westview Press, 2001), 3.

113. Robert E. Kelley, *The Power of Followership: How to Create Leaders People Want to Follow and Followers Who Lead Themselves* (New York: Currency Book, 1992), 89.

114. E.H. Potter, W.E. Rosenbach, and T.S. Pittman, "Followers for the Times: Engaging Employees in a Winning Partnership," in *Contemporary Issues in Leadership*, 5th ed. (New York: Westview Press, 2001), 4.

115. J. Raelin, *Creating Leaderful Organizations: How to Bring Out Leadership in Everyone* (San Francisco: Berrett-Koehler, 2003), 74–76.

116. Lisa M. Burke, Capella University, "Correlations of followership and leadership styles of medical science liaisons within the pharmaceutical and biopharmaceutical industry," *US Dissertation Abstracts International Section A: Humanities and Social Sciences,* 70 (4-A), 2009, 61.

117. G. Dixon and J. Westbrook, "Followers Revealed," *Engineering Management Journal* 15 (1), (2003), 25.

118. Chris Lee, "Followership: The Essence of Leadership," *Training* 28 (1), (1991), 29.

119. Ibid., 29.

120. Patsy Blackshear, "The Followership Continuum: A Model for Increasing Organizational Productivity," *The Innovation Journal: The Public Sector Innovation Journal* 9 (1), (2004), 3.

121. Ibid., 6.

122. Dean Smith, Gerald Bell, and John Kilgo, *The Carolina Way: Leadership Lessons from a Life in Coaching* (New York: Penguin Books, 2004), 25–26.

123. Patsy Blackshear, "The Followership Continuum: A Model for Increasing Organizational Productivity," *The Innovation Journal: The Public Sector Innovation Journal* 9 (1), (2004), 6.

124. Ira Chaleff, *The Courageous Follower: Standing Up to & for Our Leaders*, 2nd ed. (San Francisco: Berrett-Koehler, 2003), 6–8.

125. John Hertig, "Followership: Nontraditional Leadership Roles for New Practitioners," *American Journal of Health-System Pharmacy* 1, (2010), 1412–1413.

126. James Kouzes and Barry Posner, *The Leadership Challenge: How to Get Extraordinary Things Done in Organizations* (San Francisco: Jossey-Bass, 1987).

127. Robert E. Kelley, *The Power of Followership: How to Create Leaders People Want to Follow and Followers Who Lead Themselves* (New York: Currency Book, 1992), 29.

128. John Hertig, "Followership: Nontraditional Leadership Roles for New Practitioners," *American Journal of Health-System Pharmacy* 1, (2010), 1413.

129. Chris Lee, Followership: The Essence of Leadership, *Training* 28 (1), (1991), 35.

130. Kent Bjugstad, Elizabeth C. Thach, Karen J. Thompson, and Alan Morris, "A Fresh Look at Followership: A Model for Matching Followership and Leadership Styles," *Institute of Behavioral and Applied Management* (2006), 311–314.

131. Robert E. Kelley, *The Power of Followership: How to Create Leaders People Want to Follow and Followers Who Lead Themselves* (New York: Currency Book, 1992), 203.

132. Ibid., 205.

133. Ira Chaleff, *The Courageous Follower: Standing Up To & For Our Leaders*, 2nd ed. (San Francisco: Berrett-Koehler, 2003), 5.

134. Ibid., 7.

135. Ibid., 4.

136. Ibid., 6–10.

137. Robert E. Kelley, *The Power of Followership: How to Create Leaders People Want to Fol-*

low and Followers Who Lead Themselves (New York: Currency Book, 1992), 13.

138. John Hertig, "Followership: Nontraditional Leadership Roles for New Practitioners," *American Journal of Health-System Pharmacy* 1 (2010), 1413.

139. Chris Lee, "Followership: The Essence of Leadership," *Training* 28 (1), (1991), 33.

140. Robert E. Kelley, *The Power of Followership: How to Create Leaders People Want to Follow and Followers Who Lead Themselves* (New York: Currency Book, 1992), 187–197.

141. Ibid., 185.
142. Ibid., 194.
143. Ibid., 195.
144. Ibid., 196.
145. Ibid., 12.

Chapter 12

1. John P. Kotter, "What Leaders Really Do," in *Harvard Business Review on Leadership,* (Boston: Harvard Business School, 1998), 53.

2. Bill Parcells, "The Tough Work of Turning Around a Team," *Harvard Business Review,* (2000), 179–184.

3. Retrieved March 15, 2013, from http://dictionary.reference.com/browse/culture?s=ts&ld=1127

4. John Kotter, *Leading Change* (Boston: Harvard Business Press, 1996), 180.

5. Jeffrey Krames, *What the Best CEO's Know: 7 Exceptional Leaders and Their Lessons for Transforming Any Business* (New York: McGraw-Hill, 2003), 42.

6. Ibid., 43.

7. Edgar Schein, *Organizational Culture and Leadership,* 2nd ed. (San Francisco: Jossey-Bass, 1992).

8. Nick Saban with Brian Curtis, *How Good Do You Want to Be? A Champion's Tips on How to Lead and Succeed* (New York: Ballantine Books, 2005).

9. John Kotter and James Heskett, *Corporate Culture and Performance* (New York: Free Press, 1992), 89.

10. Marshall Sashkin and Molly Sashkin. *Leadership That Matters: The Critical Factors for Making a Difference in People's Lives and Organizations' Success* (San Francisco: Berrett-Koehler, 2003), 122.

11. Ibid., 125.
12. Ibid., 127.

13. Bill Parcells, "The Tough Work of Turning Around a Team," *Harvard Business Review,* (2000), 180–184.

14. Ibid., 181.

15. Alan Murray, *The Wall Street Journal: Essential Guide to Management* (New York: Harper Business, 2010), 39.

16. Ibid., 42.

17. Bill Walsh with Steve Jamison and Craig Walsh, *The Score Takes Care of Itself: My Philosophy of Leadership* (New York: Penguin Group, 2009), xxiv.

18. Ibid., 25.

19. Seth Godin, *Tribes* (New York: Penguin Group, 2008), 1.

20. Ibid., 126.

21. Paul Azinger and Dr. Ron Braund, *Cracking the Code—The Winning Ryder Cup Strategy: Make It Work for You* (Decatur, GA: Looking Glass Books, 2010), 52.

22. Ibid., 87.

23. Mike Krzyzewski, *The Gold Standard: Building a World-Class Team* (New York: Business Plus, 2009), 85.

24. Jena McGregor, "Game Plan: First Find the Leaders," *Bloomberg Businessweek*, August 21, 2006). Retrieved March 11, 2013, from http://businessweek.com/printer/articles/206532-game-plan-first-dind-the-leaders

25. Dave Waddell, "Cirovski Defines Leadership Formula," *The Windsor Star*, May 9, 2012. Retrieved March 11, 2013, from http://peakconsulting.ca/article-blog-8/cirovski-defines-leadership-formula

26. Sim Sitkin and J. Richard Hackman, "Developing Team Leadership: An Interview with Coach Mike Krzyzewski," *Academy of Management Learning & Education* 10 (3), (2011), 494–501.

27. Mike Krzyzewski, *The Gold Standard: Building a World-Class Team* (New York: Business Plus, 2009), 85–87.

28. James Kouzes and Barry Posner, *The Truth About Leadership: The No-Fads, Heart-of-the-Matter Facts You Need to Know* (San Francisco: Jossey-Bass, 2010), 26.

29. David Kord Murray, *Borrowing Brilliance* (New York: Penguin Group, 2004), 14.

30. Ibid., 1–2.

31. Jay Conger and Beth Benjamin, *Building Leaders: How Successful Companies Develop the Next Generation* (San Francisco: Jossey-Bass, 1999), 27.

32. Bill George, Andrew Mclean and Nick Craig, *Finding Your True North: A Personal Guide* (San Francisco: Jossey-Bass, 2008), 61.

33. Harvey Dorfman, *Coaching the Mental Game: Leadership Philosophies and Strategies for Peak Performance in Sports and Everyday Life* (Lanham, MD: Taylor Trade Publishing, 2003), 50.

34. Ibid., 51.

35. Alan Murray, *The Wall Street Journal: Essential Guide to Management* (New York: Harper Business, 2010), 170.

36. J.C. Maxwell, *Leadership Gold* (Nashville: Thomas Nelson, 2008), 28.

37. Ibid., 31.

38. Alan Murray, *The Wall Street Journal: Essential Guide to Management* (New York: Harper Business, 2010), 172.

39. Ibid., 173–75.

40. John Kotter and James Heskett, *Corporate Culture and Performance* (New York: Free Press, 1992).

41. Harvey Dorfman, *Coaching the Mental Game: Leadership Philosophies and Strategies for Peak Performance in Sports-and Everyday Life* (Lanham, MD: Taylor Trade Publishing, 2003), 31.

42. Ibid., 32–33.

43. Stewart Friedman, *Total Leadership: Be a Better Leader, Have a Richer Life* (Boston: Harvard Business School Press, 2008), 171.

44. Eric Kail, "Becoming a Leader Developer," in Major Doug Crandall (Ed.), *Leadership Lessons from West Point* (San Francisco: Jossey-Bass, 2007), 14.

45. Bill George, Andrew Mclean and Nick Craig, *Finding Your True: A Personal Guide* (San Francisco: Jossey-Bass, 2008).

46. Sean Hannah, "The Authentic High-Impact Leader," in Major Doug Crandall (Ed.) *Leadership Lessons from West Point* (San Francisco: Jossey-Bass, 2007), 92.

47. Vince Lombardi, Jr., *What It Takes to Be #1* (New York: McGraw-Hill, 2001), 125.

48. Warren Bennis and Burt Nanus, *Leaders: The Strategies for Taking Charge* (New York: Harper & Row, Publishers, 1985), 27.

49. Warren Bennis, *On Becoming a Leader* (Philadelphia: Basic Books, 2009), 65.

50. Ibid., 67.

51. James Kouzes and Barry Posner, *The Truth About Leadership: The No-Fads, Heart-Of-the-Matter Facts You Need to Know* (San Francisco: Jossey-Bass, 2010), 138.

52. Jay Conger and Beth Benjamin, *Building Leaders: How Successful Companies Develop the Next Generation* (San Francisco: Jossey-Bass, 2009), 212.

53. James Kouzes and Barry Posner, *The Leadership Challenge: How to Get Extraordinary Things Done in Organizations* (San Francisco: Jossey-Bass, 1987), 202.

54. Ibid., 204.

55. Robert Fulmer, "Business Challenge Coaching," in H. Morgan, P. Harkins, and M. Goldsmith (Eds.), *The Art and Practice of Leadership Coaching: 50 Top Executives Reveal Their Secrets* (Hoboken, NJ: John Wiley & Sons, 2005), 125–127.

56. John Kotter, *Leading Change* (Boston: Harvard Business Press, 1996), 188–90.

57. Ibid., 190.

58. James Kouzes and Barry Posner, *The Leadership Challenge: How to Get Extraordinary Things Done in Organizations* (San Francisco: Jossey-Bass, 1987), 201.

59. Annie McKee, Richard Boyatzis, and Frances Johnston, *Becoming a Resonant Leader* (Boston: Harvard Business Press, 2008), 7.

60. James Kouzes and Barry Posner, *The Leadership Challenge: How to Get Extraordinary Things Done in Organizations* (San Francisco: Jossey-Bass, 1987), 202.

61. Ibid., 203.

62. Jay Conger and Beth Benjamin, *Building Leaders: How Successful Companies Develop the Next Generation* (San Francisco: Jossey-Bass, 1999), 242.

63. Ibid., 242.

64. Ibid., 241.

65. Ibid., 132.

66. Ibid., 133.

67. Alan Murray, *The Wall Street Journal: Essential Guide to Management* (New York: Harper Business, 2010), 39.

68. Bill George, Peter Sims, Andrew McLean, and Diana Mayer, "Discovering Your Authentic Leadership," in *HBR's 10 Must Reads on Leadership* (Boston: Harvard Business School, 2011), 162.

69. Ibid., 164.

70. James Kouzes and Barry Posner, *The Leadership Challenge: How to Get Extraordinary Things Done in Organizations* (San Francisco: Jossey-Bass, 1987), 151.

71. Daniel Goleman, Richard Boyatzis, and Annie McKee, *Primal Leadership: Realizing the Power of Emotional Intelligence* (Boston: Harvard Business School Press, 2002), 157.

72. Eric Kail, "Becoming a Leader Developer," in Major Doug Crandall (Ed.), *Leadership Lessons from West Point* (San Francisco: Jossey-Bass, 2007), 5.

73. Stuart Levine, *The Six Fundamentals of Success: The Rules for Getting It Right for Yourself and Your Organization* (New York: Doubleday, 2004), 112.

74. Annie McKee, Richard Boyatzis, and Frances Johnston, *Becoming a Resonant Leader* (Boston: Harvard Business Press, 2008), 9.

75. Daniel Goleman, Richard Boyatzis, and Annie McKee, *Primal Leadership: Realizing the Power of Emotional Intelligence* (Boston: Harvard Business School Press, 2002), 109–112.

76. Ibid., 111.

77. Bill George, Peter Sims, Andrew McLean, and Diana Mayer, "Discovering Your Authentic Leadership," in *HBR's 10 Must Reads on Leadership* (Boston: Harvard Business School, 2011), 170.

78. Paul Assaiante, *Run to the Roar: Coaching to Overcome Fear* (New York: Portfolio, 2010), 80.

79. Ibid., 83.

80. Ibid., 82.

81. Jay Conger and Beth Benjamin, *Building Leaders: How Successful Companies Develop the Next Generation* (San Francisco: Jossey-Bass, 1999), 45.

82. Ibid., 46.

83. J.C. Maxwell, *The 17 Essential Qualities of a Team Player* (Nashville: Thomas Nelson, 2002), 85.

84. Jack Welch and Suzy Welch, *Winning* (New York: HarperCollins, 2005), 61.

85. Steven Sample, *The Contrarian's Guide to Leadership* (San Francisco: Jossey-Bass, 2002), 84.

86. Daniel Goleman, Richard Boyatzis, and Annie McKee, *Primal Leadership: Realizing the Power of Emotional Intelligence* (Boston: Harvard Business School Press, 2002), xiii.

87. Jim Kouzes and Barry Posner, *The Leadership Challenge: How to Get Extraordinary Things Done in Organizations* (San Francisco: Jossey-Bass, 1987), 207.

88. Ibid., 208.

89. Ibid., 209.

90. S.R. Maddi and D. M. Khoshaba, "Hardiness and Mental Health," *Journal of Personality Assessment* 67 (1994), 265–274.

91. Jim Kouzes and Barry Posner, *The Leadership Challenge: How to Get Extraordinary Things Done in Organizations* (San Francisco: Jossey-Bass, 1987), 206.

92. Ibid., 207.

93. Ibid., 209.

94. Nick Saban with Brian Curtis, *How Good Do You Want to Be? A Champion's Tips on How to Lead and Succeed* (New York: Ballantine Books, 2005), 6.

95. Ibid., 30–31.

96. Mike Krzyzewski with Donald Phillips, *Leading with the Heart* (New York: Warner Business Books, 2000), 214.

97. Linda Argote, Sara L. Beckman, and Dennis Epple, "The Persistence and Transfer of Learning in Industrial Settings," *Management Science* 36 (2), (1990), 140–154; Linda Argote and Paul Ingram, "Knowledge Transfer: A Basis for Competitive Advantage in Firms," *Organizational Behavior and Human Decision Processes* 82 (1), (2000), 150–169; G.E. Briggs and J. Naylor, "The Relative Efficiency of Several Training Methods as a Function of Transfer Task Complexity," *Journal of Experimental Psychology* 64 (1962), 505–512.

98. Jay Conger and Beth Benjamin, *Building Leaders: How Successful Companies Develop the Next Generation* (San Francisco: Jossey-Bass, 1999), 52–54.

99. Daniel Goleman, Richard Boyatzis, and Annie McKee, *Primal Leadership: Realizing the Power of Emotional Intelligence* (Boston: Harvard Business School Press, 2002), 143.

100. Marshall Goldsmith and Howard Morgan, "Leadership as a Contact Sport: You Can't Develop in a Closet," *Leadership Excellence* 36 (2004), 6–7.

101. K. A. Ericsson and N. Charness, "Expert Performance," *American Psychologist* 49 (8), (1994), 725–747; K.A. Ericsson, R.T. Krampe, and C. Tesch-Romer, "The Role of Deliberate Practices in the Acquisition of Expert Performance," *Psychological Review* 100 (3), (1993), 363–406; K.A. Ericsson and J. Smith, *Towards a General Theory of Expertise* (Cambridge: Cambridge University Press, 1991).

102. Jay Conger and Beth Benjamin, *Building Leaders: How Successful Companies Develop the Next Generation* (San Francisco: Jossey-Bass, 1999), 45.

103. Bill George, Andrew McLean, and Nick Craig, *Finding Your True North: A Personal Guide* (San Francisco: Jossey-Bass, 2008), 132.

104. Annie McKee, Richard Boyatzis, and Frances Johnston, *Becoming a Resonant Leader* (Boston: Harvard Business Press, 2008), 17.

105. Bill George, *Authentic Leadership: Rediscovering the Secrets to Creating Lasting Value,* (San Francisco: Jossey-Bass, 2003), 133.

106. J.C. Maxwell, *The 17 Essential Qualities of a Team Player* (Nashville: Thomas Nelson, 2002), 125.

107. Linda Hill, *Becoming a Manager: Mastery of a New Identity* (Boston: Harvard Business School Press, 1992), 245.

108. Ibid., 246.

109. Daniel Goleman, Richard Boyatzis, and Annie McKee, *Primal Leadership: Realizing the Power of Emotional Intelligence* (Boston: Harvard Business School Press, 2002), 233.

110. Mike Myatt, "The #1 Reason Leadership Development Fails," Forbes.com (2012, February). Retrieved March 15, 2013, from http: www.Forbes.com

111. Marshall Goldsmith and Howard Morgan, "Leadership as a Contact Sport: You Can't Develop in a Closet," *Leadership Excellence* 36 (2004), 7.

112. Daniel Goleman, Richard Boyatzis, and Annie McKee, *Primal Leadership: Realizing the Power of Emotional Intelligence* (Boston: Harvard Business School Press, 2002), 495.

113. Ibid., 233.

114. Ibid., 233–235.

115. Sean Hannah, "The Authentic High-Impact Leader," in Major Doug Crandall (Ed.), *Leadership Lessons from West Point* (San Francisco: Jossey-Bass, 2007), 101.

116. Jeff Cannon and Jon Cannon, *Leadership Lessons of the Navy Seals: Battle-Tested Strategies for Creating Successful Organizations and Inspiring Extraordinary Results* (New York: McGraw-Hill, 2003), 92.

117. Ibid., 93.

118. Warren Bennis, *An Invented Life: Reflections on Leadership and Change* (Reading, MA: Addison-Wesley Publishing, 1993), 84.

119. Ibid., 85.

120. Bill George, Andrew McLean, and

Nick Craig, *Finding Your True North: A Personal Guide* (San Francisco: Jossey-Bass, 2008), 133.

121. Bill George, *Authentic Leadership: Rediscovering The Secrets to Creating Lasting Value* (San Francisco: Jossey-Bass, 2003), 79.

122. Bill George, Andrew McLean, and Nick Craig, *Finding Your True North: A Personal Guide* (San Francisco: Jossey-Bass, 2008), 41.

123. Bill George, *Authentic Leadership: Rediscovering The Secrets to Creating Lasting Value* (San Francisco: Jossey-Bass, 2003), 82.

124. David Rooke and William Torbert, "Seven Transformations of Leadership," in *HBR's 10 Must Reads on Leadership* (Boston: Harvard Business School, 2011), 137.

125. John Kotter, *Leading Change* (Boston: Harvard Business Press, 1996), 180.

126. Jay Conger and Beth Benjamin, *Building Leaders: How Successful Companies Develop the Next Generation* (San Francisco: Jossey-Bass, 1999), 45.

127. Jay Conger, "Education for Leaders: Current Practices, New Directions," *Journal of Management Systems* (1998), 332–348.

128. Jay Conger and Beth Benjamin, *Building Leaders: How Successful Companies Develop the Next Generation* (San Francisco: Jossey-Bass, 1999), 44.

129. Ibid., 49.

130. Paul Assaiante, *Run to the Roar: Coaching to Overcome Fear* (New York: Portfolio, 2010), 85.

131. Jay Conger and Beth Benjamin, *Building Leaders: How Successful Companies Develop the Next Generation* (San Francisco: Jossey-Bass, 1999), 51.

132. Ibid., 52.

133. Alan Murray, *The Wall Street Journal: Essential Guide to Management* (New York: Harper Business, 2010), 43.

134. Anson Dorrance and Gloria Averbuch, *The Vision of a Champion: Advice and Inspiration from the World's Most Successful Women's Soccer Coach* (Ann Arbor: Huron River Press, 2002), 212.

135. Jeff Cannon and Jon Cannon, *Leadership Lessons of the Navy Seals: Battle-Tested Strategies for Creating Successful Organizations and Inspiring Extraordinary Results* (New York: McGraw-Hill, 2003), 134.

136. Anson Dorrance and Gloria Averbuch, *The Vision of a Champion: Advice and Inspiration from the World's Most Successful Women's Soccer Coach* (Ann Arbor: Huron River Press, 2002), 325.

137. Ibid., 327–329.

138. Mike Krzyzewski with Donald Phillips, *Leading with the Heart* (New York: Warner Business Books, 2000), 26.

139. Ibid., 196.

140. Ibid., 197.

141. Bill George, Peter Sims, Andrew McLean, and Diana Mayer, "Discovering Your Authentic Leadership," in *HBR's 10 Must Reads: On Leadership* (Boston: Harvard Business School, 2011), 163.

142. James Kouzes and Barry Posner, *The Truth About Leadership: The No-Fads, Heart-of-the-Matter Facts You Need to Know* (San Francisco: Jossey-Bass, 2010), 139.

143. Warren Bennis, *On Becoming a Leader* (New York: Basic Books, 2009), 188.

144. Eric Kail, "Becoming a Leader Developer," in Major Doug Crandall (Ed.), *Leadership Lessons from West Point* (San Francisco: Jossey-Bass, 2007), 3.

145. Ibid., 4.

146. Tom Rath and Barry Conchie, *Strengths-Based Leadership: Great Leaders, Teams, and Why People Follow* (New York: Gallup Press, 2008), 1.

Bibliography

ABC News. January 4, 2007. "LAX Player Files Lawsuit Against Duke University." *ABC. com*. Retrieved June 14, 2011, from http://abclocal.go.com/wtvd/story?section=triangle&id=4905060

Alexander, Chip. April 1, 2003. "Athletes' Voices Heard." In *Charlotte Observer.com*. Retrieved March 29, 2003, from http://www.newsobserver.com/sports/v-print/story/2388051.html.

Ames, Carole. Achievement Goals, Motivational Climates, and Motivational Processes. In G.C. Roberts (Ed.), *Motivation in Sport and Exercise*. Champaign, IL: Human Kinetics, 1992.

"Amount of Hours Children Spend Watching TV Could Impact Waistlines." July 16, 2012. Retrieved March 10, 2013, from http://www.foxnews.com/health/2012/07/16/amount-hours-children-spend-watching-tv-could-impact-waistlines/#ixzz2MyU2TytJ

April, Kurt, Darryn Lifson, and Tim Noakes. "Emotional Intelligence of Elite Sport Leaders & Elite Business Leaders," *International Journal of Sport Science and Coaching*, 2011.

Argote, Linda, Sara Beckman, and Dennis Epple. "The Persistence and Transfer of Learning in Industrial Settings." *Management Science*, 1990.

Argote, Linda, and Paul Ingram. "Knowledge Transfer: A Basis for Competitive Advantage in Firms," *Organizational Behavior and Human Decision Processes*, 2000.

Arnett, Dugan. December 2, 2009. "Ex-Player Accuses Mangino of Mistreatment." In *KU Sports.com*. Retrieved January 28, 2010, from http://www.2.kusports.com/news/2009/dec/02/ex-player-accuses-mangino-mistreatment/.

Assaiante, Paul. *Run to the Roar: Coaching to Overcome Fear*. New York: Portfolio, 2010.

Associated Press. "Arizona's Mackovic Vows to Change His Approach." *Los Angeles Times*, 2002.

_____. "Judge Rules Player to Be Reinstated," February 12, 2009, in *ESPN.com*. Retrieved June 14, 2011, from http://sports.espn.go.com/ncaa/news/story?id=3903336.

_____. "Laviolette: We Have Legitimate Chance at Gold," August 16, 2005, in *ESPN.com*. Retrieved June 13, 2011, from http://sports.espn.go.com/oly/news/story?id=2135849.

_____. "Players: Teammate Made to Run Till She Collapsed," February 10, 2003, in *ESPN.com*. Retrieved February 10, 2003, from http://espn.go.com/ncw/news/2003/0210/1506777.html.

_____. "QB Barkley Will Return to USC," December 2011. Retrieved December 22, 2011, from http://msn.foxsports.com/collegefootball/story/USC-Trojans-quarterback.

_____. "Sherrill Discusses Coaching Memories." *Dallas News*, 2005.

_____. "Wagner Fired After Player Exodus," June 1, 2010, in *ESPN.com*. Retrieved July 22, 2010, from http://sports.espn.go.com/espn/print?id=5240400&type=HeadlineNews&imagesPrint=off.

Azinger, Paul, and Braund, Dr. Ron. *Cracking the Code—The Winning Ryder Cup Strategy: Make it Work for You.* Decatur, GA: Looking Glass Books, 2010.

Badaracco, Joseph, Jr. *Leading Quietly: An Unorthodox Guide to Doing the Right Thing.* Boston: Harvard Business School Publishing, 2002.

_____. "The Discipline of Building Character," *Harvard Business Review on Leadership* Boston: Harvard Business School Press, 1998.

Barsh, Joanna, Susie Cranston, and Geoffrey Lewis. *How Remarkable Women Lead: The Breakthrough Model for Work and Life.* New York: Crown, 2011.

Bass, Bernard. *Bass & Stogdill's Handbook of Leadership: Theory, Research, and Managerial Applications* (3rd Ed.). New York: Free Press, 1990.

_____. *Transformational Leadership: Industry, Military, and Educational Impact.* Mahwah, NJ: Lawrence Erlbaum Associates, Publishers, 1998.

Batten, Joe. *Tough-Minded Leadership.* New York: AMACOM, American Management Association, 1989.

Bennetts, Leslie. March 5, 2012. "Women and the Leadership Gap," *Newsweek.* Retrieved May 5, 2012, from http://www. thedailybeast.com/newsweek/2012/03/ 04/the-stubborn-gender-gap.html

Bennis, Warren. "The Art of Followership." *Leadership Excellence,* 2008.

_____. *An Invented Life: Reflections on Leadership and Change.* Reading, MA: Addison-Wesley Publishing, 1993.

_____. *On Becoming a Leader.* Philadelphia: Basic Books, 2009.

Bennis, Warren, and Burt Nanus. *Leaders: The Strategies for Taking Charge.* New York: Harper & Row, 1985.

Bennis, Warren, and Joan Goldsmith. *Learning to Lead: A Workbook on Becoming a Leader.* New York: Basic Books, 2010.

Bennis, Warren, and Robert Thomas. "Crucibles of Leadership." *HBR's 10 Must Reads on Leadership.* Boston: Harvard Business School Publishing, 2011.

Berard, William III. "Coach Perspectives in the New Millennium." *NFHS Coaches Quarterly Magazine,* 2000.

Beswick, Bill. *Focused for Soccer.* Champaign, IL: Human Kinetics, 2001.

Bialek, Carl. September 3, 2010. "A Lifetime of Career Changes." In *Wall Street Journal.* Retrieved March 15, 2013, from http://blogs.wsj.com/numbersguy/a-lifetime-of-career-changes-988/

Bjugstad, Kent, Elizabeth C. Thach, Karen J. Thompson, and Alan Morris. "A Fresh Look at Followership: A Model for Matching Followership and Leadership Styles." *Institute of Behavioral and Applied Management,* 2006.

Blackshear, Patsy. "The Followership Continuum: A Model for Increasing Organizational Productivity." *The Innovation Journal: The Public Sector Innovation Journal,* 2004.

Boeree, C. George. "Limbic System Anatomy." (n.d.). Retrieved October 12, 2011, from http://webspace.ship.edu/cgboer/ limbicsystem.html.

Brady, Erik. "Coaches Who Cross the Line: Push to Win Can Become 'Abusive Tactics.'" *USA Today,* 2012.

Breakey, Patricia. "Entitlement Generation Expects It All." *The Daily Star,* 2005.

Brennan, Christine. July 9, 2009. "Player Revolt Against Commissioner Biven Latest Danger." *USA Today.* Retrieved June 13, 2011, from http://www.usatoday. com/sports/columnist/brennan/2009– 07–08-lpga-bivens_N.htm

Briggs, G.E. and J. Naylor, "The Relative Efficiency of Several Training Methods as a Function of Transfer Task Complexity." *Journal of Experimental Psychology,* 1962.

Buckingham, M. and C. Coffman. *First, Break All the Rules.* New York: Simon & Schuster, 1999.

Burke, C.S., S.M., Fiore, and E. Salas. "The Role of Shared Cognition in Enabling Shared Leadership and Team Adaptability." In C.L. Pearce and J.A. Conger (Eds.). *Shared Leadership.* Thousand Oaks, CA: Sage, 2003.

Burke, Lisa M. "Capella University, Correlations of Followership and Leadership Styles of Medical Science Liaisons Within the Pharmaceutical and Biopharmaceutical Industry." *US Dissertation Abstracts International Section A: Humanities and Social Sciences,* 2009.

Canavan, Tom. March 20, 2001. "Rutgers Fires Hoops Coach Kevin Bannon." In *USA Today.com.* Retrieved from, http://usato day30.usatoday.com/sports/basketba/ skm/2001-03–20-rutgers-bannon.htm

Cannon, Jeff, and Lt. Cmdr. Jon Canon. *Leadership Lessons of the Navy Seals*. New York: McGraw-Hill, 2003.

Chaleff, Ira. *The Courageous Follower: Standing Up to & for Our Leaders* (2nd edition). San Francisco: Berrett-Koehler Publishers, 2003.

_____. "Creating New Ways of Following." In Ronald Riggio, Ira Chaleff & Jean Lipman-Blumen (Eds.), *The Art of Followership: How Great Followers Create Great Leaders and Organizations* (Eds.) San Francisco: Jossey-Bass, 2008.

Chelladurai, P. "Leadership In Sport Organizations." *Canadian Journal of Applied Sport Sciences,* 1980.

Clarke, Liz. October 11, 2012. "Jae Su Chun Resigns as U.S. Short-Track Speed Skating Coach." In *Washington Post.com.* Retrieved February 2013, from http://articles.washingtonpost.com/2012–10-11/sports/35502307_1_hyung-yeo-canadian-skater-olivier-jean-simon-cho

Clough, P., K. Earle, and D. Sewell. "Mental Toughness: The Concept and Its Measurement." In I. Cockerill (Ed.), *Solutions In Sport Psychology*. London: Thompson, 2002.

Coakley, Jay. *Sports in Society: Issues and Controversies, 10th edition*. New York: McGraw-Hill, 2008.

"College Debts and Broken Dreams." *Business Week*, 2005.

Collins, Jim. *Good to Great*. New York: HarperCollins, 2001.

Conger, Jay. "Education for Leaders: Current Practices, New Directions," *Journal of Management Systems*, 1998.

Conger, Jay, and Beth Benjamin. *Building Leaders: How Successful Companies Develop the Next Generation*. San Francisco: Jossey-Bass, 1999.

Covey, Stephen. *Principle-Centered Leadership*. Los Angeles, CA: Fireside Press, 1992.

Cox, Richard. *Sport Psychology-Concepts and Applications*. New York: McGraw-Hill, 2001.

Crowe, Jerry. "Internet Propels Athlete Hazing Issue to Forefront." *Los Angeles Times*, 2006.

Davenport, Thomas. *Thinking for a Living: How to Get Better Performance and Results from Knowledge Workers*. Boston: Harvard Business School Press, 2005.

DeBoer, Kathleen J. "Practice Like a Girl, Compete Like a Boy: Training the Total Athlete." *US Olympic Coach*, 2006.

Dicicco, Tony, Colleen Hacker, and Charles Salzerg, 2012. *Catch Them Being Good: Everything You Need to Know to Successfully Coach Girls*. New York: Penguin Books, 2002.

Dirks, Kurt. "Trust in Leadership and Team Performance: Evidence from NCAA Basketball." *Journal of Applied Psychology*, 2000.

Dixon, G., and J. Westbrook, "Followers Revealed." *Engineering Management Journal*, 2003.

Dobson, James. *Dr. James Dobson's Focus on the Family Bulletin*. Carol Stream, IL: Tyndale House Publishers, 2005.

Dorfman, Harvey. *Coaching the Mental Game*. Lanham, MD: First Taylor Trade Publishing, 2003.

Dorrance, Anson. "Coaching Women: Going Against the Instincts of My Gender." *US Olympic Coach,* 2006.

_____. *Training Soccer Champions*. Raleigh: JTC Sports, 1996.

Dorrance, Anson, and Gloria Averbuch. *The Vision of a Champion*. Ann Arbor: Huron River Press, 2005.

Doyle, Dan, and Deborah Burch. *Encyclopedia of Sports Parenting: Everything You Need to Guide Your Young Athlete*. New York: Hall of Fame Press, 2008.

Drape, Joe. "Talking 'Bout a Revolution." *ESPN the Magazine*, 1998.

Drucker, Peter. *The Essential Drucker*. New York: HarperCollins, 2001.

Duda, Joan and H. Hall. "Achievement Goal Theory in Sport: Recent Extensions and Future Directions." In R. Singer, H. Hausenblas, & C. Janelle (Eds.), *Handbook of Sport Psychology* (2nd ed.). New York: Wiley, 2001.

Duefresne, Chris. "A Wildcat Strike May Take Flight." *Los Angeles Times*, 2002.

Dweck, Carol. "Motivational Processes Affecting Learning." *American Psychologist*, 1986.

Eagly, A.H., and B. Johannesen-Schmidt. "Leadership-Style Matters: The Small, but Important, Style Differences Between Male and Female Leaders." In D. Bilimoria and S. Piderit (Eds.). *Handbook on Women in Business and Management*. Northampton, MA: Edwin Elgar Publishing, 2007.

Eagly, A.H., S.J. Karau, and M.G. Makhijani.

"Gender and the Effectiveness of Leaders: A Meta-Analysis." *Psychological Bulletin,* 1995.

"The Echo Boomers." Aired October 3, 2004. Retrieved October 4, 2004, from http://www.cbsnews.com/stories/2004/10/01/60minutes/printable46890.shtml

Egley, A., and J.C. Howell. April 2012. "Highlights of the 2010 National Youth Gang Survey." Retrieved March 12, 2013, from https://www.ncjrs.gov/app/QA/Detail.aspx?Id=146&context=9

Eitzen, Stanley. *Sport in Contemporary Society: An Anthology,* (9th ed.). Oxford University Press, 2011.

Ericsson, K.A., and J. Smith. *Towards a General Theory of Expertise.* Cambridge: Cambridge University Press, 1991

Ericsson, K. A., and N. Charness. "Expert Performance." *American Psychologist,* 1994..

Ericsson, K.A., R.T. Krampe, and C. Tesch-Romer. "The Role of Deliberate Practices in the Acquisition of Expert Performance." *Psychological Review,* 1993.

Evans, Gail. *Play Like a Man, Win Like a Woman: What Men Know About Success that Women Need to Learn.* New York: Crown, 2001.

Eversley, Melanie, and John Bacon. "Manslaughter Charges for 12 in Florida A & M Band Hazing." *USA Today,* 2013.

Fallon, Bernie. *The Art of Followership: What Happened to the Indians?* Bloomington, IN: Phi Delta Kappa Educational Foundation, 1974.

Fields B., S. Wilder, M. Bunch, and R. Newbold. *Millennial Leaders: Success Stories from Today's Most Brilliant Generation Y Leaders.* Buffalo Grove, IL: Writers of the Round Table, 2008.

Finch, Jennie, and Ann Killion. *Throw Like a Girl: How to Dream Big and Believe in Yourself.* New York: Triumph, 2011.

Fletcher, J. *Disappearing Acts: Gender, Power and Relational Practice at Work.* Cambridge, MA: MIT Press, 1999.

Flynn, Jill, Kathryn Heath, and Mary Davis Holt. *Break Your Own Rules: How to Change the Patterns of Thinking that Block Women's Paths to Power.* San Francisco: Jossey-Bass, 2011.

Foss, Mike. September 5, 2012. "Texas Tech Coach Billy Gillespie Faces Allegations of Mistreatment." In *USA Today.com.* Retrieved February 2013, from http://content.usatoday.com/communities/campusrivalry/post-2012/09/texas-tech-coach

Frasso, Peter. April 2001. "Softball: Communication Key to Coaching Philosophy." In *The Observer On-line.* Retrieved June 20, 2012, from http:www.observer.com

Friedman, Stewart. *Total Leadership: Be a Better Leader, Have a Richer Life.* Boston: Harvard Business School Press, 2008.

Frew, D. R. "Leadership and Followership." *Personnel Journal,* 1977.

Fulmer, Robert. "Business Challenge Coaching. In H. Morgan, P. Harkins, & M. Goldsmith (Eds.). *The Art and Practice of Leadership Coaching: 50 Top Executives Reveal Their Secrets.* Hoboken, NJ: John Wiley & Sons, 2005.

Garner, Bradley J. *A Brief Guide for Teaching Millennial Learners.* Marion, IN: Triangle Publishers, 2007.

George, Bill. *Authentic Leadership: Rediscovering the Secrets to Creating Lasting Value.* San Francisco: Jossey-Bass, 2003.

George, Bill, Andrew Mclean, and Nick Craig. *Finding Your True: A Personal Guide.* San Francisco: Jossey-Bass, 2008.

George, Bill, Peter Sims, Andrew McLean, and Diana Mayer. "Discovering Your Authentic Leadership." In *HBR's 10 Must Reads on Leadership.* Boston: Harvard Business School Publishing, 2011.

George, Rachel. "E-mails Illuminate Gillispie's Fall." *USA Today,* 2012.

Giannoudis, Georgios, and Marios Goudas. "A Team-Sports-Based Life-Skills Program in a Physical Education Context." *Learning and Instruction,* 2008.

Giuliani, R. *Leadership.* New York: Hyperion, 2002.

Glenn, S.D., and Thelma Horn. "Psychological and Personal Predictors of Leadership Behavior in Female Soccer Athletes." *Journal of Applied Sport Psychology,* 1993.

Godin, Seth. *Tribes.* New York: Penguin Group, 2008.

Goffee R., and G. Jones. "Why Should Anyone Be Led by You?" *HBR's Must Reads on Leadership.* Boston: Harvard Business Review Press, 2011.

Gold, M. "The Latest Figures from Nielsen Have Children's TV Usage at an Eight-Year High. Children's Health Advocates Warn of Adverse Effects," October 27, 2009, in *Los Angeles Times.* Retrieved March 2, 2013, from http://articles.la

times.com/2009/oct/27/entertain
ment/et-kids-tv27

Goldsmith, Marshall, and Howard Morgan. "Leadership As a Contact Sport: You Can't Develop in a Closet." *Leadership Excellence*, 2004.

Goleman, Daniel. *Emotional Intelligence,* New York: Bantam Books, 1995.

_____. "Leadership That Gets Results." *Harvard Business Review.* 2000.

_____. "What Makes a Leader." *Harvard Business Review,* 1998.

Goleman, Daniel, Richard Boyatzis, and Annie McKee. *Primal Leadership: Realizing the Power of Emotional Intelligence.* Boston: Harvard Business School Publishing, 2002.

Gordon, Larry, and Louis Sahagun. "Gen Y's Ego Trip Takes a Bad Turn." *Los Angeles Times,* 2007.

Green, Thad. *Motivation Management: Fueling Performance by Discovering What People Believe About Themselves and Their Organizations.* Palo Alto, CA: Davies-Black Publishing, 2000.

Hanin, Yuri. *Emotions in Sport.* Champaign, IL: Human Kinetics, 2000.

_____. "Successful and Poor Performance Emotions." In Y.L. Hanin (Ed.), *Emotions In Sport.* Champaign, IL: Human Kinetics, 2000.

Hannah, Sean. "The Authentic High-Impact Leader." In Major Doug Crandall (Ed.), *Leadership Lessons from West Point.* San Francisco: Jossey-Bass, 2007.

Harbecker, T.B. *The Otherside of Leadership.* Wheaton, IL: Victor Books, 1987.

Hathaway, Nathan. March 4, 2005. "Embattled Coach Fired." In *The Collegian.* Retrieved March 7, 2005, from http://www.csufresno.edu/Collegian/archive/2005/03/04/news/coach.shtml

Healy, M. September 15, 2008. "Youths' Drug of Choice? Prescription." In *Los Angeles Times.com.* Retrieved March 10, 2013, from http://www.latimes.com/features/health/la-he-drugs15

Heifetz R., and D. Laurie. "The Work of Leadership." *HBR's 10 Must Reads on Leadership.* Boston: Harvard Business School Publishing Corporation, 2011.

Helgesen, Sally. *Everyday Revolutionaries: Working Women and the Transformation of American Life.* New York: Doubleday, 1998.

_____. *The Female Advantage: Women's Ways of Leadership.* New York: Bantam Doubleday Dell, 1990.

_____. "Women's Vision: Making the Strategic Case." *Warren Bennis' Leadership Excellence: The Magazine of Leadership Development, Managerial Effectiveness, and Organizational Psychology,* 2000.

Hertig, John. "Followership: Nontraditional Leadership Roles for New Practitioners." *American Journal of Health-System Pharmacy,* 2010.

"High School Dropouts in America." September 2010. Retrieved March 1, 2013, from www.all4ed.org/files/HighSchoolDropouts.pdf

Hill, Linda. *Becoming a Manager: Mastery of a New Identity.* Boston: Harvard Business School Press, 1992.

Hill, Mona. February 2, 2011. "Feather River College Players Bring Suit of Their Own." In *Plumas County News.com.* Retrieved June 14, 2011, from http://www.plumasnews.com/home/7854-feather-river-college-players-bring-suit-of-their-own.html

Hinds, Jeff. *The Republican,* 2007.

Hipple, Steven. September 2010. "Self-Employment in the United States." Retrieved March 11, 2013, from www.bls.gov/opub/mlr/2010/09/art2full.pdf

Hoover, E. "The Millennial Muddle: How Stereotyping Students Became a Thriving Industry and a Bundle of Contradictions." *The Chronicle of Higher Education,* 2009.

Houser, Thomas (n.d.). "Ten Tips to Coaching Survival." In volleyball.about.com. Retrieved May 18, 2006, from http://volleyball.about.com/od/coachingselfhelp/a/coachingsurviva_p.htm

Howe, Neil, and William Strauss. *Millennials Go to College.* AACRAO. 2003.

_____, and _____. *Millennials Rising: The Next Great Generation.* New York: Vintage, 2000.

Howell, Jon P., and Maria J. Mendez. "Three Perspectives on Followership." In R. Riggio, I. Chaleff, and J. Lipman-Blumen (Eds.). *The Art of Followership: How Great Followers Create Great Leaders and Organizations.* San Francisco: Jossey-Bass, 2008.

Hsuing, Chris. February 29, 2009. "Psychological Androgyny." Retrieved June 23, 2011, from http://uventure.net/

blog/2009/02/27/psychological-androgyny/.

Humphrey, Ronald. "The Many Faces of Emotional Leadership." *The Leadership Quarterly,* 2002.

Hums, Mary A., Glenna G. Bower, and Heidi Grappendorf. *Women as Leaders in Sport: Impact and Influence.* Reston, VA: AAHPERD, 2007.

Hunter, John. "Ageless Leaders." *ESPN the Magazine,* 2000.

Hunter, O.G. February 14, 2002. "National Statistics on Bullying in Schools." Retrieved March 2, 2013, from http://www.alicetx.com/news/article_87be339a-5658–11e1-a087–0019bb2963f4.html

Internet search retrieved June 13, 2011, from http://search.espn.go.com/player-revolt/ and http://www.google.com/#sclient=psy&hl=en&site=&source=hp&q=player+revolt&aq=f&aqi=g-v2g-j2gm1&aql=&oq=&pbx=1&bav=on.2, or.r_gc.r_pw.&fp=3ece4bbf7ce578bb&biw=1076&bih=535

Jackson, Phil. *The Last Season: A Team in Search of Its Soul.* New York: Penguin Group, 2004.

_____. *Sacred Hoops.* New York: Hyperion, 1995.

Jalonick, M.C. "Obesity Rates Soaring Over 2 Decades." *The Florida Times Union,* 2011.

Janssen, Jeff. *Championship Team Building: What Every Coach Needs to Know to Build a Motivated, Committed & Cohesive Team.* Tucson: Winning the Mental Game, 1999.

_____. *The Team Captain's Leadership Manual.* Cary, NC: Winning the Mental Game, 2003.

Janssen, Jeff, and Greg Dale. *The Seven Secrets of Successful Coaches.* Cary, NC: Winning the Mental Game, 2002.

Jayson, Sharon. "Are Students Today More Narcissistic? Survey Cites Social Networks." *USA Today,* 2009.

_____. "Gen Y Makes A Mark." *USA Today,* 2006.

Jones, Marc, Jim Taylor, Miyako Tanaka-Oulevey, and Mary Daubert. "Emotions." In J. Taylor & G. Wilson (Eds.), *Applying Sport Psychology: Four Perspectives.* Champaign, IL: Human Kinetics, 2005.

Josephson, Michael. "Cheating Nation." *PARADE Magazine,* 2006.

Kail, Eric. "Becoming a Leader Developer." In Major Doug Crandall (Ed.). *Leadership Lessons from West Point.* San Francisco: Jossey-Bass, 2007.

Kawakami, Tim. "Still Feeling The Tremors." *Los Angeles Times,* 1997.

Kelan, Elisabeth. *Rising Stars: Developing Millennial Women as Leaders.* New York: Palgrave Macmillan, 2012.

Kelley, Robert. "Rethinking Followership." In Ronald Riggio, Ira Chaleff & Jean Lipman-Blumen (Eds.), *The Art of Followership: How Great Followers Create Great Leaders and Organizations.* San Francisco: Jossey-Bass, 2008.

Kelley, Robert E. "In Praise of Followers." *Harvard Business Review,* 1988.

_____. *The Power of Followership: How to Create Leaders People Want to Follow and Followers Who Lead Themselves.* New York: Currency Book, 1992.

Kim, M.S. "Types of Leadership and Performance Norms of School Athletic Teams." *Perceptual and Motor Skills,* 1992.

Kimball, Bob. "Twitter Shutdown." *USA Today,* 2011.

Kissinger, Meg. "The Millennials." *Milwaukee Journal Sentinel,* 2005.

Klemko, Robert. "Athlete Tweets Often Create Grief." *USA Today,* 2011.

Kotter, John. *Leading Change.* Boston: Harvard Business Press, 1996.

_____. "What Leaders Do." In *HBR's 10 Must Reads on Leadership.* Boston: Harvard Business School Publishing, 2011.

_____. "What Leaders Really Do." In *Harvard Business Review on Leadership.* Boston: Harvard Business School Publishing, 1998.

Kotter, John, and James Heskett. *Corporate Culture and Performance.* New York: Free Press, 1992.

Kouzes, James, and Barry Posner. *The Leadership Challenge.* San Francisco: John Wiley & Sons, 2007.

_____, and _____. *The Truth About Leadership.* San Francisco: Jossey-Bass, 2010.

Krache, D. June 20, 2012. "By the Numbers—High School Dropouts: College Board Says 857 Drop Out Every Hour of Every School Day." Retrieved March 2, 2013, from http://www.krcrtv.com/news/national/By-the-numbers-High-school-dropouts/-/14285942/15172398/-/rdu52lz/-/index.html

Krames, Jeffrey. *What the Best CEO's Know: 7 Exceptional Leaders and Their Lessons for*

Transforming Any Business. New York: McGraw-Hill, 2003.

Krzyzewski, Mike. *The Gold Standard: Building a World-Class Team*. New York: Business Plus, 2009.

Krzyzewski, Mike, and Donald Phillips. *Leading With the Heart*. New York: Warner Business Books, 2000.

Lancaster, Lynne, and David Stillman. *When Generations Collide: Who They Are. Why They Clash. How to Solve the Generational Puzzle at Work*. New York: Collins Business, 2002.

Layden, Tim. "Mack Brown." *Sports Illustrated*, 2005.

Layton, L. March 19, 2012. "High School Graduation Rate Rises." In *Washington Post*. Retrieved March 12, 2013, from http://articles.washingtonpost.com/2012-03-19/local/35448541_1_graduation-graduation-rates-robert-balfanz

LeDoux, J. *The Emotional Brain: The Mysterious Underpinnings of Emotional Life*. New York: Touchstone, 1996.

Lee, Chris. "Followership: The Essence of Leadership." *Training*, 1991.

Lencioni, Pat. *The 5 Dysfunctions of a Team*. San Francisco: Jossey-Bass, 2002.

Leonard, W.M., T. Ostrosky, and S. Huchendorf. "Centrality of Position and Managerial Recruitment: The Case of Major League Baseball." *Sociology of Sport Journal*, 1990.

Levine, Stuart. *The Six Fundamentals of Success: The Rules for Getting It Right for Yourself and Your Organization*. New York: Random House, 2004.

Loehr, James. "Leadership: Full Engagement for Success." In S. Murphy (Ed.), *The Sport Psychology Handbook*. Champaign, IL: Human Kinetics, 2005.

_____. *Toughness Training for Sports*. New York: Penguin Books, 1994.

Loehr, James, and Tony Schwartz. "The Making of a Corporate Athlete." *Harvard Business Review*, 2001.

Lombardi, Vince Jr. *What It Takes to Be #1: Vince Lombardi On Leadership*. New York: McGraw-Hill, 2001.

Lundin S., and L. Lancaster. "Beyond Leadership: The Importance of Followership." *Futurist*, 1990.

Lussier, Robert, and David Kimball. *Applied Sport Management Skills*. Champaign, IL: Human Kinetics, 2009.

Maccoby, Michael. *The Leaders We Need and What Makes Us Follow*. Boston: Harvard Business School Publishing, 2007.

Maddi, S.R., and D.M. Khoshaba. "Hardiness and Mental Health." *Journal of Personality Assessment*, 1994.

Mangan, Katherine. *The Chronicle of Higher Education*, 1995.

Marano, Hara Estroff. *Nation of Wimps: The High Cost of Invasive Parenting*. New York: Broadway Books, 2008.

Marcello, Brandon. May 14, 2011. "Former Pitcher Suing MSU." In *ClarionLedger.com*. Retrieved June 14, 2011, from http://www.clarionledger.com/article/2011 0514/SPORTS030102/105140343/Former-pitcher-suing-MSU

Marcus, M.B. "Minority Kids Use Media More." *USA Today*, 2011.

Maroosis, James. "Leadership: A Partnership in Reciprocal Following." In Ronald Riggio, Ira Chaleff & Jean Lipman-Blumen (Eds.), *The Art of Followership: How Great Followers Create Great Leaders and Organizations*. San Francisco: Jossey-Bass, 2008.

Martens, Rainer. *Coaches Guide to Sport Psychology*. Champaign, IL: Human Kinetics, 1987.

Maxwell, John C. *Leadership Gold*. Nashville: Thomas Nelson, 2008.

_____. *The 17 Essential Qualities of a Team Player: Becoming the Kind of Person Every Team Wants*. Nashville: Thomas Nelson, 2002.

_____. *Team Work Makes the Dream Work*. Nashville: Thomas Nelson, 2002.

_____. *The 360 Leader: Developing Your Influence from Anywhere in the Organization*. Nashville: Thomas Nelson, 2005.

McCallum, J. "The Gang's All Here." *Sports Illustrated*, 2001.

McGregor, Jena. August 21, 2006. "Game plan: First Find the Leaders." *Bloomberg Businessweek*. Retrieved March 11, 2013, from http://businessweek.com/printer/articles/206532-game-plan-first-dind-the-leaders

McKee, Annie, Richard Boyatzis, and Frances Johnston. *Becoming a Resonant Leader*. Boston: Harvard Business Press, 2008.

Melnick, M.J., and J.W. Loy. "The Effects of Formal Structure on Leadership Recruitment: An Analysis of Team Captaincy among New Zealand Provincial Rugby Teams." *International Review of Sociology and Sport,* 1996.

Monson, Daniel. "Former Player Sues Guevara," February 11, 2009, CMU. Retrieved June 14, 2011, from http://www.cm-life.com/2009/02/11/formerplayersuesguevaracmu/

Moura, Pedro. "USC and Stafon Johnson Settle Lawsuit," January 19, 2012, in *ESPN.com. '11.* Retrieved February 10, 2013, from http://espn.go.com/losangeles/ncf/story/_/id/7477966/usc-trojans-settle-ex-player-stafon-johnson-negligence-lawsuit

Murray, Alan. "Leadership Styles." 2011. The *Wall Street Journal Online.* Retrieved January 3, 2011, from http://guides.wsj.com/management/developing-a-leadership-style/how-to-develop-leaders

_____. *The Wall Street Journal Guide to Management.* New York: Harper Business, 2010.

Murray, Andy. *Los Angeles Times,* 1997.

Murray, David Kord. *Borrowing Brilliance.* New York: Penguin Group, 2004.

Myatt, Mike. February 2012. "The #1 Reason Leadership Development Fails." Retrieved March 15, 2013, from http:www.Forbes.com

Myerberg, Paul, and George Schroeder. "Coaches' Rough Behavior in Spotlight." *USA Today,* 2011.

"The National Campaign to Prevent Teen and Unplanned Pregnancy." (n.d.). Retrieved March 2, 2013, from http://www.thenationalcampaign.org/national/default.aspx.

Navarro, Joe. *What Every Body Is Saying.* New York: HarperCollins, 2008.

Neal, M. "1 in 12 Teens Have Attempted Suicide: Report CDC Finds Suicide Among High School Students on the Rise," June 9, 2012, in *New York Daily News.* Retrieved March 12, 2013, from http://www.nydailynews.com/life-style/health/1–12-teens-attempted-suicide-report-article1.1092622#ixzz2My7gPcyK

News Services. January 24, 2011. "Former Player Stafon Johnson Files Lawsuit Against USC." In *The Seattle Times.com.* Retrieved June 14, 2011, from http://seattletimes.nwsource.com/html/othersports/2014028057_digs25.html-dailysentinel.com

_____. "Giuliani's Son Sues Duke," July 24, 2008, in ESPN.com. Retrieved June 14, 2011, from http://sports.espn.go.com/ncaa/news/story?id=3503157

_____. "Leavitt Fired as South Florida Coach," January 8, 2010, in *Espn.com.* Retrieved January 28, 2010, from http://sports.espn.go.com/espn/print?id=4807719&type=story

Nixon, Howard L., and James H. Frey. *Sociology of Sport.* New York: Wadsworth Publishing, 1996.

Oblinger, Diane. July/August 2003. "Boomers, Gen-Xers, and Millennials: Understanding the New Students." In *EDUCAUSE Review.*

O'Connor, Karen P. *Gender and Women's Leadership: A Reference Handbook.* New York: Sage, 2010.

Orlick, Terry. *In Pursuit of Excellence: How to Win in Sport and Life Through Mental Training.* Champaign, IL: Human Kinetics, 2000.

Parcells, Bill. "The Tough Work of Turning Around a Team." *Harvard Business Review,* 2000.

Patrick, Dan. "Just My Type." *Sports Illustrated,* 2011.

Pellerud, Even, and Sam Kucey. *Coaching and Leadership in Women's Soccer.* New York: Reedswain, 2005.

Penner, Mike. "Today's Athletes." *Los Angeles Times,* 2000.

Potter, E.H., W.E. Rosenbach, and T.S. Pittman. "Followers for the Times: Engaging Employees in a Winning Partnership." In *Contemporary Issues in Leadership* (5th Ed.). New York: Westview Press, 2001.

Pugmire, Lance. "Sports Teaching Kids to Cheat?" *Los Angeles Times,* 2007.

Raelin, J. *Creating Leaderful Organizations: How to Bring Out Leadership in Everyone.* San Francisco: Berrett-Koehler, 2003.

Raines, Claire. 2002. "Managing Millennials." In Generationsatwork.com. Retrieved September 15, 2010, from www.Generationsatwork.com

Rath, Tom, and Barry Conchie. *Strengths-Based Leadership: Great Leaders, Teams, and Why People Follow.* New York: Gallup Press, 2008.

Reid, Jason. "Sheffield Hints He Might Not Play Very Well." *Los Angeles Times,* 2001.

Reynaud, Cecile. *She Can Coach.* Champaign, IL: Human Kinetics, 2005.

Riggio, Ronald, Chaleff Ira, and Lipman-Blumen, Jean. "Rethinking Followership." In *The Art of Followership: How Great Followers Create Great Leaders and Organizations* (Eds.). San Francisco: Jossey-Bass, 2008.

Riley, Pat. *The Winner Within: A Life Plan for Team Players*. New York: Putnam, 1993.

Rooke, David, and William Torbert. "Seven Transformations of Leadership." *HBR's 10 Must Reads on Leadership*. Boston: Harvard Business School Publishing, 2011.

Rosenberg, Michael, and Mark Snyder. August 29, 2009. "A Look Inside Rodriguez's Rigorous Program." In *Detroit Free Press.com*. Retrieved June 14, 2011, from http://www.freep.com/article/20090829/SPORTS06/90829023

Rost, Joseph C. *Leadership for the Twenty-First Century*. Westport, CN: Praeger, 1993.

Rudd, Andy. "Which 'Character' Should Sport Develop?" *Physical Educator*, 2005.

Ruderman, M.N., P.J. Ohlott, K. Panzer, and S.N. King. *Standing at the Cross Roads: Next Steps for High-Achieving Women*. San Francisco: Jossey-Bass, 2002.

Rutherford, Michael (n.d.). Retrieved May 21, 2012, from http://www.brainyquote.com/quotes/ keywords/ collaboration.html#LsA6kJUCwZ0cX31K.99

Saban, Nick, with Brian Curtis. *How Good Do You Want to Be? A Champion's Tips on How to Lead and Succeed*. New York: Ballantine Books, 2005.

Salovey, P., and J.D. Mayer. "Emotional Intelligence." *Imagination, Cognition, & Personality*, 1990.

Sample, Steven B. *The Contrarian's Guide to Leadership*. San Francisco: Jossey-Bass, 2002.

Sandberg, S. *Lean In: Women, Work, and the Will to Lead*. New York: Knopf, 2013.

Sashkin, Marshall, and Molly Sashkin. *Leadership That Matters: The Critical Factors for Making a Difference in People's Lives and Organizations' Success*. San Francisco: Berrett-Koehler Publishers, 2003.

Schaefer, Richard T. *Sociology*. New York: McGraw-Hill, 2011.

Schein, Edgar. *Organizational Culture and Leadership* (2nd ed.). San Francisco: Jossey-Bass, 1992.

Schein, Virginia. "Women in Management: Reflections and Projections." *Women in Management Review*, 2007.

Schroeder, George. "Schools Try to Keep Athletes Off 'Catfish' Hook." *USA Today*, 2013.

Sherbert, Erin. "NCAA, UC Sued by College Football Players," March 16, 2011, in SFWeeklywww. Retrieved June 14, 2011, from http://blogs.sfweekly.com/thesnitch/2011/03/ncaa_uc_cal_state.php

Shields, David, and Brenda Bredemeier. *True Competition: A Guide to Pursuing Excellence in Sport and Society*. Champaign, IL: Human Kinetics, 2009.

Sitkin, Sim, and J. Richard Hackman. "Developing Team Leadership: An Interview With Coach Mike Krzyzewski." *Academy of Management Learning & Education*, 2011.

Smith, Dean, Gerald Bell, and John Kilgo. *The Carolina Way: Leadership Lessons from a Life in Coaching*. New York: Penguin Books, 2004.

Smith, Stephen. "Pistons Protest Is a Problem for Players," February 27, 2011, in *ESPN.com*. Retrieved June 13, 2011, from http://sports.espn.go.com/nba/news/story?id=6159298

Sparrowe, R.T., B.W. Soetjipto, and M.L. Kraimer. "Do Leaders' Influence Tactics Relate to Members' Helping Behavior?" *Academy of Management Journal*, 2011.

Staff. "Former Player on Women's Basketball Team Settles Bias Lawsuit Against Penn State," February 5, 2007, in *Chronicle of Higher Education.com*. Retrieved June 14, 2011, from http://chronicle.com/article/Former-Player-on-Womens/38174/?otd=Y2xpY2t0aHJ1Ojo6c293aWRnZXQ6O6jpja

_____. "Rutgers U. Women's Basketball Player Sues Shock Jock Don Imus for Slander," August 15, 2007, in *Chronicle of Higher Education.com*. Retrieved June 14, 2011. http://chronicle.com/article/Rutgers-U-Women-s-Basketball/39393

_____. "University Sued Over Alleged Promise of Scholarship," May 19, 2006. *Sports Litigation Alert Archives*. Retrieved June 14, 2011, from http://www.hackneypublications.com/sla/archive/000284.php

Stahl, Roby. September 2010. "Developing The Player-Leader." In NSCAA.com. Retrieved October 12, 2010, from http://www.nscaa.com/print2.php?id=136

Stewart, Larry. "When This Bruin Talks, Trojans Listen Too." *Los Angeles Times*, 2005.

Stone, Pamela. *Opting Out? Why Women Really Quit Careers and Head Home.* Berkeley, CA: University of California Press, 2005. *The Daily Trojan.* February 12, 2004.

Sudhin, Thanawala. February 28, 2008. "Prep Football Player Suing UH, Ex-Coach." In *Honolulu Advertiser.com.* Retrieved June 14, 2011, from http://the.honoluluadver tiser.com/article/2008/Feb/28/sp/hawaii802280375.html

Summitt, Pat Head, and Sally Jenkins. *Sum It Up: A Thousand and Ninety-Eight Victories, a Couple of Irrelevant Losses, and a Life in Perspective.* New York: Crown, 2013.

Thomas, Katie. "NCAA Sued Over One-Year Scholarships," October 25, 2010, in *New York Times.com.* Retrieved June 14, 2011, from http://www.nytimes.com/2010/10/26/sports/ncaafootball/26ncaa.html. Times Wire Reports, *Los Angeles Times,* 2004.

Tropp, K.J., and D.M. Landers. "Team Interaction and the Emergence of Leadership and Interpersonal Attraction in Field Hockey." *Journal of Sport Psychology,* 1979.

Tuckman, Bruce. "Developmental Sequence in Small Groups." *Psychological Bulletin,* 1965.

Twenge, Jean. *Generation Me: Why Today's Young Americans Are More Confident, Assertive, Entitled and More Miserable Than Ever Before.* New York: Free Press, 2006.

Twenge, Jean M., and Keith Campbell. *The Narcissism Epidemic: Living in the Age of Entitlement.* New York: Atria, 2010.

Useem, Michael. *The Leadership Moment: Nine True Stories of Triumph and Disaster and Their Lessons for Us All.* New York: Crown Business, 1999.

Vanderkam, L. "Problem With Work-Life Balance." *USA Today,* 2013.

Vealey, Robin. *Coaching for the Inner Edge.* Morgantown, WV: Fitness Information Technology, 2005.

Vecchio, Ralph. "Effective Followership and Leadership Turned Upside Down." In R. P. Vecchio (Ed.), *Leadership: Understanding the Dynamics of Power and Influence in Organizations.* Notre Dame, IN: University of Notre Dame Press, 1997.

Vecsey, George. "Living and Learning, Changing and Winning." *The New York Times,* 2008.

Voight, Mike. "Applying Sport Psychology Philosophies, Principles, and Practices Onto the Gridiron: An Interview With USC Football Coach Pete Carroll." *International Journal of Sport Science & Coaching,* 2006.

_____. "A Leadership Development Intervention Program: A Case Study with Two NCAA Final 4 Teams." *The Sport Psychologist,* 2012.

_____. *Mental Toughness Training for Basketball: Maximizing Technical & Mental Mechanics.* Monterey, CA: Coaches Choice Publishers, 2010.

_____. *A Structural Model of the Determinants, Personal and Situational Influences, and the Consequences of Athlete Dissatisfaction.* University of Southern California. Ann Arbor: UMI Dissertation Services, 2000.

Voight, Mike, and John Callaghan. "A Structural Model on the Determinants and Reactions to Athlete Dissatisfaction." *International Journal of Sports Science & Coaching,* 2006.

Waddell, Dave. "Cirovski Defines Leadership Formula," May 9, 2012, *The Windsor Star.* Retrieved March 11, 2013, from http://peakconsulting.ca/article-blog-8/cirovski-defines-leadership-formula

Wallington, P. "After You: Why Leaders Should Hone Followership Skills." *CIO,* 2003.

Walsh, Bill. *The Score Takes Care of Itself.* New York: Penguin Group, 2009.

Wang, Jin, and William Straub. "An Investigation Into the Coaching Approach of a World Class Soccer Coach: A Case Study." *International Journal of Sport Science & Coaching,* 2012.

Weber, Mike. "Millennials Reign at Olympics." *Daily Lobo,* 2004.

Weese, J., and E. Nicholls. "Team Leadership: Selection and Expectations." *Physical Educator,* 1996.

Weinberg, Robert, and Dan Gould. *Foundations of Sport and Exercise Psychology.* Champaign, IL: Human Kinetics, 2007.

Welch, Jack, and Suzy Welch. *Winning.* New York: Collins, 2005.

Wharton, David. "Two Head Coaches Prove Nice Guys Don't Finish Last." *Los Angeles Times,* 2004.

Wieberg, Steve. "End of Leach Saga, Player Ousters at Mich. State Spice Alamo Battle." *USA Today,* 2009.

Williams, G.A., and R.B. Miller. "Change the Way You Persuade." *Harvard Business Review,* 2002.

Williams, Pat. *Coaching Your Kids to Be Leaders.* New York: Faith Words, 2005.

Wilson, Craig. "Millennials: We love the 90's." *USA Today,* 2011.

Wire reports. "Dissatisfaction." *USA Today,* 1998.

_____. "Magic Number." *Los Angeles Times,* 2004.

_____. "Montgomery: 'I made a mistake.'" *USA Today,* 2013.

_____. "Player Files Suit." *USA Today,* 2011.

_____. "Police Investigate Idaho State Coach After Complaint." *USA Today,* 2012.

Wolff, Alexander. "Knight Fall," September 18, 2000, in *Sports Illustrated.com.* Retrieved January 2012, from http://sportsillustrated.cnn.com/vault/article/magazine/MAG1020376/index.htm

Wooden, John. *My Personal Best: Life Lessons from an All-American Journey.* New York: McGraw-Hill, 2004.

Woog, Dan. "A Season After Getting Ousted." *Soccer America,* 1998.

Wright, Andy, and Jean Cote. "A Retrospective Analysis of Leadership Development Through Sport." *The Sport Psychologist,* 2003.

Yoder, Jodi. "Coach-Athlete Issues." In M. Thompson, R. Vernacchia, & W. Moore (Eds.), *Case Studies in Applied Sport Psychology: An Educational Approach.* Dubuque, Iowa: Kendall/Hunt Publishing, 1998.

Youth Violence Stats (n.d.). Retrieved March 10, 2013, from http://www.childtrends databank.org/?q=node/174

Zizzi, Sam, Heather Deanier, and Doug Hirschhorn. "The Relationship Between Emotional Intelligence and Performance Among College Baseball Players." *Journal of Applied Sport Psychology,* 2003.

Index